Warfare in the Age of Napoleon

Volume 1

Napoleon, 1796

Warfare in the Age of Napoleon

The Revolutionary Wars Against the First Coalition in Northern Europe and the Italian Campaign, 1789-1797

VOLUME 1

Theodore A. Dodge

Warfare in the Age of Napoleon: the Revolutionary Wars Against the First Coalition in Northern Europe and the Italian Campaign, 1789-1797
Volume 1
by Theodore A. Dodge

Published by Leonaur Ltd

ISBN: 978-0-85706-597-1 (hardcover)
ISBN: 978-0-85706-598-8 (softcover)

http://www.leonaur.com

Publisher's Notes

Contents

To the American soldier

Who, not bred to arms, but nurtured by independence, has achieved the proudest rank among the veterans of history, these volumes are dedicated

Faites la guerre offensive comme Alexandre, Annibal, César, Gustave Adolphe, Turenne, le prince Eugène et Frédéric; lisez, relisez l'histoire de leur quatre-vingt-huit campagnes; modélez-vous sur eux,—c'est le seul moyen de devenir grand capitaine et de surprendre le sécret de l'art; votre génie, ainsi éclairé, vous fera rejeter des maximes opposées à celles de ces grands hommes.—Napoleon.

La tactique, les evolutions, la science de l'officier de génie, de l'officier d'artillerie peuvent s'apprendre dana les traités;—mais la connaissance de la grande tactique ne s'acquiert que par l'expérience et par l'étude de l'histoire des campagnes de tous les granda capitaines.—Napoleon.

Preface

The laurels worn by Gustavus Adolphus fell upon the brow of Frederick the Great; and the narrative of that great captain's campaigns, as a part of this history of the art of war, was completed several years ago. But the publication by the Great German General Staff of the early volumes of its extensive treatise on the Prussian king has interrupted the chronological sequence of this history. The abundant fresh matter and the new point of view in the splendid monument thus erected to the German national hero have made it expedient for the author to await its completion, so that he may embody in his own work many of the new facts developed by the profound research that has for years been made in the inaccessible German archives, and may recast much of what he has already finished. It has meanwhile been deemed wise to begin the publication of the Napoleonic wars, although these should properly follow the campaigns of Frederick. It is hoped that there will be no unreasonable delay in the issue of the remaining volumes.

The basis of all our information about the campaigns of Napoleon exists primarily in the letters, orders and bulletins issued from the headquarters of the armies in campaign. These, checked off by the official reports of the campaigns and battles by his opponents, and compared with other accounts from more personal sources, furnish the material from which to construct an accurate and consecutive narrative. The *Correspondence of Napoleon I.*, as far as obtainable, was published by Napoleon III. in thirty-two volumes. Some letters and orders could at the moment not be procured; a few were for other reasons omitted; but the bulk of all Napoleon's correspondence is spread before the public in the twenty-two thousand official documents printed therein. The volumes also contain Napoleon's Memoirs and other matter dictated at St. Helena. While the latter possess marked interest, they are, like all comments in after days, less reliable than the orders issued and the letters written at the moment of action. These have a positive value. Chiefly upon this correspondence the author has relied for his details, although the story of this great captain has been so often told that its bald facts may be gleaned from many sources.

The reader will remember that this work deals with only the military life of Napoleon. The political events of this era, or indeed his personality, although replete with interest, can be touched on only so far as they illustrate the art of war, or elucidate campaigns.

The bibliography of Napoleon is numbered by thousands of works, from Thiers' brilliant history of this period in thirty-one volumes to the simple brochure occasionally issued today. Most of these works contain comparatively little that can be used, although the author has made himself familiar with most of them. Some have a personal charm or a political value, but viewed from the standpoint of the art to which Napoleon contributed so much, the majority possess scant interest. Much reliance has naturally been placed on the criticisms of the well-known military historians, beginning with Jomini (*The Art of War* by Jomini, also published by Leonaur). It is difficult to say anything about the great warrior that may not already have been recorded. The *Memoirs* of some of the marshals—Victor, Marmont, St. Cyr and others—the histories and critiques of Scharnhorst, Clausewitz, Rüstow, Lindenau, Bülow, Martens, Kausler, Woerl, de Ligne, Venturini, Massenbach and many more, are full of matter. Of later books, one of the most valuable is Wartenburg's. To this work, and to that of Prince Gallitzin, which extends up to 1801, the author is greatly indebted. Wartenburg closely follows the Correspondence, and in pursuing the same path, the author has made much use of the intelligent suggestiveness of this distinguished officer. To C. von B. K., Berndt, Odon and various French text-book writers for the present generation of soldiers, thanks are also due. A preface in which acknowledgment were made by name to all the Napoleonic students who have contributed to the author's knowledge would exceed all limits; but he owes much to one and all his predecessors in this study.

It has been thought that quotations from Napoleon's utterances at the moment of action would be interesting to even the general reader, and such quotations have been largely indulged in. Most of them are *verbatim*; a few only recite the general statement or opinion. Those not otherwise credited are from the St. Helena memoirs. An occasional difference in dates may be due to the use of the Republican Calendar.

The same care in visiting the battlefields in person that was given to former campaigns has with few exceptions been exercised in writing these.

The portraits of the marshals and generals celebrated at that time, as well as those of the great captain himself, will be found interesting. It has been thought better to spread upon the pages many of these, even when of scant artistic value, than to put in a few only on account of their merit as pictures. It will be noted that most of the portraits are those of middle-aged or old men, whereas many of Napoleon's lieutenants were young; but they were too busy during their fighting years to give sittings for painters. In many cases portraits of even celebrated men seem not to be in existence. Many of the portraits are mere sketches from old engravings, which cannot be reproduced.

The cuts of uniforms and arms help to illustrate the subject treated, even when they lack the highest grade of execution. Nearly all are copied from pictures of the period, among others those of Van der Meulen, Vernet, Charlet, Lami, Bellangé and those in the Versailles Museum.

The maps and charts will be found sufficient. From the maps has been omitted everything which is not needed for the matter in hand. In the charts of battles there has been no attempt to enter into great detail, the general position of the lines alone being indicated, so that the battle in its larger features can be readily understood; for it is not the fighting of the separate divisions so much as the general plan of the leader which interests us. In the charts, the blocks or lines of troops merely indicate general position, and not numbers or specific place.

More space has been given to the strategic operations of Napoleon than to the grand-tactics of his battles. Wonderful as the latter were, the strategic marches were yet more so. They are not in most histories so amply treated, whereas the key-note of Napoleon's successes was that his strategy so led up to battle that Victory became decisive; and to the military student the strategic manoeuvres are of perhaps greater interest. This has, in fact, sometimes induced the author to give the day's routes of the various corps; but as the legends at the head of each chapter enable the general reader to skip what he cares not to read, it is hoped the prolixity will not be out of place. Much matter has also been put in small type. This matter is, as a rule, not essential to the narrative, but possesses its own interest.

This history of Napoleon is written largely from the French standpoint, although due weight has been given to the authorities of every nation. It is not possible to describe Napoleon's brilliant lessons in the art of war from the point of view of any one of his opponents. Moreover, less space has been devoted to those campaigns in which our British cousins figured than might be natural in volumes written for English-speaking people; but in the case of the Peninsular War, where so great a character as Wellington figured, and where he so often held the initiative, much has been stated from the English standpoint. The Peninsular War has, however, been so thoroughly covered by Napier, and is being again covered with so much amplitude and skill by Professor Oman, that the author has deemed it more desirable to treat these campaigns as a minor part of the great Napoleonic scheme—as indeed they were—than to seek to compete with these brilliant and laborious historians in describing the events in Spain and Portugal.

More than all are thanks owing to my collaborator for the past twenty-three years, my wife, whose patient intelligence has so often saved me from serious blunders, and whose skilful pencil has lent interest to over twenty volumes.

Chapter 1

Army Organization at the End of the 18th Century

War, substantially as it is conducted today, dates from the French Revolution. Personal service then began, and many tactical changes, some borrowed from the American Revolutionary War, were made. In 1789 the ancient, rotten royal army of France gave place to a National Guard for home defence, and a levy of the people for active armies. Every citizen being liable, half a million men were quickly raised, and all France became a factory of munitions. Every one worked on material for the army. The scientist turned his attention to war; mechanical engineers and chemists trained masters and foremen for the provincial workshops. Church-bells and statues were recast into cannon. The energy and courage of the Revolutionary leaders were equalled only by their bloody methods, and a man was safer in the army than out of it. In 1793 Carnot took hold of military affairs, and became the Organizer of Victory. All arms were improved, and the French troops partook of the leaders' enthusiasm. In the other nations improvements came more slowly, and light foot, horse and batteries were usual in France long before they appeared elsewhere. At first the ill-drilled infantry required too much artillery to sustain it, but the amount later equalized itself. Artillery schools gained in teaching-methods. Excellent polytechnic schools trained young men for the army. Miners, sappers and artificers, as well as engineer-geographers and road-builders, were joined in a special corps of exceptional utility.

The beginnings of the modern era in the art of war date from the French Revolution. It was the upheaval of the people of France which laid the foundation of personal service, and added to this patriotic gain, though in a crude manner, the changes that gradually led up to the art as it exists today. All this was later moulded into a definite form by Napoleon. Terrible as were the excesses of that rising of a down-trodden people, the good which eventually came of it was yet greater. The general social gain was also partaken by war, the old mercenary army of the kings disappeared in France, and its place was taken by the National Guard, parent of that manhood service in which every citizen pays his duty to his country.

In 1789 the French army numbered about one hundred and thirty thousand foot, thirty thousand horse, and ten thousand artillery and engineer troops, including the several foreign corps—Swiss, German, Irish—and the Guard. The army was rotten in its organization, discipline and morale. At the very opening of the Revolution the Guards and the foreign bodies were dissolved, and whatever of the militia had not deserted was mustered out. What remained was as bad as the worst of the mercenaries of the Thirty Years' War. To replace this under the existing conditions worse than useless force, a body called the National Guard was originated in Paris, and later assembled in the other large cities, by volunteering among three classes: the unmarried men from eighteen to forty-five years old, the married of like age, and the single and married from forty-five to sixty. The first class was organized in battalions which should meet once a year for drill; the second was enrolled in companies of one hundred men each for secondary use, and the third was listed for service only in its own precinct. This organization, in a population of twenty-four millions, produced a fine body of soldiers of the people; but having little discipline or education to build on, it was suited mainly for home defence. For this reason, in 1791 there were formed one hundred and seventy new battalions of infantry, and for the defence of the frontier eighty-three battalions of "national volunteers;" and the following year a number of free corps, departmental companies and legions of light troops were raised; but it was readily seen that these raw levies could not cope with the standing armies of Austria, Prussia and the other European states which were sure to combine against France,—at least in regular warfare.

As soon as France was declared a republic and war appeared on the horizon, the National Convention began the creation of a new army, and on the ground that 'the fatherland was in peril,' called upon every citizen to rally to her protection. The size of the army was set at four hundred and fifty thousand men, including the National Guard and the *gendarmes* who had supplanted the old provincial police; and meanwhile there were raised thirty thousand men in Paris, which force, with the volunteers and the relics of the old line troops, was got ready to oppose the Prussian invasion of France in 1792. At the same time all France was roused into producing army supplies, firearms and pikes, ammunition and equipments, fieldpieces and caissons, saltpetre and powder. Astonishing energy, backed by the issue of unlimited

Soldier of Legion du Midi

Old Guard Sharpshooter

paper money (*assignats*) and the ever present threat of the guillotine, enabled the Convention to raise, before the end of 1792, an army of four hundred and forty-six thousand foot, forty-three thousand horse, and twenty-three thousand men of artillery and engineers. This army was by no means of the best; and though it possessed exuberant good-will, yet it melted away so fast that in March, 1793, a further levy of three hundred thousand men was made, and in July one of twelve hundred thousand men. These enormous numbers could be raised by no method except a general enrolment, which should embrace all men from sixteen to forty-five; and this was the first time in modern history when every citizen was held liable to military duty, and the entire nation was marshalled under arms.

The act was that of the people, so-called; and a fanatical patriotism, or else the fear of the Convention and its bloody methods, led all men to seek some military duty in the rage for liberty, or as the only personal safety. In the campaign of 1793 some two hundred thousand men were lost to the ranks by sickness and wounds; yet in 1794 the army was greater than ever before.

Inasmuch, however, as this army lacked everything except men, the Convention appointed a War Committee to work out of the existing conditions a plan for an army really suited to the necessities of the time, and able to cope with regular forces; by the autumn of 1793, owing to its efforts, the French army began to assume a definite shape, and when in August of that year Carnot, then a member of the Convention, was put at the head of military affairs, the strides towards an efficient army were rapid. The old line troops, which constituted a third of the whole body, the National Guards, the volunteers and the popular levies were all consolidated. The national volunteers and the old sharpshooters made up the light infantry. The legions and the free corps contributed to the light cavalry of the line. Infantry, cavalry, artillery and engineers all received proper and simplified organization. Regiments, or, as they were denominated, "half-brigades," were placed on a more modern footing in make-up, titles of officers and tactical work. A Central General Staff was placed at the head of the army, and the whole was systematically cut up into divisions, each one comprising troops of all arms, and having its own staff and administration, thus being a body well fitted for detail on any specific duty. The entire year of 1794 was occupied in this methodical work, which in 1795 was fairly completed; and there then stood ready an army of five hundred and forty-three thousand foot, with thirteen hundred and fifty-six regimental guns; over ninety thousand horse; two hundred and eight batteries of artil-

Infantryman, 1796

Hungarian Border Hussar

lery, with twenty thousand men and twelve hundred and fifty guns; in all a force of over six hundred and fifty thousand well-organized men, not including the technical corps, invalid corps, coast artillerymen and the *gendarmes*. France had risen in her strength.

To complete the good work the Directory, which succeeded the Convention, passed in 1798 the Conscription Act, and this has practically followed into modern times. During the Consulate, 1800 to 1804, Napoleon continued and perfected the work of organization and detail, created new military schools, originated the Consular Guards, a *corps d'élite* of all arms, which later became the Imperial Guard, instituted the Legion of Honour, framed a new body of light infantry called *voltigeurs*, because they could vault on behind and be carried by a cavalryman, placed the National Guard on a suitable footing for home service, and erected the police force, or gendarmes, into a superior body. France was destined to possess a new army fit to be commanded by its new emperor. Some notable changes had also taken place in the armaments of the other European nations. Until this period wars had been conducted by the sovereigns with their standing armies, and without any voluntary participation by the people, the part of the latter being confined to furnishing such men and material as might be requisitioned by the rulers to fill gaps, and to paying without remonstrance such taxes as were laid upon them,—a duty not always cheerfully performed.

This uncertain source of supply made it difficult for the monarchs to provide by mere army chests and state economies for the enormous cost of the wars they waged, and often led to their making a peace on poor conditions for the nation, because of the exhaustion of their resources. To these rulers the French Revolution with its popular power was a revelation, and one not entirely to their taste. The whole burden of the war was borne by the French people, and when their armies conquered fresh territory, as in the Netherlands, the burden was imposed in a similar manner on the population newly added to France. In imitation of the French, Switzerland and the Black Forest region soon began a system of manhood service. And Austria anticipated much from a similar action, voluntarily taken in the Tyrol and the Slavic provinces, in the way she had always counted for recruits on the ancient Hungarian Insurrection.

At the opening of the French Revolution, Austria had about two hundred and twenty-five thousand infantry and forty-five thousand cavalry troops, from which figures might be deducted some late losses in Turkey and in the recent revolts in the Netherlands. Prussia had one hundred and seventy thousand infantry, and forty thousand cavalry. In addition to these forces were some garrison troops, in Prussia about forty thousand men, in Austria less. To compare these figures with the later enormous levies is instructive.

Infantry. In this arm there had for some years been no great change, except that light foot had proportionately increased. In France, where at first there was a dearth of muskets, the National Guard was armed in part with pikes, and indeed the Vendée troops were originally put in line and won their initial successes with only scythes, flails and pitchforks. Gradually, however, muskets enough were procured. At one time there was some use made of airguns, as among the Austrian sharpshooters, though this weapon held its place no great time. As regards organization, drill and minor tactics, the infantry of Europe remained much what it had been. The Austrian line regiments had three battalions, the Hungarian four; there were special grenadier battalions, and the light foot was composed mainly of Croats and riflemen. Each battalion had six companies, and numbered in the line regiments nine hundred and twenty-four men, in the grenadier regiments six hundred and ninety, with the Croats and riflemen, six hundred and sixty men. In 1799 there were sixty regiments of line infantry, two grenadier and eighteen fusilier regiments, each of twenty companies; seventeen regiments of Croats, two garrison regiments of eighteen companies each, and fifteen rifle battalions of six companies each. The Prussian line regiment, just prior to the French Revolution, had contained one grenadier, two musketeer, and one reserve battalions. The light infantry was made up of fusilier battalions, and there was a regiment of riflemen. Each company contained ten or twenty riflemen drilled to skirmish in open order in its front. The battalion was seven hundred strong, in four companies, the reserve battalion having but three companies. When Frederick William III. came to the throne in 1797, the line regiment had ten musketeer and two grenadier companies, in all about two thousand men; and the four grenadier companies of each two regiments were taken from it and put into a separate battalion. In England, at the end of the eighteenth century, owing to fear of a French invasion, the available forces were largely increased by the enlistment of fencibles to protect the coast. There were in all one hundred and eleven line regiments, forty regiments of fencibles, one hundred and forty-seven regiments of militia, and some five hundred volunteer corps of various kinds.

In France, when, at the beginning of the Revolution, the National Guard was originated, each first-class battalion had one grenadier, four

Austrian Light Infantryman

Officer of the Republic 1793

fusilier, and one rifle companies; and two field-guns, served by seventeen men, accompanied the body. Outside Paris, Lyons, Marseilles, Bordeaux, Rouen and Nantes, there were five hundred and forty-seven battalions, comprising four hundred and sixty thousand men. The National Guard of Paris, which Lafayette, fresh from his American training, had well organized and drilled, was the pattern for the rest. The eighty-three battalions of national volunteers raised in 1791 each numbered five hundred and sixty-four officers and men; and later these grew to two hundred and ten battalions. The riflemen of the old line regiments were detailed as light troops, and to these were added in 1792 six legions of two battalions of eight companies each, a regiment of mounted riflemen, and a corps of artificers. In 1793, after the national volunteers had been consolidated with the line infantry, each regiment (half-brigade) contained one line battalion and two volunteer battalions. The Revolutionary French foot was specially classed as line infantry and light.

Of the line there were one hundred and ninety-six, and later two hundred and thirty half-brigades, each consisting of three battalions; and each battalion comprised one grenadier company of sixty-two men, and eight fusilier companies of eighty-six men each. These numbers were increased by supernumeraries when the battalions went on foreign service. Like other foot soldiers, the grenadiers carried muskets, but these companies fought separated from their battalions. They were considered as higher in standing than the average soldier, and under special rules. Grenadiers were not to be used for escorts, they were to remain in a body with their battalion. They were not to be put on picket nor distributed with other troops. The grenadier company was always to be at the head the column, or ready to march out to sustain the picket, and by its good countenance keep up confidence; but important posts, such as bridges, might be guarded by the grenadiers.

Of light infantry there were thirty half-brigades of similar size, but in these the grenadiers were called *carbineers*. Each half-brigade, or later each brigade, had a battery of six four-pounder guns. All this made up a force of two hundred and twenty-six half-brigades, numbering over half a million men and thirteen hundred and fifty-six guns. In 1795 the half-brigades were reduced to one hundred and ten, but the grenadier companies were increased to ninety men, the fusilier companies to one hundred and twenty, the battalion, including staff, to one thousand and sixty-seven, the half-brigade to thirty-two hundred men. The light infantry companies were increased in similar fashion, which produced a relative gain in light infantry. In 1800 there were of line infantry one hundred and ten half-brigades; and of light infantry thirty half-brigades. But the regimental guns had been taken from the infantry.

Cavalry. The only general change all over Europe was towards increasing the light cavalry in proportion to the heavy. This arm had *cuirassiers* and *carbineers* who were the heavy, and dragoons, hussars, mounted riflemen (*chasseurs à cheval*), so called "light horse" (*chevaux-légers*) and some lancers, all classed as light cavalry. The dragoons were not infrequently put to use as line cavalry, having lost their original character of mounted infantry, which preferably fought on foot. In Austria, in 1789, the regiments of *cuirassiers*, *carbineers*, dragoons and light cavalry had six squadrons each; the hussar regiments ten squadrons each. There was one volunteer lancer regiment. Each heavy squadron had one hundred and sixty horses, the light squadron two hundred. In 1799 Austria had twelve cuirassier, fifteen dragoon, twelve hussar, and two lancer regiments of six squadrons each, and one regiment of mounted riflemen of eight squadrons. In Prussia there were thirteen *cuirassier* regiments of five squadrons each, twelve dragoon regiments of five and ten squadrons each, and nine hussar regiments of ten squadrons each, the squadron having one hundred and seventy-five horses. In England there were forty-one regiments of line cavalry, six regiments reserve cavalry, thirty regiments of mounted fencibles, and some two hundred and seventy-five corps of mounted volunteers.

Fewer changes in cavalry organization were made in France. In 1789 there were sixty-two regiments of line cavalry, the heavy and dragoon regiments having three squadrons each, the carbineer, mounted riflemen and hussar regiments four squadrons each. Within four years the cavalry was much increased by adding mounted national volunteers, and creating new regiments of mounted riflemen and others. In 1793 the organization was changed. The heavy cavalry had neither helmet, *cuirass*, nor carbine, being armed with only a long straight sword and pistols. There were twenty-nine regiments of heavy cavalry of four squadrons of two companies each, about seven hundred horses to a regiment. The light cavalry, consisting of dragoons, mounted riflemen and hussars, was armed with carbine, pistols and curved sword. There were twenty dragoon regiments of four squadrons each, twenty-three mounted riflemen regiments, and eleven hussar regiments of six squadrons each, the squadron containing two companies. The regiment had fourteen hundred horses. There was thus a total of eighty-three regiments with four hundred

Austrian Mounted Chasseur

squadrons, numbering nearly one hundred thousand horses, two thirds being light cavalry. In consequence of the great losses in war, the heavy regiments were cut down in 1796 to three squadrons, and the light to four squadrons; but three new regiments were raised. In 1803 the entire heavy cavalry was divided into eighteen regiments of four squadrons each, and in 1805 they were made into *cuirassiers.* There were also the mounted companies of "guides," soldiers originally intended to study the roads and lead the columns, but they later made up the emperor's escort; and the *gendarmerie nationale*, which in 1791 had taken the place of the *maréchausée* or country police, was divided into twenty-eight divisions, in which were sixteen hundred "brigades" of one non-commissioned officer (brigadier) and four *gendarmes.* The provost-marshal department of the armies was made up of military *gendarmes.* This excellent body was shortly imitated in every European country.

Artillery, The energetic men of the French Revolution initiated many improvements in this arm. The casting and boring of guns, the cleaning of saltpetre and the preparation of powder, were much improved by the clever French chemists and men of science of that day. The campaigns in the Alps originated mountain artillery which was effective, and portable enough to be really useful. Gribeauval's gun-carriage was simplified, and artillery munition-wagons and all running-gear were perfected. General Eblé invented a grapeshot, and contrived a new species of furnace for heating cannon-balls for the coast artillery. The manufacture of rockets, to throw light as well as to set fire to distant buildings, and other fire-balls, was improved. In technical artillery construction and service many fresh discoveries were made. In Prussia Tempelhof introduced small field mortars, first used to advantage at the siege of Longwy, and later against troops. Guns were cast with conical chambers, as long used by the Swedes, which gave a greater velocity to the projectile. Mortars were also cast with conical chambers, and were proved by the experiments of the Austrian Vega to be more efficient. Count Rumford and others added to the general knowledge about ballistics. On the whole, artillery was increased in proportion to the other arms, and light and horse artillery in proportion to the rest. Regimental guns were taken from the battalions and collected in batteries. And there being more room for improvement in this arm, it gained in perfection faster than the others.

In France, particularly, attention was paid to the artillery as a separate and not a merely auxiliary arm. Even before the Revolution, artillery had received an impetus among the able French scientists

Mounted Guard Grenaadier

French General 1794

and officers, and this advance continued. The arm had consisted, prior to 1789, of seven regiments of foot artillery with six companies of miners and artificers; but although Austria, Russia and some other nations had introduced Frederick's horse batteries, the French had not done so. When the Convention began its universal levy, the necessity of producing ammunition and guns became imperative; and all France, under four representatives of the people, was divided into eight sections, each supervised by an inspector, who was to oversee the production of saltpetre and powder, and the casting of guns. Most of the copper and iron mills and all the furnaces were utilized for the casting and boring of guns; church-bells were turned into cannon; and the whole of France, under requisition of the central authority, became one vast workshop. Nor was this done carelessly. The strong men of the Revolution were wise as well as energetic. Masters and foremen were trained in Paris under the most celebrated chemists and men of science, and sent into the provinces to superintend the work. As a result, in not many months, the production of all material of war grew apace. But too little heed was paid to uniformity of calibre and pattern; and in the early Revolutionary wars there was much trouble in providing proper ammunition for the guns at hand. This, however, was rectified little by little.

Field artillery was then still divided into regimental guns and batteries. The batteries had six, eight and twelve-pounders, with some sixteen-pounders for siege work; and there were six and eight-pounder howitzers. The whole field-artillery arm was divided into regiments and companies. The guns of the foot regiments were mostly four-pounders, and of these there were twelve hundred, which with the battery artillery made a disproportionate number of guns. But the object in this was to back up the courage of the ill-drilled and inexperienced conscript by means of a heavy artillery fire. The creation of a large body of light infantry led up to the production of lighter batteries which might keep pace with the men; and in 1791 there were already two companies of this light artillery, each with two eight-pounder guns and two six-inch howitzers, the men serving which were carried along in wagons of peculiar construction. But during the next year these men were mounted, as being a handier conveyance, and thus the arm grew into horse artillery. Frederick's horse batteries had been a conception of the master-mind rather than a growth. This arm suited the quick-acting French temperament so well that it took on undue proportions. When, in 1793-94, the army was reorganized, each half-brigade was given a battery of

Bavarian Sharpshooter

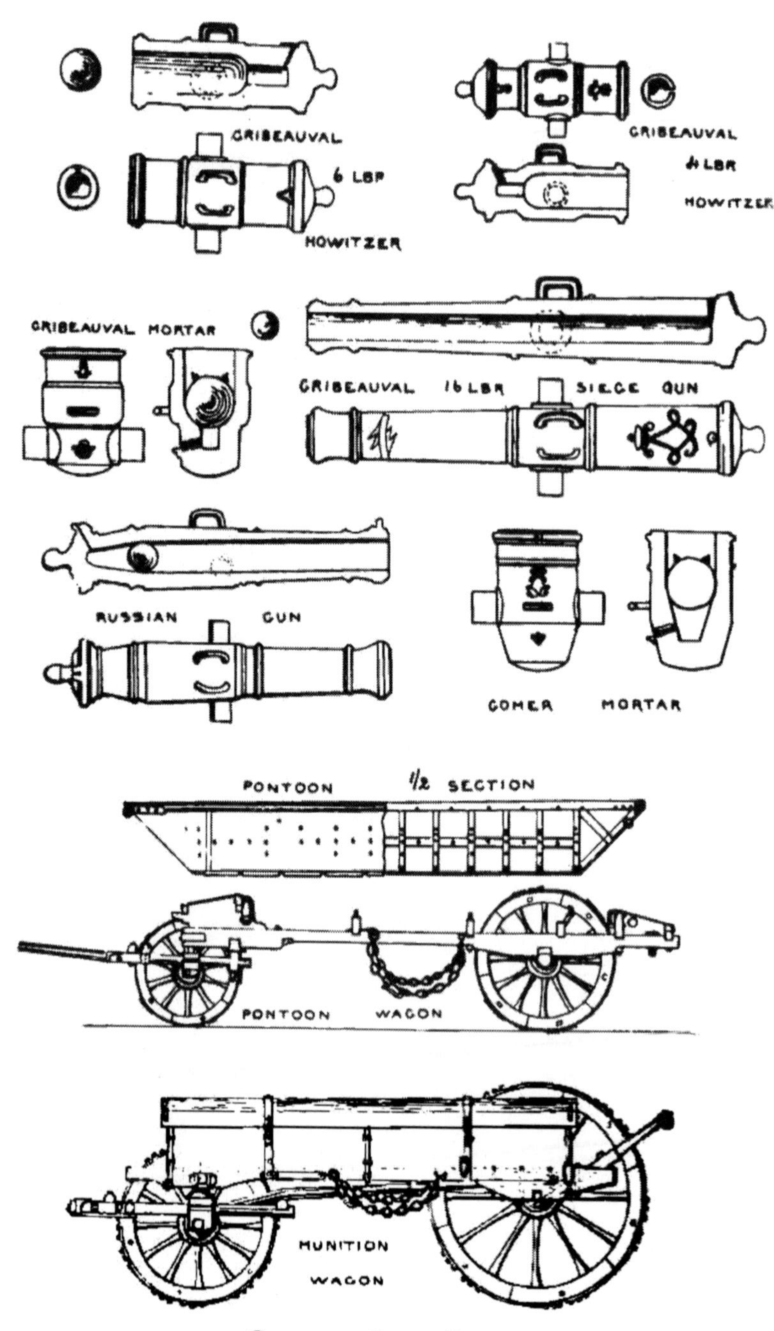

GUNS OF THE PERIOD. BETWEEN

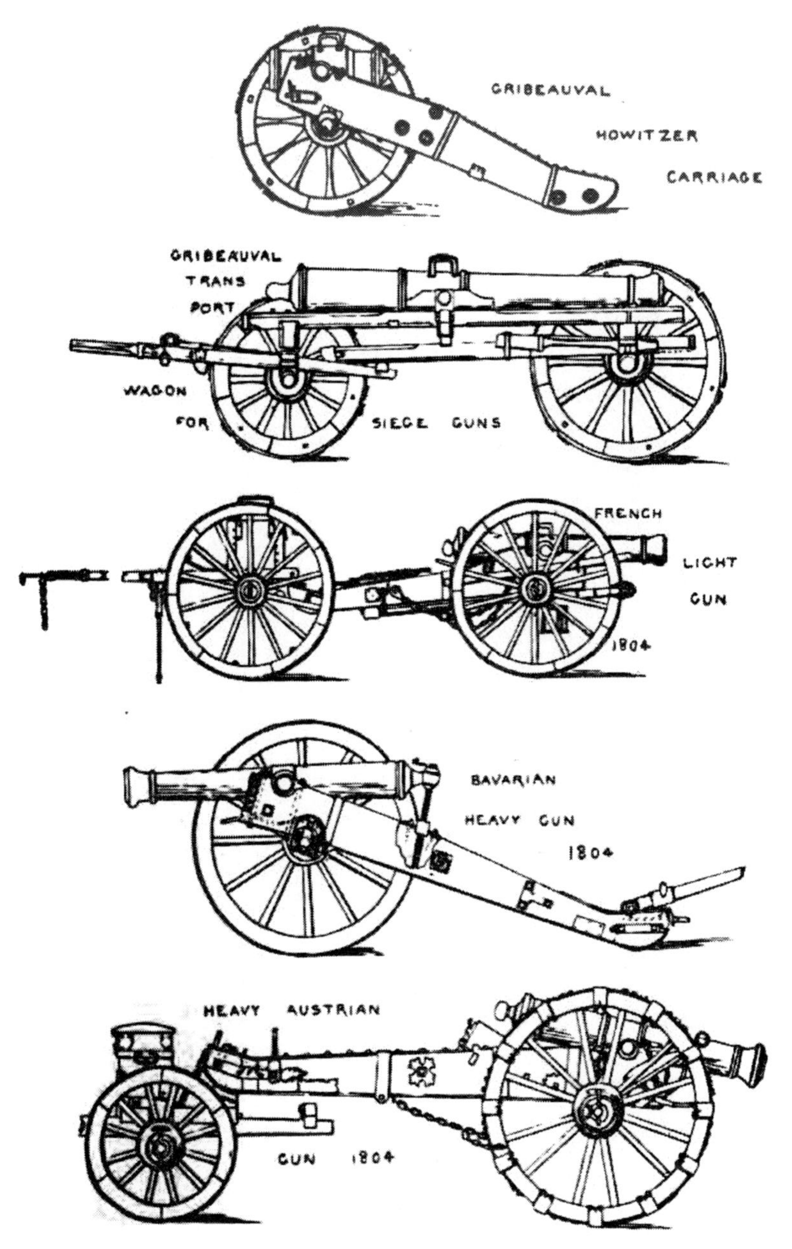

GUNS OF THE PERIOD. BETWEEN

Mameluke in French Service

Dutch Sapper

six guns, that is, the same number of two guns to each battalion was retained. As, however, it was soon discovered that too much artillery retarded the manoeuvres of the army without actual corresponding gain, this allowance was cut down to one gun per battalion, or a six-gun battery to each brigade,—a better proportion. The battalions were no longer hampered by each dragging its own gun, the guns being consolidated into one battery, which followed the brigade manoeuvres. Thus regimental guns gradually disappeared and batteries came into use, consisting of foot and horse artillery, or according to calibres of heavy and light artillery, the organization being that of regiments and companies, or batteries. (Though this distribution changed from time to time, the general trend was towards light artillery rather than heavy; and the mobility of the French armies markedly increased. In 1794 the French field artillery comprised eight regiments of foot and eight regiments of horse artillery, twelve companies of artificers and a battalion of pontoniers. The regiment of foot artillery had a staff and twenty companies; each company was a battery of six guns with eight men per gun, having also supernumeraries for general service; all of which ran the company complement up to ninety-three men. The mounted artillery regiment had a staff and six companies; each company was a battery of six guns with ten men per gun, a total of sixty men. This made nine hundred and sixty guns and fifteen thousand artillerymen in the foot artillery, two hundred and eighty-eight guns and three thousand artillerymen in the mounted artillery; a total of twelve hundred and forty-eight guns and eighteen thousand men. In charge of the corps of artillery were two hundred and twenty-eight general, staff and superior officers, including inspectors of field, coast and fortress artillery, arsenal and labouratory commanders and assistants; and there was a large corps of veteran and coast gunners. The total artillery arm counted over forty thousand men.

Of the heavy batteries, with guns and howitzers of calibres above-named, excepting the six-pounders, six or twelve were united in a *batterie de position*. The four and six-pounders and six-inch howitzers were placed in light batteries made up of four guns and two howitzers. When the French troops were consolidated into divisions, the light artillery got to be called division artillery, and the heavy artillery park or reserve artillery, often *le grand parc*. And inasmuch as the park artillery carried all the reserve ammunition, the division artillery was entirely dependent on it for supplies or for new guns. Such was the 1795 status of the French artillery. A few changes were later made by Bonaparte when First Consul. Gribeauval had long been Inspector-General, but his place was left vacant from his death in 1789 until Bonaparte filled it.

The wretched habit had long obtained of having the guns, caissons and wagons hauled by contract. This was altered in 1801 by the organization of eight "train-battalions." The seventh and eighth mounted regiments of artillery were abolished in 1802, and next year seventeen new artillery companies were organized for colonial service, one being mounted. An attempt was made in 1803 to change Gribeauval's simple calibres; but later this was given up.

In Austria the mounted batteries had six guns each, and the foot artillery was distributed among the infantry regiments, two twelve-pounder or six six-pounder guns with each one. An artillery park accompanied the army, out of which the supply could be increased, or a reserve of guns created. Archduke Charles increased the mounted artillery and added some guns to each corps of light troops. In 1799 the Austrian field artillery was divided into three regiments of eighteen companies each.

The Prussian artillery was partly mounted, partly foot, in batteries and with the foot regiments. Batteries varied greatly in guns and calibres. There were two mortar-batteries of eight ten-pounder mortars each. In 1797 the arm was divided into nine battalions of foot artillery and one battalion of mounted artillery. In the Prussian army operating in France in 1792 there were some thirty thousand foot and eleven thousand horse; and this force had two hundred guns of varied calibre, with the foot regiments and in batteries. This supply was a fair average of all the armies of Europe.

The artillery had its own regulations and tactics. The French artillery was specially speedy in manoeuvre. Artillery schools were constantly improving. The Berlin Artillery Academy, organized by Tempelhof, vied with the Chalons-sur-Marne school. But France had more polytechnic schools, to which cadets went from Chalons; and here they studied two years, and then went for practical work to the "regimental schools" at La Fère, Bésançon, Grenoble, Metz, Strasburg, Douay, Auxonne and Toulouse, where the several artillery regiments had their headquarters.

Engineer Troops, and such men as pontoniers, miners, sappers and artificers, had heretofore been a part of the artillery arm, but in France, early in the Revolutionary War, they were all collected in a special corps of engineers.

Part of the equipment of every army was a pontoon-train. In Aus-

French Sapper   Russian Chevalier Guard

tria and Prussia there were three *pontonier* companies. In France in 1793-94 there were two battalions of six hundred men each; this was reduced next year to one battalion of eight companies of seventy-four men each, and in 1799 a second similar battalion was formed. These *pontonier* companies were constantly practiced in their work, and proved very useful in the Low Countries, Italy and Switzerland, where bridges had constantly to be thrown, not only constructed of boats and pontoons, but made of any material which happened to be at hand. In addition to *pontoniers*, there existed in France bodies of expert swimmers for use in this work, to lead sudden attacks across streams, and to protect the throwing of bridges.

Of miners there were in Austria four companies, in Prussia four, in France a number varying in the several years from four to nine, which at last was fixed at six companies. *Of artificers* there were in France up to 1793 nine companies, from then on twelve companies, each with four officers and eighty-three men.

The sappers were created in 1792; in 1793 there were twelve battalions of eight companies each, the company two hundred men strong, making the battalion sixteen hundred men, and, all told, nineteen thousand two hundred men. In 1793 the sappers and miners, as above stated, were put into the engineer corps, and later the artificers. In 1797 the twelve battalions were cut down to four, and in 1799 a fifth was made, with weaker companies for all. Austria had but three sapper companies.

During the Revolution the French engineer corps at first fell into decay, because many trained officers had left the country; but the arm was later fully revived. Engineer geographers (what we call topographical engineers), road-builders and others of like profession were collected, and the graduates of the polytechnic schools little by little built up the service. In 1794 there were four hundred officers, from generals down, in the corps; later, some additions were made. This corps rose to great prominence in the Revolutionary wars, and attained a high grade of skill and utility under the Empire.

Chapter 2

Tactics and Administration at the End of the 18th Century

During this period most European nations, save France, remained under the influence of Frederick's system, which had been ill-consumed, and had degenerated into formal tactics, and what is known as the cordon system. This was such a posting of troops in small bodies over long fronts as subjected the line to be broken through with ease. For battle armies were similarly marshalled, had no reserves to retrieve disaster, and battles were rarely fought out. In the American Revolution the marksmen-farmers fought in open order behind trees and walls, and won against regular troops in line. Lafayette, Rochambeau and others carried this idea to France, and the French Revolution produced large bodies of skirmishing light foot In addition to this, to utilize the momentary courage of the French recruit, heavy columns charging with the bayonet, and backed up by plentiful artillery, were used. What this period produced was the new system of personal service and the creation of larger amounts of light foot, horse and artillery, which suited the genius of the French people, and made it easier to get value from the young conscript. In open order, sustained by columns and squares, the French soldier did wonders. The army was divided into divisions for administration. Staff duties were made more prominent. Instead of being fed from magazines, rations were requisitioned on the march. The French soldier was taught to make huts or shelters, and tents were abolished. This lightening of the train largely increased the speed of the troops. Other armies followed these movements slowly, but the French kept well ahead of them. They were a constant surprise to the enemy.

Minor and Battle Tactics

At the opening of the French Revolution the influence of the Prussian tactics, which Frederick had so splendidly illustrated, was predominant everywhere, except in France. The three-rank foot and two-rank horse formation was almost universal, but in battle the third rank, in Austria and Prussia, grew to be held superfluous, and later the foot was marshalled in two ranks. In the Austrian army the third rank of each battalion was drilled to withdraw before action, and to form into three two-rank companies, which made up a species of reserve. The English infantry had for a long while stood in only two ranks, and the Spanish campaigns proved the formation equal to all demands. The Austrian cavalry still rode mostly in three; but before action the third rank also withdrew, and ployed into column to protect the flanks. Thus the formation for both attack and defence was a long thin line, in which the foot relied chiefly upon its fire. The main evolutions of minor tactics were advancing and retiring in line, wheelings, ployments and deployments by smaller or greater bodies, forward and flank marches by platoons and sections in close or open column. The battle order of an army usually consisted of two lines of foot with light troops out in front, and a reserve too small to be efficient. Each line was under command of a general officer, and consisted of brigades of from four to six battalions each. The horse invariably stood on the flanks, unless these were leaned on obstacles which would fend off cavalry charges by the enemy; and then the horse was stationed in the rear. Each battalion had a gun or two, and at certain places in the line batteries of reserve artillery of heavier calibre were placed. The mounted artillery was generally employed in the front with the light troops, or with the reserve; or else it accompanied the light troops, if detached; the cavalry was given but little of it to complete its efficiency.

Artillery opened the action, and the skirmish line fended off the enemy's light troops. Then the first line of the attacking army advanced to within musket range of the enemy, strove to break it down by its fire, and when this was done, charged. The cavalry meanwhile sought to outflank and attack the enemy's foot and thus demoralize it. When covered by its cavalry, this had first to be driven in. If the first line did not soon succeed, it was reinforced or relieved by the second line. Should this make no better progress, and the cavalry not have beaten the opposing horse, the victory was rightfully claimed by the enemy, who had stood on the defensive. Concentric attacks were common, in front and on the flanks and rear of the enemy's army; but unless these attacks could be timed so as smartly to work together, the result was apt to be failure. The army acting on the defensive fought in place after much the same fashion, relying on its artillery and infantry fire; and the second line and cavalry assisted the first line. The retiring of the first line was wont to have an ill effect on the second. Hence, unless

Eblé

Rochambeau

Marie Antoinette

Louis XVI

Lafayette

Necker

the first line of the army on the defensive could stand off the enemy's first line and cavalry to good effect, this army would be apt, for fear of defeat, to break off the battle and retire to a fresh field, an operation in those days of slow manoeuvres much more easy of accomplishment than it is today, as the opponent was rarely ready to follow.

Frederick had given to his battles the true flavour of his own burning genius; but as a rule, in disposition for battle and in its conduct, there had since been little homogeneity or concentration. The troops were far too much spread and out of hand. They often lay in small isolated bodies, each exposed to be separately beaten. The whole mass was wont to be put into action at once, so that no reserve was left to re-establish a waning action, or renew an attack which had failed, but which, delivered afresh, might succeed. Battles were never fully fought out, and one party or the other retired from a field half won or lost. Reserves powerful (enough to give a new turn to a battle were unknown. The French troops were the first which, partly by the accident of exceptional conditions, opposed to this system the open order combined with the column of attack. The success of this new idea·quite supplanted the old Prussian lineal tactics; and it forms the most important of the tactical changes of this remarkable period.

Thrice at least in its history America has taught the world some valuable lessons in war. At Concord and Lexington it proved the superiority of good marksmen in open order, each one taking advantage of the accidents of the ground, over seasoned regulars who fought elbow to elbow. In 1812 it gave lessons in naval warfare to the English. In the Civil War, among other things, it re-established what was to be the future role of cavalry which moved in the saddle and fought on foot; what successive thin lines of attack could accomplish; it first armoured ships and effectively used them in war, and it first made many of the inventions in arms which have been the basis of modern rapid fire.

There had been firing in open, or skirmishing, order known as early as the first introduction of firearms. But at the beginning of the eighteenth century only the irregular foot, mostly irresponsible though brave men, thus fought. Then Frederick introduced it among his light infantry; but as the advancing fire of the regular Prussian line was what the king relied on to win his battles, this dispersed manner of fighting never grew to great importance in his scheme. In the American Revolutionary War the open order fighting of the sharpshooting farmers, with little discipline, lent lustre to the system by beating the marshalled lines of British or Hessian

Bavarian Dragoon

regulars, led by excellent officers. What had succeeded in America was imitated in France, many French officers who had served in America being on hand to teach the method. Such were Lafayette and Rochambeau. When the armies of the First Coalition crossed the French border, their long lines were met by irregular parties of skirmishers, who took advantage of every hedge and wall and ditch, and advanced upon them with a fire which did, much harm, though these *franctireurs* suffered little; while in the rear, under cover of the horse, the new levies formed a heavy column of attack in which multitude lent confidence. And when the skirmishers had done their work, this deep column, with true French *élan*, preceded by artillery fire and sustained by cavalry, advanced on the long thin formation of the allies with great effect, and frequently disrupted their weakened line by a charge with the naked weapon. The effect of this novelty in action upon the old-fashioned line of battle was marvellous. Not until the Gaul met the colder-blooded Anglo-Saxon in the Spanish Peninsula did this column rush tactics fail against the line.

While it is true that the use of the open order which began in Europe in the French Revolution was a direct product of American experience, and was imitated by the French under conditions similar to those which had prevailed in the New World a decade before, the ployment into a deep column of the reserve was already well known. Folard, early in the eighteenth century, made plans to draw up troops for battle in deep formation, so as to attack with the pike and bayonet. This was in part a copy of the Greek *phalanx*, or of the "battles" of the Middle Ages; but it was also founded on the French national character, which Folard aptly recognized as being better adapted to a charge in column than to long-drawn-out fire in a slender line. But there was too great formality in war in Folard's time to lend his column any proper success; and at the end of his century there was far too much adherence to the Prussian line system to enable anything but an entire change of conditions to bring about a new method of infantry attack. Two other French military authors, Mesnil-Durand and Guibert, indulged in long and bitter controversies on these points; but nothing was settled until the raw levies of the French Revolution, instinct with patriotic fervour, found that some new means of overcoming the allied troops was called for. This means proved to be the above described attack in mass with the blank weapon, covered by heavy artillery fire and sustained by horse. The endless theorizing of Folard, Mesnil-Durand and Guibert was supplanted by an instant and practical object lesson. Yet their works had pointed out the way.

Swedish Line Infantryman

Dutch Hussar

Thus arose, in France first of all European countries, a large body of light infantry trained to fight in open order; and its success also introduced a similar training in the line infantry. Following hard upon this came, as an essential sequence, the creation of battalion columns which should attack with the bayonet, a tactics which was also learned by both light and heavy infantry. These two quite opposite yet consistent ideas were united and made to work together; and their use soon rendered them effective. Later, in Egypt, the square against cavalry, long used by Russians and Austrians in battle with the Turks and Tartars, and by the English in India, came into play, and the French grew expert in combining these three methods.

Another meritorious French idea was the creation of the grand-tactical unit known as the division,, in which all three arms should be represented, and should work together jointly. This assembled an excellent body for separate action, or for action in unison with other divisions, and it was not so large or unwieldy but that a general of moderate ability and active habit could handle it. The main weakness of every army lay in the fact that there were not reserves of infantry or artillery of sufficient size to be effective. There was an artillery park, but this was rather to supply gaps than to act as reserve artillery; and the infantry reserve was always kept too small, while there was no cavalry reserve at all. The cavalry was divided up among the divisions, and even if collected, it was not habituated to operate in great masses. To the credit of Hoche, the commander-in-chief of the Army of the Sambre and Meuse in 1797, it must be scored that he first thought of collecting the cavalry (dragoons, *chasseurs*, and hussars) into special divisions. This was an important step, but it yet did not amount to a cavalry reserve. In 1796-97, in Italy, Bonaparte on several occasions took the cavalry from the divisions and collected it into a cavalry reserve. But this was an unusual step; and at the end of the eighteenth century the general want of foot and horse reserves was much felt. For this reason, too, the mounted artillery was of lessened utility, as it had no considerable body of cavalry with which to act. But though the French cavalry could not work in masses, it had become excellent for outpost, scouting and minor duties. And it learned to fight in open order like the foot, which until the middle of this century had been done in Europe only by the Turks, Cossacks, Poles and Hungarians; and this method was gradually put into practice by the line cavalry.

There were nine years of uninterrupted war following the opening of the French Revolution; and these years gave the young and able men who furthered the destinies of the new Republic oppor-

Austrian Light Grenadier

tunity to introduce and perfect the fresh system of war above spoken of. To this system the French raw levies owed their successes; the alert Gaul eagerly lent himself to forwarding it; and the Revolutionary armies attained so remarkable an elasticity and ability to manoeuvre, such speed in marching, and such energy in battle, as to lend them an unquestioned preponderance over their enemies. Moreover, the Convention ruling France, never freed from fear that the troops would rise against its merciless authority, kept the several armies in constant motion from one point on the frontier to another, never leaving them long in any one place, nor affording them idleness in which to conjure up mischief; and as a result the divisions acquired a mobility in marching and manoeuvring, a power to overcome difficulties and sustain prolonged exertion, which in a few months gave the raw French soldier the qualities of the veteran. All this gain was of course not made without much opposition to the new system, without many grievous backsets, as well as many splendid victories. There were not wanting able men who discredited the new idea, and would have put the French soldier back into the old line-of-battle rut. And it was only real and brilliant success which at length settled the new tactics as peculiarly adapted to the French genius, and as superior to the Prussian lineal-tactics. From France the new system slowly spread, forcing its way against the opposition of the old school; but during this entire period there was, in other European countries, a mixing of the old with the new, a struggle of the latter for precedence, which lent the art of war a colour far from clear, and helped to confuse the operations of armies.

There was much written discussion in these days of the rival systems. Advocates of the new system theorized about its advantages and wrought out of darkness a definite method; while the lovers of the old clung to their ancient habits. Lindenau's noteworthy *Higher Prussian Tactics*, issued in 1790, showed that what was left of Frederick's method, a mere shadow indeed, though then deemed the best in existence, was full of impossibilities and of imperfections. Other writers followed Lindenau, and by pointing out the value of the one and the weakness of the other, prepared the way for the advent of the new system. And this system was perfected much earlier and to better advantage in France than in the other European countries, and lent the French armies a marked advantage.

The Decree of the Convention of March 15, 1792, divided France into sixteen "military divisions" or sections. Each of these divisions controlled several of the so-called "departments," and all the troops, line and National Guard, therein stationed. These military divisions were kept in force for many years. They were in no sense allied to the tactical divisions, into which, as above stated, the army was divided at about the same time. This latter organization, whose administration was distinct, made a great change for the better, so far as responsibility and care of the troops was concerned. In active service the tactical divisions were homogeneous bodies well adapted to every species of duty. Four or five divisions, placed under one leader, made up an army which was convenient to handle up to a certain size, say forty thousand men. But in large armies it was found that these bodies were too small and numerous, and that they made too many units, for one commanding general to handle. This led to placing several divisions into an army corps, the first instance of which was in Moreau's army in Germany in the 1800 campaign. This army had eleven divisions; and these were consolidated into four corps, *viz.*: the reserve of three divisions under Moreau; the right wing of three divisions under Lecourbe; the centre of three divisions under St. Cyr, and the left wing of two divisions under Ste. Susanne. This excellent idea shortly spread to the other French armies. The rest of the European nations had, during peace, adopted the regiment as the unit of administration; during war, several regiments were wont to be placed in a so-called division under a general officer, whose staff was an adjutant-general, two assistant adjutant-generals and one engineering officer. The separate armies had larger but similar staffs of higher rank. But the administration was not taken from the regiments.

Administration and Supplies

For the supply departments in France there were war commissaries, and these officials, often to the confusion of all regularity, were quite independent of military control. Before the Revolution there was a general staff for the whole army, one for the artillery and infantry, and one for the cavalry; these were in 1792 consolidated into a single body. The utility of a general staff had long been recognized by military men, somewhat on the lines of those which are so efficient today, though far less detailed in organization; but no such body was actually created until the end of the eighteenth century. In France engineer officers and topographical engineers were appointed by the Convention to do duty quite similar to that of a general staff; but until the period of the Consuls, the idea was not broadened. When Bonaparte became First Consul, he began such work by or-

French Marine

Austrian Royal Infantryman

ganizing the "Depot de la Guerre," and by increasing the corps of geographic engineers. His system of maps and charts became excellent. It was then a novelty, the lack of which, as in Moreau's 1799 campaign, was grievously felt.

The entire direction of military affairs in France was held by the ministry of war, whose chief, the war minister, was responsible to the heads of the State. There was a War Council prior to 1789, which in 1790 was called a War Commission, and was made up of members of the Assembly; and later under the Convention a War Committee. During the early years of the Revolution and under the Convention, there was much disorder and irregularity in military affairs; but under the Directory and Consulate, especially by Bonaparte's efforts, matters were regulated and carried on with method. The work of the engineers and artillery was particularly to be commended.

When the reorganization of the French army was effected in the years 1793 to 1795, a number of changes were made, partly only in nomenclature, the record of which appears slightly confused. Infantry regiments became known as "half-brigades," lieutenant-colonels (or majors) as chiefs of battalions; colonels as chiefs of squadrons; brigadier-generals as commanders of half-brigades; *maréchals des camps* (or major-generals) as generals of brigade, lieutenant-generals as generals of division; marshals of France as generals-in-chief. And the staff officers were known as chief of staff, adjutant-general, adjutant-major, etc. Promotions were changed so that a third went by seniority, and two thirds among the generals by selection of the ministry, and among the lesser officers by selection of those of equal rank. Commanders of half-brigades were promoted only by seniority. The generals in chief were selected by the government from the generals of division. In 1801 there was appointed in the cavalry, and in 1804 in all the other regiments, a staff officer with title of Major, to whom was committed, as a species of assistant to the commander of the regiment, the charge of the horses and equipments, instruction and discipline.

The pay of the troops, up to the time of the Consulate, was very irregularly made, and then only in paper money. This was, in view of the condition of the French finances and the huge levies, by no means to be wondered at; but it gave rise to very great dissatisfaction and unrest, not infrequently to mutinies. Not before the consular period was this corrected. Nor was France an exception. In the German armies it was nearly as bad.

The most important change of this era was in the victualling of the armies. During the first Revolutionary campaigns the troops were fed by the long-used system of magazines, common all over Europe. It was the war commissary who served with each army to whom was committed this task; and this official handled all moneys and issued all supplies. Soon this means proved insufficient, on account of the large levies to be fed, of the rapid movements required of them over all kinds of country, in much of which supplies were hard to get, and particularly because the war commissaries commonly proved to be inefficient, and all too often dishonest. Many of these men grew rich while the troops starved; and yet the military authorities had no control over them. It was much like, and worse than the clashing of the Indian agents and the army officers in the Indian wars of the United States. These war commissaries procured influence in Paris by the usual means known to all ages and in all climes, and were thus protected in their authority and their peculations. The fact that the army commanders could not get their troops fed led them to resort to requisitions on the inhabitants of the countries traversed. Thus in 1792 and 1793 the French armies got victual partly from the magazines, and partly by forced requisitions, the latter being mostly accompanied by disorder and pillage. The next year, 1794, requisitions became the rule. From the moment the troops left their quarters, they began to levy for their food and forage on every peasant and in every village. If not willingly given, the provision was taken by force, both in France and in foreign lands. Thus arose, out of the existing evil conditions, the excellent system of victualling by requisitions, at the inception an irregular and unsystematic plan, accompanied by much plundering and suffering to the country occupied, but later worked into a methodical procedure, chiefly during the Consulate and by the efforts of Bonaparte.

This was not an entirely new means of victualling. In the Thirty Years' War, and indeed before and after, armies had been fed on the country. In fact, the reason for moving into any given territory was often not so much strategic as that it afforded good supplies; and the land traversed was wont to be left a desert. The armies of the seventeenth century moved slowly, and eat out the country before they left it. The French Revolutionary armies requisitioned as they went rapidly along. The object of the one was to find a prosperous country which might be plundered, so as to keep the mercenaries of some potentate from disbanding until some happy manoeuvre or accident yielded the advantage sought; that of the other was to enable it to live while carrying out a legitimate operation.

It was only in the French armies, at first, that this system took root,

Russian Grenadier

while the other nations continued to rely on magazines; and this accounts for the more rapid marches of the French. But it was by no means a perfect system, and much suffering among the troops and infinitely more still among the country people was the result, as well as marked deterioration of the discipline of the French levies. It was, however, well suited to the offensive character of the French wars; and as good results followed the rapid manoeuvring of their armies, the system prospered. Nothing hampers the operations of an army so much as laboured victualling; nothing leaves it so free as to live on the country, if this is rich. But in a poor land, or one long occupied, the result is sure to be a crop of the worst outrages and crimes by the men, as well as much deprivation for the troops, coupled to a complete devastation of the territory passed over. Bonaparte's orders on this subject in 1796, and frequently thereafter, show to what this system had grown. The other European armies still clung to their magazines; and it must be acknowledged that these were not much more successfully managed; for the Prussians in 1792 suffered greatly on account of defective victualling, both in strength and discipline; and the Austrian campaigns in Italy from 1796 to 1800 were vastly hampered by the difficulty of magazine-victualling, in the effort to oppose Bonaparte's more rapid operations, which were fostered by living on the country.

Baggage

In this period, too, the baggage trains began to be limited, and the abolishing of the daily transportation and erection of tents added as much as requisitions to the mobility of the French armies. In lieu of tents the French levies were taught to construct huts or shelters out of boards taken from nearby buildings, branches of trees, poles, straw and other materials, much as American Continentals had done a dozen years before. Even in permanent quarters this plan was made to work well. All people used to frontier life, or with a knowledge of woodcraft, know how comfortably men can house themselves with even limited material. The system among the French cut down the number of wagons to a small fraction of what they had been, and vastly increased the mobility of their columns. It was imitated towards the end of the century by other nations, and helped decrease the enormous trains, but scarcely in the same degree as with the French. For instance, the Prussian train in 1792 carried one hundred and eight tents for each battalion, and forty for each squadron, to transport which there were needed twenty-eight horses and sixteen men for the infantry tents, and sixteen horses and eight men for the cavalry. Each infantry and artillery company had one, and each squadron two wagons for rations; and in addition to these, each battalion was followed by four, and each squadron by two two-horse wagons to carry the tent-poles and blankets of the men. The officers were allowed wagons, horses and servants, according to rank. The result was that for an infantry regiment which had twenty-two hundred combatants, there were over twenty-four hundred noncombatants and four hundred horses in the train; for a cavalry regiment of five squadrons with nine hundred mounted men, there were nearly eleven hundred men and twelve hundred horses!

Hospital service during this period dragged on, as a rule, in the same old ruts, although many learned books were written on military hygiene, war surgery, etc., and though in some European armies an effort was made to better the practice of the art of healing.

Discipline

As regards discipline and morale, the French armies at the opening of the Revolutionary period were on the lowest possible scale; but by the efforts of the many able men and officers whom the troublous era brought to the front, this condition was changed, so that by the end of the century the evils always attending ft time of civil war and anarchy were finally and fully corrected. But the early years were one long record of mutinies against generals suspected of treachery, against officers loosely charged with appropriating the soldiers' pay and rations, and for numerous other causes. In Metz and Nancy these mutinies reached their flood-tide in extensive outbreaks. Politics invaded the ranks, especially in the National Guard and the fresh levies. This mixture of politics and war led naturally, at the first reverse, to a cry of treason by the men against the officers suspected, and to these officers being murdered on the spur of the moment, or to their being speedily brought to the guillotine. Later there was less of this wayward conduct, but real discipline consumed a decade to bring about. Infrequent pay, poor rations and the establishment by the Convention of "public denunciators" and "revolutionary tribunals" in the armies made it easy for discontent to take the form of a legal arraignment of any unpopular general as an "enemy of the country," which was wont to be followed on a half-hearing by the execution of the supposed offender. As a result, the efforts of even such leaders as Hoche, Pichegru, Moreau and others were long unrewarded by any real gain in discipline! Only those who were favourites with the men could accomplish anything. But on the other hand, the sharp, long and energetic wars bred an unflinching spirit and a power of endurance among the French troops which was of the highest type; and this in a way took the place of formal discipline. And while it is true that to the French soldiery—as indeed to nearly all other troops of the day—can be traced untold instances of cruelty, robbery, arson and rapine, yet these same troops withstood hunger, cold, toil and danger in a manner beyond all praise. Gallant and bold, though fierce and unrelenting, the Revolutionary French soldier covered himself with glory. By 1796 these good qualities rose to their greatest height, and from that year on, not only were his deeds more marked, but his general conduct became more soldierly; and the discipline in general responded, as is usual, to the character of the officer in command. But discipline as we understand it today, that discipline which tends to lessen the horrors of war by making the soldier respect the rights of others, while in no wise decreasing his fighting qualities, was never known in the Revolutionary or Napoleonic armies.

A change in military penalties was made during the Revolutionary wars. Corporal punishment, usual for centuries, was abolished. A new penal code prescribed death for the higher crimes and imprisonment for the lesser. It is curious that in this code no mention is made of duelling, though this was common, not only among individuals, but between bodies of men, whole companies indeed; a fact which led to much absurd but lamentable bloodshed. The habit may have been considered as essential to sustain the honour of a corps as well as of an individual; and the term "honour" was then more apt to be misconstrued than now. A system of military orders and decorations was instituted by the Convention. The highest reward that a French citizen could attain was public mention by the government as having well deserved of the country ("*bien mérite de la patrie*"). It was Napoleon, as First Consul, who again began the ancient tokens of reward by medals, swords of honour, pensions of soldiers, their wives and orphans, paid out of the army and navy appropriations, and the institution in 1802 of the Legion of Honour. Although the Convention had decreed that captured Vendeans and *émigrés* should be shot without trial, it is to be said to its honour that all other prisoners of war were placed under the shelter of the law, and received rations and even a small money payment. The shooting of Vendeans naturally led to retaliation, and such consequent cruelty as lent the war of the Vendée a peculiar atrocity.

BADEN MUSKETEER WESTPHALIAN GUARD GRENADIER

Balloons and Telegraphs

There were two inventions made in this period which added somewhat of interest to military matters, those of balloons and telegraphic signalling. So soon as balloons were conceived by Montgolfier in 1782, the idea of their utility in field operations was mooted. Aero-static Institutes were started in Paris to prepare airships which could be availed of to observe the enemy, and these captive balloons were actually employed in the early Revolutionary wars. Companies of aeronauts were created, and each army was accompanied by two balloons and a proper service. At first the officers who ascended used the naval signals; but they later employed telegraphic instruments, then just discovered. Teams of thirty and forty horses were attached to these captive balloons to move them from place to place; but as all other efforts to make them dirigible were fruitless, they proved to be of questionable utility. At the Battle of Fleurus in 1794, the captain of aeronauts, Coutelle by name, remained above the Austrian lines for nine hours, and telegraphed the movements of the enemy to the French army. It was not this, however, that won the battle, but it had its effect in raising the spirits of the French and in annoying the Austrians. A balloon and full equipment accompanied Bonaparte to Egypt; but we do not learn of its having been used, and after this the service declined. Telegraphic or semaphonic signalling had been well known to the ancients. In modern times, the first use in war of the new electric art was at this period. Especially at the siege of Mainz, a Frenchman named Chappé constructed a simple means of military telegraphy; and later a number of men of science improved the system.

Fortification and Field-works

Perhaps in no war were field fortifications and temporary defences put to use more than in the French Revolution. On a large scale the system of separate redoubts, mutually supporting each other, took the place of the old fortified lines. This was, it must be remembered, the era of cordon lines of defence; and it was not unusual to find, for the protection of a frontier, or of an army in quarters, or otherwise, a long line of these separate works. On the north, east and south, in the first Revolutionary wars, France was in fact surrounded by a girdle of several lines of such works, as supplementary to the large fortresses; and between these lay a dozen armies stretched out in cordon. These redoubts usually had a sharp profile and excellent obstacles in their front; and though the old form was conserved, the works were now constructed so as better to conform to the lay of the land. And yet, as always happens, even in what were called inaccessible positions, these redoubts were often captured out of hand.

Field fortifications grew apace in these wars. Many engineers and men of science took up the subject, and Fouassac, Jetze and Marquard added much to it. D'Arçon showed how isolated works could support each other, and the *terrain* be utilized to this end; Hennert in Holland wrote learnedly on permanent fortification. This latter art was also improved. War sat upon all western Europe; there was no time to build new fortresses; but much was done in improving those existing. Mainz was a good sample of such work, the city being transformed into a fortress in 1792-93. Chasseloup and Bousmard drew plans to correct the evil of leaving fortified places open to ricochet firing, and to the breaching of the main wall at any point. All the means adopted by Vauban, Coehorn and others had not been able to prevent the effectiveness of ricochet firing, except at great expense. Calibres of guns for fortresses were changed. In 1792 it was ordered that a third of such guns should be sixteen-pounders and twenty-four-pounders, a third twelve-pounders and a third smaller. One marked idea in the changes instituted was to make the work suit the existing conditions, not to construct it by hard and fast rules. The details of these improvements, however, belong to the engineer's art and not to this history.

On the other hand, the means of taking fortresses was somewhat improved. The siege-batteries were given more mortars, and guns capable of ricochet firing; and though there are no instances of the capture of large fortresses out of hand, and few by bombardment alone, yet the regular sieges were much shortened in duration, though they remained the same in form. There cannot be said to have been a distinct gain in the art of besieging in this period. As a rule, when a breach was made, a fortress was surrendered with honour, and with free exit of the garrison; or at least, the garrison surrendered as prisoners of war. Acre was one of the most noteworthy sieges of this epoch.

Rations and Pay

As all men who have seen service know, a soldier, during a serious campaign, rations himself as best he may. Messes and other means of feeding the troops may at any moment lose organization and utility, and the hard-worked man eats as, and when, and what he can. But in the French army there was supposed to be a mess for each company, the bulk of the expense of which was borne by the government, and the rest deducted from the soldiers' pay. The men largely lived on soup and bread; meat and vegetables were issued when procurable, to make a *pot-au-feu*; and issues of wine at night and brandy in the morning were usual. In garrison or on a peace footing the men lived better in the ranks than the average French peasant,—a fact which partly reconciled the raw recruit to his new life. In the field, of course, it was alternate abundance and starvation, more frequently the latter than the former.

The pay at different periods was that given in the following tables, a consider-able part of the dues to the enlisted men being consumed in mess money, and money for shoes and underclothing. For instance, in a decree of March 12, 1806, aiming to "furnish soldiers more abundant nourishment to protect their health," it was ordered—

> . . . . that from the 1st of May there should be furnished an ordinary mess administered by the captains. This mess was to be made up from the five *centimes* previously ordered plus ten *centimes* now given to the men present for duty, and from what remains of the pay,—washing, footgear and pocket-money excepted. Out of this amount, companies are to be provided with three ounces of white bread per head for soup, a half pound of meat and necessary vegetables. The captains may manage this matter as seems best to them, according to the existing conditions, but must not divert any of the money to other purposes. The colonel or other commander is to inspect this matter every month. On a war-footing, fifteen *centimes* is to be taken from the soldier's pay, for which he is to receive four ounces of bread in addition to his ration, half a pound of meat and two ounces of vegetables.

And Bonaparte wrote about the same time to Forfait, Minister of Marine:

> Why, Citizen Minister, do they give a pound of beef to the English prisoners, while the ration of the soldier is but half a pound?

Just prior to the French Revolution the pay of the troops appears to have been as follows, the *livre* being twenty *sous* or cents.

INFANTRY.

Colonel — a sinecure	3,000 livres a year.	
Lieutenant-colonel	2,000 "	"
Captain of Grenadiers	2,000 "	"
Captain of Fusiliers	1,500 "	"
Lieutenant of Grenadiers	900 "	"
Lieutenant of Fusiliers	600 "	"
Sub-lieutenant of Grenadiers	600 "	"
Sub-lieutenant of Fusiliers	540 "	"
Sergeant of Grenadiers	222 "	"
Sergeant of Fusiliers	204 "	"
Private of Grenadiers	125 "	"
Private of Fusiliers	107 "	"

CAVALRY.

Mestre de Camp (colonel)	4,700 livres a year.	
Lieutenant-colonel	3,600 "	"
Major	3,000 "	"
Sub-major	1,000 "	"
Quartermaster	600 "	"
Standard-bearer	480 "	"
Treasurer	2,000 "	"
Captain	2,000 "	"
Lieutenant	900 "	"
Sub-lieutenant	600 "	"
Maréchal des Logis (Sergeant)	13 sous a day.	
Fourrier (Company quartermaster)	12 "	"
Brigadier (Corporal)	8 "	"
Private	7 sous 9 deniers a day.	

In the dragoons and hussars the pay varied somewhat from these rates.

During the French Revolution there were a number of laws passed relating to this subject. The last one, of September 9, 1799, established the total pay of a regiment of infantry at *Frs*. 529,065.30 a year. Under the Empire the principal acts were dated December 30, 1810, and June 15, 1812.

Under the law of July 20, 1794, the pay was as follows:

INFANTRY, LINE AND LIGHT.

Chief of Brigade	21 livres 10 sous a day.
Chief of Battalion	15 " 10 " "
Quartermaster Treasurer	6 " 10 " "
Adjutant Major	9 " "
Adjutant Major's Assistant	2 " 9 " "
Drum Major	1 " 9 " "
Private	about 10 to 13 " "
Captain	9 livres "
Lieutenant	5 " 10 " "
Sub-lieutenant	4 " 5 " "

These prices varied somewhat in the grenadiers, *carbineers* and fusiliers; and there were a number of ranks, such as saddler, armourer, tailor, shoemaker, trousers-maker, artist-veterinary, etc., and various musicians.

CAVALRY, LINE AND LIGHT.

Chief of Brigade	22 livres a day.
Chief of Squadron	16 " "
Quartermaster Treasurer	6 " 10 sous a day.
Non-commissioned Adjutant	2 " 9 " "

In the artillery there were several grades of captains receiving from 6 to 10 *livres* a day, and the other officers and non-commissioned officers were paid substantially like the infantry. Successive laws made a number of changes, but none of great moment.

By the law of May 18, 1797, the following rates were established for generals and staff officers:

General-in-chief	40,000 livres a year.
General of Division	18,000 " "
General of Brigade	12,000 " "
Adjutant-general	7,000 " "
Chief of Brigade	5,500 " "
Chief of Squadron or of Battalion	4,000 " "
Captain	2,300 " "
Lieutenant	1,450 " "
Sub-lieutenant	1,100 " "
Chief Commissary of War	12,000 " "
Commissary of War	8,000 " "
Commissary of first class	4,000 " "
Commissary of second class	3,500 " "

The pay of the enlisted men varied considerably, but ran between 6 *sous* a day for privates to 32 *sous* a day for non-commissioned adjutants. A surgeon not commissioned in a regiment received from 15 to 20 *livres* a day. By the law of September 9, 1799, a

General of Division	**received**	**12,000**	**francs a year.**
General of Brigade	**"**	**8,000**	**" "**
Adjutant-general	**"**	**6,000**	**" "**
Aide Brigadier-general	**"**	**5,500**	**" "**
Aide Major	**"**	**4,000**	**" "**
Aide Captain	**"**	**2,500**	**" "**
Aide Lieutenant	**"**	**1,450**	**" "**

The commissaries of war received from 3500 to 8000 *francs*. The line was thus paid:

LINE INFANTRY.

Chief of Brigade	**5,000**	**francs a year.**
Chief of Battalion	**3,600**	**" "**
Quartermaster	**1,200**	**francs a year.**
Adjutant Major	**2,000**	**" "**
Doctor	**800 to 2,000**	**" "**
Drum Major	**292**	**" "**
Captain	**1,800 to 2,400**	**" "**
Lieutenant	**1,100 to 1,250**	**" "**
Sub-lieutenant	**1,000**	**" "**
Sergeant	**225 to 300**	**" "**
Corporal	**165**	**" "**
Private	**110**	**" "**
Drummer	**146**	**" "**

The *carbineers* were paid slightly more.

LINE CAVALRY.

Chief of Brigade	**5,500**	**francs a year.**
Chief of Squadron	**4,000**	**" "**
Quartermaster	**1,400**	**" "**
Surgeon	**2,000**	**" "**
Artist veterinary	**324**	**" "**
Master saddler	**286**	**" "**
Armorer spur-maker	**286**	**" "**
Master boot-maker	**122**	**" "**
Trousers-maker	**122**	**" "**

Tailor	122	"	"
Adjutant Major	2,300	"	"
Captain	2,500	"	"
Lieutenant	1,450	"	"
Sub-lieutenant	1,150	"	"
Private	122	"	"
Trumpeter	256	"	"

FOOT ARTILLERY

The foot artillery was paid ten to fifteen *per cent*, more, and the mounted artillery about twenty *per cent*, more, than the cavalry. Artificers and pontoniers were paid about the same as the infantry.

On May 30, 1810, an Imperial decree was issued, tabulating and settling the pay of all the troops, to begin January 1, 1811, mess money being merged into the pay of the troops. The table annexed to this decree is long and intricate, but a few items being of present interest. There was a mess to cover underclothing and foot-gear, to which the soldiers contributed thirty francs a year. The rules for employment of the ration money were made more positive. Under this decree a

Colonel received	400 to 416	francs	a month.
Major	358	"	"
Chief of battalion	300	"	"
Adjutant	166	"	"
Quartermaster Treasurer	(minimum) 100	"	"
Eagle-bearer	104	"	"
Sergeant Major	48	"	"
Wagon-master	50	"	"
Eagle-bearer's assistant	24	"	"
Drum Major	24	"	"
Musicians	16	"	"
Master workmen	9	"	"
Captain	150 to 200	"	"
Lieutenant	91 to 104	"	"
Sub-lieutenant	83	"	"
Sergeant	20 to 25	"	"
Corporal	15	"	"
Drummer	13	"	"
Private	10	"	"

To this were added rations when in the field, the supply being

Hungarian Grenadier

lessened when in quarters. The pay of cavalry was some ten *per cent*, higher; the pay of the foot artillery averaged twenty *per cent*, higher; and the mounted artillery averaged between twenty-five and thirty *per cent*, higher than that of the infantry. The soldiers of the artillery train were paid still higher, and the pontoniers and men of that class were also better compensated. Artificers generally averaged fifty *per cent*, more than infantrymen. Officers of the train were paid nearly forty *per cent*, more than infantry officers. Doctors received monthly from one hundred and sixty-six to two hundred and twenty-five *francs*, according to the length of service, in time of peace; and in the field about forty *per cent*. more. For extra distance, in addition to the regular day's march, additional pay was given, from two *francs* to the colonel down to ten *centimes* to the soldier.

To resume what has been said, in this period in France a new system of war arose, suited to the changed conditions, in which the people took part as such, and not as mercenaries. At first full of the rough earnestness of the Revolution, this system was completed by the Consuls. Infantry was divided into half-brigades (regiments) and brigades; and light infantry was increased. Cavalry was also increased, especially the light cavalry. Artillery gained much, and horse batteries were created. Engineer troops were formed into separate organizations. Tactically, open order came into use, with better fire and less loss of life as a result, and it was sustained by columns and squares for attack. The French troops surpassed all others in their new system. Administratively, the creation of divisions was the most important step; and staff duties were made more prominent. Victualling by requisition instead of by magazines grew into use. Tents gave way to huts and other temporary shelter; and the train was markedly cut down. Much increased speed followed the change.

In other European countries little was at first done to alter the old system. When the French showed the superiority of the new system, a few changes were begun. Such were the collection of regimental guns in batteries; the imitation of the French infantry formation; the creation of divisions; the giving up of tents; the increase of artillery, light foot and light horse. But no European army during these wars in any degree reached the mobility of the French. Fortification was theoretically improved; practically no great advance was made.

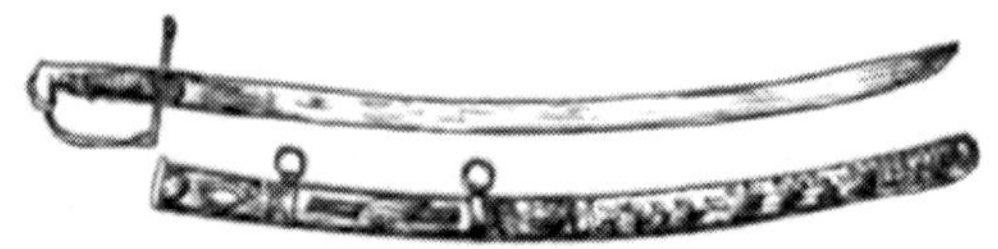

CHAPTER 3

Wars of the French Revolution

1792

The early years of the French Revolution are interesting from a historical rather than a military standpoint. Louis XIV. and Louis XV. had created an enormous debt. The peasants were downtrodden, but the middle classes had increased in intelligence. Free-thinking writers had filled the minds of all with ideas of independence, and to this the American Revolution added fuel. To raise money, Louis XVI. called together the States General in 1789. The Third Estate exerted its numerical power over the Nobles and Clergy, and formed a National Assembly. This body began to demolish the monarchy, and the king finally became the prisoner of the people. The Royalists emigrated, and urged outside nations to intervene. This the Emperor of Germany and the King of Prussia did in 1791, and the invasion of France in 1792 led up to a Reign of Terror. The people rose to defend its frontiers, and fended off attack on northern France. Another allied army expected to move through Champagne to Paris, but the advance was slow and ill-conducted. Having crossed the Argonnes, the allies under Brunswick were defeated in an artillery battle at Valmy by Dumouriez and Kellermann. This success raised the courage of the French and enabled Dumouriez to beat the allies at Jemappes in Belgium, and Montesquieu to conquer part of Savoy. After these victories the enthusiastic French soldier felt that he could face all Europe.

Before approaching the great era which Napoleon illustrated by his victories, we must make a rapid survey of the years which preceded his *début* on the military stage of Europe. The early campaigns of the French Revolution are of marked historical interest, but scarcely being within the scope of this work, they cannot be treated in great detail. The changes in organization and tactics are of more value than any lessons taught by the marches and battles. A sketch of the Revolution and a short narrative of its early campaigns is, however, essential to draw attention to the status of the art of war when Bonaparte electrified the world by his brilliant Italian campaign in 1796.

The role of France in the Seven Years' War had not been one to enhance her reputation or standing. But at its close, the French royal family, allied by marriage with Austria, Piedmont, Spain and Naples, was, under Louis XV., in a position to hold the balance of power of Europe. No country but England disputed her sway, and this at sea alone. And England, towards the end of the eighteenth century, by ill-calculated methods, succeeded in losing her American colonies, to the great weakening of her sea power.

The never ceasing wars of Louis XIV., and the heedless expenditures of Louis XV., had created for France a burden of debt beyond her power to carry. The crushing taxes called for by this debt and by the insane extravagances of the French Court should, for the sake of equity and wisdom, have fallen not only on the people, but on the nobility and the clergy as well. But the classes, though holding most of the land, steadily strove to shift the burden from their own to the shoulders of the masses, and by evading many taxes sapped the financial power of the throne. The political standing of France in Europe did not improve, and money matters finally drove the throne to call together the States General to devise means of lightening the burden. This body consisted of the Nobles, the Clergy and the Middle Classes, or Third Estate.

The leaders of the people had grown intelligent, rich and powerful. Downtrodden though the peasants still were, the middle classes had notably increased in brawn and brain. England in the prior centuries, America a few years before, had taught the masses valuable lessons. The revolutionary idea had for twenty years found a lodgement in all French minds, from peasant to courtier. Montesquieu, Voltaire, Rousseau, the Encyclopedists, Helvetius, Diderot and many other irrepressible writers, had spread abroad doctrines dangerous to the monarchy. Land, of which the peasantry and middle classes held but a small share, was miserably tilled, and the guilds limited trade and industry. Arbitrary government, rank abuses in the administration, *lettres de cachet* by which anyone could be imprisoned, *lits de justice* to collect unequal taxes, forced and unpaid labour on roads and other public works (*corvées*), had brought the middle classes into a condition ripe for any, even a violent remedy. The political hearth of France was covered with inflammable matter; to conserve the kingdom, sparks should have been kept away from it. Instead of this, the French monarch applied the match with his own hands. From

Robespierre

Danton

Carnot

Luckner

Kellermann (Senior)

Dumouriez

the standpoint of the French autocracy, a limit should have been set, and the people not permitted to transcend it, laws being meanwhile passed to do them justice. But the well-meaning king took the people into his confidence; and the people, once having gained a standing, found a means to assert their rights.

After many efforts to raise money, Louis XVI. finally fell into the financial hands of Necker, who had been director-general of finances from 1777 to 1781, and was again in 1788 and 1789; and during his administration this minister, to create a force on which to lean, began to give to the Third Estate some idea of its value in the economy of the nation. There were two parties in France, Neckerites and anti-Necherites, bitterly opposed to each other; and it was under volcanic conditions that the States General were called together in 1789.

The three orders, Nobles, Clergy, Third Estate, should by ancient custom have voted separately in the States General. As the Third Estate practically furnished a majority of its members, there being three hundred each of Nobles and Clergy, and six hundred of its own members, increased by a number from the other orders, it desired the votes to be counted in one body; but being refused this right, it organized itself into a National Assembly June 17, 1789. To this some nobles and still other strong and free-thinking men joined themselves. When its place of meeting was closed by the king, it met at the *Jeu de Paume*, and bound itself by oath to make France a constitutional monarchy. This act threatened to erect the National Assembly into the real governing power, for, glided by the Gallic temperament, these new-fledged legislators could not, like "town-meeting" Anglo-Saxons, keep within the bounds of law or wisdom. If he desired to conserve his kingdom, the king should have ruthlessly dispersed the National Assembly, and he might then have voluntarily given the people such suitable reforms as he was by nature inclined to do. He indeed appeared in the Assembly June 23, and declared it dissolved, but he did not see to it that his will was obeyed,—with the bayonet if necessary. This would have been tyranny, if you like; for the French people were right, the French monarch wrong. But Louis could only succeed against the Assembly by force, and this he did not employ when he might. It was well for France and for the liberties of Continental Europe that he did not do so. Instead of thus asserting himself, he requested the clergy and nobles to meet with the Third Estate, which they did, and Mirabeau, chief orator of the Assembly, soon became master instead of Louis. The better classes in vast numbers, headed by the Count of

Artois, second brother of the king, Condé and Polignac, foreseeing what might come, abandoned their estates, collected what they could in personal property, and emigrated.

Having gone so far, the Third Estate was compelled for its own justification and safety to demolish the monarchy stone by stone. It needed only the 14th of July (when, on a rumour that the National Assembly was to be dissolved, the people, or rather a mob of the people, destroyed the Bastille), and the creation of a National Guard under Lafayette, to enable the Assembly to gain control of the entire army. From then on the popular force grew, while the Clergy and Nobles, by seeking help abroad, denationalized their cause. The representatives of the nobles in the National Assembly surrendered the privileges which this class had for centuries enjoyed—and abused; the guilds were dissolved, and a declaration of the rights of man followed, founded on the strivings for liberty of the English peoples from Magna Charta down.[1]

Louis had retired to Versailles with some troops; but he was not the man to grapple with such a tempestuous situation. He gave way and agreed to the acts of the National Assembly, which had adopted a democratic monarchical constitution. Another revolt occurred in October, and after the excesses of the 5th and 6th, Lafayette brought the king back to Paris with twenty thousand men of the National Guard. Having stripped the throne of every attribute except a naked veto power, the Assembly seized all authority, and Louis dwelt in the Tuileries, rather as a suspect than as the king of France. On the first anniversary of the destruction of the Bastille the Constitution was accepted by the king. France was divided into eighty-three departments, and subdivided into districts containing the forty-four thousand ancient communes, with a tax suffrage. Juries were created. The

1. From 1789 to 1815 there were six governments:

1. States General and Constituent Assembly (Creation of a Constitutional Monarchy), May 5, 1789, to September 30, 1791. 2½ years.

2. Legislative Assembly (Limitation of the Monarchy), October 1, 1791, to September 21, 1792. 1 year.

3. National Convention (Abolishment of Monarchy, Reign of Terror, Wars against Coalition), September 21, 1792, to October 25, 1795. 5 years.

4. Directory (Recovery of Influence by Middle Classes. Bonaparte's Rise and *Coup d'Etat* of 18th *Brumaire*, Year VIII.), October 26, 1795, to November 9, 1799. 4 years.

5. Consulate (One Man Power), December 25, 1799, to May 20, 1804. 4½ years.

6. Empire (France the most Prominent Power of Europe), May 20, 1804, to June 22, 1815. 11 years.

There were three Coalitions formed against France; the first lasted from 1792 to 1799, the second from 1799 to 1802, the third was in 1805.

hereditary nobility was abolished. The clergy was made elective. Clubs became prominent: the Jacobins, Cordeliers, Feuillants. Paris was reorganized with forty-eight sections. Mirabeau strove to reconcile the Assembly and the king, but he died in April. Had he lived. Liberty might not so violently have purged the body-politic.

The *émigrés* had long urged Louis to flight. In 1791 he attempted this, but was arrested at Varennes, June 25, and brought back. He then accepted the revised Constitution and became a prisoner of the people.

From October 1, 1791, the National Assembly called itself the Legislative Assembly. The Jacobins and the Cordeliers—the "Mountain"—succeeded to power. While many strong and able men sat upon its sloping benches, no Cromwell arose in the Assembly who could steer the ship of state through the stormy sea into which France had drifted. A Latin race was now grappling with the problem which the English had solved five generations before.

Meanwhile the several European monarchies, each busied with its own affairs, stood as horrified but silent spectators of the upheaval. Russia had its war with Turkey and the fear of Poland to engross her attention; Austria and Prussia devoted themselves to watching the manoeuvres of Russia rather than of France; England was seeking some means to indemnify herself for the loss of the North American colonies. Italy, Spain, Portugal, Sweden and Denmark counted for little in European policy. But when the people of France had deprived the king of practically all power, and the *émigrés* had brought to bear the strong influence they possessed at every European court, the Emperor Leopold and King Frederick William held a meeting at Pillnitz, near Dresden, in August, 1791, at which the Elector of Saxony and the Count of Artois were present. As a consequence of this meeting, in the "Pillnitz Declaration" the Emperor of Germany and the King of Prussia called upon the French people to return to the old order of things and restore the monarchy, on pain of war. This academic threat was so little followed up by the powers involved, that it had no effect in France except to enable the Republican party to persuade the people that the French king had been at the bottom of it. The Legislative Assembly demanded that Louis should declare war against Austria; and when Louis declined to do so, the Assembly, seeing its advantage in opening the struggle before Austria was prepared, itself declared war April 20 against the German Empire, over which outworn skeleton of power Francis II. succeeded Leopold as emperor, and so remained until 1806. Austria, Prussia and Sardinia

Northerly frontier of France

then joined hands. The Duke of Brunswick, nephew of Frederick's great lieutenant, Ferdinand, was placed in command of the Austro-Prussian armies, and unwisely issued his threatening proclamation of July 25, 1792, from Coblenz.

This and the growing irritation against the monarchy were the origin of a fresh revolt in Paris on August 10; the Tuileries was stormed by the mob, the Swiss Guards were murdered, the king's life was imperilled, and being declared an enemy of the country, as having treasonable correspondence with its foes, he was incarcerated in the Temple. A jail-delivery and massacre of royalists, instigated by Danton, took place in Paris, September 2 to 7, and was repeated in other cities. France was declared a Republic, Louis was tried, condemned and executed in January, 1793, and the highest power devolved upon the National Convention, which was composed entirely of Republicans. September 22, 1792, became the first day of the Year 1. Later the power centred in the Committee of General Security, and then the Committee of Public Safety, a body including Danton, Robespierre and Carnot. A competing power was the Commune of Paris, under the direction of Chaumette and Hébert. In 1793 and 1794 the French Revolution culminated in a Reign of Terror all over France. Robespierre rose to power and ruled as representing the Committee of Public Safety. All manner of extravagances ensued, and the Cult of Reason succeeded the time-honoured religion of Rome.

Meanwhile England, Holland and Spain had more or less heartily followed the lead of Austria and Prussia against France; and an alliance was formed with the avowed purpose of restoring the Bourbon monarchy. Thus came into being the First Coalition. Its strategic plan was to march its armies into France and straight on Paris, from three directions, the north, the east and the south. The war was to be a sharp offensive on its part; and the early purpose of France was the simple defence of its frontiers. Such was the political status when the sword was drawn from its scabbard, to be hardly sheathed for quarter of a century.

92 the frontiers of France, on the north and northeast, ran from Dunkirk *via* Menin, Condé, Philippeville, Longwy, Sierk, Saarlouis and Bitsch to Lauterburg on the Rhine. The Meuse cut this frontier in two. From sea to Meuse the border near the coast was protected by canals and morasses, which seriously impeded military manoeuvres; the rest was open, but the entire line had a triple row of fortresses. Seven lay in first line: Dunkirk, Lille, Condé, Valenciennes, Quesnoy, Maubeuge, Philippeville. Nine lay in second line: St. Omer, Aire, Béthune, Douay, Bouchain, Cambray, Landrécies, Avesnes, Rocroy. Four

Eastern frontier of France

lay in the third line: St. Quentin, Bapaume, Arras, Amiens. The post-road (*chaussée*) from Brussels to Paris ran through Maubeuge, Laon and Soissons; there was also a post-road from Condé *via* Cambray and Senlis to the capital. On the northeast the French frontier touched Luxembourg, which then belonged to the Elector of Mainz and Trier (Trèves); and the Saar and Moselle cut at an angle through this frontier. The Meuse, the Argonnes, the foothills of the Vosges Mountains and many forests presented natural obstacles, but not serious ones, to an invader. This northeast boundary was protected by a double row of fortresses. In first line were seven; Bitsch, Saarlouis, Thionville, Longwy, Montmédy, Bouillon, Givet. In second line were four: Metz, Verdun, Sedan, Mezières. This plan of defence was ill arranged; for an enemy who should take Longwy would pierce the centre of the line, and could march on Paris practically unopposed by the other fortresses. The roads on Paris from the northeast frontier were *via* Givet, Rocroy, Mezières, Réthel, Soissons; *via* Longwy, Verdun, Chalons, or Vitry; or *via* Metz and Verdun. The entire line on north and northeast was weak in the centre, but the streams, forests, ravines, hills and other natural obstacles made its defence an easy task for a good army.

The eastern frontier ran from Lauterburg, along the left bank of the Rhine, to the fortress of Hüningen, or Basle, and was strong. On the Rhine lay six fortresses: outlying Landau, Strasburg, Vauban, Schlettstadt, Breisach, Hüningen. The second line had three: Bitsch, Pfalzburg, Belfort. The Vosges Mountains made a third line of great strength. Neutral Switzerland was the bulwark on the right of this section of the frontier. Only one good road led from the central Rhine to Paris: *via* Strasburg, Nancy, Toul, Bar le Duc, Vitry.

The southeast frontier was divisible into two parts: One part ran from Basle along the Doubs and Jura Mountains to Geneva, protected by Switzerland. The mountain passes were easy of access, but were mostly held by forts. Besançon and Auxonne were in second line. The roads from Switzerland to Paris were bad. The other part ran from Geneva along the Rhone to Belley, thence along the Savoyard Alps *via* Les Echelles, Mount Genèvre, Monte Viso, and Barcelonette, to and down the Var to the sea. This part was well protected, not only by the natural features, but by Fort Barolles, Briançon and Mount Dauphin. In second line were Grenoble and Toulon. Lyons was the "crossroads" of this section. Here also ended the highway over Les Echelles from Chambéry. The roads were not of the best, not even the highway along the coast.

The southern frontier was the Mediterranean and the Pyrenees, the western the Atlantic up to Dunkirk.

The Pillnitz Declaration and the action of France having rendered war inevitable, the Legislative Assembly decreed the putting afoot of two hundred thousand men, of which there were already one hundred and forty thousand men in the Armies of the North, Centre, Rhine and South. The two former armies of between forty and fifty thousand men each, mostly young troops, stood under Rochambeau and Lafayette along the north and northeast frontier; the Army of the Rhine, of equal strength, under Luckner, was watching the Rhine; the Army of the South under Montesquieu was yet forming, and had but twenty-five thousand men, mostly in garrison. The Coalition assembled its forces slowly. The Prussian troops, forty thousand strong, nominally under King Frederick William and the Elector of Hesse, but really commanded by Brunswick, were heading for Coblenz; Austria had but sixty thousand men available, of which half were already in the Netherlands under Sachsen-Teschen, and twenty-five thousand more stood under Hohenlohe on the right bank of the Rhine; but it was intended to double this force. Clerfayt with fifteen thousand men was advancing from the Brabant country to join the allied right wing. It was proposed in France that the armies should attack the Austrians in the Netherlands, and act on the defensive elsewhere. On the other side the allied main armies were to march through Luxemburg and Champagne on Paris, while the Rhine and Netherlands armies were to keep to the defensive. The Coalition harboured small doubt that their forces could reach the French capital in one short campaign, and dictate terms to the new Republic and its fresh levies. For, ran their argument, most of the good officers had emigrated, and were now in the allied ranks. Little they knew the cataclysmic vigour of the new men who now ruled France.

The French armies, strung along the north and northeast frontier, were faced by the Austrians, each force split into I many parts, and extending over a thin line from fortress to I fortress, as the cordon system of the day prescribed. This I altogether faulty method had gradually crept into use all over Europe, since the days when Frederick gave up war. It was diametrically opposed to the great king's tenets, for "*whoso seeks to protect everything will end in protecting nothing*," he had said; and during his campaigns he repeatedly disgarnished one position, to the last able-bodied man, in order to fall in force on the enemy in another. He was in fact the first great modern exponent of the value of massing for a single blow.

In accordance with their plan the French, early in the year, crossed into the Netherlands in a number of small columns, in the Lille-Valenciennes-Givet country. Near Jemappes one of the centre columns was thrown back by the Austrians; another fell back before it reached the enemy; the right (Lafayette's) and the left columns, though successful, then deemed it essential also to retire; for the cordon theory demanded that the advancing heads of column should keep on a level, and as the centre had retreated, so must the columns on the right and left. Both the central French columns had much outnumbered the enemy, but discipline was so lax that there had been no attempt at real fighting. One of the commanders, Dillon, was shot by his men for suspected treason; and Rochambeau was later replaced by Luckner. Quiet reigned until June. Then Luckner advanced and took Courtray; but he there arrested his operation, on the ground that the Belgians did not rise to aid him. Dillon (brother of the one killed) took command in July near Maubeuge, but accomplished nothing; whereupon Dumouriez was given control. The operations on the northern border had only gone to prove the utter worthlessness of the cordon system, with its numerous strong places and isolated columns operating between or against them, and the still greater lack of value of the French levies, as they then stood.

In Champagne, meanwhile, more important events had occurred. The Army of the Rhine, now under Biron near Weissenburg, did nothing until July. The Army of the North, under Lafayette, was near Sedan, Luckner lay under the guns of Metz, Kellermann (Senior) was near Lauterburg; all told, one hundred thousand men. Brunswick was fast approaching the Rhine with sixty-five thousand men, and with these the Netherlands forces, twenty-five thousand men under Teschen, were preparing to co-operate by a diversion. The allies proposed to thrust themselves in between the French armies and move straight on Paris, on a line from Coblenz *via* Longwy and Verdun, where the French frontier was to be ruptured; thence to Chalons and down the valley of the Marne. The *émigrés* had assured the allies that the people would spontaneously rise in favour of Louis, and the Coalition felt convinced that the Republic would speedily succumb. Should the rising against the Republic occur, all would go well from the start; but even should it not, a secondary base on the Mouse would at all events be gained. In August Treves was reached by the Prussians, while eighteen thousand men, under Hohenlohe, opened the blockade of Landau August 10, and later advanced on Thionville; Longwy, after two days' bombardment, fell August 23; Verdun, early in September, capitulated to the Netherlands army under Clerfayt, which, operating by its left, here joined Brunswick; and the latter had already forced Kellermann

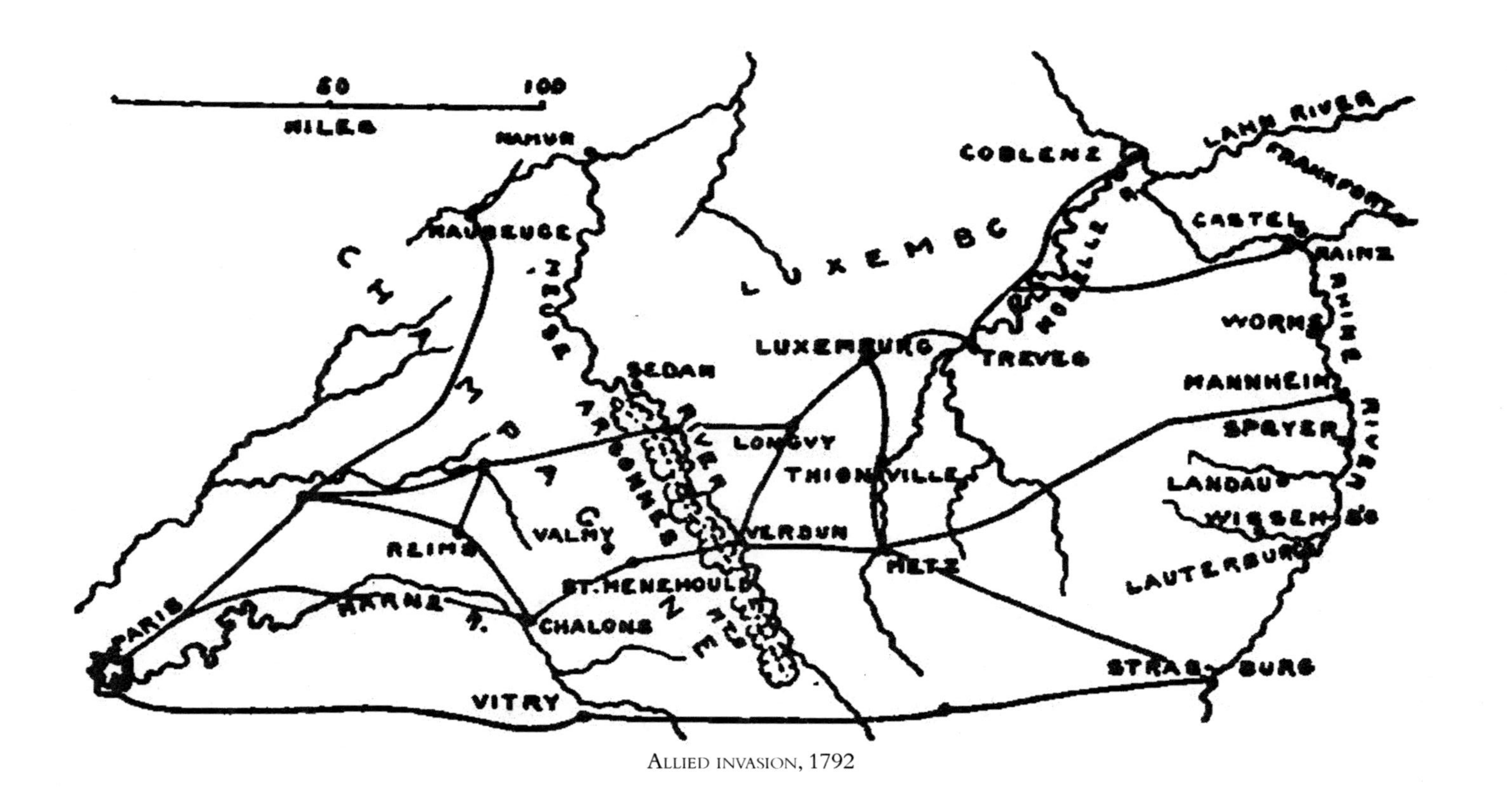

Allied invasion, 1792

to fall back on Metz. All this promised success; but the allies had in many ways been careless, having, as an instance, neglected to provide for a safe retreat across the Rhine in case of failure. Even Mainz was not occupied in force. The advance was slow, at the rate of only five miles a day, owing to pedantic tactics, the result of blind imitation of the letter of Frederick's methods without the spirit, the putting of the men nightly under canvas, and the feeding from magazines. Yet, despite their errors, the allied oncoming seemed like an irresistible flood. The outlook for the Republic was a desperate one.

The French leaders meanwhile were striving to bring order out of chaos in their forces. This advance on French soil of an army led by generals trained in the methods of Frederick seemed perilous indeed; but they had abundant courage, and aimed to place themselves athwart the lines of advance of the allies on Paris. Kellermann had felt compelled to fall back towards Metz; Luckner had retired to the Chalons country; Lafayette, at Sedan, being suspected by the Assembly of an intention to use his forces to sustain the monarchy, was proscribed, fled the country, and was replaced by Dumouriez, who shortly joined the army. Separated from Kellermann by the enemy's advance, Dumouriez was also constrained to retire, and both French armies crossed the Meuse in retreat, leaving much fertile country to the allies, and producing a disheartening effect on the raw levies. But this withdrawal operated as a concentration, and it was the only proper step they could well have taken. Elated by apparent success, the allies under Brunswick kept on their slow advance, but failing to catch the French armies separated, tarried long at Verdun to close up their interminable column, and to collect victual. Time was afforded Dumouriez to make his plans, and to call in troops from the Maubeuge region. Fall was coming on; the country roads were bad; continual rain spread disease in the allied ranks.

Still, as his line of advance was now headed for the French left flank, Brunswick felt that his strategic success was assured. The Meuse was crossed, and in his front lay the Argonnes Mountains, through which ran a number of passes, the Chêne Populeux, the Croix au Bois, Grand Pré, La Chalade and Les Islettes. This range, and the marshy woods and valleys of the Aire and Aisne, might well have been stoutly defended by the French, especially as in crossing the mountains the allies were much split up. Dumouriez ought at least to have held Chêne, but he weakened his force there and at Croix to strengthen Grand Pré; and the allies, by using the first two, turned him out of the last, and forced him also to vacate La Chalade and Les Islettes and to retire behind the

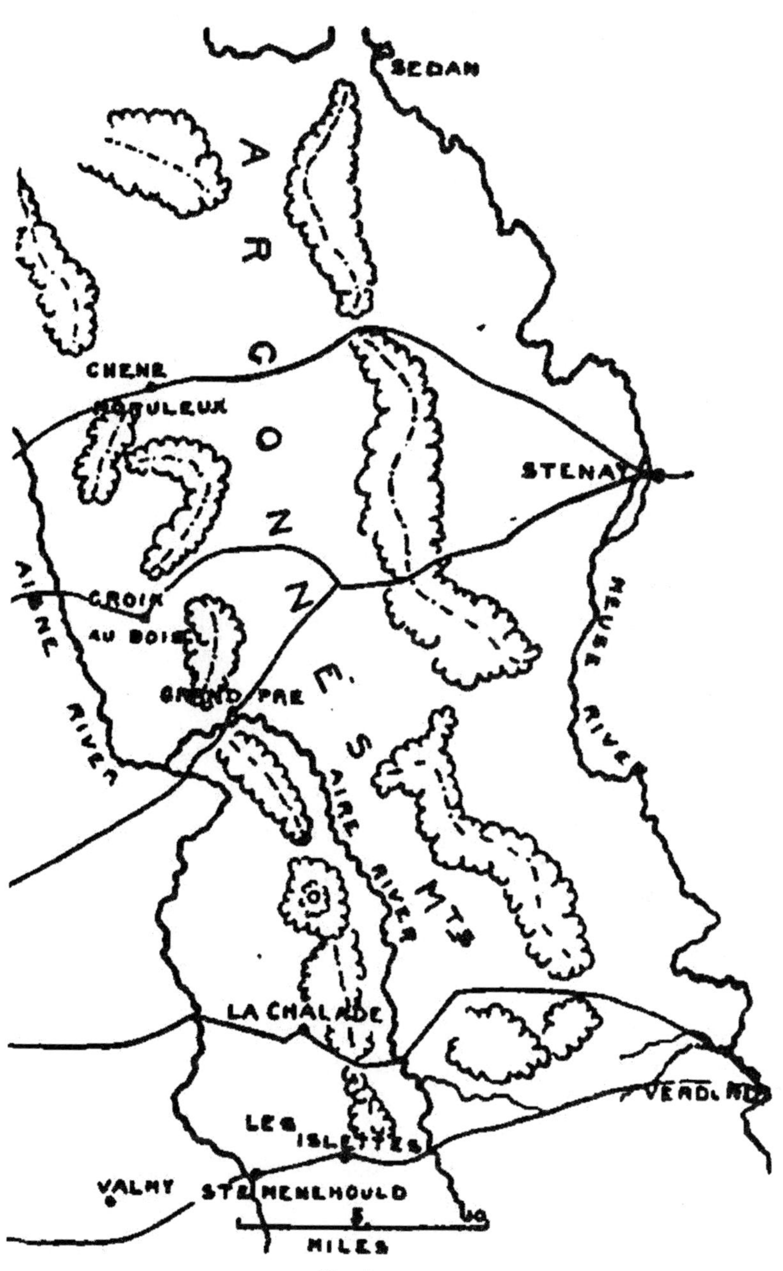

THE ARGONNES

Aisne. Not far from Ste. Ménéhould he took up a defensive position at Valmy, and here Kellermann joined him by the long circuit he had been obliged to make from Metz. Dumouriez was actually farther from Paris than Brunswick, should the latter move by way of Reims. But having thus manoeuvred himself into a fatal strategic position, though perhaps unaware of it, Dumouriez put on a bold front, and determined to invite an attack from the allies. Failing to secure this, it was his purpose to follow them, should they march on the capital; or perchance turn against the allied line of operations, and threaten theirs as they were now threatening his own. Although the first stage of the dose manoeuvring had been quite in favour of the allies, this latter was the manifest strategic operation for the French, for all that would be left for Dumouriez and Kellermann to do, if the allies marched on Paris, was to seek to deter them by a movement *via* Metz on their communications, however questionable this might prove with a bold opponent, who had an-other line of retreat to Flanders. But the allies feared to advance on the French capital, with an army on their rear, and finally, reduced to some forty-five thousand men by details and shrinkage, Brunswick advanced towards Ste. Ménéhould, purposing to take possession of all the Argonnes passes, and then to seize the Chalons road in the rear of the French army, when, as he imagined, he would have it at his mercy. Such, indeed, might have been the result, had his boldness only equalled the position chance had yielded him.

The so-called Battle of Valmy, which should rather be called the cannonade of Valmy, for there was no infantry fighting, decided the campaign and the fate of the new Republic; but the French victory was due rather to utter lack of energy on the part of the allies than to the exceptional bearing of the raw levies of Gaul. On the 20th of September, 1792, at day-break, the allies broke up, and soon reached the Chalons post-road at Cabaret La Lune. Here they were surprised by an occasional cannon-ball which fell into their column and indicated the enemy in their front; but the fog prevented their gauging the value of his position. The shots came from the guns of Kellermann, whose scouts had reported the allied advance, and who held a position near Valmy; while Dumouriez, on his right rear, stretched out as far as the Aisne at Chaude Fontaine, and leaning his left on the Chalons road, had put a heavy detachment with artillery out on the hill of Maffrecourt, and his cavalry van along the Bionne. Kellermann had purposed that morning to occupy a fresh position on Dumouriez's left behind the Auve and Jèvre, but the unexpected allied advance held him in place; and moving up to the windmill hill south of Valmy, he ran his

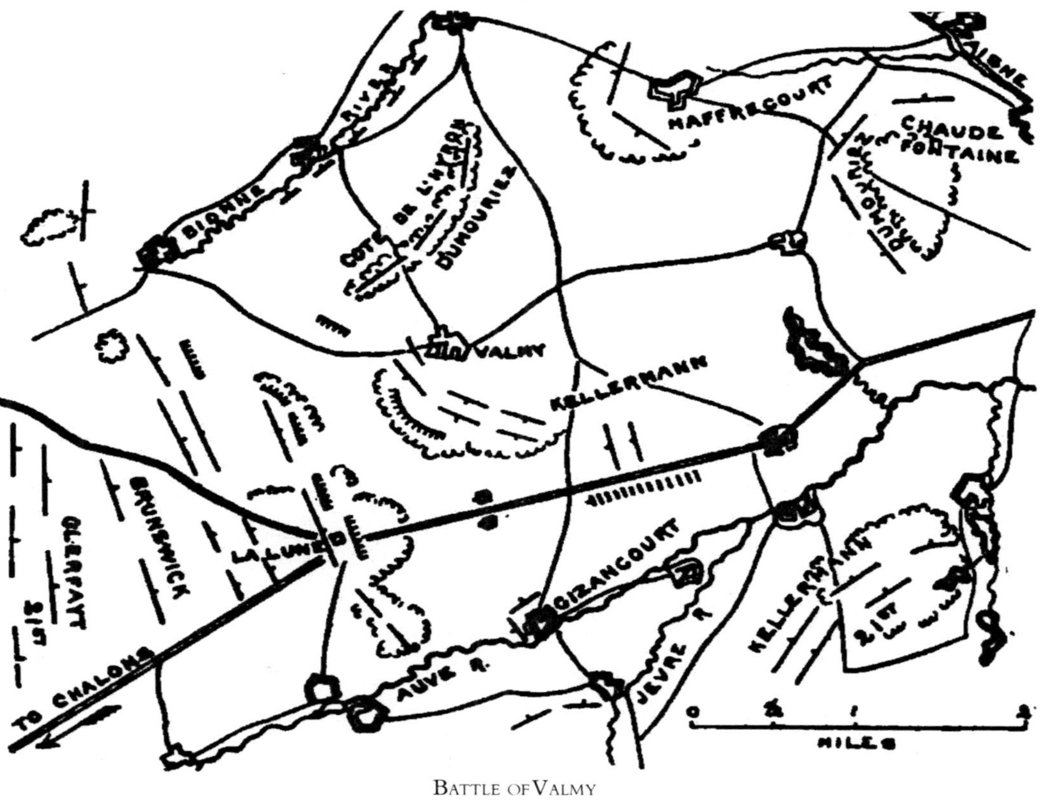

Battle of Valmy

guns in battery and deployed his foot, sending a detachment to Gizancourt and. placing his cavalry on the Chalons road. Dumouriez on his part sent sixteen battalions to Côte de l'Hyron on Kellermann's right, dispatched a small force across the Bionne to threaten the allied left, and ordered a column towards La Lune heights.

As the allied brigades successively came up, they deployed to the left of La Lune, with the artillery in front of the fork in the road, and along the line; and later in the day three columns of attack were formed to move up on Valmy hill. So soon as the fog lifted, the artillery opened, and though Kellermann replied heartily, the allied fire was so much more effective that after an hour or two the French troops began to weaken. Everyone knows how disheartening artillery fire is to young troops ignorant of its slight effect and held in hand without action. Kellermann's horse was shot, and an aide was killed at his side; a French munition-wagon was exploded by a shell; alarm seized the young conscripts. Had the allies pushed in their columns of attack at this moment, the battle would have been won before contact was reached, and perchance the French Republic, with all that it promised for the future, might have perished in the smoke of the Valmy batteries. But Brunswick could not see his chance; and the pause gave Kellermann the time to rally and hearten his men. In this he measurably succeeded. He then put in his reserve artillery, and formed three columns with battalion front, purposing in his turn to attack, should the opportunity offer. But all the allies did was to send a detachment to Gizancourt, and this accomplished nothing. Neither would the French assume the offensive, so long as the allies did not. In all the actions hitherto delivered, the French levies had decamped almost at the first fire, and Brunswick had good reason to expect them now to withdraw, if not retire in confusion. As they did not do so, the allied commander failed to follow up what was really the turning-point in the action, but continued to rely on the fire of the artillery to do the work; and this fire, which, owing to the good conduct of the French generals, failed to accomplish the usual result, died out by five o'clock.

Not to win was for the allies to lose the battle. The casualties were barely five hundred men on either side; but the French gained immensely in morale by finding that they could withstand the enemy, while the allies lost whatever heart they had left for this campaign.

No battle ever exhibited the influence of success on the bearing of an army, or of a nation in arms, as did that of Valmy. It is in any event probable that the shrinkage in the allied forces by heavy marching, exposure and disease would have prevented their reaching Paris in condition to accomplish their task, unless heavily reinforced. But Valmy shortened the campaign, and furnished the spark which electrified the half-alive body of the French raw levies into an alert and self-confident power. Valmy was in truth one of the Decisive Battles of the World.

Clerfayt came up at night and went into line behind Brunswick. Kellermann moved next morning to the position previously chosen, and Dumouriez returned to that he had held anterior to the battle. Brunswick remained ten days lazily facing Valmy, and then retired towards Verdun and Longwy, proposing to go into winter quarters in that neighbourhood. Clerfayt marched to Belgium *via* Namur; Dumouriez slowly followed up Brunswick; but whether owing to the misunderstandings between Kellermann and himself, or owing to an arrangement made with the Duke of Brunswick, or to general mistrust of the situation, cannot be said, no pursuit worthy the name was undertaken.

Dumouriez now turned towards the Netherlands, leaving Kellermann to drive the allies out of France. Brunswick, seeing that he could not maintain himself without further battle, vacated Verdun and Longwy, and at the end of October retired into Luxemburg. Kellermann followed slowly, and put his troops into winter quarters near Longwy. The news of Custine's approach to Mainz, down the Rhine in the allied rear, drove Brunswick back on Coblenz, the magazines of which were thus threatened. He crossed the Rhine in mid-November.

The allies' plan had been good, but its execution was of the very worst. The capture of Longwy and Verdun gave a proper base, and the moral preponderance was on their side. But the slothful advance was indicative of what was to come, and the retreat after a little cannonading exchange at Valmy was ludicrously weak for generals pretending to know war. The French made a grave error at the inception of the campaign in dividing their forces, and another in not defending the Argonnes passes. And even when the Meuse and these were passed by the allies, had Dumouriez only manoeuvred to keep the enemy on the constant move, he could have quite exhausted his army and rendered it unfit for the campaign, without the grave risk of a battle. Previous to Valmy he was quite outnumbered; at Valmy he ran an unnecessary danger, in view of the fact that the French had as yet never stood the oncoming of the enemy's line. But Brunswick's fortunate want of enterprise saved him. After Valmy, it has been said, had Dumouriez been active, had he drawn in the Army of the Rhine and marched sharply

CUSTINE

LOUIS PHILIPPE

KLEBER

PICHEGRU

HOCHE

JOURDAN

on the allies, he could have seized Mainz, Coblenz and Cologne; and, having paralyzed the allied army, he could have taken the Netherlands in reverse and overrun the whole land. But Dumouriez was not this species of general. We cannot fairly hold him up to the standard which Napoleon later established.

In this Valmy campaign there is nothing new. The old hidebound system of cordons and divided forces was apparent at every turn. But it serves to show how low, since Frederick's day, the art of war had fallen.

While operations on the northern frontier and in Champagne were thus going on, Custine with his seventeen thousand men had not been idle in the Landau region. Until September he had been held in check by the superior forces of the allies, but at the end of the month, the enemy having dispersed his divisions (the greater part having gone to the Aisne), he advanced downstream and captured Speyer and Worms; and, encouraged by this easy success, determined to move on Mainz, with some of whose inhabitants he had entered into a secret understanding. This bold idea was well carried out, and Mainz fortress was taken October 20, without a show of resistance. Frankfort was captured in like manner, and the country between the Rhine and Lahn was overrun by the French. Custine then sat down in Mainz and built a bridge-head at Castel on the opposite bank. By sending a corps on Coblenz he also could have destroyed the allied magazines, and markedly aided the other French operations; but he did not attempt this manoeuvre. Custine's triumph was short-lived. In December the Prussians recaptured Frankfort, and Custine withdrew to the left bank of the Rhine, still holding Castel. But what he had done was of itself a great moral gain.

Kellermann's going into winter quarters lost him the command. He was sent to the Army of the South, and Beurnonville took his place. But the latter accomplished nothing in his attempts to again drive the allies across the Rhine.

In the Netherlands, the allies besieged Lille without result, and then took up a position near Mons, which they strongly fortified, but which was too long, and had its left, by which they must retreat if defeated, ill-protected. After Valmy, Dumouriez had, as stated, moved into the Low Countries with his superior forces, but in several columns. In Champagne the French had proved their ability to stand on the defensive against the allies; they were now to essay the offensive. Valence, with the Army of the Ardennes, twenty thousand strong, was manoeuvring on the Meuse, while Labourdonnaye, with the Army of the North, of nearly equal strength, was operating on the Scheldt, the

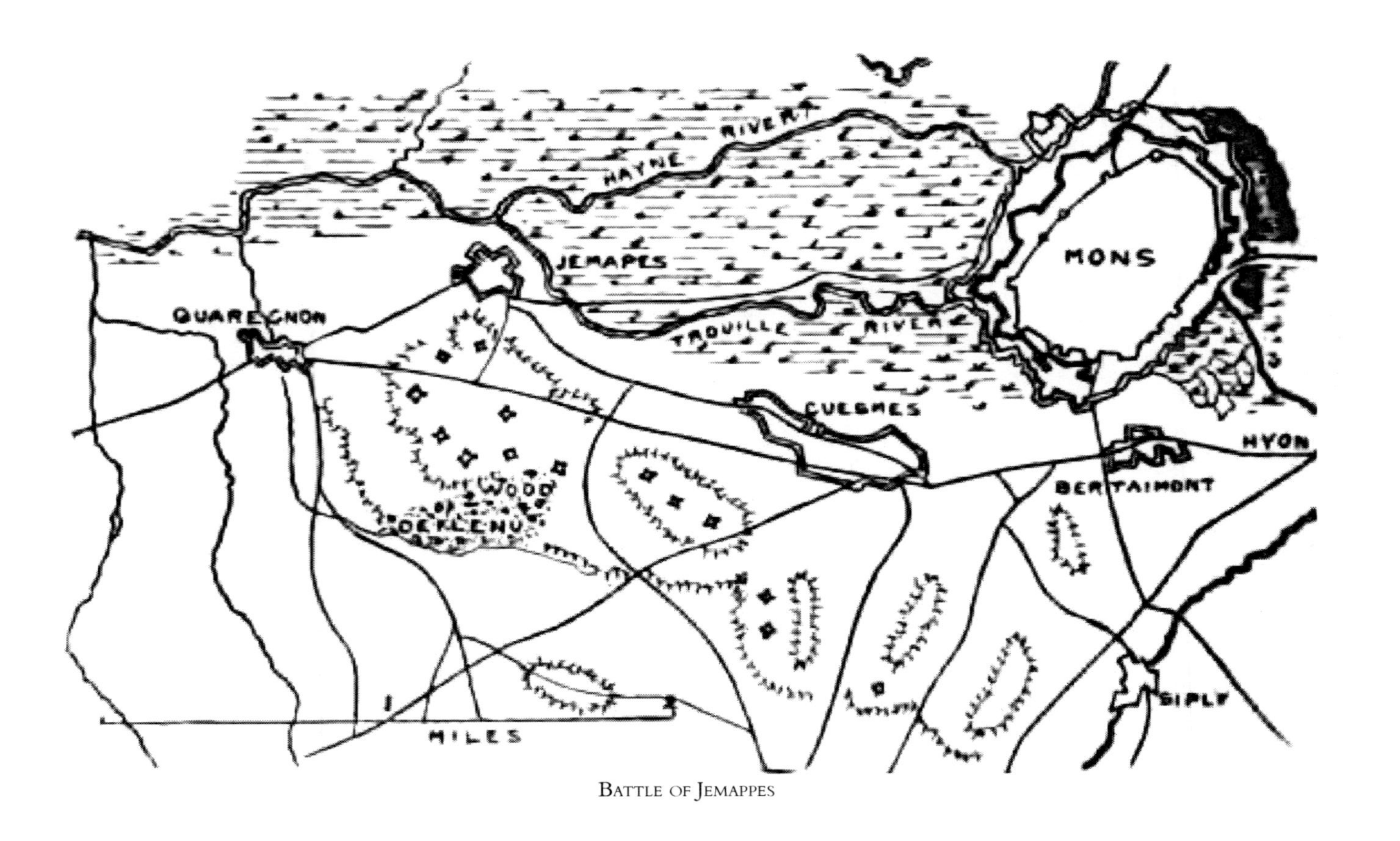

Battle of Jemappes

two being intended to threaten the allied flanks, and thus divert their attention. Dumouriez was in the centre with nearly fifty thousand men. The Austrians, under Beaulieu, Latour, Teschen and Clerfayt, had some forty thousand effective, and held the debouches of Namur, Mons and Tournay. It being on the route to Brussels, they strove to make Mons unapproachable.

This fortress lies in the marshy confluence of the Hayne and Trouille. In its south front lies a chain of moderate hills, between which and the rivers, like outlying works, stand the villages of Jemappes, Cuesmes and Bertaimont, while Quaregnon flanks the hills on the west. On this highland the Austrians had built fourteen redoubts and manned them with fifty-four guns; and here Clerfayt, Teschen and Beaulieu, with about twenty-five thousand men, proposed to arrest the French advance. Dumouriez had the divisions of the Duke of Chartres (Louis Philippe), Miranda, Ferrand, Beurnonville, Dampierre and Harville, and with these, forty-five thousand strong, he started from Valenciennes and Maubeuge, while a column from Condé was ordered forward to observe Tournay. On November 6, 1792, he came in presence of the Austrians, and speedily moved upon them, holding in hand a good reserve.

Ferrand attacked Quaregnon with his foot; Dumouriez in the centre and Beurnonville on the right opened on the Austrian redoubts with artillery. Harville with a flying right wing was intended to debouch from Siply, take Bertaimont, turn Mons by the right and cut the Austrians off from retreat on Brussels. But he went at his task in a slothful manner, also opening with his guns alone, instead of advancing with his foot. All along the line the Austrian defence was hardy. But French numbers told. At ten o'clock Quaregnon was taken. At twelve Dumouriez advanced his troops in battalion columns under Dampierre and Beurnonville . The wood of Deflenu offered a stout defence, but when Ferrand captured Jemappes and took it in reverse, the Austrians vacated the shelter. On debouching from it, however, the French were thrown into unsteadiness by the heavy fire from the Austrian line and guns, and were on the point of falling back in a panic, when Chartres rallied them, and at their head gallantly stormed the heights and captured the redoubts. Beurnonville at the same time got possession of Cuesmes, and drove back the enemy's cavalry. At two o'clock the Austrians beat a retreat, which, owing to Harville's failure to accomplish his task, was easy.

Dumouriez would have done better had he attacked the Austrian left, which was the strategic flank, as covering the road to Brussels. But

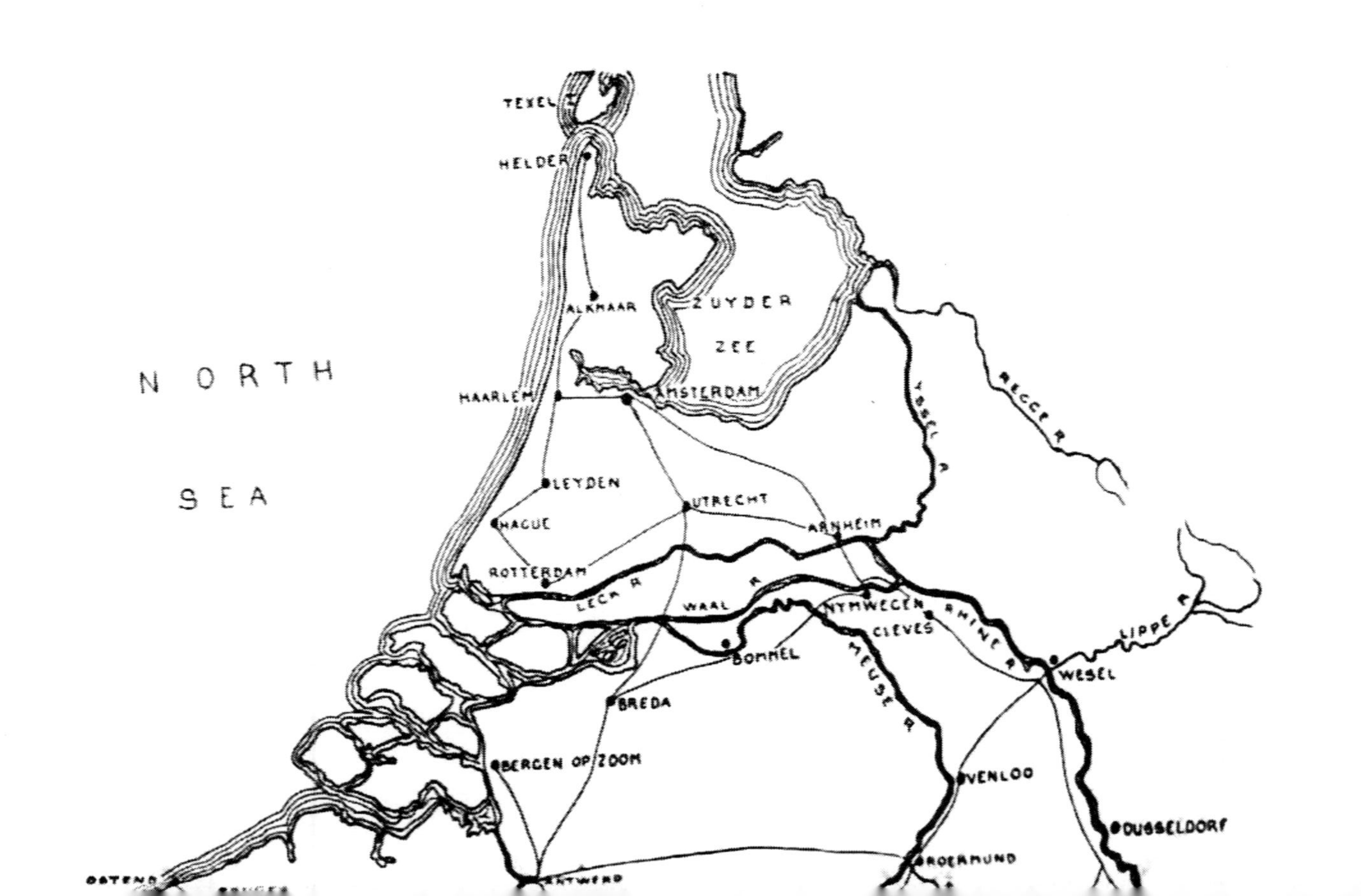

NORTH
SEA
TEXEL
HELDER
ALKMAAR
ZUYDER
ZEE
HAARLEM
AMSTERDAM
LEYDEN
HAGUE
UTRECHT
ARNHEIM
ROTTERDAM
LECK R
WAAL R
NYMWEGEN
CLEVES
RHINE R
MEUSE R
BOMMEL
BREDA
BERGEN OP ZOOM
VENLOO
WESEL
LIPPE R
YSSEL R
RECCE R
DUSSELDORF
ROERMUND

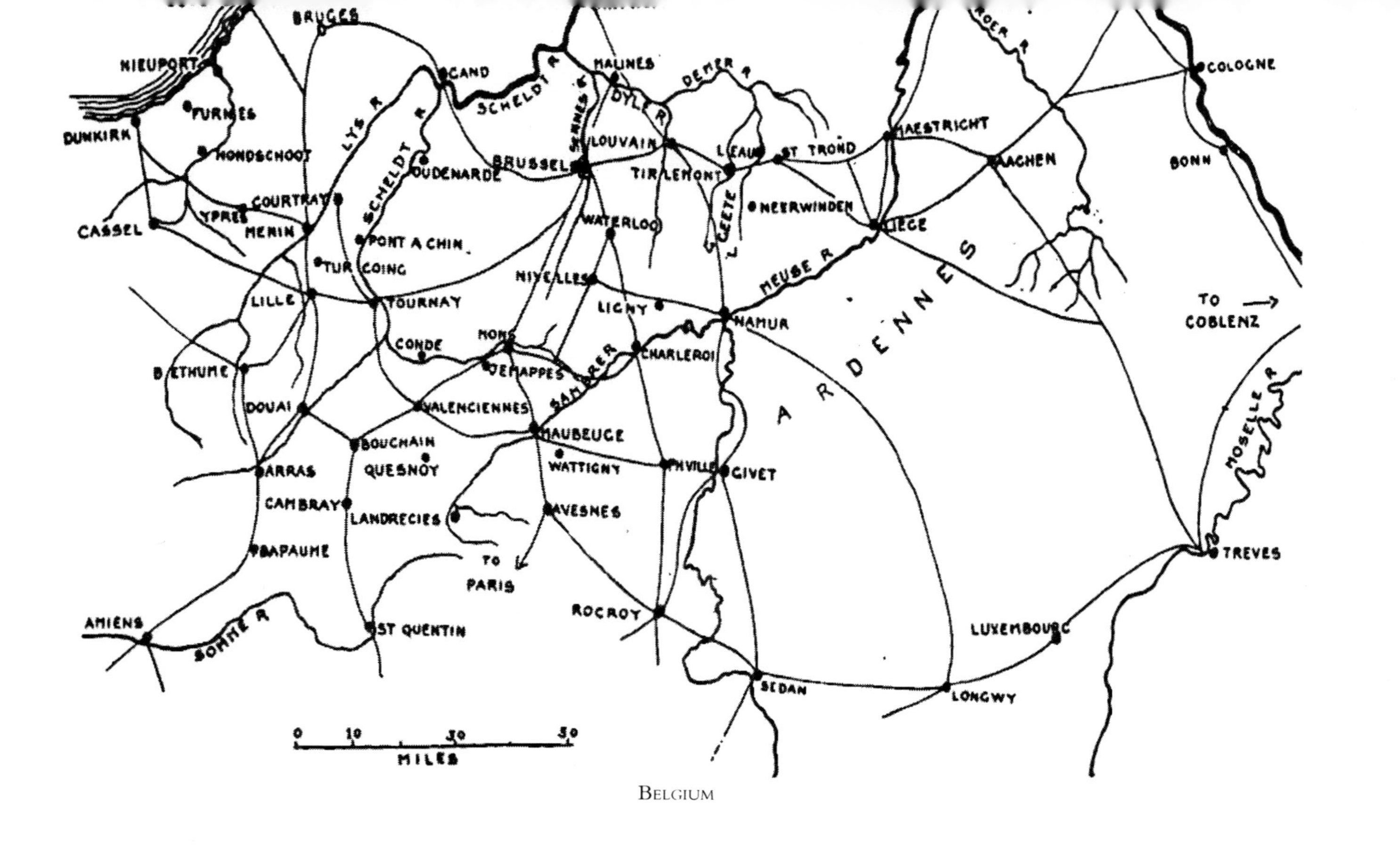
BRUGES
NIEUPORT
FURNES
DUNKIRK
HONDSCHOOT
CASSEL
YPRES
COURTRAY
MENIN
LYS R
SCHELDT R
GAND
OUDENARDE
PONT A CHIN
TURCOING
LILLE
TOURNAY
BETHUNE
DOUAI
ARRAS
BAPAUME
AMIENS
SOMME R
CAMBRAY
BOUCHAIN
QUESNOY
LANDRECIES
ST QUENTIN
CONDE
MONS
JEMAPPES
VALENCIENNES
TO
PARIS
SCHELDT R
MALINES
DYLE R
SENNES R
BRUSSEL
LOUVAIN
TIRLEMONT
WATERLOO
NIVELLES
LIGNY
CHARLEROI
SAMBRE R
MAUBEUGE
WATTIGNY
AVESNES
ROCROY
PHVILLE
GIVET
DEMER R
LEAU
ST TROND
GEETE
NEERWINDEN
NAMUR
MEUSE R
LIEGE
MAESTRICHT
AACHEN
ROER R
ARDENNES
COLOGNE
BONN
TO
COBLENZ
MOSELLE R
TREVES
LUXEMBOURG
LONGWY
SEDAN
0
10
30
50
MILES

Belgium

he had not yet risen to the comprehension of this now simple idea. He did, as stated, send Harville's column to attack the allied left, but this officer, it is urged, had orders, according to the cordon system, to keep on the same level with the other columns; and thus hampered, the attack came to naught. The fighting was the first creditable work of the French levies. Elated by what they had done at Valmy, they carried the field-works of the Austrians with praiseworthy courage. The loss was not far from four thousand killed and wounded on each side, and the victory raised the spirits of the French conscripts to a singular degree. The next day the victors occupied Mons. The Austrians retired to Brussels, which a further French advance soon induced them to vacate and retreat behind the Meuse, along which river Dumouriez took up winter quarters. He had overrun all Belgium. The Austrians had lost the land by their absurd adherence to the cordon system. But Dumouriez did not understand how to utilize his vast preponderance of forces so as to destroy the Austrian army.

After this pronounced success, the Convention unwisely declared the country out of danger, a proceeding which was followed by wholesale desertion from the French ranks.

In the southeast, during 1792, Sardinia, allied to Louis XVI. by marriage, raised a force to meet some forty thousand French in the Army of the South, of which latter army part was ordered to operate against Savoy and part against Nice. The Sardinian regular army consisted of twenty battalions, say ten thousand men of foot, forty squadrons of cavalry, scarcely over five thousand men, and, including fortresses, some four thousand artillery. Its discipline was good. The French invaded both Savoy and Nice, and overran part of each land. It is quite noteworthy that Montesquieu, who commanded the Savoy expedition, concentrated his forces and advanced into that country in one body, thus throwing aside the shackles of the cordon system. This was in a way prescribed by the topography, but still the idea was good. The execution was, however, so faulty that less came of it than might have been expected. An expedition undertaken against Naples, moreover, bore no fruit.

On November 19, 1792, the Convention issued a proclamation offering the assistance of France to any people desirous of throwing off the yoke of its existing government. This was a challenge to all Europe, and its effect was to knit together the not overstrong purpose of the allies.

On the whole, the campaign of 1792 proved that France could hold her own against the Coalition. Belgium had been conquered.

Light Infantryman, 1791

Mainz, a salient on the Rhine in the enemy's territory, had been taken. Savoy and Nice had in part been added to the French dominions. The allies had set themselves the task of marching on Paris and dictating terms to the new Republic. Had they fallen markedly short of this end, the French would have deemed the campaign won. But not only had their armies been driven back across the French frontier, but the allies had lost a substantial territory beside. And the main thing gained by the French was self-confidence, and ability to do better work in future. The raw levies of the Republic had met the allied regulars and had beaten them. Up to Valmy, the French recruit or national guardsman was altogether lacking in morale. After Valmy, with his Gallic exuberance, he felt that he could face all Europe. The troops gained, the generals learned, the requisition system worked well, gaps were easily filled in the ranks, and the attitude of the French armies was strengthened out of all proportion to the gain actually made, which was small. What they had won, to be sure, they owed to the allies' slothful method and foolish cordon system, rather than to their own good conduct. A strong allied commander could have marched into Paris and restored the monarchy; but no words can describe the utter weakness of the operations of the Coalition.

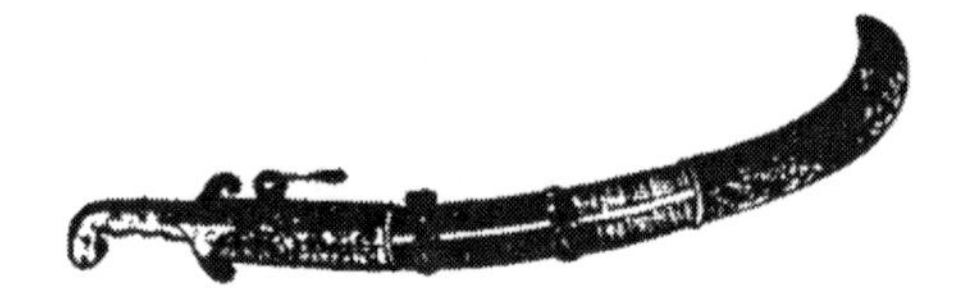

Chapter 4

The Wars of the French Revolution

1793

The execution of Louis XVI. markedly strengthened the Coalition against France, and the civil war of the Vendée, the want of money and internal troubles of many kinds made a difficult task for the French leaders. Yet they raised a million men, and had armies at every point on the frontier. The merciless system of the guillotine kept the army full, and obliged generals to do their best work. Hoche and Pichegru held the Rhine. Despite hearty effort, Hoche was beaten at Kaiserslautern, but his gallantry saved his head. Dumouriez took Holland, but lost Belgium at Neerwinden. Still the allies parcelled out their forces, and accomplished no worthy result. Kellermann evacuated Nice, and lost, but later recaptured, part of Savoy. The English took Toulon, a heavy blow to France. Spain joined the Coalition, and the rival armies fought south of the Pyrenees. But though the French lost battles, the allies made no advance. Meanwhile the Vendée gave great trouble, and required large armies to keep this part of France under control. At first the Vendeans had much success; later they were put down by the Republican forces.

In 1793 the situation of France was complicated by the fact that the execution of Louis XVI., on January 21, arrayed against her many of the other powers. So soon as the National Convention had thrown off the mask, most of the nations hitherto neutral cast in their lot with the Coalition. England had delayed actual participation in the struggle, but on February 1, 1793, France boldly anticipated her by declaring war. Holland was dependent on England, and. the decree equally included her. Spain had remained neutral until the execution of the king, but on March 7 France declared war against Spain also, rather than await such an act on her part. The German Empire had been making preparations ever since the capture of Mainz, and on April 30 issued a formal challenge. Protected by an English fleet. Naples joined the enemies of France. Portugal, also dependent upon England, offered troops. The Pope threw in his lot with the allies out of religious policy. Excepting the Scandinavian kingdoms, Russia and neutral Switzerland, all Europe was in effect arrayed against the Republic. At home matters had gone from worse to worse. Disorder reigned. The finances were at a low ebb. The army was depleted by' deserters and absentees, who had construed too literally the last year's decree that the country was out of danger. So shrunken was the army that on February 24, 1798, a levy in mass was ordered. The decree recited that until the complete expulsion of the enemy out of the land, and beyond the frontiers of France, the entire male population was to stand in readiness to seize arms at the first call. Unmarried young men and childless widowers should be drawn first to complete the active armies; the married and less fit for field duty should be used for interior duty and the repair of arms. All weapons in private hands were to be delivered to the war authorities, for distribution to the armies. All horses not absolutely needed for agriculture were to be taken for the cavalry and artillery. Other equally stringent provisions were made. It was not alone the foreign danger that the Republican leaders had to contend with; for the Vendée and other uprisings against the Convention—in Marseilles, Lyons, Bordeaux, Caen and later at Nantes and Angers—obliged the authorities during the whole war to draw from the already depleted frontier armies battalions by the wholesale for interior use.

The operations of 1793 were conducted on the border, against the Netherlands, Germany, Italy and Spain. Under the February decree, three hundred thousand additional men were to be raised and distributed among the several existing armies, which would give a total of half a million men, including fifty thousand cavalry and twenty thousand artillery. But actually not much over two hundred and seventy thousand men were at any one time present under the colours. These were parcelled out along the frontier, in the Army of the Rhine, the Army of the Moselle, the Army of the North, the Army of the Alps and the Army of Italy, the Army of the Eastern Pyrenees and the Army of the Western Pyrenees. The Army of the North was ninety thousand strong, the Army of the Rhine half as large; the others were much smaller. Garrisons and reserves considerably swelled the number. Most of this force was raw.

The allies had three hundred and seventy-five thousand men, well-disciplined and in good heart. The general plan was again to attack the north and north-eastern French frontier. On the Rhine were to operate one hundred thousand men in two armies under

Commissary of Wars

Brunswick and Wurmser, with Hohenlohe and Beaulieu in support. On the north-eastern frontier were eighty thousand allies under Coburg. Piedmont had forty thousand men. Spain put a force of thirty thousand men afoot. Dumouriez drew up the French plan of campaign. The general idea was to complete the conquest of Belgium and of Nice; and to act along the Rhine and Spanish frontier as occasion demanded. The allies proposed to recover Mainz, and to push the French back across the Meuse.

The allied forces on the Rhine were ill parcelled out from the Lahn to Basle, and these were faced by the Army of the Rhine in Mainz, and the Army of the Moselle behind the Saar. There was so scant a co-operation between the allied armies, that had the French debouched from Mainz across the Rhine and turned against the Prussians, they might have quite upset the allied plans. But the French held to the defensive. On the other hand it was open to the allies to cross the Rhine at Mannheim and cut the Army of the Rhine and the Army of the Moselle asunder, an operation which would have thrown these forces back from the river. As it was, they crossed in the Hundsrück country, turned the left of the Army of the Rhine, and beat part of Custine's forces at Bingen. Custine withdrew the balance of his force to the left bank at Mainz, and the two French armies being now put under his command, he left that city with an ample garrison to its own defence, and retired up river to the Landau region. The allies laid siege to Mainz, and Custine's several operations remained fruitless. In May Custine went to the Army of the North, and Beauharnais (first husband of Josephine) succeeded him. Several attempts were made to relieve Mainz, but the city, though defended valiantly by Kleber, Meunier and Dubayet, fell to the allies in July. Beauharnais ascended the scaffold for thus abandoning Mainz, and was succeeded by Landremont. Being a noble, Custine was easily suspected of not having done all that he might have done to save this city; and accused of such failure, he suffered the same fate. Houchard was put in command of the Army of the Moselle. One commander replaced another, all to the destruction of good discipline and morale, and to the utter ruin of pending operations. During the summer a number of small actions were fought, and on September 1 the Army of the Moselle was defeated at Pirmasens, with loss of four thousand men against a few hundred by the enemy. But owing to the lifeless attitude of the allies, no strategic ill resulted. Change still succeeded change, and in the frequent small affairs the French were more often worsted than successful.

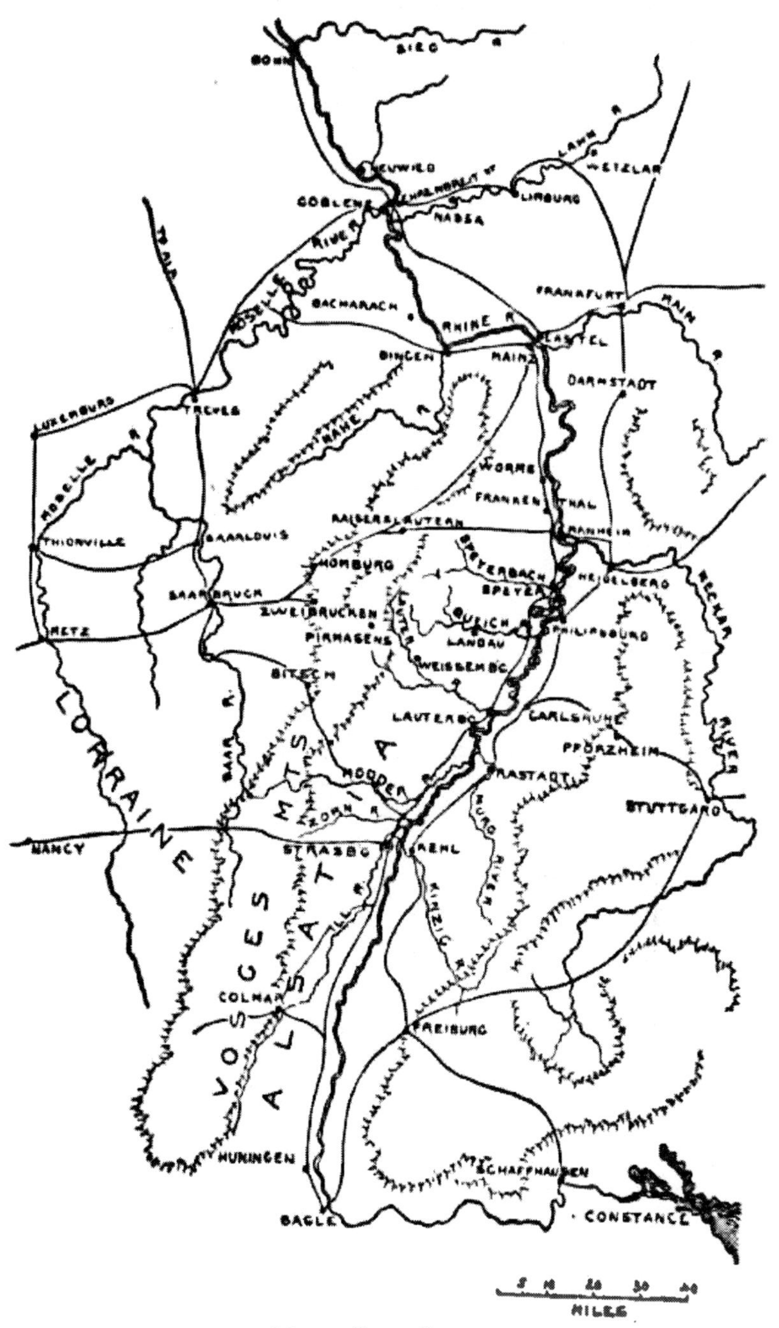

Middle-Rhine Country

These constant defeats led the Convention to raise the cry of "Traitors!" One after another incompetent general was put in command, and one after another of the unsuccessful commanders was driven to the guillotine. But no gain was made until Hoche and Pichegru were put at the head of the forces operating between the Rhine and Moselle; while until Pichegru reached headquarters, Carlin, an obstinate old captain of dragoons, the latest appointment, almost completed the ruin of the army.

The allies had finally prepared to invade Alsatia. The first step was to drive the Army of the Rhine from the lines of Weissemburg, an ancient series of fortifications along the Lauter between the Rhine and the Vosges Mountains, which in the past had played an important role. The Army of the Moselle was first attacked at the end of September and driven behind the Saar, and this uncovered the left flank of the Army of the Rhine. On October 18 Wurmser gallantly assaulted and took the Weissemburg lines, and the French retired to the Zorn, just below Strasburg. Landau was besieged; and Wurmser, urged on from Vienna, penetrated into Alsatia and threatened Strasburg.

Such was the situation when Hoche took command of the Army of the Moselle, and Pichegru of the Army of the Rhine; they were given some substantial reinforcements, and ordered summarily to attack the enemy. A levy in mass was ordered, so as to provide a suitable reserve. Pichegru at once began his task, and pushed the allies in his front back to the Moder, where they entrenched.

Hoche's duty required more extensive operations. He projected the relief of Landau by an advance down the left bank of the Queich, crossing the Vosges at Zweibrücken and Homburg. But about the same time, late in November, the Prussians and Saxons under Brunswick, who was proposing to go into winter quarters, took position in the neighbourhood of Kaiserslautern with twenty thousand men, Hohenlohe being at Pirmasens; and in his advance Hoche found that he had in his front a powerful army. The rest of the allies were distributed over a line nearly one hundred miles long, up the Rhine. Hoche, who had forty thousand men and abundant energy, moved against Kaiserslautern, and on November 27 came in presence of the enemy, whom he struck first at Vogelweh, and pushed in on the Galgenberg, the gallows hill, which was now crowned by a redoubt. Another French column occupied Katzweiler. After reconnoitring, and finding that Brunswick had entrenched himself on the west and north of Kaiserslautern, Hoche determined to turn his right by capturing Erlenbach and Morlautern, and for this purpose set up a battery of sixteen heavy

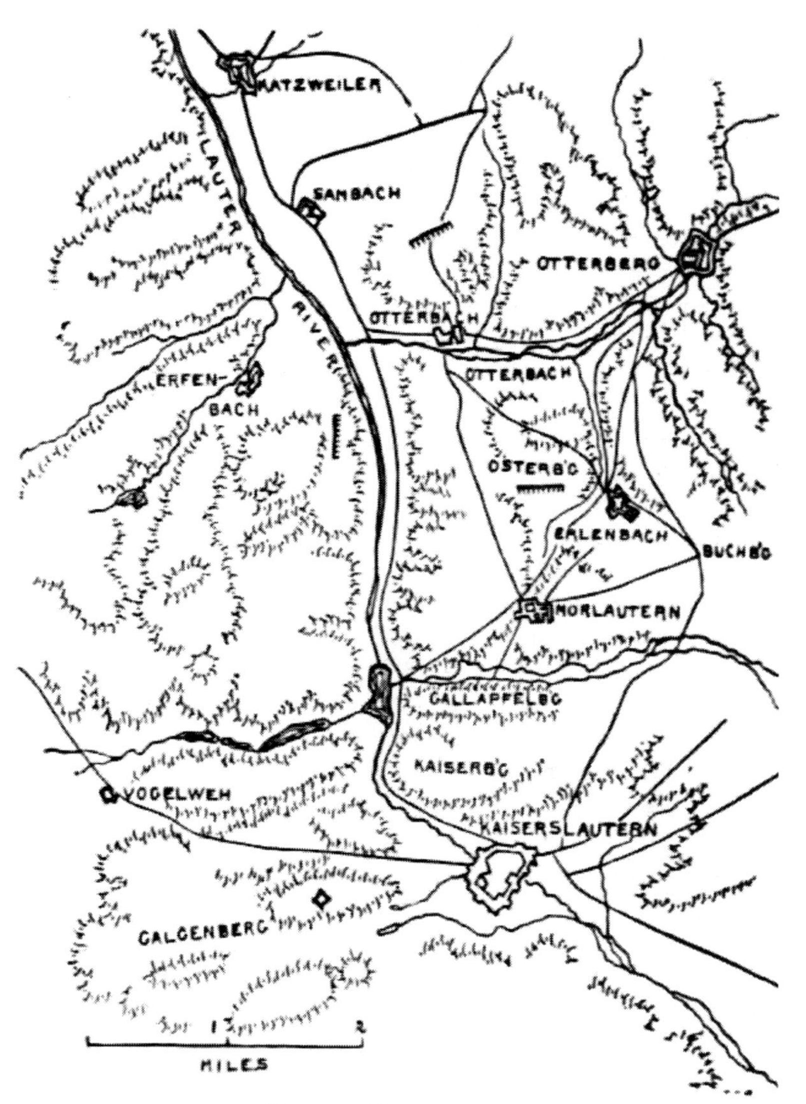

Battle of Kaiserslautern

guns near Sambach on the right bank of the Lauter stream which flows past Kaiserslautern. The allies held the Kaiserberg, where they had built another redoubt; and on the high land south of the Otterbach they had constructed a third one, and back of it stationed the cavalry. Erlenbach was filled with riflemen.

Early November 29 Hoche debouched from Katzweiler in three columns against the villages of Otterbach, Erlenbach and Otterberg. A cross-fire from the French batteries at Erfenbach and Sambach drove the enemy out of the lower land and towards Kaiserslautern. Hoche followed, crossed the Otterbach and took position on the Osterberg, where he established a battery of twenty-nine guns. A cannonade of several hours followed, when a French column of ten thousand men, which had formed under cover in the valley, debouched on Morlautern. The allies received the gallant assault of the French with stanchness, replied by a countercharge and sent a body of cavalry to take the French column in the left flank. This was too much for the young conscripts, who retired back to the cover where they had formed, and the Prussian pursuit was stopped by the French horse. Each side withdrew to its old location. The French columns sent on Erlenbach and Otterberg likewise failed to make a gain; and on the left bank the allies stood off the French attack. By six o'clock the fire ceased. During the night Brunswick reinforced Morlautern and Erlenbach.

Determined not to score a failure, at daybreak of the 30th Hoche opened his batteries, and shortly sent forward a column of foot in the Erlenbach valley on Buchberg. But Kalkreuth, here stationed, took the French column in flank, drove it back, and even threatened to take in reverse the position at Osterberg. About the same time the French made an unsuccessful attack on Galapfelberg; and on the other bank two assaults on the Galgenberg, and nearby it, were driven back by Weimar. At three o'clock the fighting was over. Hoche was forced to retire to Zweibrücken December 3. Brunswick went into winter quarters.

Although Hoche had lost at Kaiserslautern, the Convention recognized the heartiness of the attack, and weary of changes, reinforced the Army of the Moselle. Meanwhile Pichegru with sixty thousand men was pushing Wurmser, and tiring out the allied troops by restless enterprises; and when Hoche moved by his right to join him, the allies, sixty thousand strong, retired to the right bank of the Rhine. Landau, Worms and Frankenthal were relieved. The Army of the Moselle went into winter quarters on the Saar, the Army of the Rhine on the Queich. At this point on the French frontier the allies had once more quite failed to accomplish their end. The Republican forces, despite frequent backsets, had firmly held the French frontier.

In the Netherlands, in 1793, Dumouriez commanded the French, one hundred thousand strong, against allied armies of equal force. The Army of the Netherlands was strung out, cordon fashion, from Antwerp to the Meuse; the allies were parcelled out all over the land. The French proposed to conquer Holland, and to give to the people the power held by the *Stadholder*; the allies to reconquer Belgium. About mid-February Dumouriez invaded Holland with a small part of his force, and in three weeks captured several strong places; but on hearing of the allied inroad into Belgium, he personally returned to the Meuse. The allied leader, Coburg, under whom were serving Archduke Charles, Wurtemberg, Latour and Clerfayt, advanced on the Roer in March, drove away the French troops there lying in cantonments, occupied Aix-la-Chapelle, threw the French back beyond the Meuse, took Maestricht and Liège, and forced Miranda and Valence back on St. Trond and towards Louvain. The French finally concentrated on the Dyle, where Dumouriez joined them, and at once assuming the offensive, took Tirlemont after a lively fight, and the heights between the Great and Little Geete. The Austrians retired behind the latter stream, and drew up in a position about Neerwinden, with thirty thousand foot and ten thousand horse. Dumouriez had some forty-seven thousand men in line, but only half the cavalry. This was the ground on which one hundred years before the French under Luxemburg had won a great victory against William III.; and the memory of this triumph was no doubt used to cheer up the Gallic levies for the coming battle.

On the Austrian right, extending up to Halle, stood the van under Archduke Charles, later so renowned; in the centre, Colloredo with Wurtemberg in second line; on the left, south of Neerwinden, the reserve under Clerfayt; light troops occupied all the villages along the Little Geete. The French right was under Valence; the centre under Chartres; the left under Miranda; a flying wing was on right and left; and a reserve lay behind the Great Geete. Never doubting success, for he had won so often and now outnumbered the enemy, Dumouriez marshalled the French army in eight columns of attack, three under Valence, which crossed the river and advanced on Racour and Oberwinden; two under Chartres, which also crossed and pushed through Laer on Neerwinden; and three under Miranda along the post-road on Halle; while the reserve was given the task to take Leau and debouch to the right on the same village.

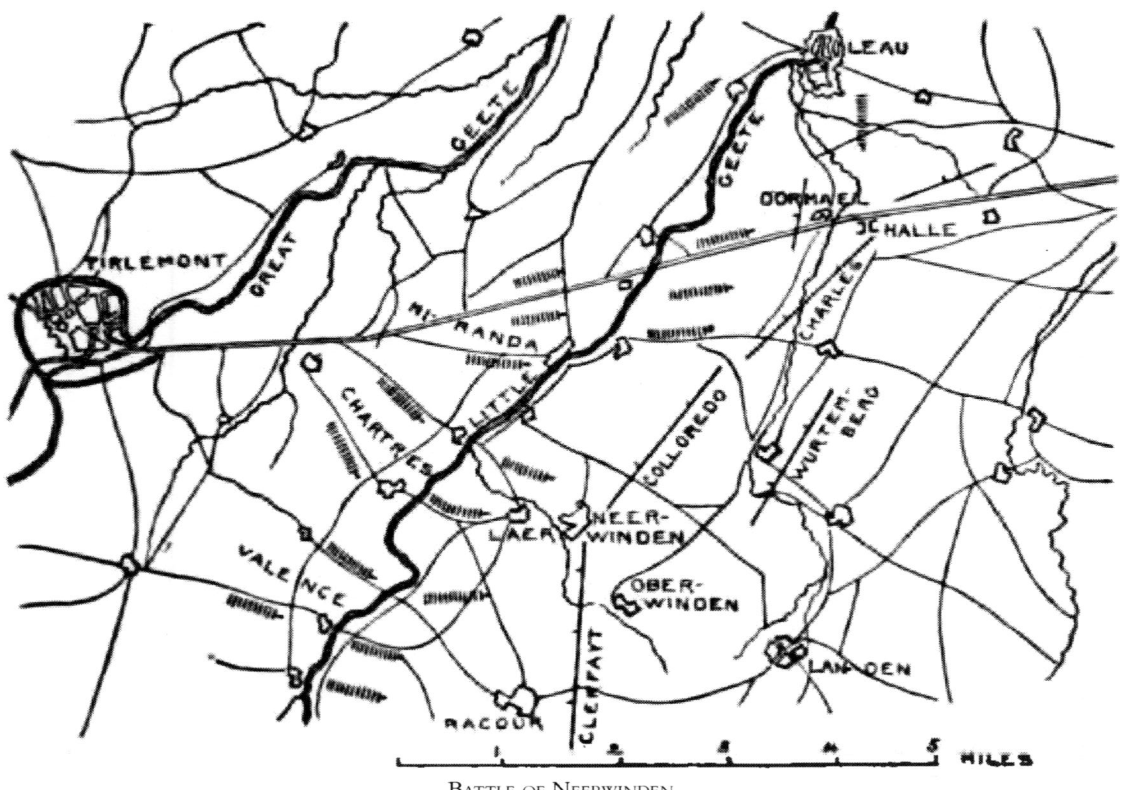

Battle of Neerwinden

The first news received by Coburg early on the 18th of March was from the announcement of attacks on his right; and fearing for his line of retreat along the highway, he withdrew a heavy force of foot and horse from the centre, and sent it to protect Halle. Meanwhile the French right and centre had captured Racour, Oberwinden, and later Neerwinden; the French left had driven the Austrians back on Dormael; and the reserve had occupied Leau and advanced on Halle. But shortly Coburg recovered himself, while the French onset had exhausted the young recruits. The reserve was thrown back on Leau, and the Austrians held firm in Dormael. This moment was seized by Archduke Charles to advance. His sharp onset pushed the French back along the post-road, and afforded the cavalry the chance to ride down on the weakening French left, and push it behind the Little Geete. The blow delivered by Charles had been well timed and heavy. So demoralized did the French left wing become, that only at Tirlemont could Miranda rally a part of it.

Meanwhile on the Austrian left, after making splendid efforts to regain Neerwinden, Oberwinden and Racour, and after a murderous defence of these villages by the French, during which the two last were taken and retaken again and again, the troops succeeded in tiring out Dumouriez's raw infantry, and aided by the cavalry, which charged in the open between the villages, drove them out of all three places. The Austrian work had been strong, and the battle was theirs. The French cavalry handsomely covered the retreat of the brigades, and the line held itself in front of the Little Geete until next morning, when, on account of the serious defeat of his left by Charles, Dumouriez saw that he must definitely retire. This he did, and took position southeast of Tirlemont.

The ill effect of the defeat on the French was such that they deserted wholesale, and made for France. Even the Convention could not guillotine an entire army, and demoralization was rampant. Three days after the battle, Dumouriez had but twenty thousand men. The allies recovered a great part of Flanders; while the French kept but a section, and this by severe measures only. In taking Holland, Dumouriez had lost Belgium.

Whether or not this defeat was the result of treachery on Dumouriez's part is not certain; but treachery was charged, and when the deputies of the Convention came to headquarters to hold him to task, he openly proposed to the army to march on Paris and restore the monarchy. Met, however, by stem refusal, he fled to the allied camp. The Army of the North was consolidated into the Army of the

Heavy Cavalryman, 1795

Ardennes. Coburg was at this moment afforded a fine opportunity for a fatal blow to the Republic by an advance on the capital, but he failed to utilize it. He was indecisive and slow. Neither were the French in any position to assume the offensive, and the allies managed to capture Valenciennes, Condé and le Quesnoy, and besieged Dunkirk during the summer months. They had a quarter of a million men on their line from Lille to Basle, but as usual infinitely divided their forces. The Convention raised fresh levies, and placed Houchard in command of the Flanders armies.

Despite their excellent chances this year, the allies practically accomplished nothing in the Netherlands. Houchard, who received orders to cut the English off from Fumes and drive them into the sea, beat the Dutch at Hondschoote and saved Dunkirk; but as he took no advantage of his victory and had failed to accomplish the task set him, he was recalled and guillotined, "*pour encourager les autres*." The allies, with a second army out for protection, laid siege to Maubeuge. In place of Houchard, Jourdan was put in command of all the armies along the northern frontier. With forty-five thousand men the new leader advanced on Maubeuge, beat the protecting army at Wattigny, and relieved the fortress. The allies retired across the Sambre. After some unimportant additional manoeuvres in Flanders, both contestants went into winter quarters. The allied work in the Netherlands had practically come to naught. The French had maintained their frontier, though they had lost part of their outside holdings.

In Italy, in 1793, after some changes, Kellermann (Junior) came into command of both the Army of the Alps and the Army of Italy. His operations were not, however, followed by much good fortune. The allies recaptured Savoy, and the French were compelled to vacate Nice. Later, part of Savoy was again taken by Kellermann; but on the other hand Toulon was captured by the English. Yet, weighing the *pros* and *cons*, the allies had made no greater gain on this field than in the north.

The execution of Louis had brought Spain into the Coalition. She had a force of ninety thousand foot and fifteen thousand horse, of which thirty thousand men were on the frontier, in Catalonia, Navarre and Aragon. In the Eastern Pyrenees Davout, and later Thureau and Doppet, were held in check in their attempt to invade Catalonia by Ricarod. A number of minor engagements were fought, and much manoeuvring done over this difficult terrain, with no decisive result, and the French went into winter quarters near Perpignan. In the Western Pyrenees no greater result was obtained; nor indeed in Aragon. The French had not been able to get a foothold in Spain. But they had made secure the Republican frontier.

The important recapture of Toulon from the English, which occurred this year, and in which Bonaparte first played a leading role, will be detailed later.

The results of 1798, then, were unimportant for the allies, who in their project of invading France and changing her new government had made no substantial headway. On the whole the French had, even with their raw levies and poor conduct, more than held their own against the regular troops of the allies, which, led by hidebound exponents of the old methods of war, had done themselves scant justice.

The war of the Coalition on the French Republic was largely one of Anglo-Saxon business methods pitted against the furious energy of the Gaul. While England put few British regiments into the field, she was lavish of her money in subsidies to those who could furnish men. Still striving to bring all the European powers into the Coalition, by 1794 she was in good part successful with the smaller ones. Portugal, Naples and Tuscany mobilized. Holland did the same. Genoa wavered. Venice refused French advances and armed. Prussia had been tempted to leave the Coalition, but was persuaded by England to remain in it and furnish sixty thousand troops, to be fed and paid by England. Switzerland remained neutral, which was of vast gain to France, and Russia held aloof. England raised her army to sixty thousand men, subsidized forty thousand foreign troops for her own service, and put her navy on a war footing of eighty-five thousand men. The Vendeans were furnished aid, and an expedition was sent against Corsica.

Perhaps no leaders of a great national uprising ever had more difficulties to face than the men who fathered the French Revolution. There were great men in those days, not always men such as peace and plenty breed, but men of the moment, fierce, intractable, ruthless, who sought by any means, fair or foul, just or unjust, to accomplish the one object they had at, heart—the liberation of the French from the yoke of centuries of oppression. However much hatred they engendered, however much the world may shudder at the recital of their doings, no one can withhold his meed of admiration for their courage and ability.

The difficulties before them were not only those of foreign interference fostered by the Royalists who were driven out of France, but those of internal struggles, which necessitated the keeping of large armies to suppress civil war, and made the tenure of office by the parties

Officer of Light Infantry

in power one of extreme uncertainty. As there was much civil bloodshed, and as no tyranny was ever worse than that which succeeded the deposal of Louis XVI., so there were many men in power whose guiding motive was merely self-seeking; but amongst these men there was also a leaven of true patriots, and it was eventually the influence of these men which prevailed.

Foremost among the difficulties which the Revolutionary leaders had to face was the war in the Vendée. This struggle has little to do with a history of the art of war, except for its interest as the insurrection of a people. As such, a few words may be devoted to it.

The Vendée began in 1793, and lasted with more or less intensity and after sundry truces and pacifications, until 1799, when it was suppressed, only to break out spasmodically thereafter, especially in 1813, 1814 and 1815. It was a war for the throne and the rights of the Bourbons, and was characterized by extraordinary courage and self-sacrifice on the part of the Vendeans.

The theatre of the *Vendée Militaire* was that which is known as the departments of the Vendée, the Sevres, the Loire Inférieure, and the Maine et Loire, that is to say, the country lying on the north-east of the Bay of Biscay, sheltered by the peninsula of Finisterre. It contained a population of eight hundred thousand souls, and was topographically divided into Le Bocage, or forest land; Le Marais, or marsh land; and La Plaine, or flat upland. The forest land comprised two thirds of the area, and contained isolated farms and estates closed in, as were also the fields, by ditches, live-hedges and fences, and connected by mere semblances of roads, which during the rainy weather could scarcely be used. Le Marais was near the sea, open and flat, and cut up by many canals, ditches and small shallow ponds, through which, as in many parts of Holland, nearly all communication between town and town, and farm and farm, was kept up by means of flat-bottomed boats. Pedestrians were forced to carry poles by means of which they might vault over the canals and ditches. Open stretches of country could be found only near the mouth of the Loire. There were scarcely any highways which could be used for the operations of an army. Over most of this land troops would have to move by squads, or even in single file.

The Vendeans were a robust people, moderate, laborious, of strong and stubborn character, and fixed though narrow religious views. They were strong partisans of the Bourbons, but the priesthood had greater influence than the nobility. These men never became soldiers, but everyone responded to the call to arms, shouldering such

The Vendée Militaire

weapons as he could collect, with clothing and victual; and having received absolution from the priest, he sallied forth to help the cause. After victory or defeat alike, these peasant warriors melted back into the population and resumed their every-day work; while only a few leaders and some men, in small part mounted, kept on foot to act as patrols and news-carriers.

When the war broke out, the Vendeans had only pikes, flails, scythes and pitchforks, with an occasional fowling-piece or carbine. Little by little, however, they seized from the enemy weapons of a more regular kind. There was no drill or discipline; the men merely marched in a crude mass as directed by their leaders. The advance was nothing but an irregular mob following the men in whom they had confidence; and the only value of the body was the weight of a mass of men whose purpose was strong. There could be no greater difference between two classes of men fighting for independence than existed between the Americans of the Revolution and these Vendean patriots. Those of the men who were armed with muskets, usually fowling-pieces loaded with buckshot or scraps of iron, were placed in front or on the flanks. When the enemy (*Les Bleus*) was met, the leaders ordered: "*Egaillez-vous, mes gars!*" whereupon the whole body would move to right and left into a long line, so as to encircle the body of the enemy, and at a signal boldly rush forward with loud shouts. A special body was detailed to capture the enemy's guns. This was not infrequently done by volunteers, who would creep out towards the guns, throwing themselves on the ground when they saw these about to fire, hiding themselves behind obstacles, dashing forward at intervals, and finally throwing themselves in a crowd upon the guns, though armed only with iron-shod clubs. There were few mounted men, and these unreliable. Superstition made the Vendeans worthless at night, and discipline was so lax that sentries commonly slept on post.

It was the decree of the Convention in 1793 for raising some three hundred thousand men which gave the signal for the rising in the Vendée, already much wrought up against the Republican government because of the execution of Louis XVI., and the action taken against religion, churches and holy orders. In March, 1793, the insurrection began in Anjou, and in the Marais and the Bocage, under their leaders, Cathelineau, Stofflet, D'Elbée, Bonchamp and Charette. The Vendeans seized a number of places, beat several of the bodies of Republican troops sent against them, and captured some artillery. Hereupon the Convention declared the insurrectionists to be outlaws, and ordered La Bourdonnaye, who commanded in this district, to form two columns of three thousand men each, to guard the communications with Brittany. At the same time it called out fifteen thousand men under Berruyer, composed of fresh levies. In Angers Berruyer divided his army into four parts, purposing to move on the Vendeans from different directions and push them into the ocean; and, in fact, he did win a victory at Beaupréau against thirty thousand Vendeans; yet Larochejaquelin, leader of the Vendeans, beat one of his advance bodies at Aubiers, collected a number of the insurrectionists, threw part of the Republican troops across the Loire, and shut up others in Bressuire and Fontenay. On May 5 the main Vendean army, twenty thousand strong, under D'Elbée and Cathelineau, surrounded and captured a Republican army, taking six thousand muskets and twelve guns, and the patriots were joined by the experienced Lescure, and many less valuable friends, among them an adventurer who called himself Bishop of Agra. On May 9 this force closed in Parthenay, and on the 13th *Chataigneray*; but the booty collected induced many of the men to desert. Even patriotism is not always proof to the seduction of loot. On May 16 the Vendeans attacking Fontenay were beaten; but Bonchamp and Larochejaquelin came up to their assistance, and the Republican troops on the 24th were defeated with the loss of forty guns and much material, victual and money.

Biron now took charge of the Bleus, but his forces were still undisciplined; they were in fact no better than the forty thousand men that the Vendeans collected in Chatillon and Vihiers. The Vendeans took Doué and Saumur early in June, but were shortly driven back to Tours by Menou, who commanded ten thousand Bleus. Cathelineau was then elected "*Generalissimo* of the Royal Catholic Army." He determined to move on and capture Nantes as a central base. Bonchamp wanted to move into Brittany and Normandy and on towards Paris; but the Vendeans, in fact, moved down the right bank of the Loire, took Angers and reached Nantes the end of June, being joined by Charette, who had marched by the left bank. Here fifty thousand Vendeans shut in ten thousand Bleus under Canclaux, but the Vendeans could not get possession of the city. Cathelineau was killed. Canclaux was joined by other Republicans; and Westermann, who commanded Biron's cavalry, beat the Vendeans in several engagements, but earned a bad reputation for cruelty to prisoners. On July 5 he was entirely defeated by Bonchamp and Larochejaquelin, whereupon, in retaliation, the Vendeans cut down all the prisoners they took. Another

Republican force marching from the Saumur country was defeated, but the southern Vendeans failed in their effort to capture Luçon. D'Elbée succeeded Cathelineau, but there was much disagreement among the Vendeans as to leaders and management.

In five months the Vendeans had created a strong and fairly well-armed force, and their successes over the Bleus had been so considerable as to compel the central power to raise large forces to put them down, and as they phrased it to "destroy the race." The bitterness of the Republicans was equalled by their cruel measures. It was essential to put better troops in the field against the Vendeans; and the garrison of Mainz, which city had lately been surrendered to the Austrians, was sent to the Loire. Here the army was parcelled into three divisions, one so called of Brest under Canclaux, six thousand men and twenty guns; one of La Rochelle, ten thousand men and thirty guns, under Rossignol; and one of the Mainz troops, eighteen thousand men and thirty guns. These forces, thirty-five thousand strong, were to operate from Nantes, cut the Vendeans from the sea, push them into the interior and surround them. On September 9 the Republicans broke up from Nantes in two columns, the Brest column against Machecoul, the Mainz column (Kleber commanding van) against Légé. The La Rochelle column also moved on Saumur and Cholet, but the Vendeans managed to beat the latter separately, and to force back Kleber and Canclaux. The Republicans retired to Nantes. Hereupon the Convention joined the Brest and La Rochelle divisions under the name of the Army of the West, and Lechelle was put in command, a poor soldier, who during his short term of office moved into the Vendean country in two concentric columns. On October 15 twenty-three thousand men of the Army of the West, under Beaupuy, Marceau and Kleber, got in the rear of the Vendeans, forty thousand strong, at Cholet. Here D'Elbée and Bonchamp were defeated October 17, and driven back to Beaupréau with heavy loss. Charette, busy with other operations, had failed to sustain his brother officers. The Vendean army was compelled to cross to the right bank of the Loire, followed by many old men, women and children, to escape the fury of the Republicans.

Larochejaquelin succeeded D'Elbée; Chalbos, Lechelle. The Vendeans strove to enlist Brittany in their cause, and in October took Laval. Here Kleber was defeated by them, despite which, however, he was left in command of his division. The Republicans reorganized, after repeated defeats, in Angers. The Vendeans, though above all they needed union, disagreed as to plans, and finally, in the hope

KELLERMANN (JUNIOR)

LAROCHEJAQUELIN

CATHELINEAN

MARCEAU

CHARETTE

WESTERMANN

of English aid, moved in force to Granville, on the Normandy sea-coast. But they could capture neither this town nor Avranches.

The Republicans collected a force of levies and peasants behind the Vire, and the troops from Angers and Rennes followed the Vendeans into Normandy. Seeking to move back to the Loire country, the Vendeans won a battle at Dole, but instead of pursuing the enemy, turned to bombard Angers, hoping to cross the Loire on its permanent bridge. This vicinity, however, they soon had to leave on the approach of the Republican army under Marceau, who had now been put in charge. The Vendeans again strove to reach the left bank of the Loire, but the Republicans headed them off, and they moved back into Maine. On December 8 they were nearly defeated at La Flèche, being saved only by the clever management of Larochejaquelin. Marceau now marched from Angers towards Laval, and obliqued on Le Mans in three columns. The left column, in advance of the others, struck the Vendeans a heavy blow, but was beaten off; and the second column attacked and took the suburbs, December 12. Kleber with the right column came up in the succeeding night, fell on the Vendeans, and drove them back on Laval with the loss of ten thousand men and all their artillery and train. Very many old men, women and children were ruthlessly cut down. A detachment occupied Angers to prevent the Vendeans reaching the other side of the Loire.

After this defeat the Vendeans could not hold head to the Republican forces. Marceau followed them up sharply, and the garrisons of Saumur, Angers and Nantes prevented their crossing the river. On December 16 they attempted to steal a passage between Angers and Nantes, but fruitlessly. They were driven back to Sarenay, where on December 22 the body was attacked by the Republicans and cut to pieces. The few who escaped the sabres of Westermann's cavalry went to the guillotine. Only a handful saved their lives. South of the Loire, Haxo's Republicans had been equally successful; and the year 1798 ended with the almost total destruction of the Vendée and its population. The first six months had been favourable for them, but from September to December their chiefs disagreed, and they worked in detail instead of together, and thus could not meet the better troops and generals the Republicans continued to send against them. Instead of sticking to their proper role of a popular uprising, moreover, and fighting in small bands on the defensive, they undertook a regular warfare to which they were not suited. In the beginning of 1794 the Vendée was still further ravaged by the Republicans, and on the other hand the Vendeans revenged themselves by killing all captured

Bleus. It became a war of extermination. Larochejaquelin alone held the Vendeans together. Westermann, whom Larochejaquelin had defeated at Vezins, was guillotined; and Larochejaquelin fell in battle.

The further operations in the Vendée are less interesting; but France had to struggle with civil war until Hoche finally pacified the country in 1796, and Bonaparte subdued the *Chouans* of Brittany in 1800. After this the outbreaks were spasmodic.

There is no end to the stories of heroism, on the part of men and women alike, in this hopeless struggle for faith and king; but these may not be dwelt upon. The war is mentioned solely to show the method of the Vendeans, as well as to draw attention to the serious internal difficulties with which the Republican authorities had to contend while facing all Europe in arms.

CHAPTER 5

The Wars of the French Revolution

1794-1796

The Reign of Terror and the finances were at their worst, yet, dragooned by fear, the people of France proposed to raise a million and a quarter men. The Coalition, subsidised by England, raised a million men. Pichegru commanded the French on the northern frontier, along which several costly battles were lost and won. Jourdan made several crossings of the Sambre, in June captured Charleroi, and somewhat later fought the Battle of Fleurus. This was really lost, but the allies retired. Pichegru again advanced, and the allies retired into winter quarters, while Pichegru overran Holland. All these operations were weak and ill-considered, but the French had shown much energy, and the Coalition armies, which were to enter France and march on Paris, could gain no real foothold within the frontier. On the Rhine the French were again defeated at Kaiserslautern, but on the whole, under Moreau, they held their own. In the Alps Kellermann, and on the Riviera Massena, did good work. The campaign of 1794 was a failure for the Coalition. In 1795 only Austria and the German empire remained in the field. The French had more than six hundred thousand men all told, two thirds campaigning against the Coalition. In September Jourdan crossed the Rhine at Düsseldorf, and Pichegru crossed and took Heidelberg. Pichegru turned traitor, and the allies recaptured Mainz. In 1795 Kellermann did no more than to hold his position in the Alps, but Scherer, aided by Massena, won the Battle of Loano in November, and drove the enemy back across the mountains. If during the first years of the Revolutionary wars France was able to defend her frontiers, in 1794 and 1795 she advanced into the enemy's territory, and showed energy and ability far beyond those of the allies. The year 1794 saw the Vendean struggle largely quieted.

As 1794 opened, the internal conditions of France were at their worst. All power was held by the Committee of Public Safety, and the Reign of Terror was in full blast. The finances were desperate, the pa-

Republican general and his orderly

per money worthless. Civil war added to the burdens of the country; and to forestall famine food had to be got from Italy, Barbary and even North America. Despite all this, enormous preparations were made for the approaching campaign by the men in power, with whom it literally was neck or nothing. By the decrees of August and September, 1793, a million and a quarter men of all kinds were ordered to be raised; and throughout the several armies the old soldiers were mixed with the new, one old battalion and two new ones in each half-brigade, as a means of easier education and better discipline, and to steady the bodies in action.

The bulk of the French forces were on the northern and eastern frontiers. The Army of the North numbered one hundred and sixty thousand men; the Army of the Ardennes was thirty-five thousand strong; the Army of the Moselle had sixty thousand men; the Army of the Rhine forty-five thousand men; the Army of the Upper Rhine numbered nearly fifty thousand effective; the Army of the Alps forty thousand men; the Army of Italy fifty-five thousand men; the Army of the Eastern Pyrenees seventy thousand men; the Army of the Western Pyrenees fifty thousand men; and there were three armies in the interior. These were, however, paper figures, never actually reached and by no means representing men under the colours. Opposed to this force on the northern frontier of France were the troops furnished and subsidized by England. Austria, despite her losses, got into line a quarter of a million men, most of which force went to the Netherlands. The Prussian troops were fed at a large cost by England and Holland, and numbered over fifty thousand men. Holland furnished its usual contingent. The German Empire did the like. The Coalition in one way or other had nearly a million men of all kinds afoot, but as this comprised home and garrison troops, not half of the numbers were actively engaged. The Upper Rhine forces numbered sixty thousand men; sixty-five thousand men stood near Mainz; twenty thousand were in Luxemburg. The main army in the Netherlands had fully one hundred and fifty thousand men for duty. In Italy stood forty thousand, and in the Pyrenees fifty thousand men.

The purpose of the allies was to push hard on the northern and north-eastern frontier of France, and perhaps this year to open the long essayed path to Paris. In Italy the troops would stand on the defensive, or assume the offensive only if good chance offered; and the Spaniards were to push through the Eastern Pyrenees and act on the defensive in the Western Pyrenees, so as to draw French forces away

Line Infantryman

French Grenadier, 1795

from the northern armies. The allies' plan was good, but they forgot to take into account the tremendous momentum of the popular uprising in France.

Pichegru, high in favour, commanded the Army of the North, which was strung out from Dunkirk through Lille, Douay and Cambray to Maubeuge, with the Army of the Ardennes sustaining its right. The fortresses were mostly garrisoned by new levies. Coburg commanded the allies in the Netherlands, and these were also strung out from the ocean to the Rhine, the English under the Duke of York on the right. The French had several fortresses to recapture. They were superior in numbers, but not as good in discipline. Carnot, now French minister of war, drew up the plan of campaign, which, under his pet theory, was to comprise the turning of both allied flanks in the Netherlands. Each opponent was again about to operate on the old cordon system, which had fully taken possession of men's minds, to the exclusion of every sound strategical idea that Gustavus and Frederick had taught the world.

In March, 1794, the allies advanced upon Landrecies with eighty-five thousand men and closed it in. The fortress surrendered April 30, and the French fell back after two rather faint attempts to relieve it. The capture of Landrecies in a way ruptured the centre of the French line, and foreseeing the danger, the Committee of Public Safety ordered Jourdan up with the Army of the Moselle, and Pichegru was otherwise sustained. On April 25 the latter general advanced in two columns on Menin and Courtray. Menin was smartly taken by Moreau. Clerfayt advanced to meet Pichegru, but was beaten at Courtray May 11, and the allied right wing fell back. Ypres was blockaded by the French about the end of April.

At the same time the Army of the Ardennes attempted to cross the Sambre in several columns on a front extending from Charleroi to Maubeuge; but after some heavy fighting, was defeated, with a loss of four thousand men and twelve guns, on May 13. All the battles of this period, however stoutly contested and costly, seem to have remained without result. Nor even when the details which remain to us suffice, do they present points of interest salient enough to make a lengthy narrative useful. In a renewed effort to place the French armies beyond the Sambre, Kleber's troops suffered a defeat with considerable loss May 21, and again on the 24th. Despite these three defeats, the French showed admirable activity; but still they clung to the fatal system of many columns. Operations and attacks in one mass were reserved for Napoleon to revive. Frederick's lessons had been apparently forgotten.

After the battle of Courtray the allied right wing advanced again in a number of columns on the French, who had for unexplained reasons retired to their old lines. As a matter of course these columns did not work together, and one of them was defeated May 18 and 19 at Turcoing, with loss of four thousand men and all its artillery. The records of these several serious engagements are very crude. In no respect did the French utilize their victory as they might. The allies returned to Tournay, where they took up a position in a half-circle around the town. On May 22 Pichegru attacked them here, and heavy fighting occurred at Pont-à-Chin; but though the French were defeated, with a loss of over five thousand men, and retired to Courtray, this battle also remained without immediate result. Coburg and York were at odds; and the allies quite failed to work for a common purpose. The French, who showed great vigour if not good strategy, kept on their advance along the coast towns, and took Ypres June 18, and Ostende and Nieuport in July.

In the centre, at the end of May, the French made another, the third, attempt to cross the Sambre, but after an advance barely worth mentioning, again retired.

The Army of the Moselle meanwhile, under Jourdan, had marched to the Sambre, Moreau being placed in command on the Moselle; and a new army was created, under Jourdan, to be called the Army of the Sambre and Meuse. About mid-June, for the fourth time, the French under the new leader crossed the Sambre, but after a defeat north of Charleroi, in which they lost three thousand men and sixteen guns, they still again retired. Later in June, urged on by the never-to-be-satisfied Committee of Public Safety, Jourdan's army for the fifth time crossed the Sambre, and laid siege to Charleroi, shutting up all avenues to the place. The left was at Trazegnies and Forchies; the centre at Gosselies and Heppignies; the right at Fleurus and Lambusart. Here on June 16 the Prince of Orange attacked Jourdan's centre and right and drove them across the Sambre, and the rest of the French array was constrained to follow; but Orange's heavy losses induced him also to retire. Coburg then came up with thirty thousand men to his aid; but with praiseworthy energy Jourdan had already re-established order, recrossed the Sambre and again blockaded Charleroi. By a hearty bombardment the city was made to capitulate June 25, just as Coburg' got ready to take decisive action. The possession of Charleroi gave Jourdan a marked advantage, and added the French besieging forces to the fighting line.

The allies had forty-six thousand men; the French are given as

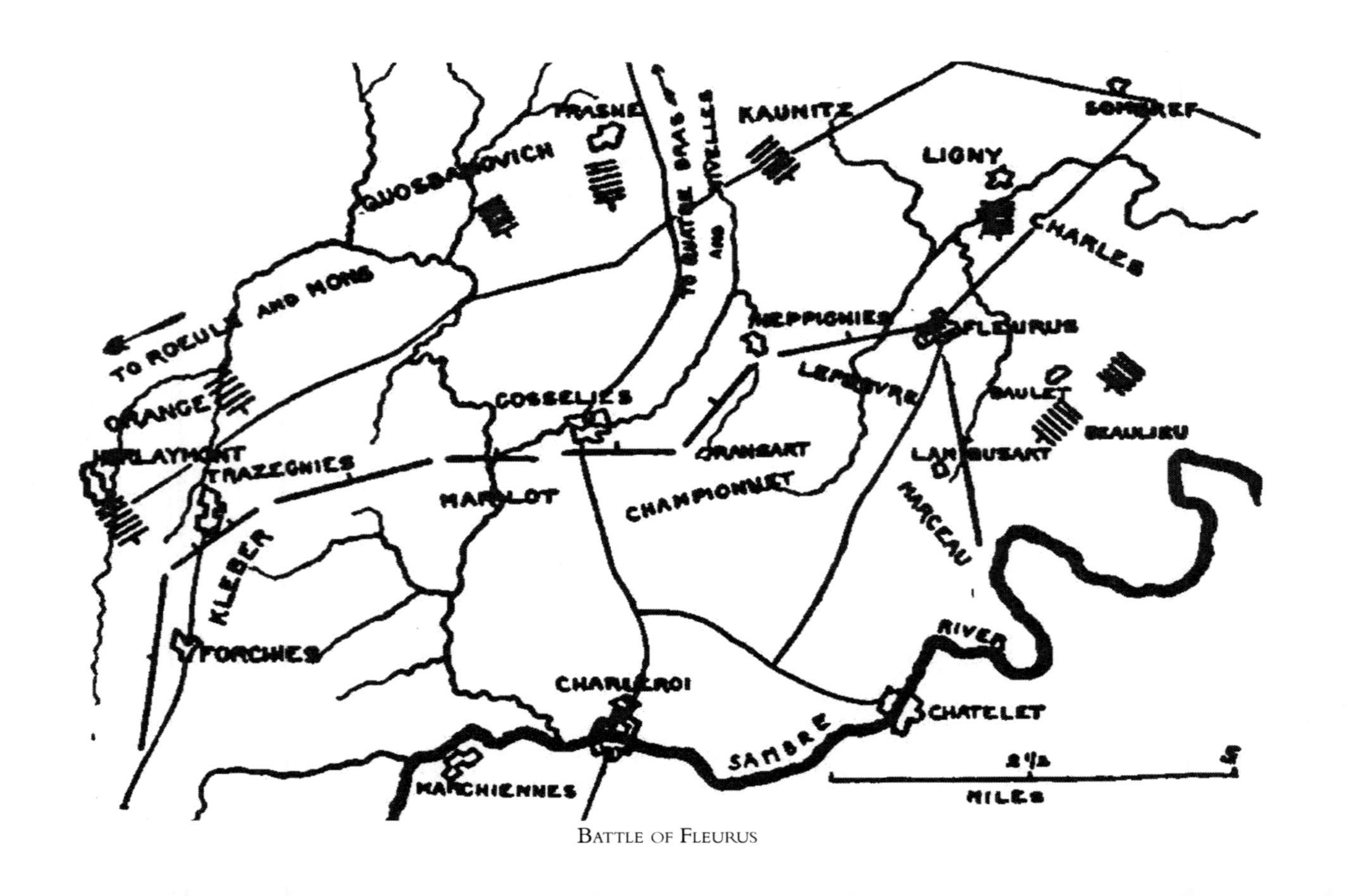

Battle of Fleurus

seventy-five thousand, but they were of far inferior quality. Coburg drew up his line on the usual cordon plan in a huge semicircle around the French position, and formed five columns of attack widely separated, each one subdivided into other columns. On the right, Orange was to debouch from Herlaymont; next came Quosdanovich from Frasne; then Kaunitz, who was to operate towards Fleurus to help the Archduke Charles, after taking which, both would advance on Ransart; finally Beaulieu was to debouch through Baulet on Lambusart.

Jourdan's line ran from river to river, through Trazegnies, Gosselies, Heppignies, Fleurus, Lambusart, the divisions standing in order, Kleber, Marlot, Championnet, Lefebvre, Marceau. Considerable forces were out beyond the line in the several villages.

At daybreak of June 26 the allied leader threw all five columns on the French lines. Exhibiting great gallantry, they met with uniform success. Orange had three columns of attack, and speedily drove in Kleber's division as far as Marchiennes, where, learning that Charleroi had surrendered, he paused, and afforded Kleber time to mass his guns on the hills and force the allies back. Quosdanovich pushed in Marlot's advanced parties to Gosselies, and Kaunitz forced Championnet in to Heppignies, where he waited until Charles ousted Lefebvre from Fleurus; but Kaunitz was shortly driven out by Jourdan, who brought up his cavalry for the purpose. Meanwhile Beaulieu had attacked Marceau's division, broken the young troops, and forced the bulk of them across the Sambre. But, collecting a few brigades, Marceau held fiercely on to Lambusart, where Lefebvre came up to his aid. Here was the bloodiest fighting of the day; and this village became the key-point of the field. Finally the haystacks and thatched roofs of the village caught fire, but the battle raged on in the midst of flames, with surprising tenacity on either hand. Jourdan brought up all the reserve troops he could gather, and the place was held. The day, with more energy, would have proved an allied victory, but Coburg, on the news of the fall of Charleroi being confirmed by Beaulieu, elected to retire, which he did in many columns on Sombref, Quatre-Bras and Nivelles, Roeulx and Mons.

The French loss is given as six thousand men. The allies quoted their own losses as sixteen hundred, and the French claimed the allied loss to be thirteen thousand. It is probable that the allied casualties exceeded five thousand. The battle of Fleurus was followed by a fresh advance of Pichegru's army during the summer, by the retreat of the allies behind the Meuse, and the occupation of Belgium and

West Flanders by the French. Brussels was entered July 10. The persistency of the Republican leaders had been as admirable as their military methods were lacking.

Clerfayt succeeded Coburg. Jourdan, late in August, marched against the former and pushed him back to the Boer, on which river he defeated the enemy October 2; and after a number of smaller exchanges the allies retired behind the Rhine into winter quarters. On either side these armies of seventy or eighty thousand men had been ill-handled. Upon Clerfayt's retreat the Duke of York and the English army felt constrained to retire behind the Waal, upon which York went to England, leaving Walmoden in command. The Army of the North followed up the allied retreat Pichegru crossed the Meuse and the Waal on the ice and, taking Bommel by assault, reached Utrecht January 19, and Amsterdam next day. The whole of Holland was overrun by the end of January, 1795. To show how oddly warfare is at times conducted, the fact may be mentioned that the French hussars rode out into the Helder Strait upon the ice, reached the Dutch fleet, which was frozen in near Texel island, and captured it,—as strange a cavalry exploit as ever occurred. The Army of the North then went into winter quarters. Holland had no recourse but to make a treaty with the French.

There is much in the campaign in Flanders which is of interest; but as it is no part of this history, furnishing as it does no lesson in the art of war, except to exhibit the folly of the cordon system and the status upon which Bonaparte grafted his new method, these otherwise important events must be passed over with only brief mention.

The result of the Netherlands campaign of 1794, during which the allies had proposed to invade France and push on to Paris—a purpose by no means dulled by three successive failures—had resulted not only in their not entering France, but in their being pushed back behind the Rhine, and being compelled to abandon Belgium and Holland. Whatever criticism may be passed on the lamentable strategy and tactics of both sides, it is to be said to the credit of the French that, during each of the years 1792, 1793 and 1794, they had placed more men and better generals in the field as time went on. The energy of Pichegru and Jourdan, under the lash to be sure of the Committee of Public Safety and its horrible methods, was much to be commended. Four times they failed after crossing the Sambre; the fifth time they succeeded; and while this success was largely due to the bad system, quarrels and utter lack of energy of the allied generals, yet the French commanders deserve none the less

French Hussar, 1795

credit for what they accomplished. It is to be noted that here and on the Rhine were a number of Bonaparte's later opponents. Mack, Beaulieu, Wurmser and others, practicing in a subordinate command those errors of the cordon system of which the great soldier was by and by on a larger scale to teach them the worthlessness.

While the Netherlands armies were waging a warfare in detail, which eventuated in favour of the French, the allies concentrated one hundred and fifty thousand men on the Rhine. Facing this array of allies were the Army of the Moselle and the Army of the Rhine. The purpose was to stand on the defensive along this part of the French frontier, and up to May little occurred beyond small-war. In July the French made an advance movement, but without result. Later, under orders from Carnot, another movement forward was made in the Vosges region, and part of the allied army retired across the Rhine at Mannheim. In August Moreau advanced on Treves and took it; and though its recovery was attempted and the French were a second time beaten at Kaiserslautern, yet the general effect of the French advance in September and October was that the allies retired to their side of the river. Mainz was then blockaded. Thus on the Rhine, as well as in the Netherlands, the French had held their own, and more. According to the strict rules of the cordon system, when the main army in the Netherlands retired, the Rhine forces had to do the like; and although the French also followed the cordon system in a way, they displayed much greater decision and intelligence in their operations.

In Italy the Army of the Alps and the Army of Italy, respectively of thirty-five and forty thousand men, were faced by not exceeding forty thousand allies all told. The Army of the Alps under Kellermann got possession of the little St. Bernard and Mont Cenis. The Army of Italy under Massena did some good work. A plan drawn up by Bonaparte, who was then serving in the Army of Italy as an artillery officer, was begun; but lacking, as it did, its author's vigour of execution, it failed of the largest result. The pirates were, however, driven out of Oneille; and chiefly by the efforts of Massena, Saorgio was also taken, and the Austrians driven back to Ceva. Seizing the Col di Tenda, the French forced the allies down to the foothills, where they concentrated around Coni. In July an advance was made on this fortress, but the 9th *Thermidor* and fall of Robespierre arrested the undertaking. The French retained the watershed. The allies in September, attempting to take Savona, were beaten off; and the place being occupied by a French garrison, the coast as far as Savona was

Map Battle of the Mainz

covered by the French winter quarters. The allied winter quarters lay in the shelter of the fortresses beyond the mountains. Scherer took command of the Army of Italy, and to Kellermann was given the joint control of both armies.

In the Pyrenees the western Spanish army was intended to remain on the defensive, the eastern one to advance across the French frontier. But the French anticipated the Spanish, and Augereau, the later so distinguished Marshal of the Empire, won some credit for a victory at Seret; after which the Spaniards retired across the border, followed by the French. Constant exchanges took place during the campaign, in which the names of Victor and Sauret also appear with distinction. The campaign ended by the capture of Figueras. In the Western Pyrenees there was also much secondary fighting of no particular interest. On the borders of Aragon a number of expeditions were undertaken, and swords crossed without important effect.

On the whole, then, the result of the campaign of 1794 was naught on the part of the Coalition, and of marked value on the part of France. The allies had accomplished no part of their vast undertaking, while the French Republic, in three years, had pushed forward its frontier on all sides in a manner which Louis XIV., after nearly fifty years of warfare, had been unable to attain. The Committee of Public Safety, and especially Carnot, had conducted the defence of France with an offensive method which, allowing all its faults, had produced great results. The campaign had shown what an active organization like the new Republic could succeed in doing against a lifeless body like the Coalition. The raw levies and new generals of France had proved more than a match for the veterans of the allied armies, led by officers long trained in war.

The fine results of the French operations in 1794 led to a peace with Prussia in April, 1795, by which France remained in possession of some of the conquered Prussian territory on the left bank of the Rhine. Hesse-Cassel made a later peace, and Holland concluded an offensive-defensive alliance with France. England remained stubbornly opposed to the French regime, and increased her navy to two hundred thousand men; but the English-paid German troops were discharged. Only Austria and the German Empire continued in the field as, since the execution of Marie Antoinette, they were in a way constrained to do. From financial stress, indeed, the emperor would have been glad to make peace, but England subsidized Austria, and determined her to keep the field.

Russia now joined in the fray, and sent a few ships to join the

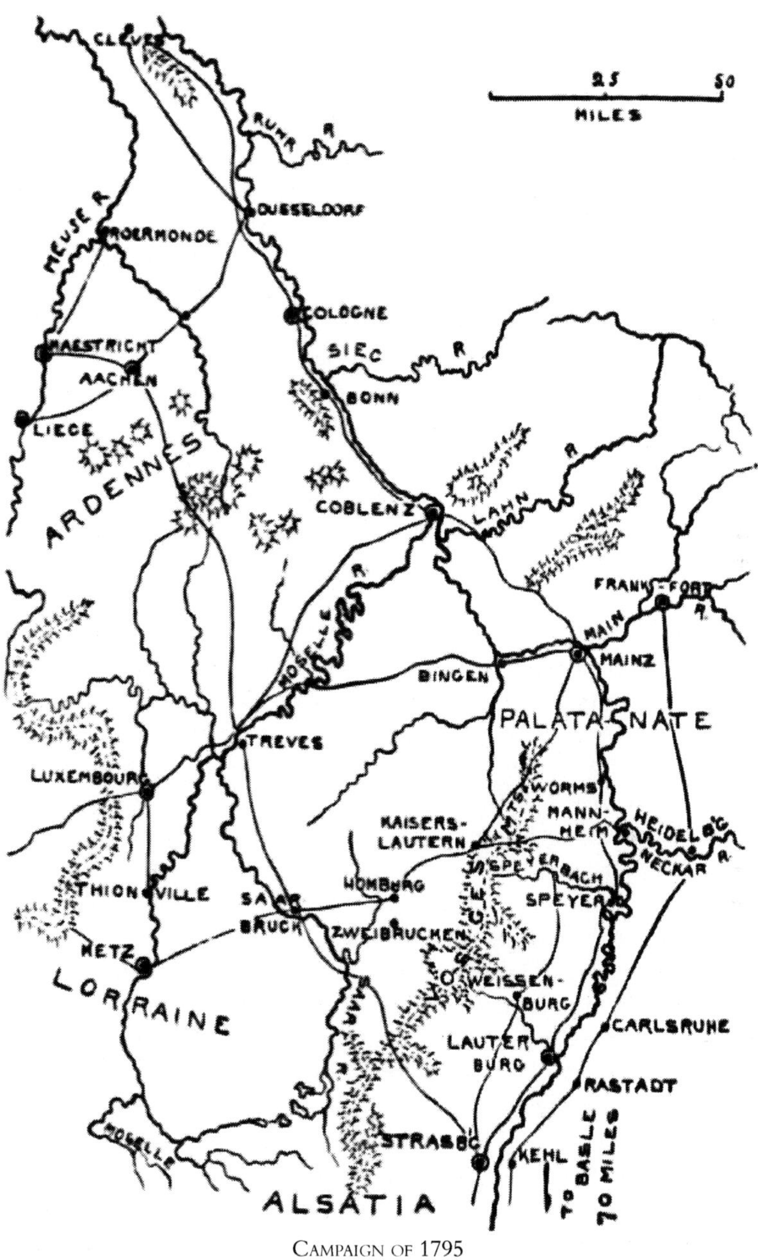

Campaign of 1795

English fleet. Denmark and Sweden remained neutral. Spain entered into negotiations with France. All Italy, except Genoa and Tuscany, remained in the Coalition, but Sardinia would have rejoiced to be quit of the war. Thus in reality England and Austria were the only great powers which still faced France. But though the Republic had won in arms, the internal difficulties of the country grew. There was little food, and the English fleet captured a great part of the corn-laden ships. The Vendeans made a temporary truce, but one hundred and twenty thousand men had to be kept afoot in the armies of the interior. The French forces in 1795 numbered less than six hundred thousand men, of which not exceeding two thirds were disposable for use against the Coalition.

Moreau commanded the Army of the North, fifty thousand strong, with an equal number garrisoning the fortresses, and was closely watching neutral Prussia. The Army of the Sambre and Meuse under Jourdan numbered nearly one hundred thousand men, with ample garrisons in the strong places along the Rhine from Cleves to Coblenz and Bingen. The Army of the Rhine and the Army of the Moselle under Pichegru in Alsatia and the Palatinate, ninety thousand effective, had nearly as many more in garrison along the Rhine from Mainz to Basle, and four divisions were blockading Mainz to keep the allies from debouching on the left bank. The Army of the Alps of twenty thousand men and the Army of Italy of ninety thousand men remained under command of Kellermann. The two Pyrenees armies of seventy-five thousand each stood as before; and the so-called Army of the West faced the Vendée, seventy thousand aggregate. The above were really paper figures, never reached. Two armies stood at Cherbourg and Brest to prevent landings by the English. The French plan was to assume the offensive all along the line, and the Republic particularly aimed to capture Luxemburg and Mainz.

Along the Rhine lay the allies with eighty-five thousand men under Wurmser, in detachments from Basle to the Neckar; and nearly a hundred thousand men under Clerfayt from the Neckar to the Ruhr. In Italy were seventy thousand men. The Spanish armies were smaller than before. The allies hoped this year to reconquer Belgium.

Serious questions of food, equipment and munitions of war delayed the opening of the campaign. In June, 1795, Luxemburg, after a busy siege of eight months, was captured by the French. Both parties held the long line of the Rhine on the cordon system, and spread their forces in small isolated bodies over the entire distance. In September Jourdan crossed the Rhine and took Düsseldorf, the Austrians falling back behind the Lahn and Main; and Pichegru, who being in correspondence with the enemy was slow at his task, also crossed and occupied Mannheim and Heidelberg, where vast stores were found. Jourdan followed up the Austrians to the Lahn and beyond, but in October the latter, under Clerfayt, by manoeuvres threatening his flanks, and facilitated by Pichegru's treachery, forced him back and across the Rhine. Pichegru also retiring, the allies turned to the relief of Mainz.

Mainz had been well fortified, and the French lines were also elaborate, mounting over two hundred guns. These lines began at Laubenheim near the Rhine, and ran *via* Hechtsheim, Mariaborn, Gonzenheim, to near Monbach, where they again reached the river. Their main fault lay in leaving a gap between Laubenheim and the Rhine. General Schaal, in command of the French, had about thirty thousand men in the blockading lines, and the division commanders stood from right to left: Courtot, Gouvion St. Cyr, Mengaud, Rencauld. So soon as Clerfayt reconnoitred this position on October 25, he saw that the gap of over half a mile between Laubenheim and the Rhine opened a good chance of breaking the blockade. He arranged to make stout feints on the French left, and under cover of these, *via* Weissenau and across the Rhine, to take the French right in reverse. This attack was carefully prepared during the night of October 28-29. Early on the 29th Monbach was smartly attacked, and the French generals drew troops from the right to reinforce the left. Bodenheim, in Courtot's rear, was taken by a column which crossed the Rhine in boats. The Weissenau column advanced without firing a shot, captured the outlying works of Laubenheim with a rush, and pushed in on Courtot's division; while a second column advanced on Hechtsheim, a third on Brenzenheim, and still another column captured Gonzenheim. Courtot retired after a good defence, and St. Cyr was thus taken in flank. The column at Bodenheim was heavily reinforced, and advancing rapidly captured Gaubischofsheim. The French were fairly turned out of their position, much to Clerfayt's credit, and retired from the blockade, with a loss of over four thousand men, and all their guns and material. The allied loss was less than half as much.

The allies now in their turn kept on in their advance, and in November both French generals fell back behind the Vosges. Mannheim was occupied by the Austrians and later Kaiserslautern, Homburg, and Zweibrucken; and when the Army of the Sambre and Meuse was withdrawn to the Moselle, the Army of the Rhine withdrew behind the Speyerbach. From January until the spring, a truce kept the armies on the Rhine quiet.

Carlo di Bonoparte

Letitia di Bonoparte

Lefebvre

Massena

Gouvion St Cyr

Moreau

In 1795 Austria strengthened her army in Italy, and Sardinia did the like. There were seventy thousand men on paper, fifty thousand under the colours. The Army of Italy stood along the coast from Savona to the Finestre and Tenda passes; the Army of the Alps still held the Alpine passes from the Little St. Bernard to the Argentières. All these forces were in poor condition, numbering barely thirty thousand men for duty. The Austrians proposed to drive the French back to the Var, and occupy the coast; the French to force the Bocchetta pass. Kellermann was given a free hand to advance or retire, as circumstances might dictate.

The Army of the Alps accomplished little but to hold its own. The Austrians advanced in June against the Army of Italy, and forced it back some distance to the line Borghetto-Ormea-Tenda. The English fleet cut off its supplies and reduced the troops to great straits; and reinforcements did not reach the army until August. Kellermann's lack of success resulted in his being left in charge of the Army of the Alps alone, the sole command of the Army of Italy being confided to Scherer.

Late in the year the allies had gone into winter quarters, their left covered by a twofold line of field-works from Rocca Barbena to Loano and from Bardinetto to Finale, and the right extending across the mountains to Ceva. They were well provided with food from Genoa. Fresh from compelling peace in Catalonia, Scherer proposed to surprise the enemy in his quarters, especially as many of the Austrian officers had left their command for the greater comfort of the towns, and he himself had received reinforcements, including Augereau's division from the Eastern Pyrenees, which ran the Army of Italy up to nearly fifty thousand men. Loano and Finale lie at the foot of valleys whose upper ends were closed by strong works at Rocca Barbena, Bardinetto and Melongo; and as these had to be taken to insure the success of any advance on Loano, the task was confided to Massena, who, born in Nice, happened to be familiar with the country and its mountain paths.

On November 23 Scherer formed three columns, to advance at the same moment. Serurier on the left made his way down into the Tanaro valley; Augereau on the right advanced straight on Loano; Massena in the centre headed the column destined to clear the enemy away from the works at the headwaters of the valleys. His knowledge of the country here came into play; he led his men through ravines and over hills with a secrecy and ardour which proved him to be a born mountain fighter, and quickly surprising and successively capturing the redoubts at Rocca Barbena, Bardinetto and Melongo,

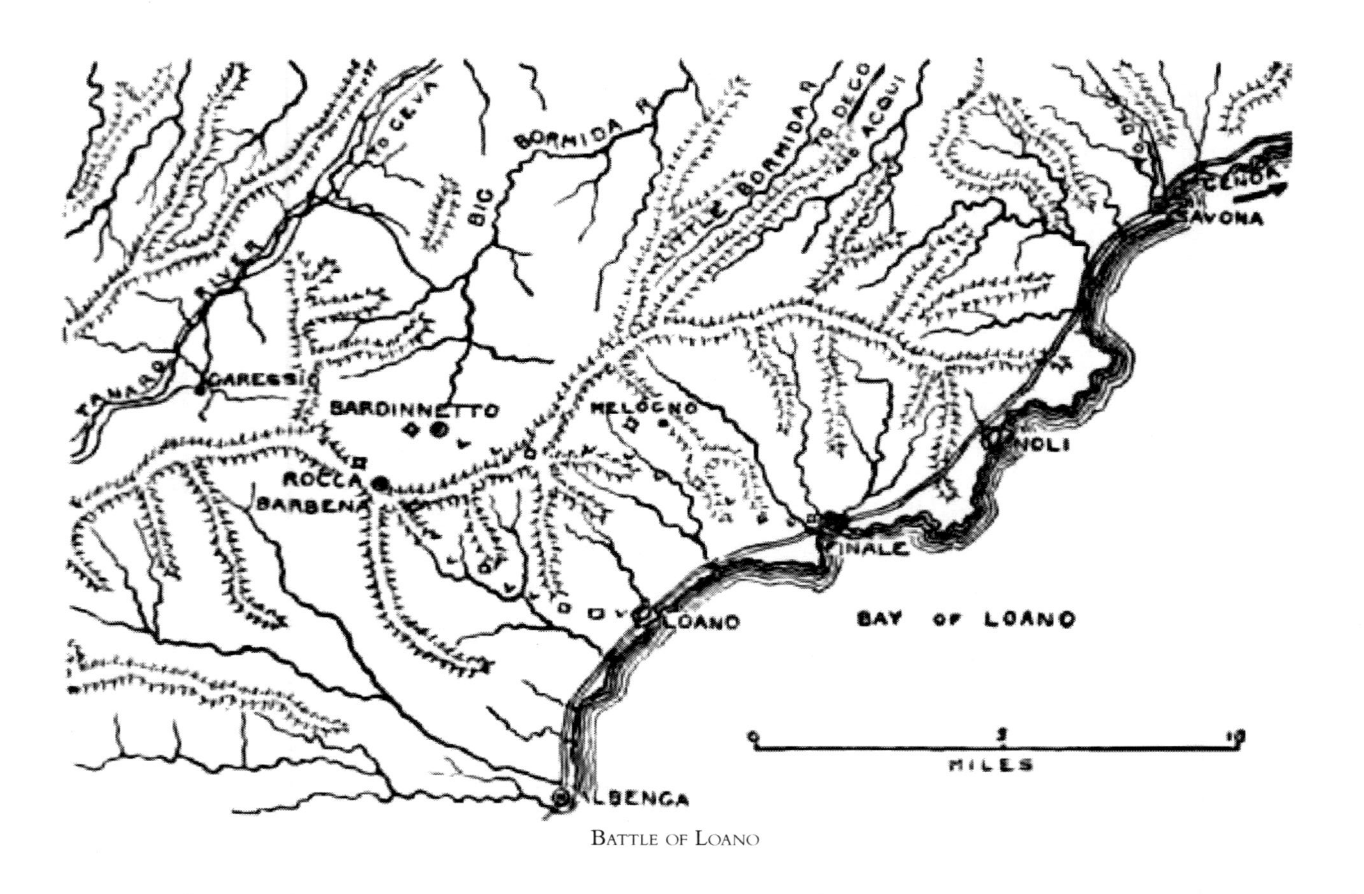

Battle of Loano

he then swung to the right and swept like a whirlwind down upon the rear of the allied positions. The next day a heavy engagement was fought in front of Loano. Argenteau, surprised, and soon finding his position turned, was fain to decamp from Loano, which Augereau at once occupied, and was able to hold Finale but a short while. Serurier pushed down the Tanaro, captured Garessio, and forced the Piedmontese back to Ceva. Massena, following up his gain, pushed Argenteau behind the Bormida, and the Austrians did not stop their retreat until they had reached Dego and Acqui. They had lost in this short and sharp winter operation three thousand killed and wounded, five thousand prisoners and forty guns. This victory opened for the French the road to Genoa, and gave them control of the passes in the Apennines. Though the plan for the operation was drawn up by Bonaparte, who was then working in the department of war in Paris, its conduct reflected great credit on Scherer, and particularly on Massena. And, moreover, it gave all the French generals a better knowledge of the country in which they were next year to campaign to such good effect under the new leader.

In the Eastern Pyrenees region there was much manoeuvring to and fro without especial result; among the hills of the Western Pyrenees there was more activity, but equally unfruitful. In July peace was concluded between Spain and France.

The campaign of 1795 had been quite as disastrous for the Coalition as that of 1794. The total forces operating in the field were on each side something over three hundred thousand men. On the Rhine, Jourdan and Pichegru had been active enough to prevent the allies from winning much beyond what they had held at the opening of operations. In Italy, the French had gained more than the allies. On the whole the offensive of the Coalition had weakened into defensive, and the French were now in better condition to carry forward their projects. The entire scheme of the Coalition was crumbling.

The first four years of the French Revolution were the beginning of the wars of the new era. Not only did France introduce a new system of war, but the Republic showed itself fully able to defend its frontiers against all Europe; and the years 1794 and 1795 proved France ready to conquer territory outside her old borders. Though there was no special gain in a strategic sense on either side, for both opponents held firmly to the cordon system, yet the French exhibited a great excess of moral force over the allies. However much their methods may be questioned, to the Convention and the Committee of Public Safety must be attributed wonderful intelligence, unanimity and energy in conducting the wars of France. This was complemented by the extraordinary public spirit of the people, partly controlled to be sure by the tyranny of the governing power, but largely due also to the strong innate love of country. Every available man was in arms, every one learned his lesson in the ranks, and the whole population of France became instinct with military fervour. Although the feats of arms attempted by the French troops often tamed out to be lamentably weak, yet the constant work along the border from Dunkirk to the Pyrenees, in daily conflict with the enemy, was a good school for officers and men. Many of the ancient and well-educated officers, being nobles, had left France, but the Republic bred up others, and the rule of making success the sole test brought the able men to the front, though it buried from sight many who had failed from no fault of their own.

On the other side there was little unity and less moral force; the operations of the allies had no general method; they were conducted largely by the Vienna Aulic Council, and the men at the head of the armies were hampered by red tape, apt to be at odds, and rarely worked together. As a rule the allied operations lacked energy; the unnecessary dread of being turned or cut off from their base appeared to be a constant motive for retreat. As to their army organization, this had not been changed for fifty years. The armies were loaded down with immense trains and impeded by magazines, and they could not tear themselves loose from the glaring defects of the cordon system and concentrate any respectable force for a single operation. The four years on the part of the allies had been a war of fortresses and field fortifications. The French armies, on the other hand, with small trains, and feeding themselves on the country, were able to accomplish better results, despite their own adherence to the cordon system, which had been less formal; and while these campaigns were on their part defensive, they took the shape of offensive operations.

In these four years the French showed by far the greater ability in war, and the operations of their generals and armies during this period laid a foundation upon which Napoleon could erect his magnificent schemes. Circumstances were building up for him an army with which to essay his new theory of war, much as Philip and Frederick William had trained armies to be later led to victory by Alexander and Frederick.

In the Vendée, in 1794, Thurreau was in command of the Republicans, who numbered forty thousand men, more or less raw. The Vendeans had half as many and were still in disagreement as to plans, and could consequently make no progress. In June the Committee of Public Safety withdrew the bulk of the forces from the Vendée, which encouraged the revolutionists. The year 1794 had no occurrences of value. In 1795 Canclaux took command of the Republican army, and on the 5th of February Charette made a treaty of peace with him, and his lead was followed by Stofflet. The rest thus given lasted no great time. The *émigrés* started the Vendeans afresh, and the uprising broke out in Poitou. In June the Vendeans were again in full insurrection, and the utmost cruelty was exhibited by both parties. On August 10 an English squadron brought supplies to Charette at St. Gilles, and an English fleet soon followed. The Republicans strengthened the Army of the West by some troops from the Pyrenees. Hoche succeeded Canclaux, and marched on Belleville against Charette. He had fifteen thousand men, and used these cleverly cordon-fashion, pushing Charette farther and farther towards the ocean. At the end of the year the whole coast from Bordeaux to Cherbourg was placed under Hoche, who practically pacified the Vendée.

The year 1793 was the most important one in the Vendée war. In 1794 only isolated attempts made by Thurreau and Hoche against Charette and Stofflet were noteworthy. The fault of the Vendeans had been that instead of carrying on a people's war, they attempted to wage a regular war in masses, for which they were not suited. On the Republican side, poor generals and poorer troops had kept the war dragging beyond any necessity.

But we must now turn to the young officer, whose future exploits are to be the burden of these volumes, and see what he has been doing to qualify himself for the extraordinary campaign of 1796, which at once raised him to the level of the greatest captains of all time.

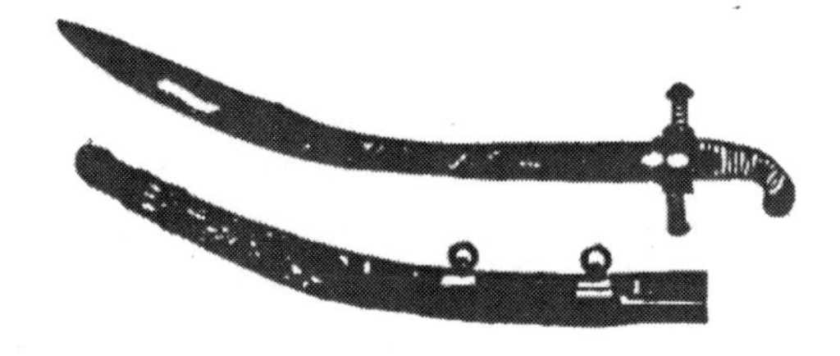

Chapter 6

The Youth and the Company Officer

1769-1793

Napoleone Bonoparte was the fourth child of a poor but noble family in Ajaccio, Corsica. His father was an easygoing man, his mother a woman of character. Born in 1769, he was educated at home, at ten was sent to the military school at Brienne, and later to that of Paris. He was a small, strange boy, morose and obstinate, capable in some studies, neglectful in others, but with intelligence and character. Looked down upon by his rich classmates, he yet in a way impressed himself upon them, and in 1786 received his commission as artillery subaltern in the French army. For a number of years, instead of serving with his regiment, young Bonoparte managed to be much absent in Corsica, where he was at first an adherent of the patriot Paoli, and harboured an ambition to free his native island. But later he deemed it wiser to accept the French occupation. He was pitifully poor. When off duty in Paris, he would live on bread to buy books. He wrote much, read voraciously and made prolific notes. Little by little he rose to be captain, but, probably on account of his usefulness to the French in Corsica, was allowed to be much away from regimental duties. During the early Revolutionary struggle he paid vastly more heed to his birthplace than to France. Though energetic, he seemed to fail in all his undertakings, and made as many enemies as friends. This ill success and his French leanings were so marked that finally the whole Bonoparte family was compelled to leave Corsica and become refugees, subsisting in Provence on a pittance allowed them by the government. This was small promise for the future.

About no great character in history has there been so much to dispute as the wonderful son of Corsica, who for two decades kept Europe aflame. Even disagreement as to the date of his birth exists; but in military history it has long been accepted that Napoleone di Bonoparte first saw the light at Ajaccio, August 15, 1769.

A legend exists that, on the night of the birth of his successor as captain, Frederick the Great had a singular dream, which he next day narrated to the members of his household. In the west arose a star, which, as it ascended above the horizon, grew to huge proportions, descended upon the earth, and covered it with a brilliant light. Surrounding this star was a luminous sea, extending out into a comet's tail. In seeking to free himself from the oppressing glare of this awful body, the king awoke.

Napoleon was the fourth child, two having died in infancy, and his brother Joseph being the third. As nine children followed, it was fortunate that one of the family should make his mark, so as to be able to aid the others.[1] Madame Bonoparte was a woman of much activity and ambition. Though her time was near at hand, she personally assisted at the *fête* of the Assumption at Ajaccio; but no sooner had she reached the church than—as is narrated—she was compelled to seek her home, and, unable to reach her bedchamber, gave birth to her famous son in her parlour, on an old rug representing characters from Homer. Little is known as to his boyhood, though he spoke of himself in late years as having been of a domineering, restless nature; but as, despite a life well calculated to breed quick temper and impatience, he exhibited in his trying days at St. Helena a singular amiability and equipoise, we are led to believe that some of the gentler qualities were inborn.

Some historians have found much that was exceptional in his youth. He himself denied that there were any such characteristics, in much the same way that he denied the necessity of ancestors for one who by his own merit had re-erected the throne of Charlemagne. Except that the lad possessed the true Corsican hatred of its tyrants, Genoa and France, and strove to tread in the steps of Paoli, the liberator, there is nothing in the youth of Napoleone Bonoparte which may not be found in that of many boys who have risen only to mediocrity.

Endless origins have been traced to distinguish the ancestors of the family; and in a way the Buonapartes had possessed a past on the Italian mainland. One William, a Ghibelline of Florence, took the name of Buona Parte (the good part) in the thirteenth century; but when the Guelphs chased their opponents out of the city, this citizen, who had apparently chosen the worse part, retired to Sarzana in Tuscany.

---

1. Thirteen children were born, of whom eight grew up. The list is as follows: Joseph (king, first of Naples, then of Spain), Napoleon, Lucien, Eliza (Princess Bacciochi), Pauline (married first to General Leclerc, afterwards to Prince Borghese), Caroline (married to Murat, became queen of Naples), Louis (king of Holland), Jerome (king of Westphalia). Of these the eldest was born in 1768, the youngest in 1784.

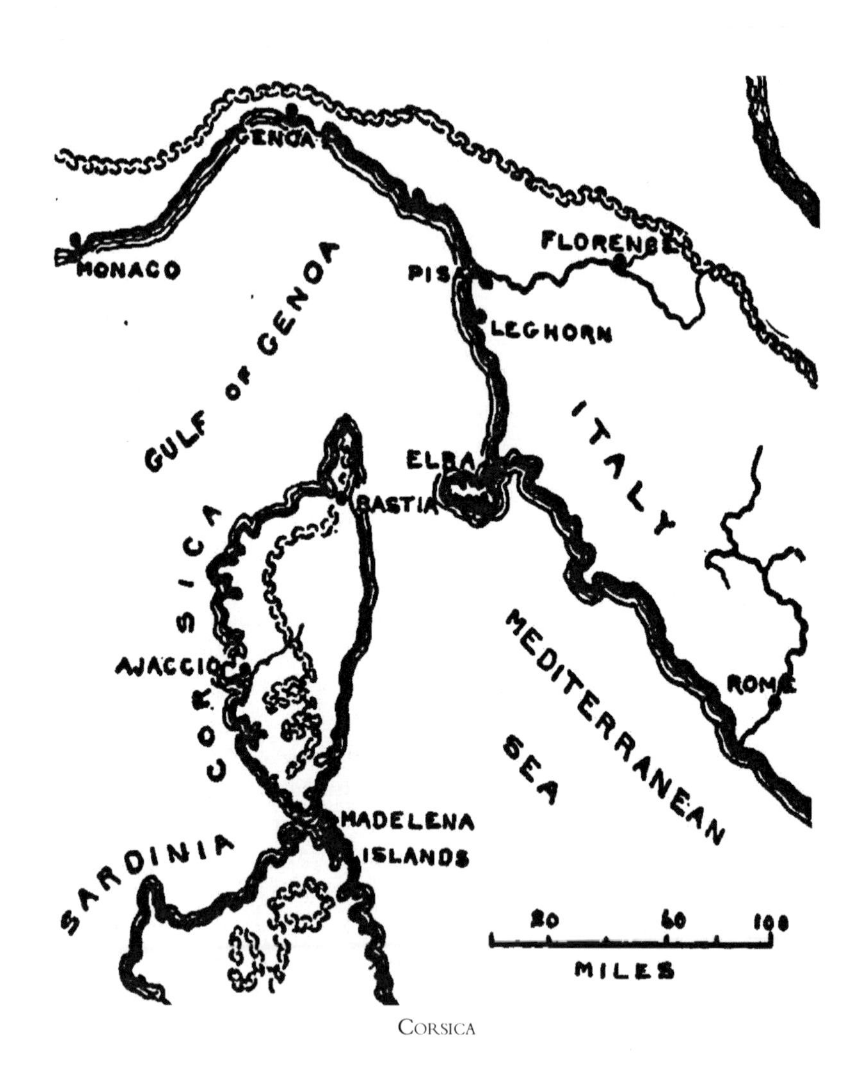
GENOA
MONACO
GULF OF GENOA
PISA
FLORENCE
LEGHORN
ELBA
BASTIA
ITALY
CORSICA
AJACCIO
MEDITERRANEAN
SEA
ROME
MADELENA
ISLANDS
SARDINIA
20
60
100
MILES

CORSICA

Here the family hid its poverty, until in 1529 it migrated to Corsica. So much distinction might be claimed in the ancestry of almost any family. Yet it remains true, if it has any value, that the Bonapartes had held titles of nobility from both Genoa and Tuscany.

When the Emperor Francis, before the Russian campaign, showed Napoleon what he had dug out with regard to the Buonapartes, from old records and parchments at Treviso, a mass of matter which he considered much in their favour, Napoleon replied to his father-in-law, "I attach no price to these old parchments. My nobility dates only from Montenotte, and the 18th *Brumaire*. I prefer to be the founder rather than the descendant of an illustrious race. I wish to be the Rudolph of Hapsburg of my family."

Corsica had from ancient times been under the dominion of every nation whose navy ruled the Mediterranean, but this dominion had never overthrown the hardy, turbulent population of the mountainous interior. This race possessed in a rare degree the virtues of courage, devotion and fidelity; but they were engrafted on habits as savage as those of several other mountain dwelling peoples, where a shot precedes a word, and honour sullied requires bloodshed to the seventh generation. In Ajaccio the Bonapartes were adherents of the patriot Paoli, and indeed Charles, the father of Napoleon, was educated at the University founded by him.

Carlo di Bonoparte was an easy-going man, who relied throughout life rather on what his influence could procure from the efforts of others, than on what he might him-self create, in order to care for his constantly increasing family. Napoleon's mother, Letitia Ramolino, was a beautiful woman with much force of character. She, too, came of Florentine ancestry which had emigrated to Corsica, and the young people were married at a very early age. Though she gave evidences of good extraction, Letitia's frugality was bred of Italian economies as well as of the family necessities, and it was largely due to her that on the slender means provided for the family budget, there was anything substantial accomplished towards the proper nurture and education of the children. She lived to be eighty-six, and the extraordinary rise of her great son never dazzled her, as his downfall did not dishearten. It was she who chiefly moulded her son Napoleon.

Genoa had been succeeded by France as protector of Corsica; and Paoli, who had ejected the Genoese, would gladly have done the same thing with the French; but his efforts ended in failure, and he and his chief adherents fled to England. Carlo Bonoparte accepted the French amnesty, and when, as a part reward for this conduct, the gift of an appointment to the military school of Brienne was secured by him through the French governor of Corsica, Count Marboeuf, young Napoleon's future was first determined.

In his tenth year, April 28, 1779, after three months' schooling in French at Autun, the future leader of men, a small, thin, strange boy, entered upon his early training in arms. Curiously, the school of Brienne stood at that time under the direction of Benedictine monks. The lad naturally possessed a scant knowledge of French; indeed, at every stage of his life Napoleon was crude as a linguist, though he could use language in a most incisive way; and his comrades, many of whom came from rich if not noble families, looked jeeringly at the poverty-stricken, half-savage islander, who was educated at the royal charge, and treated him after a fashion that often forced him to a quarrel, or else to seek solitude, and taught him to keep his own counsel. He was nicknamed "the Spartan." The lad had a large store of pride in his make-up; he was silent and obstinate; and a letter written in his eleventh year to his father shows that this treatment not only excited his anger, but also stirred up a determination some day to do that which should place him on a par with, if not beyond his companions. Many a boy would have succumbed to the treatment he received; this one rose superior to it, and he is represented in many accounts, despite his low social standing, as having succeeded in impressing himself upon his schoolmates, both in their games and studies, as he later did on all who met him. He was imperious in his way, and irascible; but he was able enough to accomplish some things the other boys could not do. His schoolmate, Bourrienne, tells of his directing the construction of snow forts in the schoolyard in the winter of 1783-84, after a fashion unequalled by any comrade. He learned some things more easily than others, especially the exact sciences, but he was not noted for general excellence in his classes. His memory was, however, of the best, his mind alert, and anything which he willed himself to do he could accomplish. He thought so quickly that he had time to reconsider a question which others had just mastered. His imagination was keen, his mental equipment left nothing to be desired; and he was known for a self-will which often overrode others. But the lesson mainly impressed upon him at Brienne was that some social change was demanded which might give him an even chance with the rest of the world, to stand or fall in the military or political arena. At that time all France was permeated with the revolutionary idea—peasantry, middle classes, clergy and nobles alike; even the Court was not free from discussions on this subject; and we may well believe, that the new idea penetrated more or less into every school. The American Revolution had taught a lesson for all to study; and the Gallic temperament was then what it is now, the Gallic mind much narrower.

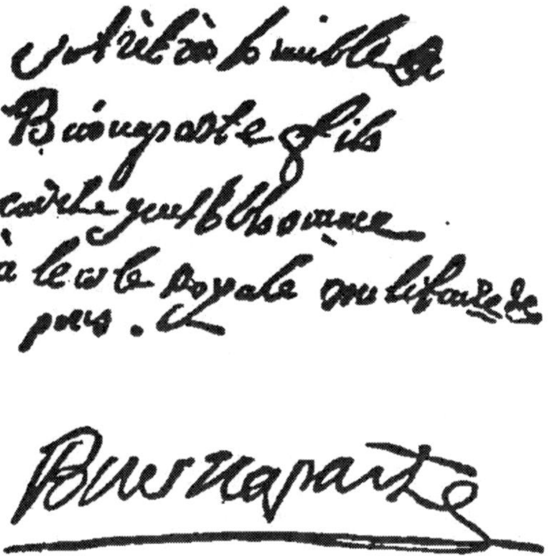

AUTOGRAPH OF BONOPARTE

The character and native intelligence of the young Napoleon continued to grow beyond his scholarship. He was outspoken, if an act or word chanced to gall him. When he was being confirmed, the archbishop seemed astonished at the name of Napoleone, when the future monarch, annoyed, and not diverted by the holiness of the place or the dignity of the churchman, replied, "He is a Corsican Saint, and, moreover, are there not more saints in the Book of Martyrs than there are days in the year?" In 1784 the lad, then but fifteen, wrote a letter to his great-uncle Fesch about his elder brother Joseph's future, which, though full of errors of spelling and diction, clearly shows that in self-poise and in habit of thought he was more than abreast of his years; and the letters written the next year, at the time of his father's death, exhibit exceptional stability and clearness of thought in one so young. He read with avidity Plutarch's *Lives* and Caesar's *Gallic War*, it was a delight to him that a son of Italy should have conquered Gaul, and he was an ardent lover of Paoli. But France was not in his thoughts; all his aspirations were centred in his beloved Corsica and her eventual freedom. His future commission in the French army was in his view but a means to an end. On leaving Brienne, in October, 1784, Monsieur de Keralio, the inspector of the twelve French military schools, thus judged the young man:

> Monsieur de Bonaparte (Napoleon), born the 15th of August, 1769, four feet ten inches ten lines tall, has finished his fourth class. He has a good constitution, excellent health and a character submissive, honest and grateful; very regular conduct, has always distinguished himself by his application to mathematics. He knows fairly well his history and geography. He is rather feeble in the lighter studies and Latin. . . . He would be an excellent sailor, and deserves to pass into the school at Paris.

This same inspector had said to the monks who wished to keep Napoleon an additional year, so as to perfect him in Latin, "No, I can see in this young man a spark which cannot be too highly cultivated."

Domarion, his professor of *belles-lettres*, said of his rhetoric, "It is granite heated by a volcano," an indefinite but easily understood phrase. His teacher of mathematics was Father Patrault, whose assistant, Pichegru, was later so famous.

Thus equipped, on October 17 Napoleon was transferred as "*cadet-gentilhomme*" to the military school in Paris, to prepare for an artillery commission, the suggested purpose of going into the navy having been abandoned. His standing among his comrades here, too, was similar to what it had been at Brienne; the school, created by Louis XV., gave the cadets far too much luxury; and there is an essay of the lad's written at this time which suggests as a means of discipline a much simpler life for the future French officer, and leads one to believe that he still harboured the feelings of antagonistic pride with regard to his richer classmates. The reforms suggested in the essay also show that the young Napoleon's mind early began to dwell on creative things.

On September 1, 1785, the gentleman-cadet passed his final examinations with credit, but not high marks. The certificate from the military school is, however, in a way prophetic:

> Reserved and laborious, he is more fond of study than of any pleasure; likes to read good authors; very diligent in abstract sciences, little inquiring in others, he knows thoroughly mathematics and geography; silent, loves solitude, obstinate, haughty, exceptionally given to egoism, talks little, is energetic in his answers, prompt in action, and severe in meeting opposition; has much self-esteem, is ambitious and striving for all things. This young man is worthy of being favoured.

He was sent to the La Fère regiment at Valence, where, on about eighteen dollars a month, he had three months' work to qualify himself for his lieutenancy in the service of Louis XVI. His talent was recognized by his superiors, he got a fuller view of what a military life meant, and in due season he received his commission as second lieutenant.

Stationed at Valence, for the first time the young officer found congenial surroundings and society, and, as contemporary letters tell us, showed himself at times frank and amiable. Taking small part in the usually frivolous recreations of his brother subalterns, he was noted rather for scrupulous attention to duty, and for a special aptitude for the artillery arm. He affected the society of the better *bourgeoisie*, and it was here that his earliest love story was told to a young lady named Caroline de Colombier, who seems to have grown fond of the young officer in earnest. His flirtation, however, he said in later life, never went beyond eating cherries with his lady love, at a rendezvous which she gave him one day at sunrise, in her father's orchard. Though he kept steadily at work, as all through life it was his habit to do. Napoleon was peculiarly devoted to military studies only in so far as they applied to mathematics useful in his profession, and history, whose great military heroes aroused in him the ambition, not to conquer the world, but solely to follow in the steps of Paoli, and free his native Corsica. He also began to read Rousseau, whose Swiss blood led him to admire the hardy pride and courage of the islanders.

Though in 1786 Napoleon was promoted to be first lieutenant in the Grenoble regiment, his constant work did not keep him from serious fits of despondency. His father had entered into speculations which ended in financial ruin; and after participation in the putting down of the riot in Lyons, he asked for leave of absence and in September went to Corsica, where the Bonoparte family matters were at their worst. Mixed with these griefs was, however, a joy at revisiting his native land, of which his expressions were youthfully overwrought. With the confidence of ignorance, at the end of 1787 the young subaltern went to Paris, thinking in some fashion to obtain money from the national treasury for his family's services in Corsica. It was not until after an absence of twenty-one months that he rejoined his regiment. Unless we assume that his superiors recognized that the Buonapartes were useful in Corsica, one can scarcely understand his obtaining so long a leave.

Returned to his regiment at Auxonne, from June, 1788, to September, 1789, Lieutenant Bonaparte resumed his work and studies. His books were his only friends, and he used his pen much. In the lowlands of the Saone his health suffered markedly from malaria, as later it did at Toulon from a skin disease (?*sarcoptes scabiei*), which constantly annoyed him until he became emperor, when better living and skilful treatment enabled him to throw it off. But he allowed ill-health to make no difference in his work. In April, 1786, he wrote his first manuscript now extant, on the right of the Corsicans to revolt. If a people elects a prince, he argues, he is bound to do its will; if the prince gets his authority elsewhere, yet he is bound to make and execute laws for the happiness of the people. So soon as he fails so to act, the people may throw off his yoke. This manuscript was manifestly inspired by Rousseau's *Contrat Social*. His next one was on *Suicide*, which he justifies, and at times he was assuredly in a mood for it. In 1790 he produced a *History of Corsica*; and the next year he received from the Academy of Lyons a prize for an essay under the title, *What are the Principles and Institutions to be inculcated to Mankind to render them the most happy possible*. Later in life this essay was unearthed by Talleyrand and brought to the emperor, who at once threw it in the fire. A less perfect copy was afterwards discovered, and published in 1826. One phrase from the original is worth preserving. "Great men are like meteors, which shine and consume themselves to give light to the earth." A voracious reader and endless in his notes, the young officer made a Summary of English History down to 1688, and came to the conclusion that few kings deserved their thrones. There was an unceasing struggle between his aristocratic feeling and his republican tendencies. Yet every fibre yearned for the freedom of his well-loved Corsica, with which sentiment only his love of kin, and his innate sense of superiority—always a dominant note in his character—conflicted.

The French Revolution was in the throes of its birth. The seed sown by England and America had fallen on soil all too fruitful, soil which was destined to produce a tropical exuberance of good and evil. No doubt all the extravagant happenings of the day were very real to a mind like that of the young lieutenant, and produced their due effect. "Revolutions," said he, "are good for soldiers with intelligence and courage;" and to his ambition, not limited by over-active moral principles, the great upheaval in France seemed to offer a rare chance. But as, at the outset, he personally thought only of a struggle for freedom by Corsica, he again asked leave, and returned thither in the fall of 1789. He would have been glad to essay afresh the role of Paoli. Indeed it was fortunate that what he did and strove to do at this time bred no evil results in his French career. There were larger dramas to enact, and his small but questionable by-play in Corsica was overlooked, or was perhaps deemed to have been useful to the Republic.

In the autumn of 1789, then, we again find Lieutenant Bonaparte on leave in Corsica, where he preached democratic ideas, all tending to the independence of the island, and urged the formation of an insular National Guard. His name appears at the head of a petition to the National Assembly of France for Corsican civil liberty. Much disorder reigned on the island, and on November 5 there was an affray between the royal troops and the populace. Meanwhile Paoli and his adherents were amnestied and allowed to return, in the belief that they would now aid the French *régime* in Corsica. But while Paoli worked for liberty, he yet was far from being a Republican in the Paris sense; he was indeed of an autocratic mood; and Napoleon soon found himself drifting away from his idol. This may have been in part due to the fact that the young author had dedicated his manuscript on Corsica to the great patriot, with a panegyric, and that the latter had declined the praise as being strained, and mislaid the manuscript as having scant value. Yet Paoli seems to have admired Bonaparte to begin with. "This young man," he is said to have observed, "is cut antique-fashion. He is a hero of Plutarch." But his fancy was short-lived. In February, 1791, our subaltern again returned to his regiment. He had prolonged his leave by certificates of sickness; but his means, unless political, of satisfying his superiors as to his long absences cannot be guessed. On his return journey he found all the peasants, as well as every enlisted man in the ranks, heartily in favour of the Revolution. Despite his shallow purse, he at this time brought with him his brother Louis, and looked after his education. "I lived like a bear," said he. This meant that black bread was often his only food, in order to save money for books; but this was not the only occasion in life when Napoleon's kindliness of heart came to the surface. He never forgot his family, placing them indeed in positions to which many of them did small credit.

In the summer of 1791 Lieutenant Bonaparte was transferred to another regiment in Valence. Later in the year he went to Paris to see whether the seething of the Revolution would afford him a chance of rising. The extraordinary laxness in army discipline which could afford a subaltern so many absences was but typical of the times. Not only did he visit Paris, but in September he returned to Corsica, to which he was devoting so much fervour. It can scarcely be deemed curious that he failed to see the outcome of the Revolution in France; few people did. In the first trying days of 1861, many later stanch Unionists were of doubting spirit. And to Napoleon at this period Corsica was greater than France. He remained in the island until the succeeding May. It was at this time that the break occurred between him, who was a revolutionist, and Paoli, whose sober tendencies led him away from the wreckers of solid government.

The young man's ambition at this time scarcely reached beyond the epaulets of a general of artillery; and when, on February 6, 1792, the regular course of promotion gave him his commission as captain in the Fourth Regiment of Foot Artillery, he began to see life expanding before him. But the untold ambition of the future does not at this early age seem to have shown much growth.

In the National Guard that had been created in Corsica, Napoleon had been made major, and aspired to be lieutenant-colonel. His tenure of rank in the French artillery appeared to be a secondary thought. In seeking election to the higher rank, he is said to have resorted to questionable methods, even to sequestrating one of the Commissioners who was working for Paoli's interests—a prototype of future *coups d'état* But these were the ordinary tricks of the day and place.

By this time the Legislative Assembly was master in Paris; the king was a prisoner, and the First Coalition had been formed against France. Still the young man's thoughts remained centred on Corsica. He did not yet see his future in France. As is wont to be the case in civil wars, he scarcely knew which side to embrace. Whether, indeed, he followed the military preparations of France at this juncture, we have no means of knowing. He said later:

> As a general I would have sustained the Court; as a lieutenant without fortune, I had to place myself on the side of the people.

The island was divided between the French revolutionary methods and the ancient ways of the Corsicans. Loving their church, the populace rose against the French acts of clerical repression; and the National Guard was called in to subdue the riot. Napoleon not only endeavoured to seize the citadel of Ajaccio,. but he went so far as to strive to seduce the enlisted men of the French troops from their duty to their aristocratic officers. The entire scheme failed, and the young officer awoke to the fact that he had placed himself in opposition to both the native majority of the island and to the government whose commission he held. His enemies accused him of having fermented revolt against the French in Corsica, for the sake of making the island independent; and not only was he obliged to go to Paris to exculpate himself from the charge of desertion in again overstaying his leave, but his attitude towards the French troops had been little short of treason. Just what he had purposed to accomplish cannot be said.

Shortly after he had reached Corsica, in September, 1791, his great-uncle Fesch died, and Napoleon henceforth looked upon himself as the head of the house of Bonoparte. His brother Lucien says that he permitted no contradiction, and ruled in everything. Apparently blind to the fact that he had overstayed his leave, and that his regiment had been put on a war footing, Napoleon's tarrying in Corsica had actually resulted in his being rated, according to the orders of the law-making powers of the day, as a deserter, and being stricken from the rolls of the army. Though he claimed to have been serving the French Revolutionists, it is a wonder that he was able to return to France at all, without suffering disaster from his to say the least extravagant conduct But the young man was even then ready to beard the lion in his den. With a certificate in his favour from the French authorities on the island, he journeyed in May, 1792, to Paris, and strove to get restored to the service, while struggling along on the slenderest means. The rising of June 20, when the mob invaded the Tuileries and insulted the king and queen, he observed from a room near the palace, and though he himself may have been fresh from an attempt to overturn the French regime in Corsica, yet in viewing the excesses of the populace, his strong feeling for order and authority—for he was always an aristocrat at heart—was expressed in the exclamation, "*Che coglione!*" (What rabble!), and the desire to blow away the revolutionists with his guns. The 10th of August, 1792, when the monarchy fell and the Republic succeeded it, was for him salvation. Officers of talent were in demand for the National Guard, and to replace those who had emigrated; small misdemeanours were cast into the shade by grave events; the past was overlooked, and Napoleon again received his old commission as an artillery captain.

The French patriotic fervour had risen to white heat. The Prussian invaders met their match in the memorable battle of Valmy; Dumouriez beat the Austrians at Jemappes and won all Belgium; and Custine pushed by way of Mainz to the Lahn. Savoy and Nice were wrested from Piedmont. The Jacobins became unduly excited by so much success,—and Louis XVI. ascended the scaffold.

This act set the rest of Europe against the French Republic; and the tide of victory turned. Striving to conquer Holland, Dumouriez was beaten at Neerwinden and lost Belgium, the Prussians crossed the Rhine, and Condé and Valenciennes were besieged. The Sardinians re-entered Savoy, the Spaniards came close to invading France; the Vendée rising of royalists brought on civil war. To the Committee of Public Safety—Robespierre, Danton, Marat—the situation was confided; the "Mountain," with the aid of the Paris mob, had driven out the Girondists, and these raised the standard of revolt in many towns; but against the superior organization of the Jacobins, and its possession of the central power, they could accomplish nothing. To add to the difficulty under which the Committee staggered, England now headed the Coalition, and furnished the needed funds to carry on the war; and to her business methods the Convention could only oppose its fervid energy and a million men. "From Alps to Pyrenees and from Rhine to Ocean the tricolour fell back." The military situation was desperate, when Carnot was added to the Committee of Public Safety on August 14, 1792; a levy in mass was ordered August 23, under the motto, "*Le Peuple Français Debout Devant Les Tyrans;*" and "*Aux Armes, Français!*" rang throughout the land.

During this violent period, instead of serving with his regiment in Savoy, Napoleon on a flimsy pretext again managed to return to Corsica, reaching the island in September, 1792. It was not long after the Convention had seized the reins of power in France, September 21, that disagreement followed between it and Paoli, whose influence made him the practical ruler of the island; and when Napoleon, who was a pronounced Republican, as Paoli had always been the head of the aristocracy, took the side of the French, he was made Major and Inspector-General of Artillery of Corsica, October 19.

The French party in the island was declining. The action of Paoli had not resulted, as the rulers in Paris had, from their efforts to conciliate him, hoped it would do, in reconciling the Corsicans to Republican terrorism; and French influence steadily decreased. While, early in January, 1793, Major Bonaparte was working one way and Paoli another (the hero and the hero-worshiper were now far apart), six thousand French volunteers landed at Ajaccio on a filibustering expedition to Sardinia. The coarse brutality of these men, mostly from the slums of the maritime cities of France, raised a riot in Ajaccio, and when the French soldiers caught and in their zealous fury hanged three of the citizens, the excitement grew intense and was hard to be allayed. The Corsicans refused to march to Sardinia in company with the French troops. The Inspector-General suggested a purely Corsican invasion of the Maddalena Islands, lying between Corsica and Sardinia. This was undertaken; but internal jealousies, perhaps fostered by Paoli, brought about failure, and Major Bonaparte, who was almost captured at the time of the landing and attack, returned to Ajaccio March 3, now a strong anti-Paoli man.

French commissioners were appointed to disband the Corsican

National Guard, to investigate this expedition and pass on Paoli's conduct; and these sought to seize the patriot. One of the commissioners, Saliceti, and Major Bonaparte strove in vain to get possession by stratagem of the citadel of Ajaccio, held by the Paoli party; and in trips to and from Bastia at the north of the island, where the French commissioners sat, the young officer had a series of quixotic personal adventures which might well have put an end to his career. An armed attempt was now made on the citadel by the French, but this also failed. Almost to a man the Corsicans became enemies of the French, and the English fleet was asked to cooperate with Paoli and his adherents. During these days Major Bonaparte wrote many lurid pamphlets.

It was quite natural that the Corsicans should take umbrage at the conduct of the Bonoparte family, and the whole tribe found it wise to leave the island early in June, 1793, to land at Marseilles, and wander in Provence on a pittance allowed by the government to Corsican refugees. Napoleon reported to his regiment at Nice. In July the island drifted into the hands of the British.

Thus we see that, instead of serving with his regiments and learning his profession, the greater part of the time of this French company officer, from the date of his leaving school, had been spent in what appears to have been a striving to liberate Corsica, and to turn its population towards republican doctrines. There is not much promise to be extracted from these early years on which to found the hope of a great future for the young man. Perhaps his native ability can, however, be put to no higher test than by the fact that he grew proficient in the artillery arm, when he devoted so little time to regimental service in his early military years. For no one will deny that, at every age, Napoleon knew his profession as few others did, although he never became, as Carnot says, a truly scientific man. Out of these years only the energy, persistency and, if you like, the gambling instinct, or readiness to take chances, stand out from the other traits of the half-formed character. He was twenty-four years old, and he had so far failed in every undertaking. Even his motive in devoting himself to Corsica is obscure. Whether by nature he was more governed by a love of fame or a love of power can hardly be determined.

"One can scarcely say," writes Madame de Remusat, "that he really loved fame, he never hesitated to prefer results."

On the other hand: "Fame, always fame, that is what he wished, for France and for himself;" and, "In all his business the present moment disappeared in the future centuries," says Bourrienne.

Paoli

Marat

And to Carnot, from Verona, January 28, 1797, with regard to things said against him, Bonaparte wrote:

> . . . . So far as I am concerned, whatever they may say, they do not reach me. The esteem of a small number of persons like you, that of my comrades and the soldiers, sometimes also the opinion of posterity, and above all the sentiment of my conscience and the prosperity of my country, alone interest me. . . .

While we cannot always give full credence to Bonaparte's own expressions, which were apt to be coloured by the demands of the moment, yet there may be a glimmer of truth in this one.

As with all ambitious, hard-working, successful men, so in Napoleon's case, fame and activity were consuming fires. But if he was working for either fame or results, his judgment as to what he might accomplish in Corsica had been lamentably at fault. He had, however, shown two of the essential factors of the great captain, force of intellect and force of character. Would the third factor, opportunity, ever come?

Chapter 7

Toulon

August 1793-March 1796

The Coalition did not work harmoniously, though it won success on the French frontiers. The execution of the queen practically arrayed all Europe against France. But the French overran Belgium and the Palatinate, while the English held the sea and the French colonies went lost. In the south there had been Royalist uprisings, and here Major Bonaparte first attracted attention by a paper favouring the Revolution. In 1793 the French made a strong effort to take Toulon, and the most active artillery officer present with the army was Bonaparte. He suggested that Toulon should be captured by taking the promontory which commanded the harbour, and thence bombarding the enemy's fleet.

This plan was put into execution. The most necessary point, l'Eguillette, was taken by storm, and the English fleet was at once compelled to sail away. The Republican commissioners recognized Bonaparte's ability, and he was made brigadier-general. Bonaparte had so far accomplished little except this, but the whirl of events worked in his favour. As commandant of artillery of the Army of Italy he drew up a plan for capturing Saorgio, which succeeded. He later drew up plans for operations in Italy, which, though sound, were rejected by the commanding generals as impossible. Some thought Bonaparte an intriguer, some welcomed his ability. He was sometimes in the army, sometimes out of it. His military life was a series of ups and downs, during which he saw little active service. In 1795 he was put in the geographical bureau to work up plans of campaign, but few people could see the value of his ideas.

When the Sections rose against the Convention, Barras took control for the latter, and among his lieutenants was Bonaparte. In charge of the artillery he blew away the forces of the Sections and saved the Convention. By this act he rose to a marked position; and early in 1796, after his marriage with Josephine, he was made commander of the Army of Italy.

As has already been narrated, the members of the Coalition did not work with much unanimity. To be sure, Mainz and Valenciennes were captured; the English and Spaniards were admitted to Toulon; Dunkirk was besieged by the British, Quesnoy and Maubeuge by the Austrians, Landau by the Prussians; the Austrians captured the lines of Weissemburg and Fort St. Louis, and threatened Strasburg. All this work, however, though effective, lacked the *ensemble* essential to real success.

These irruptions the Committee of Public Safety met with vigour. Jourdan marched on Maubeuge and pushed the Austrians back. Kellermann put down the uprising in Lyons, and drove the Sardinians across the Alps to Piedmont. Dugommier recaptured Toulon, as we shall see. Kleber and Marceau for a while checked the Vendée at the Battle of Le Mans. Then came the fatal mistake of the execution of the queen; and soon France had arrayed against her England, Austria, Spain, Prussia, the Empire, Russia, all Italy and Holland.

But even this did not dishearten the strong men of the Revolution. While the campaign in the Alps was discouraging, three hundred thousand French overran Belgium and the Palatinate, boldly claimed victory over the allies at Turcoing, Fleurus, Kaiserslautern, on the Ourthe, on the Boer, drove them behind the Rhine, entered Brussels, Antwerp and Maestricht, Amsterdam, Cologne and Coblentz; and turned the tables on Spain. On the sea, however, the English were supreme; the French Atlantic and Mediterranean fleets being neutralized, the French colonies all went lost, from the Antilles to India; and England, having declared the French ports in a state of blockade, began to confiscate neutral vessels trading therewith.

In the south of France there had occurred an uprising against the Convention, centring in Lyons, Marseilles, Toulon and other places, to meet which General Carteaux, an ancient artist turned soldier, was sent to Avignon. Hither also came Major Bonaparte, sent from Nice to assemble artillery. While the batteries were being got together, in August, 1793, Major Bonaparte was intrusted with a mission to Marseilles, to persuade the insurrectionists to withdraw from Avignon, at which point they prevented supply trains from moving to the Army of Italy. Inspired by certain events on this trip, he wrote a paper entitled *The Supper at Beaucaire*, in which he placed himself firmly on the side of the "Mountain," then in power, sketched in a masterly manner the political and military situation in the south, and prophesied the success of the Republican arms. The essay was prompted by and was in the form of a conversation between an officer (no doubt himself) and several citizens, in which the former urges all classes to rally to the side of the party in power, as representing France in arms against European despots. Any concession to save the nation and the Republic was its tone. This paper came into the hands of the people's representatives, Saliceti, Gasparin and the younger Robespierre, who had just arrived at Avignon, and of whom the first named already knew the author; and, printed at public cost, it was Bonaparte's first introduction to the powers that be, to whom he soon proved that he could act as well as write. He had now sloughed off his Corsican dreams, and could see his future in France. The tone of the *Souper*, unlike his overheated pamphlets up to this day, was as cold and cynical as it was business-like and convincing.

Toulon, the key of southern France, whose harbour was then held by the English and Spaniards, was the burning question of the hour. It was essential to recover control of the place. The Royalists had called in outside aid, and on August 28, 1793, the English fleet, under Admiral Hood, had sailed into the harbour and taken possession of the city for the king of France. This was only the day before the van of the Republican army, under Mouret, appeared in the defile of Ollioules, on the road from Marseilles and Lyons; and even here it had not been able to hold itself. The work of retaking the defile was begun September 7, and on the wounding of Dommartin, the commandant of artillery,—an accident which left only one captain and some sergeants in charge of the batteries,—Bonaparte, on his arrival September 16, was made second in command, and put in his place by Saliceti, who was on the ground. He went actively to work. About these days Mouret had been succeeded by Carteaux; but the latter had been able to undertake nothings definite against Toulon until reinforcements could come up from the Army of Italy, and material and men could be got from Lyons; but when the division of Lapoype had arrived from the Riviera, a blockade was at once begun, and a regular siege was projected. Carteaux, who quite lacked ability, was shortly replaced by Doppet, an ex-doctor, and he finally by Dugommier, a veteran and an excellent soldier.

Admiral Hood had taken possession of all the works as well as the harbour of Toulon, and had disembarked a motley array of sixteen hundred Royalists, seven thousand Spaniards, five thousand Neapolitan and fifteen hundred Piedmontese troops, to leaven all which two English regiments of twenty-two hundred men under Colonel O'Hara were on hand. This ran the garrison up to seventeen thousand men, a goodly force, but hardly sufficient to man the very extensive outlying works. The city had only a simple bastioned wall, but it was defended by a circuit of excellent forts and redoubts. On the shore, east of the city, lay Fort Malque, and thence, running around the rocky ridge of

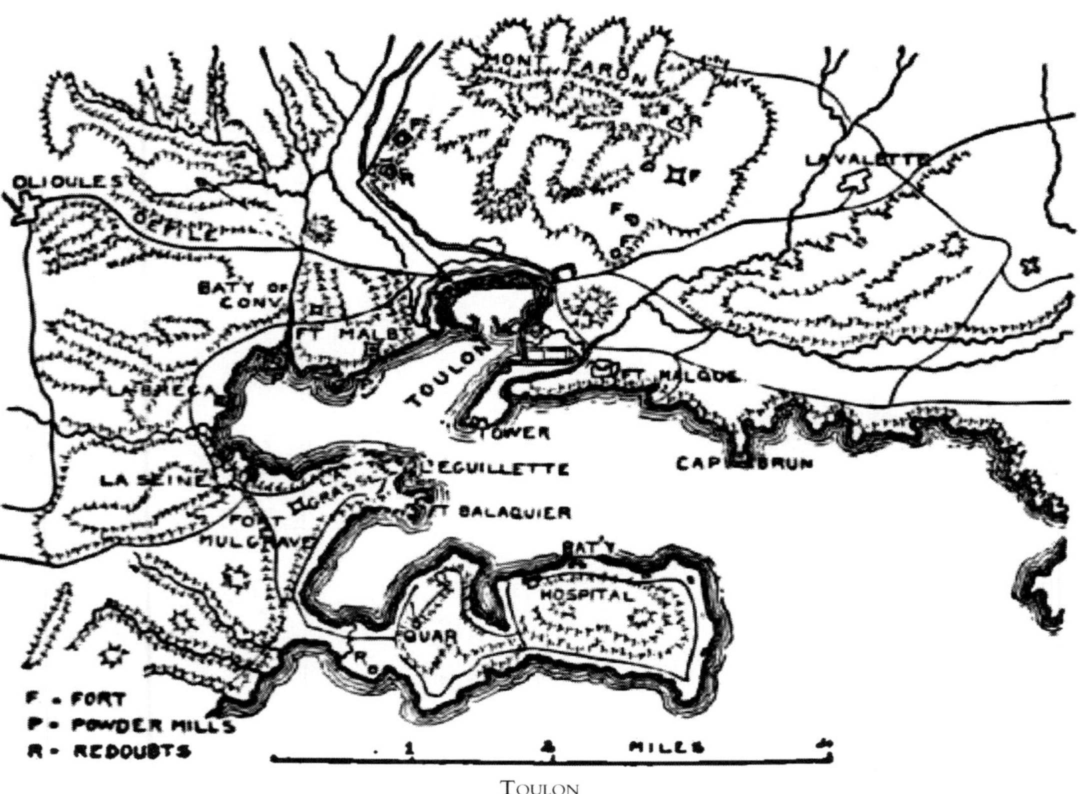
MONT FARON
LA VALETTE
OLIOULES
DEFILE
BATY OF CONV
FT MALBT
TOULON
FT MALGUE
LA BREGA
TOWER
L'EGUILLETTE
CAP BRUN
LA SEINE
FT BALAQUIER
FORT MULGRAVE
BATY
HOSPITAL
QUAR
F - FORT
P - POWDER MILLS
R - REDOUBTS
1
2
MILES

Toulon

Mont Faron, which stood like a vast protecting wall to the city, was a succession of works, well placed on east and west of Faron, and ending in the strong Fort Malbosquet on the inner harbour. To protect the harbour there were also a number of forts, chiefly l'Eguillette and Balaquier; but they could play no part in the operations of an attacking land army, so far as the French generals could see.

Carteaux had but eight thousand men, with the three batteries under Dommartin, west of Ollioules; Lapoype, from the Army of Italy, had brought little over five thousand men and two field batteries; and there were but eight twenty-four-pounders, which had come from Marseilles. Of these Bonaparte had placed five at La Brega to annoy the English fleet; and on September 28 had opened so hearty a fire that the enemy recognized the danger, and landing three thousand men at l'Eguillette, took possession of the hill of La Grasse and built Fort Mulgrave, otherwise called "Little Gibraltar," manning it with heavy guns and a garrison of eight hundred men. The position of this fort was ably chosen. So long as it was held, the French could not reach ground which would enable them to command the harbour, and no pains was spared to make It strong. Purposing to reduce this fort, Bonaparte constructed a number of siege-batteries. One day, having an order to give, he called for a non-commissioned officer to act as clerk. A young man stepped out of the ranks and wrote, from his dictation, on the *epaulement* of the battery. Just as the letter was finished, a ball striking nearby covered the paper and the writer with dirt. "So much the better," said the scribe with consummate coolness, "I shall need no sand." This youngster was Junot.

After the capture of Lyons on October 9, the army in front of Toulon gradually rose to forty thousand men, and several artillery officers senior to Bonaparte arrived. A series of batteries was erected against all the forts protecting the city, and regular operations were begun. The original plan suggested by the Committee of Public Safety,—the work, says Napoleon, of General D'Arcon—had been to capture all the forts about Mont Faron, and then to open trenches against Toulon on the north. The Commissioners with the army, of whom Barras was one, had written the Convention, September 13, that whenever the siege-guns came they would be so placed as to reach the fleet with hot shot; and thus by driving it out of the harbour, would enable the army to capture the town; but how far their plan had been matured cannot be said.

At a council of war held November 25 (there had been two previous ones), to approve and adopt means to carry out one or other plan, there were present Dugommier, Lapoype and Mouret, two generals of brigade, Chief of Artillery Duteil, three battalion chiefs, including Bonaparte, and two captains of engineers. Bonaparte appears to have written the report of the council to the Paris authorities, and as he had already, on November 14, sent to the minister of war a detailed scheme for capturing Toulon, which had been received with approval, he was able to argue his plan with effect, as he did with force and intelligence. In the scheme referred to he said:

> Citizen Minister, the plan of attack for the City of Toulon which I presented to the generals and the representatives of the people is, I believe, the only practicable one; if it had been followed from the beginning with a little more warmth, it is probable that we should be in Toulon. . . . To drive the enemy from the harbour is the preliminary point to a siege in form; and perhaps this operation alone will give us Toulon. (*Then follow extended details of what it is desirable to do.*) It is more than a month ago that I told the generals that the artillery on hand at this moment was sufficient to stop the fire of the English redoubt placed on the summit of the promontory of l'Eguillette. (*Then follows the detailed work to be done by each of the eleven batteries he had constructed.*) If this has not been done, it is because the general persisted in thinking he had not sufficient infantry.

Four long collateral reports are appended, giving every essential detail. In one of them Bonaparte claims that the allied attack on the upland of l'Eguillette to build Fort Mulgrave might by proper measures have been beaten back.

At the council of war it was concluded that the right wing should make a feint on Fort Malbosquet and take it if possible, while its main attack should be on the Eguillette promontory; that the left wing should make a feint on Cap Brun and its main assault on Mont Faron, which it was to seize and hold; that Toulon was to be bombarded so soon as proper ground between the Battery of the Convention on Arènes heights and Fort Malbosquet could be seized, meanwhile protecting the former work from a *coup de main*.

No one will deny Bonaparte, beyond all others, the ability to cast aside minor considerations and keep in view the main object to be attained. His sense of perspective was perfect, though perhaps at this day not fully matured. Here at Toulon it is in evidence that most of his superiors seemed to see no other means of capturing the place than a regular siege from the land side—and steps were to this end taken.

Bonaparte went into the subject deeper, and (whether he originated the scheme or not seems immaterial) insisted that if Toulon harbour could be commanded, the allied fleet, no longer able to protect the town, would withdraw the defending garrison; for the latter would have no means of retreat if the fleet had left, and must sooner or later succumb to siege or starvation. He next pointed out the fact that to control the roadstead and prevent the allied ships, for fear of being burned by hot shot, from there riding at anchor, Point l'Eguillette should first be taken; and to accomplish this he drew up in writing a feasible plan, as above quoted. And there appears to be no other scheme in existence by any other hand. The earliest suggestion may not have been Bonaparte's; his detractors claim it was not; but it was his advocacy which determined the matter, as indisputably it was his courage and skill which carried it through; With slight variation the young officer's ideas were adopted.

It is clear that Bonaparte was the busiest man at Toulon; that above all others he exhibited intelligence, courage, power to lead men and to make them willing instruments for his purposes. He embraced this, his first chance, and showed the stuff that was in him. He had not liked his early superiors. While Doppet was in command, Bonaparte had, on November 15, organized a demonstration on the works at Fort Mulgrave, or, as his St. Helena narrative has it, two or three battalions had started an attack. This in the carrying out grew into a hearty engagement. The garrison made a sortie and drove the French back. Bonaparte rallied his men, and, deeming it safer to go on than to discontinue the operation, was heading his column to make a rush which distinctly promised success, when Doppet sounded the recall,—an act which discouraged and angered the young officer and all his men. The latter loudly railed at the "painters and doctors" who were at their head; and Dugommier was heartily welcomed, when, a few days later, he came to take supreme command.

Lapoype now commanded the left division of Dugommier's forces, and Mouret the right one. In the shifting of commands, Duteil became chief of the corps artillery; Bonaparte, to begin with, had had charge of only that of one brigade of Mouret's division. Duteil was old and not over active, and his junior's views, always fresh and original, were frequently accepted by the chief and acted on. No one showed activity in the siege equal to Bonaparte's, and practically he was after a while left in charge of all the artillery business of the right wing, where the important work was being done. But he does not appear to have been technically chief of the corps artillery, or appointed by the government to take charge of all the artillery, as in his St. Helena papers he suggests that he was, though as *locum tenens* he acted as such; and it seems that he had a comparatively free hand.

There is no doubt that Bonaparte's lead, as the best, or certainly the most energetic and suggestive artillery officer present, was commonly followed. As a first step he had erected the Battery of the Convention on the heights of Arènes, at a point which commanded Fort Malbosquet, and in November—the date is in dispute—surprised its garrison by a rapid and annoying fire, which dismounted several guns. To suppress this annoyance O'Hara landed twenty-three hundred men and attempted to capture the battery. His assault was stanch, and his force entered the works and spiked several guns; but Bonaparte marched a battalion through the trenches leading to the battery and took the English in flank. O'Hara, wounded, fell into his hands. On Dugommier's coming up from a direction which threatened to cut the English off, they retired with a loss of nearly five hundred men, and without having silenced the battery. Dundas succeeded O'Hara. The French now moved down more forces and began regular approaches on Fort Mulgrave. In the effort to reduce this fort, Bonaparte constructed a number of batteries, one of which was within pistol-shot of the enemy; and so dangerous was the manning of it that he could get few volunteers until, relying on the fact that his countrymen do not calmly take a challenge, he aptly dubbed it the "*Redoute des Hommes Sans Peur*." The soldiers then vied with each other for the duty; and Bonaparte was ever first in their company. Having by December 14 got thirty guns and fifteen mortars in position, the young officer directed a heavier fire against both this Little Gibraltar and l'Eguillette, and after a steady two days' bombardment, the works of the enemy were much broken; and as they do not appear to have been substantially reinforced, an assault was set for December 18. Lapoype was at the same time to assault the Faron forts.

In the night of December 17-18 the storming column of eight thousand men started from La Seine towards Fort Mulgrave, the capture of which meant the evacuation of l'Eguillette. It was hoped to reach the fort unobserved, for the garrison was apt to remain under cover during the bombardment; but at the foot of the hill of La Grasse the French van ran across some pickets, and the resulting fire alarmed the garrison and called it to the walls. Bonaparte's horse was shot under him—according to some authorities this was the third during the siege—and he accompanied the men on foot. The first assault was thrown back; but a small party climbed the heights unobserved, entered by a broken casemate and thus captured a portion of the wall. Followed sharply by more and more men, the gain was maintained, the garrison was overpowered and the fort was taken. Bonaparte received a slight wound in the leg. By five o'clock in the morning the allies had decamped towards Fort Balaquier, where they were picked up by boats from the fleet. At the same time Lapoype seized the hill and redoubts of Faron.

Though an old man, Dugommier had accompanied his troops; but he was much worn out by the fatigue. So soon as the fort had been taken, Bonaparte, who was nearby, turned to him with, "Go and rest yourself, general, we have captured Toulon. You will sleep there to-morrow."

Having occupied Fort Mulgrave and L'Eguillette, Bonaparte immediately turned every available gun on the enemy's fleet. Recognizing that the harbour was untenable, Dundas called a council of war; and the effective garrison of Toulon having fallen to twelve thousand men, it was decided to evacuate the place. This was set about at once, and during the day of December 18 the troops were embarked, and the fleet passed out under the French guns. The arsenal and twenty ships of the line and frigates were burned. Next day the Republicans entered the town. To prevent pillage, all the property of the citizens was declared forfeited to the army. This property was soon redeemed by the payment of two million *francs* by the citizens.

Saliceti and Robespierre recognized that in Bonaparte the Republic had a man of original ideas and abundant energy for its service, and the hero of Toulon profited accordingly. He had seen his opportunity, and had seized it with the sure hand of genius. And it was in this siege that Bonaparte discovered the qualities of Junot, Marmont and Victor, his later so able lieutenants.

It is quite true that Bonaparte's later overshadowing success may have led historians to exaggerate this first feat of arms; but in view of his exhaustive written reports, and of the work he confessedly did at Toulon; in view of the fact that he was rapidly promoted at and after the siege; inasmuch as no documents exist to show that his then superiors disputed his written claim to have suggested as well as carried out the scheme that won Toulon, which, had it been false, they had abundant chance to do, it may fairly be assumed that to him, largely at least, was due the idea and the work which produced the success there gained, and that he fairly earned his laurels.

The rapidly succeeding events of these whirling years, as good luck would have it, had all worked in favour of Bonaparte. Although he had taken no active part in the stirring campaigns in the Netherlands and on the Rhine during the first four years of the wars of the French Revolution, the frequent gaps made by the *émigrés*, by the attrition of service and by the lack of able men, afforded him promotion. We have seen that he had but recently become chief of battalion (major) in the Fourth Regiment of Artillery; and now for handsome services in the subjection of the Marseilles Federalists (although for ordering the rehabilitation of the ante-revolutionary Fort St. Nicholas, to which the populace objected, he was reprimanded and temporarily placed in arrest), he received promotion to a colonelcy. This was no doubt due in part to the influence of Saliceti and Robespierre, who had gauged his ability at Toulon. The new colonel was set to work to place the Riviera and Provence in a state of good defence; and on February 6, that is as soon as promotion could be secured from the authorities in Paris, he was made general of brigade.

That as a result of his work at Toulon Bonaparte rose from a junior major to brigadier-general cannot, however, be wholly referred to the influence of Robespierre and Saliceti. To be sure, promotions were at that day made rapidly and by favour. Anyone whom the Convention believed to be capable or brave might find himself in a dangerously important post at a moment's notice; and many there were whom fame, thus thrust upon them, led to the guillotine. It was otherwise with Bonaparte. From Toulon days on, his promotion was due to solid work, founded on that exceptional ability which kept him on the upward path to the zenith of his career. That his friends should help him so long as he needed help was but an accident.

In April, 1794, the Army of Italy moved from Nice forward in order to take possession of the passes of the Maritime Alps. Bonaparte had joined this army as general commanding the artillery; and as Commissary of the Convention with the army stood the younger Robespierre, to whose good sense much of its success was due. Bonaparte had drawn up a plan to turn the famous position of Saorgio, which, as already told, was duly adopted; and in the absence of Dumirbion, who was general-in-chief, but sick, Massena, second in command, carried out the plan with entire success. In the St. Helena Memorial Napoleon claims, perhaps with too much breadth, to have "carried the Army of Italy to Savona and the gates of Ceva, which advance freed Genoa, then menaced by the Coalition." But he did play a distinguished part in it. Late in May there was a general consultation as to future plans, and Bonaparte was selected to draw up the scheme, which fairly presents his views on war, as then held.

Wartenburg aptly divides the career of this great captain into three periods. The first comprises the years when he was only one general out of many, and when in what he did he was compelled to pay heed to the ideas and prejudices of others, being hedged and hampered accordingly. In the second period he was in sole command of his army, but had behind him a government which controlled the resources, and from whom he must receive general orders. The third period is that in which all the resources of France were in his sole control and he could act as he saw fit. We are now in the first period, which lasted until Bonaparte received the sole command of the Army of Italy; the second lasted until the Consulate came in on the 18th Brumaire, 1799; the third lasted until 1815.

The plans, then, which Bonaparte drew up for the operations of the Army of Italy before he received its command in chief exhibit less boldness and more sense of limitation than the later ones. There are a number of these monographs: two dated respectively May 21 and June 20, 1794, four dated July 20, 1795, and two dated October 12, 1795, and January 19, 1796. The first-named even from its contents appears to have had a lost predecessor, which was probably the one on the taking of Saorgio. Each plan is worked out at length. The same intellectual conceptions are apparent in all. He begins by saying:

> One cannot enter the Piedmont plain except with forces superior to the enemy's; in order to obtain this superiority, one must unite the Armies of the Alps and of Italy. . . . Whatever plan is adopted, this is a preliminary.

The desire to outnumber the enemy was his principle all through life, and very different from Frederick's readiness—bred, to be sure, of dire necessity—to fight double or treble his own numbers.

> The junction of the two armies can only be made in the valley of the Stura, in order to take advantage of the positions and debouches won by the Army of Italy.

And after indicating that both armies were heading for a point where the Stura enters the plain of Lombardy, and that this plain was their natural meeting-place, Bonaparte goes into detail. The Army of the Alps was to create several columns, the task of some of which would be to attack, of others to protect the attacking columns, and of yet others to make feints to deceive the enemy as to the point of attack. The eventual objective would be the Stura valley. Meanwhile the Army of Italy would watch the gaps leading from the Tinea valley to the Stura, and out towards the right to Mondovi, and form several columns of attack, with similar tasks; and would eventually force its way to Borgo San Dalmazzo, and co-operate with the Army of the Alps in the Stura valley. The advance of the Army of Italy would, by monopolizing the enemy's attention, have the effect of making the work of the Army of the Alps easy.

In a mountainous country there is more excuse for dividing an army into a number of columns. A mountain pass is practically forced only by the head of column and a few flankers; the rear is useless, if not dangerous; while a second column moving by a parallel pass may possibly take the enemy in reverse, and thus insure his retreat. Bonaparte's usual habit all through life was to work in masses and not in detached bodies; but here he probably had other than purely military problems to face. He was by no means free from interference, and had superiors, whose very marked ideas of their own importance he must respect. The plan shows close study of the topography and a sharp eye for the key-points; but its weakness lies in the fact that, like all work in separate detachments, it depends on the success of each and every column to produce the desired result; and the failure of any one column, from a fact unknown to the commanding general or not under control of the column commander, might upset the entire scheme. The detailed daily operation and the means of subsistence of each column are well worked out in the papers, and each commander is held strictly to its performance—another weakness. The entire plan exhibits wonderful adaptation to what was apparently strong pressure from many seniors.

At Nice, on the 2nd Mesidor (June 20), Bonaparte made a change in the plan, also probably brought about by some pressure from several generals, by which the Army of the Alps was to send fewer columns into the Stura valley, and the Army of Italy was also to operate in fewer columns. The one destined to sustain the Army of the Alps in the Stura valley is lessened; and the columns which are to march on Dalmazzo to close the pass and to secure the whole operation are respectively increased. "This," says he, "is really the corps which is the key of the whole army and the whole system, from Castel Delfino to the Tanaro." In this changed scheme, more freedom is left to the several commanders of columns, and it is by thus much simpler and better.

But neither plan was destined to be put into practice. The upheaval of the 9th Thermidor (July 27, 1794) and the fall of Robespierre menaced Bonaparte with disaster, for the favours he had received from the Robespierres had made him enemies at headquarters. Sent on a secret mission to Genoa, which was threatened by the British from the sea and by the Austrians and the French by land, he had done well; but upon his return in August some unwarranted suspicion caused his arrest and imprisonment in the fort at Antibes.

A strong friendship had existed between the younger Robespierre and Bonaparte, although the former acknowledged that he never quite understood, perhaps never fully trusted the general. Bonaparte had come out flatly for the Jacobins: whether or not he agreed that Terrorism was an evil necessary to purge the body politic, cannot be said; but he was either with the Terrorists or truckling to them, and the latter is unlikely. He saw, as others did, that Terrorism had become a bogy to the French peasant, who feared the soldiers as *infidels* and as upholding the high-handed and bloody methods of the Convention, and was thus less ready than he might be to aid in furnishing them food and shelter; and that to this extent Terrorism was a failure. But in act and word Bonaparte had been faithful to the ruling party. His plan for the Army of Italy had, however, made him enemies in the Array of the Alps, which had no desire to play a second role; still the general suspicion no doubt came from his intimacy with the Robespierres, and it took form on their downfall, which had just occurred. But Saliceti remained his friend; a war commissary was a power in the army; and, as nothing definite could be alleged against him, he was released August 20, 1794, and restored to duty. The reason given was that better than any other he knew the coast and mountains along the Maritime Alps, and was too able and useful a man to spare.

How everything that Bonaparte had to do with Corsica seemed to go wrong is a noteworthy fact. In the spring of 1796 an expedition had been fitting out by the French to recapture the island from the English, and Bonaparte was put in charge of the artillery. But as matters turned out, the British fleet drove the French convoy back to the coast; and on his return Bonaparte found that he had not only once more lamentably failed, but owing to a reorganization of the arm, had lost as well his berth as Inspector of Coast Artillery. From his activity, slow Scherer had classed him as too ambitious and intriguing. Very much to his disgust he was, in lieu of his artillery command, given a commission as brigadier-general of infantry, and was assigned to the Army of the West, which was facing the Vendée. On the score of ill-health, however, he managed for a while not to report for duty with that force.

With his brother Louis, Marmont and Junot, he travelled to Paris in May, 1795, to protest against what he deemed an injustice. The Deputy Aubry, recently created general, was at the head of the military committee. He had never seen service. He reproached Bonaparte with his youth. "One ages quickly on battlefields, and I have just come from them," replied Bonaparte. In the capital he spent some time, hoping to be on hand for the next political upheaval. He was alone, the Jacobins having been elbowed to one side; but not being on duty, he had more leisure to devote to his pen, and he prepared his *Mémoire militaire sur l'Armée d'Italie, Paris, premiers jours de Thermidor III.*, about July 20, 1795. In this memorial, which he opens by the significant words, "In the present position of Europe, one can turn the Army of Italy to great account, and enable it to deliver blows decisive for peace and of marked effect on the House of Austria," he lays bare the kernel of the 1796 campaign: the advance through the gaps between the Alps and Apennines; the idea that a military severance of their armies would at once result in the political severance of Austria and Piedmont, the former army to rush to the protection of Lombardy, and the latter to that of its own country; then the forcing back of the Austrians on Alessandria, while a threat against Turin would compel a peace from Piedmont.

Only to true genius or to arrant incapacity is ever given the power to see perfection in the plans it draws up. In this memorial Bonaparte argues out, in burning phrases and with entire confidence, the value of his plan, and tells what its immediate results must be. The paper first exhibits the man's exceptional far-sightedness and breadth of view; for be goes on to show how the Army of Italy, after peace forced on Piedmont, may conquer Lombardy, march towards the Tyrol, unite with the Army of the Rhine on the Danube, and dictate terms in the heart of Austria. Even Carnot had never conceived so bold and true a plan.

As a wonderful proof of Bonaparte's genius, it has been pointed out by some authors that he took command of the Army of Italy in 1796, and at once proceeded out of hand upon the marvellous campaign which first illustrated his career. But one must not forget that genius, apart from study and hard work, has never yet accomplished its end. Bonaparte's success in 1796 was due to years of office study of the country and the situation. While other generals of higher or equal rank were spending their leisure in wondering what was to be done next, or how they could strike a safe blow, or indeed in trivial pleasures, Bonaparte set himself to work out the problem with his maps and charts; he weighed each factor until he found its true value in the whole scheme; he studied the theatre of war until he knew its every hill and river; and he only then felt that he could command success. Like every great captain, his imagination was boundless, and in his brain there revolved at all times problems of what might thereafter be. Whenever he was confronted by a new proposition, he found its answer in the work of many sleep-less nights of his restless past. Bourrienne says:

> All great things that one saw him do as emperor, were but the carrying out of projects long ago made, when his future greatness was only a dream, or rather a demand of his own imagination.

The man was indeed a dreamer, but his dreams were full of reality, and peopled with facts; and his imagination mainly wandered over those fields upon which he was thereafter actually to play his part.

How much this memorial, how much the recommendations of Saliceti and other friends weighed, we do not know, but, on August 21, 1795, instead of being sent to bury himself in the command of a brigade in the Army of the West, Bonaparte was assigned by the Committee of Public Safety to its geographical bureau (the "Direction of the Movement of the Armies of the Republic"), to work out plans of campaign; and here he speedily gained the confidence of its members, who utilized his suggestions constantly. The leaders of the several armies to whom these suggestions were sent received them, however, with little patience. Kellermann wrote back that the originator belonged in an insane asylum; and Scherer answered that the man who had made the plan for the Army of Italy had better come and carry it out himself. Curiously prophetic suggestion!

Bonaparte remained no great time in this position. Opinions and men changed rapidly in those weeks. With apparently small desire to give his best days to the service of France, and perhaps with his first symptoms of Oriental fever, he made a request to the Committee of Public Safety to be allowed to go to Turkey to reorganize the Sultan's artillery,—a matter he must have been preparing for some time; and this request was being favourably considered by the sub-committee he was specially serving when, not having reported to his brigade in the Army of the West, he was, under the technical regulations made for the reorganization of the levy in mass, stricken by the Central Committee from the list of active generals. Here was apparently a violent end to the career of a man who had so far succeeded in but one under-taking in life, in a subordinate though prominent position at Toulon. But Providence was reserving him for greater things. His loss of rank was but a step upward. Remaining in Paris he busied himself with many projects, yet often nearly at the end of his resources and without friends. But the 13th Vendémiaire (October 14, 1795) came on, and with it active work.

In 1795, as already stated, treaties had been made with Spain and Prussia, and a more moderate political situation had come in. The *émigrés* had been dispersed by Hoche at Quiberon. Jourdan and Pichegru had but half succeeded on the Rhine. In Italy Scherer had, under the plan claimed by Bonaparte as his own, and ably seconded by Massena, won the battle of Loano, which gave the Army of Italy a position on the Apennines as far as Savona. Matters began to wear their old-time aspect, and France was apparently recovering from the awful disease which had nearly buried the nation.

Paris was then, as now, *toujours gai*. The Reign of Terror had been a nightmare, and the city had awakened to fresh social life. In this Bonaparte mixed little. Politically, in 1795, France was in a struggle between Jacobins and Royalists, in which the latter, in the provinces at least, came close to winning, until Hoche put an end to their hopes in Brittany. France was again threatened, as she has at stated intervals been ever since, with the danger of anarchy from the masses, tyranny from the governing power, or a *coup d'état* by some ambitious schemer. A new constitution was being made, under which tax-paying residents might vote, and a Council of Ancients should have a steadying influence on the Deputies. The Committee of Public Safety was to become a Directory of five members, with more moderate powers. Extreme measures had seen their day.

But the Convention did not willingly cede its enormous powers, and shortly the Sections rose against it. To Barras, who had commanded the Army of the Interior with energy, was given the task to protect the Convention. He already knew Bonaparte. There were thirty thousand National Guards without artillery arrayed against the Convention's five thousand regulars with several batteries. Barras is said to have appointed seven lieutenants, among whom, though he was but one, Bonaparte was the ruling spirit; the entire operation was in his control, and from the first word spoken all followed in his steps. While his sentiments were always with the people ("he was ever the peasants' General, the peasants' Consul, the peasants' Emperor"), his action was in favour of the ruling party of law and order. In addition to the five thousand line infantry there were fifteen hundred citizens, and when Barras authorized him to get guns from Sablons, he dispatched his subordinate Murat thither to bring them up. The latter was only just in time: the Sections had sent to seize the cannon for their side. With guns well served the Convention had a distinct superiority, unless the Sections should happen to be unusually well led, as it turned out they were not. General Menou had been in charge for the Convention, but he had weakly dallied with the Sections. After Bonaparte took the matter in hand, the day was still spent parleying and awaiting a movement of the Sections. But Bonaparte had for hours been ready, with his guns trained on the Louis XVI. bridge (now Pont de la Concorde), the Pont Royal, the *rues de* Rohan, *du* Dauphin, St. Florentin and St. Honouré, and with matches lighted. The members of the Convention were also armed, and the whole great mass of solid buildings making up the Louvre and the Tuileries was held by its troops. About 4 p. m. a few stray shots were fired from adjoining houses, and the Sections advanced on the Convention army by the issues of the rue St. Honouré, and first near the church of St. Roch, where they had their headquarters. Waiting for nothing, and although but a single gun could be trained up the narrow rue du Dauphin, Bonaparte so ably managed his batteries that the troops of the Sections were blown away with a few rounds of grape and canister. A similar attack from across the Seine by the Pont Royal was somewhat later dispersed in like manner. By six o'clock the matter was finished, the Sections had played their cards and lost, with casualties on each side of about two hundred men. The Convention had won by Bonaparte's quick and uncompromising measures, and he was promoted to be general of division, and made second in command of the Army of the Interior, with headquarters in Paris.

After the defeat of the Sections, the disarmament of the citizens was decreed, and it was strictly carried out. No arm of whatever kind was left in the hands of the people. A few days later, one morning, a lad of thirteen came to see Bonaparte, and though received kindly, could explain with difficulty through his tears that he was the son, Eugene, of General de Beauharnais, and that his dead father's sword had been taken. Touched by the gallant bearing of the lad, Bonaparte saw to the return of the weapon. Madame Josephine de Beauharnais later came to thank the soldier, and this was their first introduction.

Bonaparte now busied himself with reorganizing the National Guard, and formed the Guard of the Directory and Legislative Assembly,—a body which later became the Consular and Imperial Guard. He found himself at once a lion in society, and shortly in Barras' *salon* he again met Josephine, with whom, though she was six years his senior, he fell desperately and honestly in love. (*Napoleon's Letters to Josephine* by Henry Foljambe Hall, also published by Leonaur).

In this year there was much suffering from hunger in Paris. One day, while inspecting the issues to the multitude. Napoleon and his

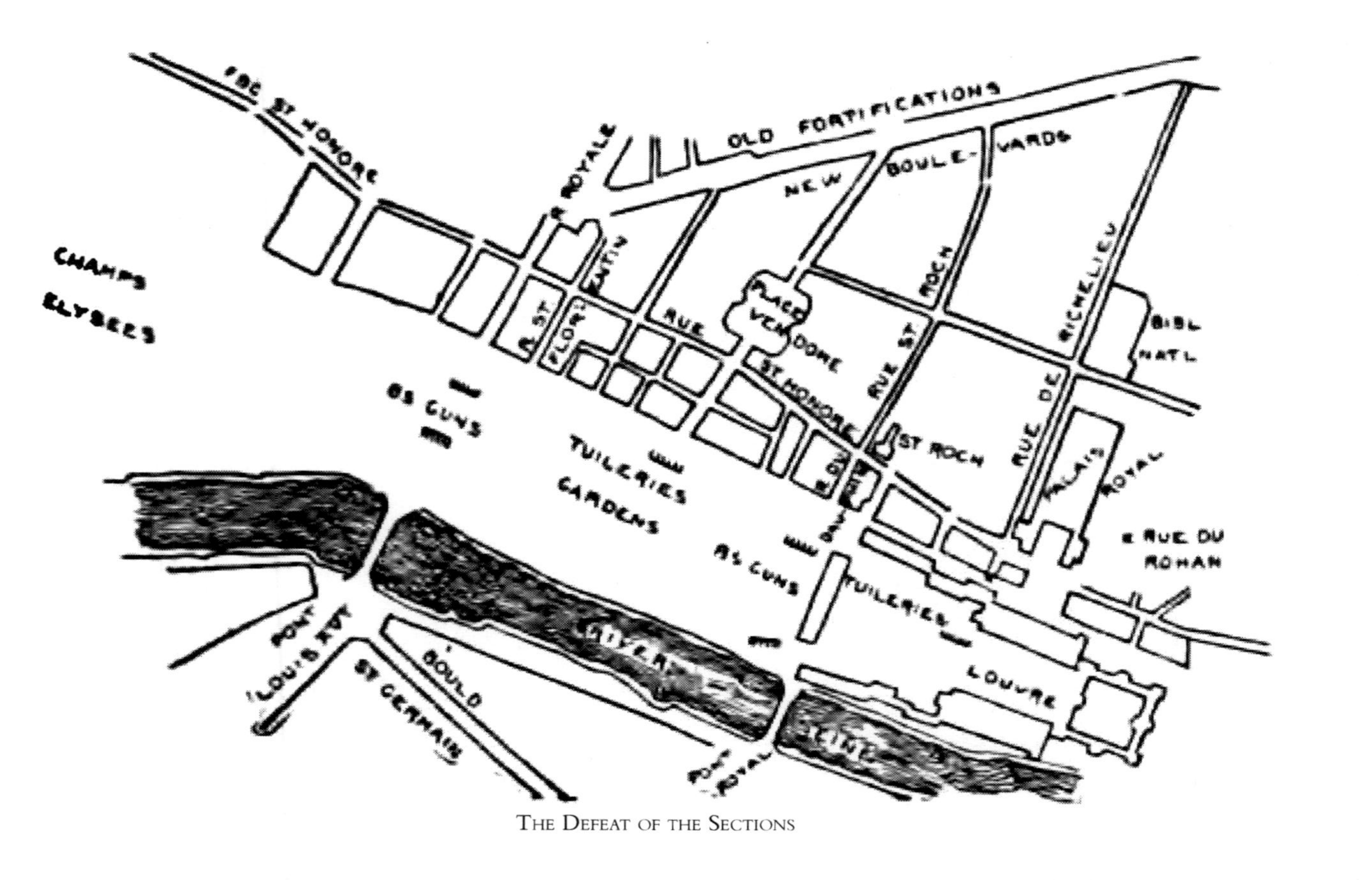

The Defeat of the Sections

staff were surrounded by a riotous group of women clamouring for bread, which threatened a critical result. The leader was an extremely tall and fat woman, one of the notabilities of the great market near-by. "All these epauleted men," she cried, "well cared for and fed, are mocking us. As long as they eat and grow fat, little care they how many poor die of hunger."

Bonaparte good-naturedly turned towards her with "My good woman, are you or am I the fatter?" This turned the laugh against the woman, and broke up the riot, as a French laugh will always do. Ridicule is the strongest Gallic argument.

Early next year Bonaparte was given command of the Army of Italy. Barras's claim that the appointment was owing entirely to him cannot be substantiated. The man who made such appointments was Carnot; and this able administrator was not slow to recognize the strength of the young general, for whom, moreover, much later correspondence shows that he harboured a sincere regard. Barras may indeed have been Bonaparte's backer, or one of them. The new Directory had come in; Carnot asked Bonaparte to redraw his plan for the Army of Italy, which he did in January, 1796; and Scherer having given small satisfaction and being more-over in bad health, Bonaparte was put in his place.

Marmont, who became his adjutant-general, tells us that he found Bonaparte transformed into a man positive of what he knew and could do, and with a full sense of his own importance. In every way he made his appointment tell in his own favour, and one of its immediate results was his marriage to Josephine, of which Barras, in his *Memoirs*, tells us so much and suggests more.

What Josephine narrates of Bonaparte's manner in those days is of marked interest. "I admire the courage of the general," says she, "the breadth of his knowledge in all things, of which he also talks well, the liveliness of his mind, which allows him to understand the thoughts of others almost before they speak; but I confess I am frightened at the dominion which he seems to desire to exert over all who surround him. His inquiring eye has something peculiar which is inexplicable, but which even impresses our directors." She further tells that Bonaparte said to her, "Think you that I need influence in order to rise? All will someday be happy when I give them mine. My sword is at my side, and with it I will go far." Josephine adds: "I do not understand it, but sometimes this ridiculous positiveness so impresses me that it makes me believe everything possible that this extraordinary man puts into my head; and who knows what, with his imagination, he may not undertake."

At that time Madame de Beauharnais was fairly well off. Her notary, a certain Raguideau, who was drawing up the marriage contract, remonstrated with her. "How can you," said he, "marry a soldier who has only his cloak and his sword? "Bonaparte, who was sitting in the adjoining room, chanced to overhear this remark; and eight years later, when he was being dressed for the imperial crowning, and Raguideau was nearby, having indeed been employed by Bonaparte as his own notary, he showed him the imperial mantle covered with golden bees, and beside it the long sword of Charlemagne, with the remark, "There, sir, are the cloak and the sword!"

Chapter 8

Montenotte and Dego

March-April, 1796

The position of France was critical. The Coalition was strong. England had captured the French colonies. Finances were at lowest ebb. The three main armies were those of Jourdan on the lower Rhine, Moreau in Alsatia and Bonaparte in Italy. The two former were to cross the Rhine and unite against the allies under Archduke Charles. Bonaparte took command with firmness, and all quickly recognized his authority and ability. He corrected the bad strategical position of the army, which had been strung out along the coast, with communications in prolongation of the left He equipped and fed the troops better than before, roused their enthusiasm by his masterful work, and won their affection by his hearty words. The allies in Italy (the Austrians and the Piedmontese) were so ill-posted as not to support each other. Bonaparte ployed his forces into one mass, crossed the mountains and defeated the Austrians at Montenotte; then turned on Dego, again beat them, broke through the centre of the allied line, and separated the two armies. His speed and audacity had never yet been equalled in modern days. He worked his divisions in a marvellous manner. Then leaving small forces to hold the Austrians in check, he advanced on the Piedmontese, beat them repeatedly, and drove them back towards Turin with such rapidity that the Austrians could not help them. Piedmont was glad to sue for peace, and the Austrians withdrew behind the Po. The campaign was fairly startling in its energy and skill.

Appointed to command the Army of Italy March 2, 1796, Bonaparte, accompanied by his faithful comrades, Marmont, Junot, Berthier, Murat and Duroc, left Paris the 21st, and on the 27th assumed command at Nice. He at once issued the following proclamation:

Headquarters
Nice
7 Germinal, IV
Soldiers! You are naked, ill-fed; the government owes you much,

it can give you nothing. Your patience, the courage you exhibit in the midst of these rocks, are admirable, but they bring you no glory; no lustre is reflected on you. I will lead you into the most fertile plains of the world. Rich provinces, great cities will be in your power; there you shall find honour, fame and riches. Soldiers of Italy, shall courage or constancy fail you?
Bonaparte

This proclamation showed a keen sense of the strength as well as weakness of the French soldier's character. Bonaparte promised them food, fame, spoils. The Gallic conscript was about to fight for his rations, as many European armies had done before, but with the additional incentive of loot.

France was in a critical situation. In coalition against her were England, Russia, the German Empire, Austria, Naples and the Pope, who had formally joined the allies September 28, 1795; while Prussia and Spain, which had recently made peace at Basle, were still far from reliable as neutrals, though Prussia had reason to hope for an increase of territory. Russia had gone so far as to send ships to the North Sea. Sweden and Denmark, Hanover, Saxony and some other German States were friendly, and Portugal would have been glad to leave the Coalition. Holland had established a republican government, and Beurnonville was there in command of the joint Dutch and French forces. Poland had ceased to exist, and Turkey had no interest in European politics. Switzerland remained neutral. All the French colonies had been alienated or seized by the English; the French fleet had been destroyed; the small foothold of France in India had been lost. On the other hand Belgium had been formally reunited to France, though without the consent of Austria, who viewed the loss of the Netherlands as a grievous blow to her prestige; and the Austrian victories on the Rhine in 1795 gave small hope that Vienna would voluntarily cede this territory. The German armies were expected to make an attempt to cross the Rhine. Finances were at such low ebb that the Directory resorted to the offensive quite as much to subsist the armies it could not feed upon the enemy's soil, as for strategic gain.

There were three main armies, Jourdan's, Moreau's and Bonaparte's, and two in reserve: Kellermann's Army of the Alps, and one in Provence and on the Var. Jourdan had upwards of seventy thousand men on the lower Rhine, with which to mask Mainz and advance into Franconia with forty-five thousand. Moreau had an equal number in Alsatia, with which to mask Mannheim and advance into

Swabia. The two were then to unite, and descend upon Bavaria. The Army of the Alps and the Army of Italy, while near each other, did little work in common, and the former commander of the Army of Italy, Scherer, after the victory of Loano, had sat down to rest upon his laurels in a useless defensive.

Although Clerfayt had done well in 1795, Archduke Charles had superseded him, and with his ninety thousand men was expected to recapture Belgium. On the Upper Rhine, Wurmser with eighty thousand men was to hold head to Moreau; and Beaulieu, with sixty thousand men in Italy, was ordered to drive the French from the Riviera and follow them into Provence.

In 1796 Italy, divided up into twenty petty principalities, existed only on the map. Sardinia, with Savoy, Nice and Piedmont, Genoa, Lucca, Lombardy, Venice, Modena, Tuscany, comprised the northern part; the States of the Pope took up the centre; and Naples covered the southern part of the peninsula, including Sicily. Corsica was French. Victor Amadeus III. of Piedmont, "*le portier des Alpes*," had married his daughters to the brothers of Louis XVI.; and his fear of republican doctrines, his family ties and English subsidies, all induced him to cling to the Coalition. And yet, in truth, for in her alliance he had everything to lose and nothing to gain, it was but a feeble fealty that he harboured towards Austria. Lombardy was Austrian. Tuscany was governed by a scion of the Hapsburg family. Modena and Lucca were under the thumb of Vienna. Ferdinand IV. of Naples was allied by marriage to Austria, and sent a contingent to her army in Italy. The execution of Marie Antoinette had exasperated everyone who had pro-Austrian tendencies. The Pope, Pius VI., was governed by his religious motives. The oligarchies of Genoa and Venice had fallen from their old estate, but might still be of weight in the balance. Austria had essayed to create an Italian league against France, but though she had not accomplished much, all Italy was really anti-French to the last degree. Yet there existed among the middle classes in Piedmont and Lombardy, and in other states, as Bologna and Ferrara, a distinct striving towards liberty, bred of the French Revolution and the iniquities of their present rulers.

Strategically there were two theatres, Germany and Italy. In northern Italy the Alps and Apennines play the great topographical role, inclosing as they do on north and south the valley of the Po. Though in a way the two are the same range, the point of geographical division is at the Colle di Tenda. The mountain ranges on the south lie near the sea, leaving only a narrow territory along the

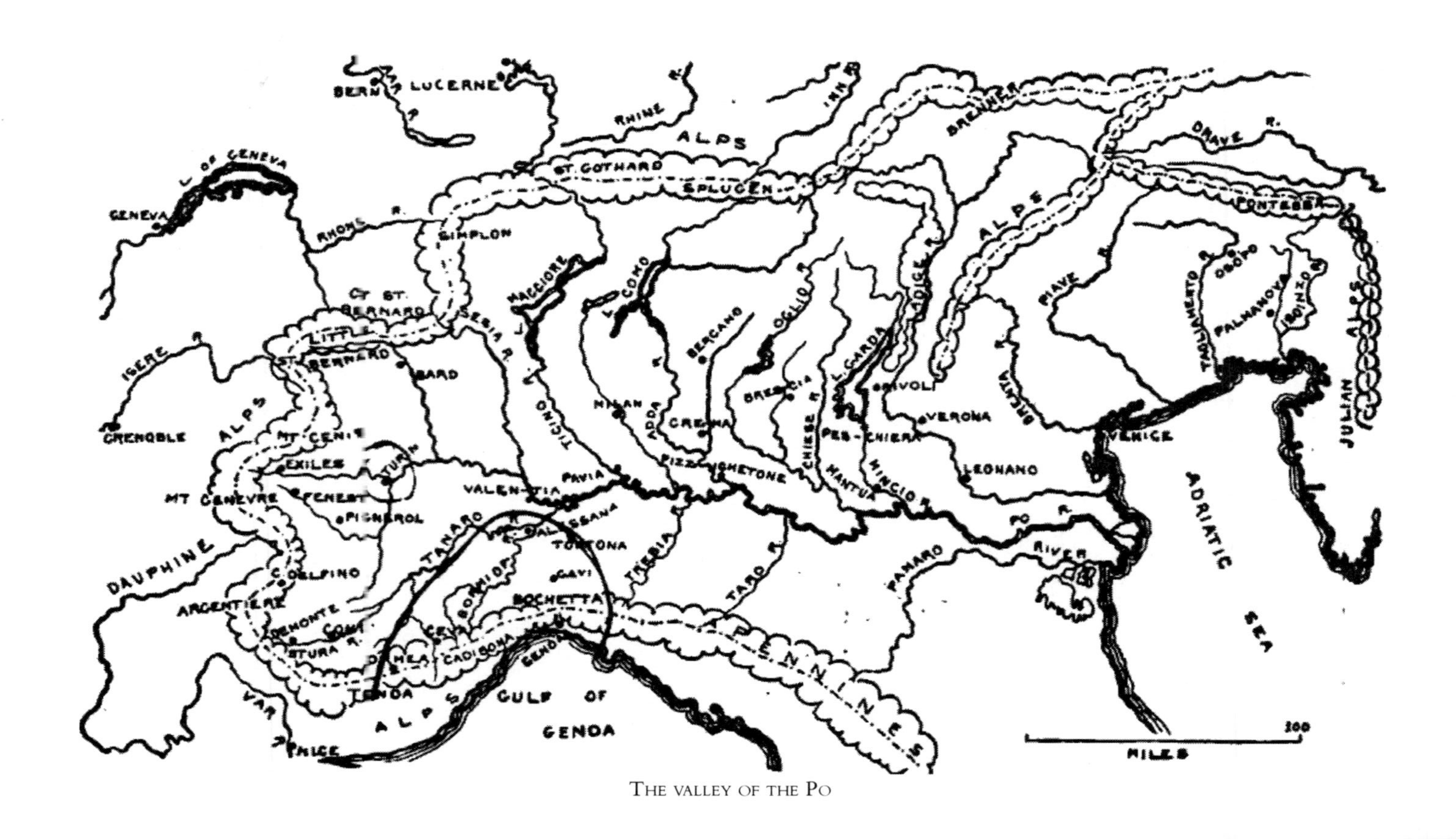

The valley of the Po

Gulf of Genoa. The Po valley is practically shut in from the north and west. From the south it is approachable by easy passes across the Apennines; from the east by fairly good ones over the Julian Alps, and by the passes of the Tagliamento (Pontebba) and of the Piave; on the north and west, however, it can only be entered by the rugged passes of the Adige (Brenner) and of the Brenta; by the Splügen, St. Gothard, the Simplon, and the St. Bernard, Great and Little; by Mont Cenis, Mont Genèvre, Argentière, Tenda. All the latter French and Swiss passes were at that day protected by more or less strong forts; the eastern gaps were not. The debouches from the Riviera to the Po valley were covered by the fortresses of Coni, Ormea, Ceva; and that all these passes ran through valleys into the Padane plains at nearly a right angle lent greater value to these strong places. From the coast, between the Bocchetta and Tenda passes, the roads across the mountains over the Ormea and Cadibona passes were poor.

From Turin down the Po is navigable. It is about as wide as the Danube, but not being deep and having a quiet current, it is in many places easily crossed by troops. The Isonzo protects northern Italy from the east, and the Palmanova aids in its defence; but these rivers can be turned by the pass of Pontebba *via* Osopo into the valley of the Tagliamento. The Piave protects Venice. The Brenta has many fords. All these rivers are torrential in the mountains. They can all be turned by the upper waters of the Adige, along which run roads from the Tyrol and Bavaria into Italy. From this it follows that the Adige is the strongest barrier of the Po valley on the east, as the line of this river can only be turned by the difficult passes farther to the west. Down to Rivoli the Adige is protected by Monte Baldo, and the position at La Corona, just above Rivoli, practically prevents artillery from moving along the road. Verona commands the Adige at the outlet of the mountains, and still farther down Legnano, below which the country is too marshy for military operations. The Mincio, from the Lake of Garda to the Po, is watched by the fortresses of Peschiera and Mantua, but between the former and Goito there are many fords. About Mantua lie much marsh land and many lakes. The line of the Mincio can be turned south of the Po, or by the north of the Lake of Garda. The Adda, which flows through the Lake of Como and to the Po above Cremona, has several fords, but Pizzighetone protects its lower course, while Lecco, Trezzo, Cassano and Lodi are strong points above. The Ticino flows through Lago Maggiore, and divides Piedmont from Lombardy. Navigable, with many affluents and uncertain fords, it is a good defensive line, Pavia being its strongest place. Opposite the mouth of the Ticino lies the pass of Stradella, between the Po and a rugged spur of the Apennines; and all roads along the left bank of the Po, practicable for an army, must pass through this defile. We remember that Hannibal saw and seized its advantages.

Mantua was the best fortress in Italy, lying on an island in the Mincio in the midst of marshes and flanked by a citadel and by Fort San Giorgio. Venice, from her position and her forts, was of marked value. Verona had good walls, and on the left bank a strong fort. Legnano was fairly strong. Peschiera was small but important. Pizzighetone had considerable value. Palmanova was a new fortress. Milan possessed a six-bastioned citadel, but was not otherwise strong. Pavia held the Ticino bridge and was strengthened by walls and a citadel. Brescia had like defences. Bergamo had a citadel and the fortified castle Capella. Crema was strong. Turin boasted good walls and a fine citadel. Alessandria, Tortona, Valencia, Gavi, Ceva, Coni, all strong fortresses, protected Piedmont on the south, while the forts of Bard, Exilles, Fenestrelles, Pignerolo, Castel Delfino, Demonte, performed like office on the west. Such was the theatre which lay open to the new commander of the Army of Italy.

At this date Bonaparte's appearance had little that was attractive. Short of stature, being a scant five feet five, spare, and with features so pinched that their real beauty of outline was quite hidden, high broad forehead, thin lips, long yellow hair, not always well kempt, wearing his clothes in a loose and ungainly fashion, ill-groomed to the last degree, there was nothing to suggest his real character, except the big, deep-set, blue-gray eyes, which never failed to fascinate, and his voice, whose words none could fail to heed. Apparently lacking physique, he yet possessed unlimited nervous strength, and he soon proved that he could outwork almost any man in the army. On his first appearance the older generals in the Army of Italy looked with small favour on this twenty-seven years old commander-in-chief; but in a few weeks they were heart and soul his willing lieutenants.

> Headquarters had not left Nice since the beginning of the war. . . . The administrations considered themselves as at a permanent post, and busied themselves more with the comforts of life than the needs of the army.

The new leader at once showed the strong hand of authority. He disbanded one battalion for refusing to march for want of shoes and: pay, and consolidated the men in groups of five into other commands, "the officers not having shown enough nerve" in the mutiny. He raised money from local bankers to partly pay the troops, and began to gather food and forage with an energy and success not yet seen. Everything was done for the men; everything was demanded of them. He wrote the Directory:

> I am compelled to threaten the agents, who have stolen much and who have credit, and I accomplish a good deal by following up my threats with caresses. The army will hereafter eat good bread and have meat.

And to Commissary Lambert he wrote, April 7, concerning a complaint as to the weight of the rations and forage, and stating that larceny had been proven:

> The general-in-chief orders you to make an official report on the weight of the bundles of hay which remain and which have been placed under charge of the guard. You will have Citizen Michel arrested until you can find out who bundled the hay, and the storekeeper who received the lettuce.... It is important, Citizen Commissary, that not a single rogue shall escape. For a long time the soldiers and the interests of the country have been a prey to cupidity. An example is necessary at all times, particularly on the opening of the campaign.

To Scherer's credit be it said that he received the new commander-in-chief cordially, and gave him all the aid he could. In return Bonaparte suggested him for the post of ambassador. He wrote the Directory March 28:

> I have been particularly satisfied with the frankness and integrity of General Scherer. By his loyal conduct, and by his promptness in giving me all the information which can be useful to me, he has acquired a right to my gratitude.

And to Carnot:

> I have seemed to see in Scherer a man pure and enlightened. He appears to me tired of war, which has broken his health. Could you not employ him as ambassador? He has knowledge of men, and moral breadth.

The Army of Italy, whose soldiers the allies derisively called "heroes in rags,"—as indeed they were, for "privations, poverty, misery, are the school of the good soldier," said the emperor at St. Helena,—was perched upon the watershed along the coast of the Gulf of Genoa, over too long a front, from Ormea, at the headwaters of the Tanaro, to Savona. Its communications with France ran along the sea parallel with its front—always a dangerous situation—and were thus liable to be cut at any time. Supplies had to come by the seashore road, as an English flotilla under Nelson and Jervis held the sea, and could cut off French ships sailing from Toulon. The condition of the army was pitiable. "Bread was ill-assured; for a long while no distribution of meat had been made." The men and officers alike were unpaid, ill-clad, unshod, ill-fed.

From France into Italy there were many roads: by the Colle di Tenda, the Argentière, Mont Genèvre, Mont Cenis, the Little and Great St. Bernard, and farther along the Simplon, the Splügen and the St. Gothard. But none of these could really be called practicable for an army, most of them being snow-bound except for a brief summer period, and few of them having wagon-roads. From Nice into Italy there were at that day but two highways. The present fine *chaussée* from Nice to Genoa and Florence was not begun until 1805, at the same time as the military roads over the Simplon and Mont Cenis. One of the roads then existing ran across the Colle di Tenda *via* Coni to Turin; the other was the Corniche, winding its narrow, tortuous way along the coast; and beyond Genoa on to Alessandria the road ran over the Bocchetta range, the pass through which was protected by the fort at Gavi. By his march across the Colle di Tenda, Bonaparte was really turning the Alps. From the coast at Fort Maurice to Ceva ran a third road across the mountains, practicable for artillery; while less good roads were those from Loano to Garessio and Ceva; from Savona to Carcare, and thence either to Dego or Ceva; from Savona *via* Montenotte to Sassello; and from Voltri to Campofreddo. Country roads, fit enough for infantry or pack-mules, ran along every valley and over every pass from town to town; but for guns or cavalry most of them would serve only in case of necessity.

The French thus held the Riviera coast and the steep southerly foothills of the Apennines; the allied Piedmontese-Austrian armies held the northerly slopes of the range, which were much less pronounced. In the Alps, on Bonaparte's left and with communications running back through Savoy, stood Kellermann's forces, over which Bonaparte had no control. It is plain that by way of Coni, had it so wished, the Army of Italy could have reached out towards the Army of the Alps and worked in unison with it; but there was actually no intimate cooperation. Each commander paid heed to his own front only.

The distribution of troops was as follows: on the left of the army

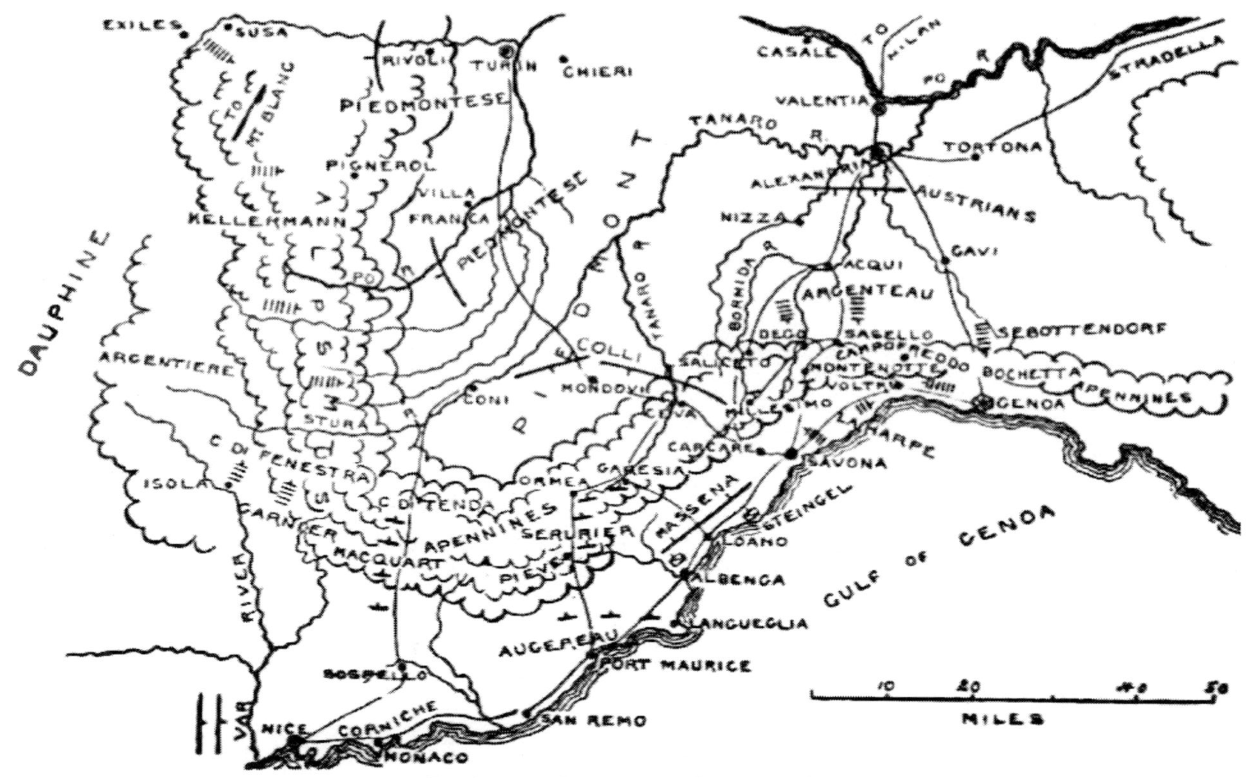

The Army of Italy on the Riviera, 1796

stood Garnier's division of thirty-two hundred men along the Colle di Finestre towards Isola; then came Macquart's division of thirty-seven hundred men along the road from Sospello up to the Colle di Tenda. These two were intended to keep up connection with the Army of the Alps by the Coni road, and to block the way to the Piedmontese, so that the French communications should not be cut by the enemy's advance through the Tenda pass. Serurier's division, seven thousand strong, lay on the road Pieve-Ormea-Garessio as if ready to push on Ceva and Turin, with Augereau's division of eight thousand men stationed behind its right and leaning its own right flank on the sea at Langueglia. There were two divisions in the van, .Massena's of nine thousand men, and Laharpe's of eight thousand men; and these held the coast-from Augereau's position out to near Voltri. The artillery boasted but sixty guns. All the troops were in cantonments, and far from being in marching order. Of cavalry Bonaparte had not exceeding three thousand men. These he placed under the command of the veteran Steingel, and stationed them in two divisions near Loano, in rear of the foot. In a limited sense both Kellermann's Army of the Alps and the troops on the Var were a reserve to the Army of Italy. But they were not subject to Bonaparte's control. As a fact, Kellermann was none too eager to cooperate with his new associate.

The forces of the allies were equally ill-distributed. After the battle of Loano they had been crowded down from the watershed to the northern foothills of the mountains, and lay covering the approaches to Turin and Milan. Over twenty thousand Piedmontese were contained by Kellermann in the passes of the Alps from Mont Blanc down to the Argentière, so as to be of practically no present use against the Army of Italy; and to this extent Kellermann was doing useful work. But in the immediate problem which Bonaparte was to work out, he was playing only a neutral role.

In the valleys of the Tanaro and the Great Bormida, about Ceva and Mondovi, stood Colli, and under him Provera and Latour, with the rest of the Piedmontese, twenty-five thousand effective, covering Turin, with his left on Millesimo; and the Austrians, thirty-five thousand strong under Beaulieu, a veteran of seventy-one, who was, indeed, supposed to be in command of both armies, extended their left out towards the Bocchetta pass, thus covering Milan, and with a flying wing near Genoa. The Austrian centre was at Sassello, with outposts along the ridge of the Apennines; the right was at Dego on the Little. Bormida. The main body, which had been in winter quarters on the Po and Adda, was yet assembling in the plains near Alessandria.

Beaulieu had good lieutenants: Argenteau, Melas, Wukassovich, Liptay, Sebottendorf. The entire allied line thus extended from the fortress of Coni, which strongly protected its right flank, to the Bocchetta pass and the great city of Genoa. They numbered about sixty thousand men under the colours, and had one hundred and fifty guns. This line was long, and was so placed that, owing to the trend of the watersheds, intercommunication between parts was over difficult ground; if interrupted at any one point, it could be re-established only by a considerable circuit The entire allied force was marshalled cordon fashion: Sebottendorf, opposite Voltri, was supposed, while advancing down the coast, to keep in touch with the English fleet and Genoa; Argenteau was to advance from Acqui towards the coast with his mass at Sassello; Provera, with a brigade at Saliceto and Millesimo, was to keep up contact between the Austrian right and Piedmontese left; and Colli, with the main Piedmontese army, was to hold firm in Ceva.

Bonaparte's orders from the Directory were to separate the allies and force peace on Piedmont, in accordance with his own plans already mentioned, and for which he had been ridiculed by his associate, Kellermann, and his predecessor, Scherer; and though he was resolved to undertake the offensive at an early day, yet there remained a host of things to be done before he could move. Many have portrayed Napoleon as a man always pushing forward, "following his star," without regard to logistics or lines of retreat. The truth is, that no man was ever more scrupulous in his care of victual, clothing and material than he; no man ever knew more certainly what he should do in case of disaster. He was far removed from a Charles XII. Napoleon, to be sure, always made "war nourish war" (excepting the cost of his wars with England, his campaigns were made to pay for themselves); but he none the less calculated everything relating to administration with a nicety of detail which was marvellous; and woe betide that officer who failed him in the department of supplies. It is, however, true that he relied on the country, rather than on magazines, as Frederick had to do. This system he had inherited from the bold recklessness of the early Revolutionary generals. But on the other hand, the valley of the Po, whither he was bound to push his way, was rich, as were not Bohemia and Moravia, where the Prussians campaigned in the seventeenth century. Inasmuch as, in this particular case, what Bonaparte was resolved to do would demand great speed, so the question of supplies had all the more to be considered and provided for. And the greater part of his early days in command were devoted to this task.

It seems that Bonaparte had for a moment conceived an idea that he might persuade or compel Genoa to give him passage, so that through the Bocchetta pass he might, by a threat to the Austrian left, throw Beaulieu back on or beyond Alessandria, detach Piedmont from the Austrian alliance by advancing between the allies from that direction, and, taking their defences in reverse, call in the Army of the Alps and move in mass on the Tyrol. In fact, his advance on Voltri was in part owing to this idea, and was in part a threat on Genoa, to persuade her to pay an indemnity for the burning by the English of a French ship in her neutral waters. But on due weighing of the chances, he reverted to the 1794 plan, which he had so carefully worked out in his *Memorial* and other papers, and which would be much more effective if successful. In general, as already shown, this plan was to break through the enemy's centre across the western Apennines, strategically separate the Austrians from the Piedmontese, force peace on the latter, and then turn upon the Austrians. The point of attack was to be along the Savona-Carcare road; and to carry out this plan he must first concentrate on his right. "To change from the defensive to the offensive formation is one of the most sensitive of operations," said he, as he began this work. A few months later, when his hand had got used to his tools,—or perhaps we should say used to holding the baton,—he found it easier; and thereafter he paid small heed to tactical difficulties, which he always felt he could overcome when met.

Bonaparte's chief of staff was Berthier, then forty-three years old, the man who served him as such throughout his campaigns, except the last. He had been lieutenant-colonel on the staff of Rochambeau in America, had served in the Vendée and under Kellermann in the Army of the Alps. Berthier was a most useful officer, brave, exact and reliable in every part of the practical business of war, but "of an indecisive character," and without the slightest conception of its intellectual side. Napoleon gave him fame, riches, friendship, and this, said he, Berthier later repaid him by betrayal. At St. Helena he characterized Berthier as a gander whom he had in a way transformed into an eagle. This was scarcely a fair simile, but the emperor was then embittered. Untiring at work in the tent or in the saddle, master of all the details of administration, Berthier was invaluable to the great army leader; but he was not strong in any place except beside his master. On Bonaparte's staff were also Marmont, Murat and Junot, later to rise to fame; and in subordinate positions were serving Lannes, Joubert, Bessieres, Suchet and Victor. As lieutenants, each worked up to the top of the ladder.

All the regiments capable of work on the fighting line were now ordered up, and as soon as they could be relieved by garrisons, came on from Nice and Albenga to Savona. These were all places essential to be held to protect the line of communications with France. Bonaparte left his Nice headquarters for the front on April 2, to set the army in motion. His purpose was to concentrate at Savona, push at once up to Carcare on the Little Bormida, where the road forks towards the capitals of Piedmont and Lombardy, and having seized this fork, he might advance on either road at will.

The allies had also been contemplating active operations. Napoleon narrates:

> The minister of France had demanded of the Senate of Genoa a passage through the Bocchetta, and the keys of Gavi, announcing that the French desired to penetrate into Lombardy, and lean their operations on Genoa.

Beaulieu had thus conceived fears for the safety of Genoa, and by March 31 had begun to reinforce the troops which lay in front of the French extreme right at Voltri, while Argenteau should debouch from Sassello, *via* Montenotte, on the French left. The *Memoirs* say:

> Had General Beaulieu reflected on the topographical conditions, he would not have marched on Voltri to cover Genoa; he would have moved on Acqui and on Cairo; from here he would have debouched . . . in three columns . . . by Montenotte on Savona, . . . by Cadibona, . . . and on Finale. . . . The French army would have quickly fallen back from Voltri and Genoa to defend these three important positions.

Certain Austrian movements in this region equally demonstrated to Bonaparte that there was no further chance of surprising the allies in their winter quarters, as at one time he had hoped to do. And meanwhile Colli, also alive to a possible advance of the French, had got his troops together into close cantonments about Ceva and Mondovi, and in an extensive camp near the former town. From Albenga, April 6, Bonaparte wrote the Directory:

> The Piedmontese army is of the strength of forty thousand men of infantry and five thousand men of cavalry; that of the Austrians is of the strength of thirty-four thousand men of infantry and three thousand of cavalry. I have disposable only forty-five thousand men, all included. They have held back many troops

> in the rear and beyond the Rhone.... The King of Sardinia has made a requisition of young men over fifteen years of age. He has condemned to be shot those who do not join, and as a matter of fact has had some shot in Turin.

The effective for the field would be nearer stated at twenty-five thousand under Colli, and thirty-five thousand under Beaulieu, as against not over thirty-seven thousand French. Even this was a superiority which the enemy might well have utilized; and the French status furnished a problem not easy of solution, especially as the allies had an unlimited supply of artillery, and the French had far less.

Bonaparte also wrote the Directory, April 6:

> I have found in Oneille some marbles which are valued at quite a sum. I have ordered them to be estimated, and to be put up at auction in the Genoese Riviera. That might give you a sum of thirty to forty thousand *francs*.

This was the beginning of the habit of seizing works of art as lawful booty, later so pronounced.

It would appear that Beaulieu could have threatened the French to better strategic advantage by an operation in force against their left by way of Ceva, while with a small force retaining his hold on the Bocchetta pass; for this operation might have compelled Bonaparte to retire summarily to the line of the Var; but the manoeuvre did not appeal to the Austrian leader, and he chose to push in where Bonaparte was strongest, forgetting that the latter might advance on his own line where he himself was weakest. But Beaulieu, like nearly every other general of that day, had limited views as to what strategy meant. His desire to work against the French right may have come from fear for Genoa; or perchance he had orders from Vienna not to lose touch with that city. Remembering the capacity of the Aulic Council for blundering interference, one might almost assume this to be true.

Colli had in fact advised Beaulieu to concentrate on his right, across the Apennines between Loano and Savona, and by thus cutting off the French right at Voltri force the Army of Italy back to the Var—an excellent operation. But Beaulieu's conception of the offensive was markedly tame; and in preparing for it he lost sight of the demands of his own defensive. Still it was not left to Bonaparte to open the campaign. His advance on Voltri had roused the Austrian leader from his quiet. On April 9 Beaulieu sent Sebottendorf with the bulk of his seven thousand men forward on Voltri, while Argenteau, who disposed of a column of nine thousand men, pushed forward from Sassello, intending to march on Savona by the Montenotte pass. Beaulieu apparently thought that between Argenteau and Sebottendorf, with a fraction of the force they should have got in line, the French right wing could be cut off and destroyed. Colli, commanding the Piedmontese, while advised of the operation, merely retained his position at Ceva, where Serurier by feints from Garessio held him fast, lest he should open the road to Turin. The Austrian commander may have purposed to pivot on Ceva, and after pushing in the French, form a new line from this fortified place across the mountains to Loano. This on the face of it was practicable; but the result of the operation would have been to separate the centre so far and by so bad a route from the right at Ceva and the left near Genoa, that the French might fall on it in force and destroy it Whatever Beaulieu may have intended to do, what he actually did fitted into Bonaparte's plans with nicety.

Bonaparte had been purposing to inspect Serurier's force and position, but on hearing the news from Voltri, speeded to Savona, to ascertain how much the Austrian activity there might mean. On April 10 Sebottendorf's division seriously attacked Cervoni's brigade, which held the extreme right; and though the French made a gallant all-day fight for the position, they were at eventide forced to fall back on the main body, and reached Laharpe next day near Savona. Nor, indeed, was Argenteau idle. At noon on April 11 he met and pushed the French outposts back of Montenotte, until he was checked by the fierce resistance of a French force (whether under Rampon or Fornésy is disputed), in one of three old redoubts on Monte Legino. There are two Montenottes, Superior and Inferior, one almost on the watershed, and one below on the northerly slope. From the Superior ran a road *via* Monte Legino to the sea. It was this pass Bonaparte had sent a body of thirteen hundred men to hold, and these were the troops Argenteau had struck. Thrice the Austrian forces advanced on the brave Frenchmen's post; thrice they were thrown back with loss. French infantry has often defended positions such as this with admirable constancy.

The meaning of the two attacks could not be misapprehended. No doubt was left in Bonaparte's mind that the Austrians had set out with a determination to drive the French back to Nice. It was for him to counter the blow.

There was nothing to indicate how large a force the allies had put in motion, nor at what point the bulk of it might debouch. But Bonaparte was not slow to recognize the fact that the two operating Austrian columns were separated by a mountain chain, and that he might easily hold one with a small force and fall on the other with enough men to crush it. At the very outset the enemy had committed the error of moving on him in two concentric columns, an operation which generally endangers them both; and here in effect did so. Bonaparte elected to deliver his main blow on Argenteau, because, should he defeat this general, he would place himself between Colli and Beaulieu, to the assistance of neither of whom could the other come, except by a long detour, and he might thus be able to move upon one or the other of the main armies to marked advantage. To this effect, then, his orders were at once issued on April 11. With Augereau, Massena and Laharpe, Bonaparte purposed to cross the Apennines near the sources of the Little Bormida, while Serurier should descend the mountain slopes towards the plain of the Tanaro. His minor operation was to be a tactical advance against the right flank of Argenteau's column at Montenotte; his major operation was to be a strategic breaking through the centre of the whole allied line.

Augereau, who with his six thousand men had been marching on Savona, was ordered to head on Mallare, and next day on Cairo, where further orders would be given him. This he proceeded to do in good style, forcing back whatever small outlying parties he met. Massena, collecting his nine thousand men, advanced as ordered by way of Altare. This manoeuvre was intended to project these two divisions around the right flank of Argenteau. Laharpe, with seven thousand men, leaving a small force to act as rearguard on the Voltri road, started at daylight on the 12th to sustain the Montenotte battalions in their gallant stand at Monte Legino; and on arrival filed into place on each flank of this small force. Information of the manoeuvre was sent back to Serurier, with instructions to demonstrate sharply but safely against Colli down the valley of the Tanaro. Personally, Bonaparte accompanied Massena's column.

This plan, rapidly formed and stoutly carried out as a counterblow to the attack of Sebottendorf already inaugurated, deserved and met with complete success. The Austrians were but ill-prepared for larger operations. Argenteau had apparently got together not exceeding half his force (Beaulieu stated it at one third), and finding himself sharply attacked by Laharpe in front and his right about to be turned by Massena, whose van had pushed over country roads towards Montenotte Inferiore, he was compelled from the outset to fight in retreat. Laharpe followed him up sharply, while Massena strove to reach his right. Bonaparte, from a hill near Carcare, which dominated much of the surrounding country, directed all the manoeuvres. Argenteau did his best, but it was a losing game; and lest he should be cut off from Dego, where lay considerable Austrian forces, he soon beat a disastrous retreat down the mountain roads, with a loss of nearly twenty-five hundred men in killed, wounded and missing. Augereau did not reach the field, as sundry movements of Piedmontese scouting parties up the Great Bormida valley called his attention thither, for fear the French left flank should be threatened; in fact, before reaching Carcare he retired upstream some distance lest the enemy should get in his rear. Serurier at Garessio contented himself with his role of containing the Piedmontese by a feigned attack.

Having found Voltri abandoned, and learning of the combat at Montenotte, Beaulieu now threw up his initiative and strove to reach Dego by such mountain roads as were available. But his progress was necessarily slow, and he could do nothing to arrest the impending disaster.

For the nonce Argenteau was checked, and retired down the Erro valley in the effort to reach Dego by a circuit across the hills. He was followed by a party sent in pursuit by Laharpe. Bonaparte had crushed him by concentrating superior weight at the point of contact. Believing that the Austrian corps was quite neutralized and would not again advance, the young leader now saw that he might at least for a moment turn his attention to Colli. Assembling ten thousand men, the whole of Augereau's division with part of Massena's, he sent them *via* Millesimo towards Montezemolo on the road to Ceva; and meanwhile Serurier, learning Napoleon's advance, also worked his way down the Tanaro; seeking with his left to envelop the enemy's right, and with his right to reach out towards the French forces heading for Montezemolo. Laharpe, and Massena with what was left of his division, marched across the hills to Dego, to fend the Austrians off from interfering with the attack on Colli, and perhaps to push on to Acqui, which they could now threaten down both the valley of the Little Bormida and that of the Erro.

In order to co-operate with Beaulieu, Colli should not have leaned his right on Millesimo, but on Dego. It was not necessary to stand astride the highway in order to protect Turin. At Dego he would have been covering the road to Milan, but he would have equally protected Turin, because he was lying on the flank of any column moving towards that capital. And at Dego he could not have been so speedily cut apart from his allies.

On the morning of the 13th Augereau struck the left wing of the Piedmontese, as he was marching on the pass of Millesimo.

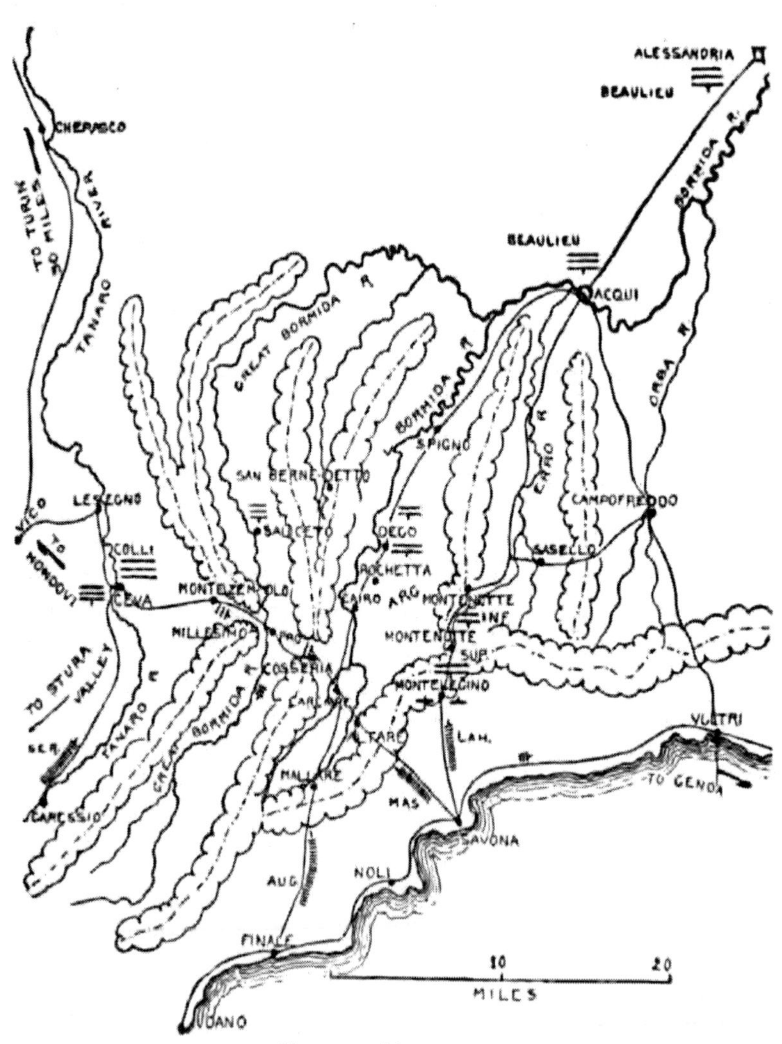

Battle of Montenotte

Provera, in command there and at Saliceto, in a commendable effort to maintain connection between the allied armies, and recognizing the importance of holding himself at the upper waters of the two Bormidas until the allies could assemble their forces, had sent part of his men back to Colli, and with part had thrown himself into the ancient castle of Cosseria, in which, as it lay between the valleys of the Great and Little Bormida, he hoped to arrest the French columns in their attempt to advance down towards the plain. And here he held himself stanchly for a day and a night, for Augereau could not advance another step until he had taken the place. To clear the way, Augereau attacked, and Bonaparte soon brought up a brigade to his aid. Provera resisted two stout assaults; but as Colli being unable to reach him, he could receive neither reinforcements nor further orders, want of water and ammunition compelled him next day to surrender with fifteen hundred men. The Piedmontese army being also for the moment neutralized by the French capture of the head-water passes, so that Colli would be more apt to look to his own safety than strive to assist his allies, Bonaparte now sharply turned on Dego, to meet a fresh Austrian column which he heard was on the way thither, and by taking and holding this key-point to fully secure the French right in further operations against the Piedmontese. Dego was in the hands of some three thousand Austrians, and Laharpe and Massena were already in its front. There had been ample time, while Provera held Cosseria, for the Austrians to reinforce Dego, but Beaulieu was not only slow by nature, he was hampered by bad roads. Until the French could drive the Piedmontese back on the Stura, Dego was of the utmost importance; and the force had been placed there by Beaulieu's orders, to hold the town as an outpost until he could for further operations concentrate at Acqui, whither from the Bocchetta country he had betaken himself on hearing of Bonaparte's sudden onslaught on Argenteau. His advance on the French right at Voltri had been quite suspended. Bonaparte had snatched the initiative from his hand.

The assault on Dego, with its six hillocks each crowned by a redoubt, began at noon of April 14. Bonaparte pushed in from the direction of Cosseria to aid Massena and Laharpe, and between them the place, with nearly all the garrison and eighteen guns, fell to the French by evening. Thus in these two days, the French had, as they claimed, won two smart combats, which are usually called the Battle of Millesimo, and inflicted on the enemy a loss of six thousand men, killed, wounded and missing, thirty guns and five

DORA B R
IVREA
ROMAINO
ORCA R
CHIUSELLA
CHIVASSO
VERCELLI
NOVARA
SESIA R
VERRUA
MONT CENIS
SUSE
EXILLES
DORA R
TURIN
CASALE
FENESTRELLA
BRIANCON
VALENTIA
ASTI
BESSIGNANO
PIGNEROLA
TAMARO R
ALESSANDRIA
MARENGO
NOVI
CAVI
AQUI
PO R
SALUCES
BORMIDA R
ERRO R
DEGO
SASSELLO
MONDOVI
CEVA
CAIRO
CONI
VICO
CARCARE
MONTENOTTE
ARGENTIERE
S. DALMAZZO
COL CADIBONA
SAVONA
ORMEA
GARESSIO
COL DI TENDA
FINALE
LOANO
BORCHETTO
ALBENCA
ALLASSIO
TENDA
TINEA R
GULF
GENOA
VAR R
ST REMO
PORT MAURICE
VINTIMILLE
NICE
MONACO
VILLAFRANCA
20

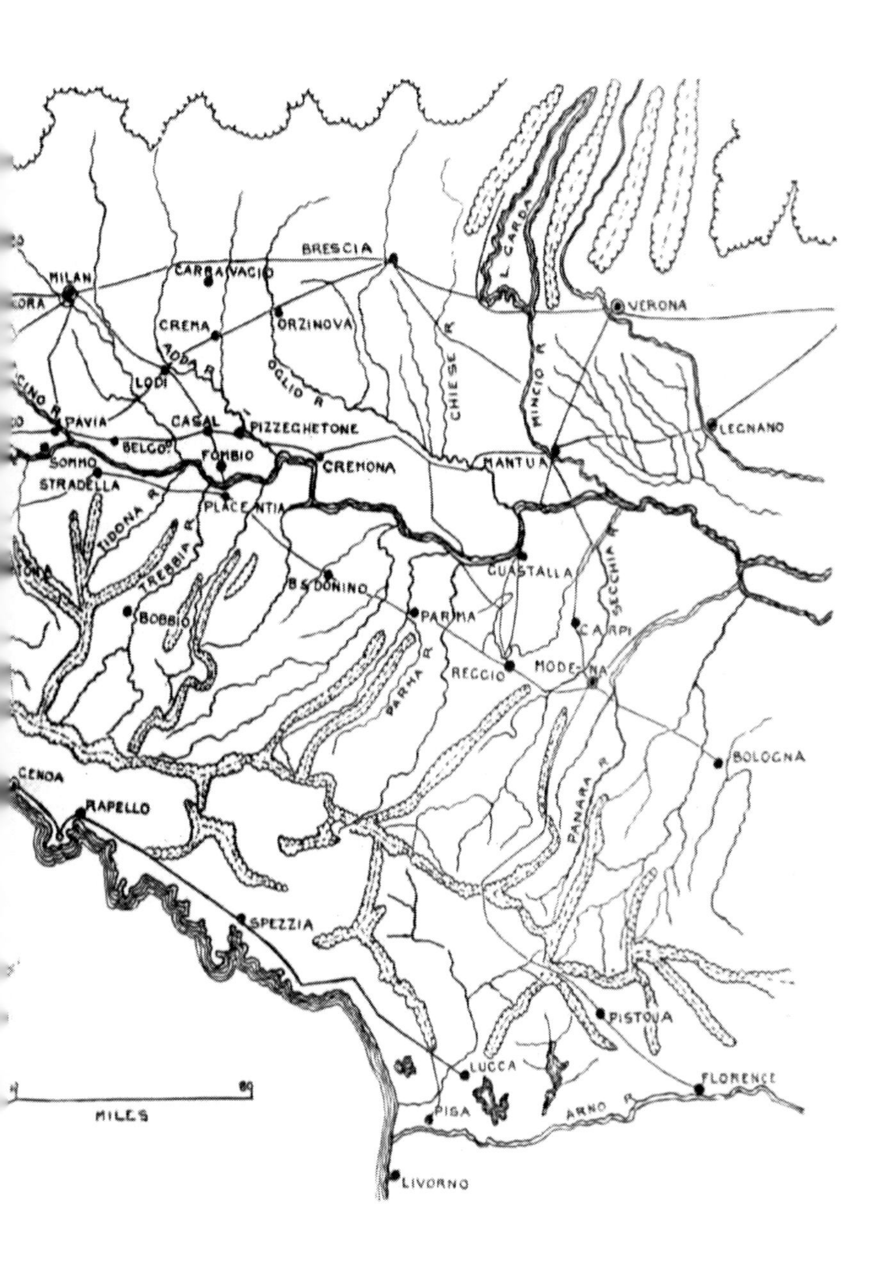
MILAN
BRESCIA
CARRAVACIO
CREMA
ORZINOVA
VERONA
ADDA R
OGLIO R
CHIESE R
MINCIO R
L. GARDA
LODI
PAVIA
CASAL
PIZZEGHETONE
LEGNANO
BELGO
FOMBIO
CREMONA
MANTUA
SOMMO
STRADELLA
PLACENTIA
TIDONA R
TREBBIA R
GUASTALLA
SECCHIA R
B S DONINO
BOBBIO
PARMA
CARPI
REGGIO
MODENA
PARMA R
BOLOGNA
PANARA R
GENOA
RAPELLO
SPEZZIA
PISTOIA
LUCCA
FLORENCE
PISA
ARNO R
LIVORNO
MILES
80

flags. The French loss was very much less. Bonaparte gives it at four hundred men; but owing to his intentionally perverse arithmetic, it is never possible to procure acceptable figures of the French casualties. They always have to be estimated.

Beaulieu was now fully cut off from Colli. Nothing but an advance in force sufficient to overwhelm the French could re-establish his connection with his ally on their original line.

From Dego Bonaparte returned to Carcare, determined to push in without delay on the Piedmontese and bring them to terms. Massena was ordered to gather his regiments and hold Dego; and by 8 a. m. of the 15th, with all the rest of his forces, Bonaparte was on the way back to Montezemolo. The cavalry was ordered up to Carcare, and Bonaparte felt secure as to his right flank.

But Dego was not safe yet. No sooner had Bonaparte turned his back then, owing to careless French outpost service and the absence on foraging of too large a party, an Austrian column of three thousand men, being five battalions from Sassello, under Wukassovich, who was to have reached the place for the fight of the 14th, but had been retarded by bad mountain roads, appeared before the town, and with a sudden dash, by 11 a. m. of the 15th had driven the French out. A rumour had reached Bonaparte that Beaulieu proposed in person to march on Dego, and before hearing from Massena of this new onset, he had already given Laharpe fresh orders to halt at Rochetta. So soon as he heard of the disaster, he hurried to the spot; about 2 p. m. the French again assumed the offensive, and drove out the Austrians with loss of a thousand men and eighteen guns, and pushed them back on Spigno. Lanusse especially distinguished himself; and here, too, Bonaparte first saw Lannes in action, and noticed his ardour. Dego was left in good hands. This last effort made the right flank safe; and on the left, on this same day, Serurier had marched down the Tanaro valley well towards Ceva, while Augereau, forcing in the Piedmontese, reached Montezemolo and established connection with his brother officer. Colli withdrew to his entrenched camp at Ceva.

In these four days Bonaparte had given the first illustration of the value of his mass-theory as opposed to the cordon system.

When from the heights of Montezemolo the French army contemplated the gigantic, snow-clad chain of the Alps, which they had faced with dread, but which now seemed to be behind them in their march, Bonaparte encouraged them with the remark, "Hannibal crossed the Alps; we have turned them!"

Personally the young commander had been omnipresent, galloping from column to column, cheering and directing every movement. Scarce Alexander could have excelled him in bodily efficiency. In a strategical sense be had worked so rapidly and skilfully as to convince Beaulieu that the French were superior in numbers, and to set that officer to concentrating all his forces at Acqui, not indeed for advance on his opponent, but for the bare protection of Lombardy. The Austrians had lost not far from ten thousand men; and the French blows had succeeded each other with such astonishing rapidity, and on such unexpected places, that the veteran Austrian commander was completely dazed. He had never conceived of such abnormal speed; it appeared to him quite outside the rules of the game of war; and he recognized too late that Colli was cut off from touch with his Austrians. Beaulieu was slow of thought, slower of action; Bonaparte was as rapid in both. Still on the 15th, himself delaying for neither rest nor food, while Beaulieu was wondering what he could do to meet this half-comprehended peril, Bonaparte made arrangements to take the Piedmontese left in reverse from Dego, while his own left should attack them in front It began to look as if this new strategist could actually bring the Piedmontese to sue for peace, as he had planned to do. He was taking Scherer at his word.

Of the two armies of the enemy, the Piedmontese was the one to attack first. It was manifestly useless to move against the Austrians. Beaulieu would have retired from the French advance, and have led them away from the main scheme. And Bonaparte was all the more intent on following up his success against Colli, lest the Piedmontese should retire to Turin and there delay him by a siege, for which he was ill-prepared, having neither siege-guns, material, nor equipment. Nor did he forget the difficulty Prince Eugene had laboured under in 1706, in his masterly operation up the Po against this capital city. In any event, whatever idea may have tempted Bonaparte to follow up his success against the Austrians instead of Colli he summarily dismissed, and kept in view his main and original plan: first, the separation of the allies; second, the forcing of a Piedmontese peace. Many a general fails by forgetting his first and better intention, and in being led astray by an unimportant gain to do what is not in natural strategic sequence. A sense of proportion, of the relative value of things, is one of the highest qualities in the captain—as in every other workman.

Though there seems to have been no further need of anxiety about the French right flank, yet Bonaparte, on April 16, joined part of the divisions of Laharpe and Massena in still another advance on Sassello. Just why this was done is not indicated by any contemporary evidence. It is probable that reports came in of further bodies of Austrian troops seeking a junction with Argenteau from Voltri. To lose no time, he seems to have left full orders for his other lieutenants to go on during his absence with the work cut out for them. On the 16th Augereau left Montezemolo, and reaching Ceva, attacked with marked vigour the redoubts in front of the entrenched camp of the Piedmontese near this city. The camp was held in force, and after several hours' hot work Augereau was thrown back. A second and a third assault met with the same fate; but soon Serurier and Massena came up to his aid, and each moved in from a direction to threaten one of the enemy's flanks. With this additional force the French had by evening ousted the enemy from his camp, and driven him back on the roads leading to Lesegno and Mondovi. Early on the 17th Serurier occupied the town of Ceva and invested the citadel. On the 16th also Laharpe was called back from Dego and left at San Benedetto to observe the Austrians, and Steingel's cavalry, as useless in the mountains as it would now be valuable in the plain, was added to Serurier's column. Headquarters was changed to Saliceto.

This section of country is cut up by watersheds, all running substantially northeast and southwest, and in each valley between these watersheds flows a torrential stream. Behind any one of these rivers was an opportunity for the Piedmontese to make a strong defence; but Colli seemed to have no such thought. He had too hearty a fear for Turin. As for Bonaparte, having apparently neutralized Beaulieu for good, he could begin in earnest his attack upon Colli. On April 18 Serurier moved towards San Michele, seeking to turn Colli's right flank and cut him off from Mondovi; Augereau, with part of his division, marched about his left flank *via* Castellino; Massena's division, accompanied by Bonaparte, moved up to Ceva. Bonaparte could now more accurately ascertain Colli's position, and issue his orders with a precision hitherto impossible. Some of Augereau's troops were placed under Massena, who was ordered to Lesegno; the remaining part of Augereau's division which had not been dispatched to Castellino was pushed on to the Monbarcaro gap, to head off any possible approach of the Austrians up the Bormida valley. Thither also Laharpe was ordered, a brigade only of his division being left to occupy Ceva, with a rearguard out at Cairo to connect with Dego.

Passing the Tanaro, Massena marched to Lesegno before daylight on April 19, while Serurier was ordered across the Cursaglia at Torre,

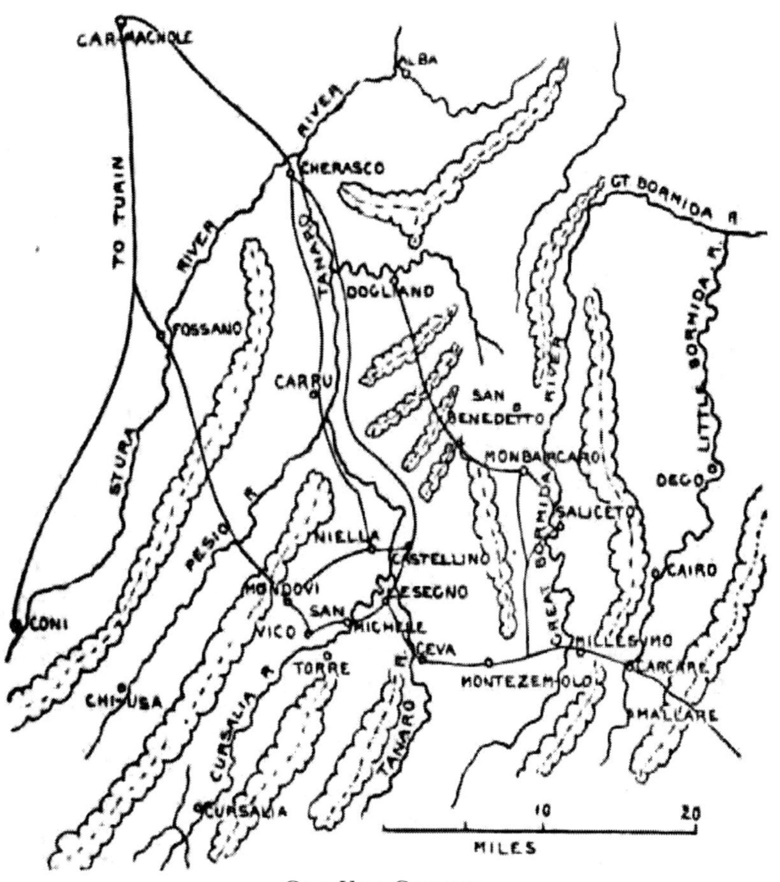

Ceva-Vico Country

to turn by a longer circuit the right flank of the enemy, who, since his fight at Ceva, lay behind that stream with his right leaning on Vico. From here Serurier was to push on to Mondovi. Collins position was a good one—on the high and steep left bank of the Cursaglia. He had broken all the bridges and erected strong field-works. Here Bonaparte attacked him the same day, Serurier falling on the position from the left, while Massena moved up in front, and Augereau around the right flank of the enemy. Massena's front and Augereau's flank attack, owing to the difficulties of the ground to be passed over and the fact that the river was not fordable, proved fruitless; and Colli, drawing from his left to reinforce his right, threw back Serurier, who had fought his way across the stream, with loss. The Piedmontese on this day claimed the victory with a show of right.

The French troops had long been ill-fed, were wearied with fast marching and heavy fighting, and needed rest; but as Bonaparte could not sit down after a backset, lest he should encourage the Piedmontese to continue the struggle and give the Austrians time to resume their advance, he made preparations on April 20 for a renewed attack on Collins position for the morning of the 21st, manoeuvring to find a weak spot, and throw the enemy off his guard. He proposed to force his way to Mondovi, and by a turning manoeuvre compel Colli to vacate his strong position. But Colli had little stomach left for battle; he and his Piedmontese did not await another attack, but retired through Mondovi towards Fossano. Early on April 22 the French in pursuit reached the rear of the retiring Piedmontese, and a lively combat began in the village of Vico. Guyeux moved round to the left towards Mondovi; Fiorella and Dommartin attacked the centre. Colli made no great defence, and abandoned the field of battle with a loss of one thousand men and eighteen guns, and the French entered Mondovi at night. Gallant Steingel was killed in the pursuit. On reaching Mondovi Bonaparte took a short survey of the situation, gave orders for further operations, and then, with his usual extraordinary activity, rode back to Lesegno to hurry forward his troops and material.

On April 22 the French army lay on the line Mondovi-Niella-Castellino. Bonaparte was not certain as to what Colli might do, and his troops had, by their wonderful exertions, earned some hours for rest and for realigning the divisions. But the respite was short. All through his campaigns Napoleon called on his troops for the same exertions that Frederick demanded from his. Exceptional situations must be met by exceptional exertions; and on the 23rd he pushed Serurier

Augereau

Kilmaine

Berthier

Clerfayt

Serurier

Barras

forward on the road to Fossano beyond the Pesio, to harry Colli's rear, and Massena on that to Cherasco near the Tanaro; Augereau moved to Dogliano, and Laharpe in reserve next day came up to Niella. Colli still had the strongest of his positions on the Stura, with the fortress of Coni on his right and Cherasco on his left; but his sense of resistance had been broken. He had small mind to keep the field. On April 25 Serurier was in Fossano, Massena in Cherasco, and Augereau at Alba. Macquart and Garnier were ordered on Coni to capture the place. Colli retired to Carmagnole. Here he resigned from the Piedmontese, and later entered the Austrian service.

There had been a great deal of pillaging by the long-starved, ill-clad French troops, and the Piedmontese common folk were incensed at this treatment by the men who came in the guise of friends to wreak woe upon them. Bonaparte determined to stop this by summary means, and issued orders to punish every soldier caught in pillage. He always used the resources of the country he traversed to the utmost extent, but at this period he was strenuous to stop excesses by the men, not only for the effect on a perhaps friendly population, but principally because it loosened all the bonds of discipline. "I will restore order, or cease to command these robbers," said he at this time. Not even as a reward for the great exertions of his men could he tolerate the evil, which had grown beyond all bounds. On the 22nd of April he published an order on the subject which deserves attention. It has no uncertain sound. The "morality" referred to applies, of course, only to courage and discipline.

Order
Headquarters
Lesegno
8 Floréal, Year IV
The general-in-chief expresses to the army his satisfaction with its bravery, and with the successes it obtains every day over the enemy; but he sees with horror the frightful pillage indulged in by wicked men, who straggle behind their corps until after the battle, so as to devote themselves to excesses most dishonouring to the army and the French name.
Consequently he orders:

1. The general, chief of staff, to make him within twenty-four hours a report on the moral conduct of the adjutants-general and other officers attached to the staff.

2. The generals of division will send within twenty-four

hours to the general-in-chief a note on the morality of the superior officers who have been under their orders since the opening of the campaign.

3. The chief commissary in charge will make the same report on the conduct of the war commissaries.

4. The general-in-chief reserves the right to decide with regard to the superior officers or war commissaries against whom complaints are made.

5. The chiefs of brigade, the chiefs of battalion, will assemble at the quarters of the general of the brigade; they will make a note of the officers of each half-brigade, and of the moral conduct they have shown since the opening of the campaign. The general of brigade will forward this note to the general of division, accompanied by his remarks.

The generals of division are authorized summarily to cashier and even to send in confinement to the castle of Fort Carré, at Antibes, the officers who by their example authorized the horrible pillage which has been going on for several days.

The generals of division are authorized, according to circumstances, to have summarily shot the officers or soldiers who, by their example, shall excite others to pillage, and thereby destroy discipline, introduce disorder in the army, and compromise its safety and glory.

Every officer or non-commissioned officer who has not followed his flag, and who without a legitimate reason is found absent at the moment of a combat, shall be dismissed, and his name shall be sent to his department, in order that he shall be branded in the opinion of his fellow-citizens as a coward.

Every soldier who shall be convicted of having remained away from his flag (*i.e.*, straggled) twice in succession, shall be published in orders.

Every soldier who shall be convicted of not having been in one combat shall lose his rank of seniority, and shall be carried on the roll at the foot of the company, and if he be a grenadier or *carbineer*, he shall be stricken from the company roster. A soldier who shall be convicted of being absent twice from a combat shall be degraded at the head of the battalion; he shall be stripped of his uniform, and he shall be sent beyond the Var to mend the roads as long as the campaign shall last.

The commanders of battalions, or of companies, when they

are detached, will make the report to the superior officer commanding the column, who will order the above punishment, and report the same to the general of division.

The generals of division, the generals of brigade and the chiefs of the corps are held responsible for the execution of the present order.

By order of the General-in-Chief

This order accomplished its end. Bonaparte shortly wrote the Directory:

Everything goes well. Pillaging is less. This first thirst of an army deprived of everything is being quenched. The wretches are excusable. After having groaned three years on the summit of the Alps, they arrive in the promised land, and they want to taste it. I have had three shot, and have put six at work with the pickaxe beyond the Var.

The proclamation which was issued April 26 was aimed to convey a political hint to Piedmont, to encourage the army, and to threaten those who plundered. As thoroughly Napoleonic, it also is quoted entire.

Headquarters
Cherbasco
7 Floréal, Year IV

Soldiers! In a fortnight you have won six victories, taken twenty-one flags, fifty-five guns, several strong places, and conquered the richest part of Piedmont; you have taken fifteen thousand prisoners and killed or wounded more than ten thousand men! You had been fighting for sterile rocks, illustrated by your courage, but useless to the country; today you equal, by your services, the Army of Holland and the Rhine. Deprived of everything, you have supplied everything; you have gained battles without guns, crossed rivers without bridges, made forced marches without shoes, bivouacked without brandy and often without bread; republican phalanxes, soldiers of liberty alone were capable of enduring what you have endured! Thanks be to you, soldiers! The grateful country will owe you its prosperity; and if, victors of Toulon, you foretold the immortal campaign of 1796, your present victories foretell a yet finer one.

The two armies which recently attacked you with audacity are fleeing in terror before you; the perverse men who laughed at your misery, and rejoiced in their thought of the triumph of your enemies, are confounded and trembling.

But, soldiers, you have as yet done nothing, because things remain for you to do. Neither Turin nor Milan are yours: the assassins of Basseville yet tread upon the ashes of those who vanquished the Tarquins.

At the opening of the campaign you were naked of all things; today you are abundantly supplied. The storehouses taken from the enemy are numerous. The siege and light artillery has arrived. Soldiers, the country has the right to expect great things of you: will you justify its expectations? The greatest obstacles are overcome, no doubt; but you have yet combats to deliver, towns to take, rivers to pass. Are there any among you whose courage will weaken? Are there any among you who prefer to return and bear patiently, on the summits of the Alps and the Apennines, the insults of soldiers enthralled? No! There is none among the victors of Montenotte, Millesimo, Dego and Mondovi! All burn to bear to distant parts the glory of the French people, all wish to humiliate the haughty kings who thought to put irons upon us; all desire to dictate a glorious peace which shall indemnify the fatherland for the immense sacrifices it has made. You all wish, in returning to your villages, to be able to say with pride: "I was of the conquering Army of Italy."

Friends, I promise you this conquest; but there is a condition you must swear to fulfil, and that is, to respect the peoples which you deliver; to repress the horrible pillaging in which indulge some wretches encouraged by our enemies. Without this you would not be the liberators of the peoples, you would be their scourge; you would not be the honour of the French people, it would disavow you; your victories, your courage, your successes, the blood of your brothers who have died in battle, all would be lost, even honour and glory. As for me and the generals who have your confidence, we should blush to command an army without discipline, without rein, which knew no law but force. But, invested with the national authority, strong with justice and law, I shall know how to make the small number of men lacking courage and heart respect the laws of humanity and honour which they trample under foot; I shall not suffer brigands to soil your laurels; I will carry out with vigour the rules I have published in orders.

Pillagers will be pitilessly shot; several have already been, and I have had occasion to remark with pleasure the alacrity with which the good soldiers of the army have sought to carry out the orders.

Peoples of Italy, the French army comes to break your bonds! The French people is the friend of all peoples! Come confidently to meet it! Your property, your religion and your customs will be respected. We wage war like generous enemies; we bear ill-will to none except the tyrants who enslave you!
Bonaparte

That all the calculations of the new commander of the Army of Italy were accurate was clearly proved on the 23rd, while the columns were crossing the Pesio, by the arrival of a dispatch from Turin praying for a truce. It has been said that the truce was first suggested by Bonaparte, and that Turin promptly replied. But so limited by the Directory was the army leader that he had no power even to agree to an armistice, and did so only on the surrender of some fortresses. On the 28th the truce was signed at Cherasco, after an interview with Generals Latour and Beauregard, to whom had been given power to treat. At the meeting Bonaparte bore himself in a courteous, but cold and haughty manner. For the first time he had led an army; for the first time he had conducted negotiations of the highest importance; and in both, the wonderful character which dominated all who met him, in the cabinet or the field, came at once to the fore. He told the procrastinating envoys that the army had orders to advance at 2 p. m., and that, while he might lose battles, he would not be taxed with losing minutes. Quite browbeaten, the envoys signed the truce. The French leader was glad thus to put a glorious term to this his first campaign, especially as it neutralized one of the armies he had to meet, and enabled him to turn in force against the other. It was a welcome crowning of a series of victories, glorious and fruitful, but which yet left the French in far from a secure situation; and Bonaparte was fortunate in being able to impose on the enemy the surrender of two out of three fortresses,—Coni, Alessandria and Tortona,—and to insist that negotiations for a permanent peace should at once be begun. And the terms he informed the Directory they could prescribe, as he possessed the certain means of enforcing them. He wrote to Paris:

The King of Sardinia will be obliged to make a peace such as you wish to dictate to him because, independently of the coun-

> try comprised between Coni, Cherasco, Alba and Alessandria, we have the town and the fortress of Coni, and the towns and the fortresses of Tortona and Alessandria. . . . You can dictate, as masters, peace to the King of Sardinia.

So soon as the armistice was signed, Coni and Tortona were delivered over to the French. This armistice served the Directory as the basis of the Treaty of Paris, which was executed in that capital. May 15. Alessandria and Tortona were to remain in French hands during the war, Susa, La Brunette and Exiles were to be razed, and Piedmont agreed to keep open the routes over the Mont Cenis and Argentière for French uses.

Colonel Murat, first *Aide-de-Camp*, was sent to Paris with the flags and papers, as Junot had been dispatched from Millesimo. The French legislature decreed on five separate occasions that the Army of Italy had "well deserved of the country" during this short campaign.

In order that there should be no halfway measures about the negotiations, Bonaparte continued to push on towards Turin, the Piedmontese retiring before him, and on April 27 the French army crossed the Stura. Next day orders were issued providing garrisons for all the strong places taken or surrendered, as a base for further operations; for so disposing the army as to head it towards Tortona; and for Macquart's and Grenier's divisions to march in *via* Coni, as reinforcements to the Army of Italy. Bonaparte would thus have, after deducting garrisons, a force of thirty-five thousand men under the colours with which to march against Beaulieu, who had but twenty-six thousand effective left for field service. The French now possessed the advantage of numbers.

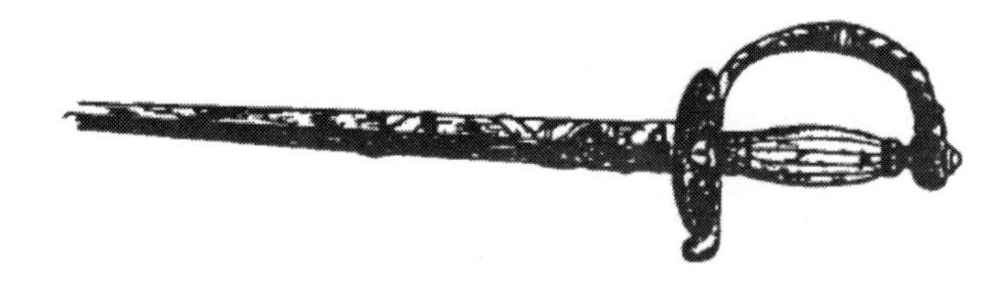

Chapter 9

Lombardy

April 28-May 14, 1796

In two weeks Bonaparte had done what the Army of Italy had striven for years to do. In these few days he had rectified the bad position of the Army of Italy, he had fed and encouraged it, he had beaten the Austrian army, nearly equal to his own in numbers, and had forced peace on Piedmont; he had opened a free line of operations, and had swept the ground in his front clean. He had worked in concentrated masses. He had led these against the decisive points; and with weaker forces, whenever he came in contact with the enemy, he had outnumbered him. So soon as he had divided the allies, he held one with small forces and advanced in mass against the other. In what he had done resided the whole theory of modern war. Beaulieu crossed the Po, and placed himself so as to defend it. Bonaparte feigned a crossing opposite Valencia, quietly massed his army, marched rapidly down river to Placentia, where he passed, thus turned Beaulieu's left, beat his outlying parties, and forced him to summary retreat With an audacity which enheartened his troops, he stormed the bridge of Lodi, defeated the Austrian rearguard, and drove the army into a hasty withdrawal to the Mincio. Thus Lombardy was also conquered in a bare two weeks, as Piedmont had been. The Directory now suggested that the army be divided, and that Bonaparte should move with part of it down the peninsula. This he declined to do, and the Directory annulled the order. In a month Bonaparte had won several sharp combats, three well-contested battles, made twelve thousand prisoners, taken several fortresses and two capitals, detached Piedmont from the Coalition, overrun Lombardy and opened the road into Italy through Savoy. So magnificent a piece of campaigning had not been seen since Leuthen.

In two weeks Bonaparte had accomplished more than the Army of Italy under its former commanders had done in four campaigns. The masterful grasp with which he had under-taken his work was in correct sequence to the exhaustive preparations he had undergone by his study of the terrain and the conditions, while in his poverty, years before, he was preparing his *Memorial on the Army of Italy*. Neither Alexander nor Hannibal had set to work with a firmer hand than the young French general who was destined to follow in their footsteps. The strategic situation of the army had been a false one. Strung out along the Maritime Alps, with an English fleet in his rear, and confronted by two powerful armies; with his line of communications running out from his left flank and in prolongation of his front; liable to be cut off from Nice and Marseilles by a strong column of Piedmontese with which any enterprising commander might debouch from the Colle di Tenda, the Army of Italy could hardly have been in more parlous case. Out of this danger, in two weeks' time. Napoleon had wrought a marvellous situation: he had beaten one of his enemies, practically equal in force to his own army, and had thrown him back into Lombardy; he had forced the other to sue for peace, and to surrender two of his fortresses; and he had opened a free line of retreat in rear of his centre, and had swept for himself a clean front from Saluzzo to Savona. Though outnumbered by the enemy, wherever he had struck him he had put more men into fighting contact. He had developed his paper theory of action by masses in actual manoeuvres on the field, and he had again and again demonstrated the exceptional marching power of the French soldier. As Jomini's rules put it, in *The Fundamental Principles of War:*

> Bonaparte had by strategic calculation led the mass of his forces against the decisive points of the theatre of war, usually the communications of the enemy, and this without endangering his own; and he had so manoeuvred that he had hurled the mass of his force against divided portions of the enemy.

In 1794 Bonaparte said:

> To conduct war is like besieging a fortress; you must unite your fire against one point. When a breach is made, the balance is broken, all other work is useless, and the fortress is taken. . . . You must not divide your attacks, but unite them.

And on first meeting Moreau in 1799, when that able soldier asserted that it was always the greater force that beat the lesser, Bonaparte agreed with him; but, said he:

> . . . with the lesser force you can, by rapidity and skill, hurl the greater force on the enemy, and by successive attacks on different points by your mass, always retain the advantage of numbers.

To be thus superior in numbers at the point of fighting contact is the basis of Napoleon's conduct of war; but it requires a Napoleonic coup d'œil, speed and decision to carry it out. Frederick enunciated the same idea and acted on it; and both Alexander and Hannibal, because always outnumbered, were compelled to act on the theory. During the American Civil War, partly owing to their interior lines, often to better management, the Confederates as a rule had as many men at the point of contact, tactically if not strategically, as the numerically superior Federals. Especially was this true in Virginia. What is needed is an eye to see the key of the field, and moral courage to disregard everything else, and to push in straight and hard upon the one essential point, affording the opponent no leisure to take advantage of any opening one may thus give him. When Bonaparte had concluded the entire campaign of 1796-97, and was dictating terms to Austria on her own territory, he said:

> Many good generals exist in Europe, but they see too many things at once; I see but one thing, and that is the masses; I seek to destroy them, sure that the minor matters will fall of themselves.

Here, then, he closed his eyes to Beaulieu at Genoa and to Colli watching the Tenda pass, merely leaving a suitable force under a good commander to contain each of them; and from April 11 to 15 he destroyed the allied centre by the superior mass he hurled upon it; whereupon both the Piedmontese and the Austrians yielded up Genoa and Ceva. Napoleon always made keen political guesses subserve his strategy; he knew that Savoy hoped for accessions of territory from the Milanese; and he was wise in divining that the Piedmontese and Austrians would not long hold together when once strategically severed, but that the former would think first of the safety of their own country. This they did, though from a military standpoint their real safety lay in a junction with the Austrians and the delivery of one great battle, in which their total numbers would have told.

Again, as soon as Beaulieu was neutralized, acting on the same theory, Bonaparte pushed his mass in on Colli, merely containing the Austrians with a small force. From the 17th to the 23rd was all the time he needed to force the Piedmontese to sue for peace. He even drew from the force left to watch the Austrians, so soon as he saw that Beaulieu was so stunned as to be apt to keep quiet, and that the immediate theatre of operation was getting distant from him. This was one of those risks which tells, but which only the active, able leader dares assume. He concentrated to fight, and in time for action, just as he was wont to separate to feed the army. Add to all this his scrupulous care in the matter of supplies, his protection of his base, his untiring labour and his disciplinary measures, and we have a picture which no other modern captain has given us at the opening of his career.

In his dispatches home, Bonaparte greatly exaggerated matters in his own favour; but this is the common prerogative of the campaigning leader. He wrote April 29 and May 1:

> The combined armies were eighty-five thousand strong, I have beat them with thirty-five thousand men all told. . . . Beaulieu flees so fast that we cannot catch him; . . . he told the King of Sardinia that he would not unshoe himself until he reached Lyon; but he is not on the road thither.

Yet while his attitude towards the Directory was strong and self-confident, he never failed in showing good-will in word as well as deed. "Be sure that we shall do everything that is feasible," he wrote.

No sooner had Bonaparte accomplished this first success than he began to urge the Directory at home to add at least a part of the Army of the Alps to his own, and to send him reinforcements to complete the great work. His tone in addressing the Directory was that of a successful man, who proposed to make himself necessary. Instead of sitting down on his laurels, he at once looked forward to fresh ones. While waiting for the truce to be ratified, he wrote the Directory April 28:

> I march tomorrow against Beaulieu. I shall force him back across the Po; I shall immediately follow him over; I shall take possession of all Lombardy; and before a month, I hope to be on the mountains of the Tyrol, to find the Army of the Rhine, and with it to carry the war into Bavaria. This project is worthy of you, of the army, and of the destinies of France.
>
> If you continue to give me your confidence, and you approve these projects, I am sure of the result: Italy is yours.
>
> I have justified your confidence.
>
> I shall constantly seek to give you proofs of zeal.

These phrases from his letters speak the man's purpose as well as his independence.

Among other failings Beaulieu was wanting in enterprise. He might at an early day have struck Bonaparte's rear by an advance on Laharpe at San Benedetto, and thus have seriously hampered the French operations; and in fact, by April 26 he rather feebly set out to do this thing, but it was then too late; and shortly hearing of the truce, he gave up any idea of a counter-blow.

Having failed in an attempt to get possession of Alessandria and Tortona, and thus to retain a foothold on the right bank of the Po, Beaulieu retired before the advancing French, and on May 1 crossed the Po at Valencia, where, breaking the bridge, he took up a position at Valeggio, and along the Ogogno near Lomello, with van out at the Sesia, and detached parties along the Po down to the mouth of the Ticino. He thought he might hold the line of the Po, especially with his excess of cavalry. This was, however, a task which as a general proposition was impossible of accomplishment, unless for the temporary purpose of giving battle on favourable terms whenever the French should cross the river. Colli, now one of his lieutenants, was stationed at Buffalora, to hold the road to Milan against an attack from the west; and a force was placed at Sommo to protect the left. To defend Milan, which was his first duty, Pavia on the Ticino would have been a better town to hold in force; but Beaulieu did not suppose the French would undertake to march across neutral Parma, to which the territory here on the south bank of the Po belonged. Bonaparte had cleverly inserted in the negotiations with the Piedmontese an article giving the army permission to cross the Po near Valencia, without having the remotest intention of so doing; and into this crude trap the enemy fell. Beaulieu imagined that Bonaparte would attack him in front, and the latter did all he could to encourage the error, making a marked show of forcing a passage at Cambio. On May 2, when the Austrian commander retired behind the Ogogno, Massena was near Castellaccio, Laharpe at Rivalta, Augereau in the rear; and the army headquarters was at Bosco, while Serurier was still a full day's march behind, at Alba. All this, so far as he knew of it, had a distinct appearance to Beaulieu of a French passage nearby his front. The Austrian general would have defended the Po to better advantage against a manoeuvring army by a position astride the river connected by several good bridges near Stradella. This would have compelled the Army of Italy to cross above, and have left Beaulieu both the Ticino and the Po as defensive barriers.

Beaulieu's having crossed the Po at Valencia gave Bonaparte just the chance he desired and had hoped for; he had no idea of forcing a river almost as formidable as the Rhine in the face of a numerous army not yet defeated in one body in battle, nor of successively forcing several other streams, when, by a speedy and well-calculated manoeuvre, he might turn them all. He could now without danger move down the Po on the right bank, take possession of a large territory which could be made tributary to the French army; cross at any one of several places farther below, and take Beaulieu and his army completely in reverse. This, too, by rapidity and skill he might manage secretly, and have his crossing of the great river unopposed. He feared the enemy's horse more than any other thing.

"If I have any chances to run in Lombardy, it is on the score of the enemy's cavalry," he wrote the Directory April 29; and "The Austrians are redoubtable only for their cavalry, of which they have six thousand," he later said.

> From headquarters, now moved to Tortona, Bonaparte on May 8 ordered an élite corps, made up of four grenadier and two carbineer battalions and fifteen hundred cavalry, to be ready May 5; and these as a van he proposed should seize on the crossing-point he aimed at; but meanwhile he kept up an active semblance of preparation to force the river near Valencia, by pushing his divisions to the neighbourhood of Sale and Castelnuovo, by taking possession of all the boats he could gather, and by writing to the governor of Alessandria that a division would surely cross at that point—which misinformation soon reached the Austrian commander, and was credited in full. All communication with the left bank was then cut off, and Beaulieu, completely in the dark, strove to hold all the territory north of the Po, by distributing his forces in small parties all along the threatened river. He was doing everything in his power to aid Bonaparte in his projected operation, and yet what he did was strictly in accordance with the rules of his precious cordon system, which in those days was a positive disease. While on the 4th the six élite battalions above named assembled at Casteggio under General Dallemagne, and were joined by the cavalry and six guns, the army was being secretly prepared for a rapid march by the right down the Po.

Bonaparte here began to show his peculiar force of apprehension and character. Having gauged his opponent and his weaknesses, and

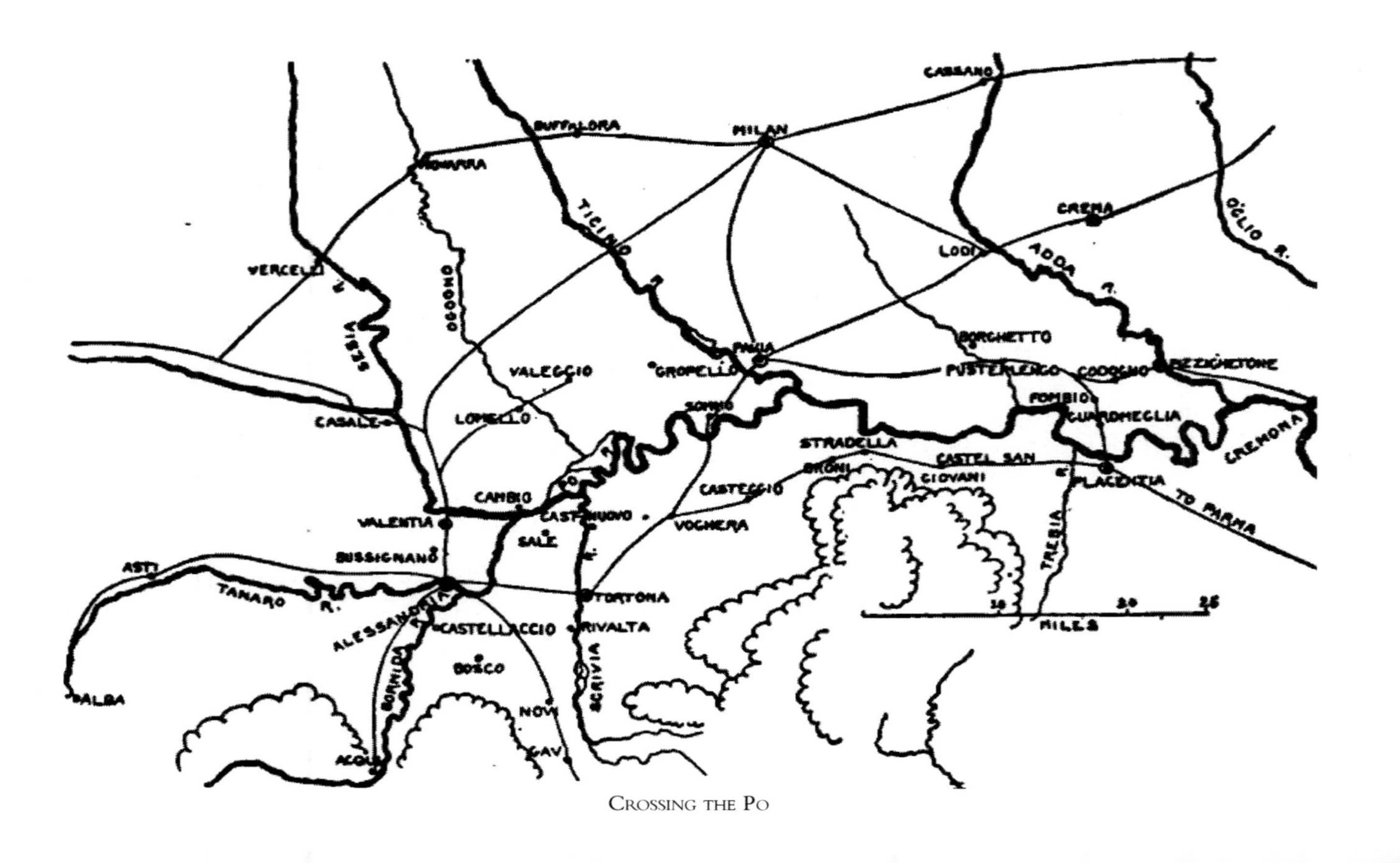

Crossing the Po

feeling that he could certainly rely on his committing those errors into which he chose to lead him, and which were essential to his own success, he forged ahead with his plan, never doubting that Beaulieu would second the French manoeuvres. This would not have been wise, or indeed possible, with some generals in his front; but all great captains have habitually based their action on a knowledge of their opponent's strength or weakness, and this one never met an antagonist to whom he did not feel superior. At the beginning this self-reliance bred success; later in his career the virtue grew to an excessive fault, and bred failure. In some of the qualities of the great captain Napoleon outranked Frederick, but in one quality Frederick was markedly his superior: the king learned a lesson from each victory and each defeat; Napoleon was sometimes unteachable. Not to recognize defeat is in one sense the guiding strength of the great soldier; but it may be carried too far.

On the 6th of May Bonaparte headed his column for Placentia. Dallemagne reached Castel San Giovanni, Augereau Broni, Laharpe and the cavalry under Kilmaine got to the pass of Stradella. Serurier still stood opposite Valencia and Massena near Sale, and their presence kept the enemy from fathoming the French commander's design. With respect to this situation, Bonaparte wrote the Directory, May 6:

> If my movement on Placentia leads Beaulieu to vacate the Lumellina, I will quietly cross at Valencia. If Beaulieu remains twenty-four hours in ignorance of our march on Placentia, and I can find boats or material for rafts in that town, I will cross in the night.

In order to keep in touch with both his wings, Bonaparte retained his headquarters in Tortona, but was personally much at the front, while Berthier conducted the formal business. In this he had the further object to keep Beaulieu as long as possible subject to the delusion of a crossing near Valencia; for as, in order to succeed fully, he must steal the passage at Placentia, it was essential that Beaulieu should send no large body of troops thither. Throughout life Napoleon was fertile in this species of stratagem, and judged with great astuteness what would or what would not deceive the enemy.

It took all day of May 6 to determine how the conditions were shaping themselves, and the crossing had in effect to be done by daylight, and not by night as Bonaparte had intended. Late on the 6th, from Tortona, he ordered Massena to Voghera, Augereau to Castel San Giovanni, Dallemagne, with Laharpe in support, to Borgo

San Antonio, near Placentia, prescribing early morning hours for each division to start He himself came on to Castel San Giovanni, reconnoitred the neighbourhood and collected some boats. By 4 a. m. of May 7 Dallemagne started, reached Placentia by 9 a. m., and found on the farther side of the Po but a single squadron of Austrian horse. The column d'élite had marched from Tortona to Placentia, forty-four miles, in thirty-six hours. Upon the absence in force of the enemy being reported to headquarters, all the French divisions, which so far had been cautiously advanced for fear that the calculations might by some untoward accident be upset, were ordered by forced marches forward to Placentia. It was now certain that the passage could be effectuated here; and the town being on the right bank, the difficulties were much diminished. Lannes, "as brave as he is intelligent," then commanding a brigade under Dallemagne, was the first to cross with the van, and to put foot ashore; and by 2 p. m. Dallemagne had got over the rest of his detachment. Had the army been equipped with a pontoon bridge, Bonaparte could have dealt Beaulieu a fatal blow; as he was compelled to rely on boats and rafts alone, the passage was slow and laborious. Some flat-boats had been captured on the river above Placentia, carrying five hundred wounded Austrians and a large quantity of medical stores. There was also a big ferry-boat at Placentia, which could make a trip every half hour, with a considerable number of men and horses, across the river, which here is rapid and some quarter of a mile wide. The bridge did not get finished until the 9th. Laharpe's division was the first to follow Dallemagne. Bonaparte could truthfully write to Carnot:

> Beaulieu is disconcerted, he calculates rather ill, he falls constantly into the snares one lays for him. Perhaps he will wish to deliver battle, for the man has the audacity of madness and not of genius.

Cremona has been pointed out by many military critics as the better place to cross in order to cut off Beaulieu. But as Placentia was nearer and on the right bank, it was chosen rather than Cremona, though it is true that by crossing at the latter place the French would have got beyond the Adda. Moreover, time was of the essence in this manoeuvre.

As a matter of fact, expeditious and secret though the manoeuvre had been, Beaulieu had received abundant notice of the proposed crossing at Placentia to enable him, with the French army's accidental delays, to concentrate forces which could offer serious resistance to the operation. But he was all strung out in the effort to hold the Ticino with his right and extend to the lower Adda with his left, so as to protect Milan. He had no sense of perspective. He could not see that if the French crossed below him, Milan would still be compromised. Wise enough in his effort to hold the Adda, he was mistaken in his desire not to leave the Ticino. But Beaulieu naturally judged that an advance would now be made by the Army of the Alps in support of the Army of Italy. This indeed Bonaparte had been asking for, and it would have been good policy for the Directory to order it.

On hearing of the French appearance at various points down the river, Beaulieu, on May 4, ordered Liptay with five thousand men to march towards Pizzighetone to dispute any crossing the enemy might attempt, and especially to cover the Austrian communications with that city and Mantua. Sebottendorf marched to Pavia, and Beaulieu followed. Colli was left in Buffalora to fend off the expected attack by Kellermann.

Bonaparte utilized the enforced delay at Placentia in compelling the Duke of Parma to sign an armistice, to pay two million francs, and deliver up ten of his best museum pictures as purchase money for his neutrality; and to furnish, moreover, large supplies, and many horses for the artillery and cavalry. It was here Bonaparte systematically began that habit of collecting works of art from captured cities which has so wonderfully enriched the French capital. The Duke of Modena had fled to Venice, but his territory was none the less mulcted in ten millions of francs and twenty chefs-d'œuvre. Both these rulers had rather haughtily refused Bonaparte's recent overtures, and were treated with corresponding harshness.

Late on this same 7th of May the French advance on the north bank struck the head of the enemy's column, which the Austrian commander had ordered downstream, and which had been all too leisurely coming on. Liptay's van had reached Guardamiglia, and from here he managed to throw the French van back towards the river. But by May 8 Bonaparte, who had now got across enough men, pushed forward Lannes, who struck Liptay at Fombio, where the Austrians had collected twenty guns and entrenched. Dallemagne's grenadiers attacked on the right; Lanusse headed a column on the high-road; and Lannes fell to on the left. After a lively combat, Liptay was hustled back on Pizzighetone with loss of twenty-five hundred prisoners, some guns and three flags. "The success of the combat of Fombio is in great part due to the courage of the Chief of Brigade Lannes," reported Bonaparte. By night Laharpe had got to Codogno, and Dallemagne advanced towards Pizzighetone. About 10 p. m. a fresh Austrian de-

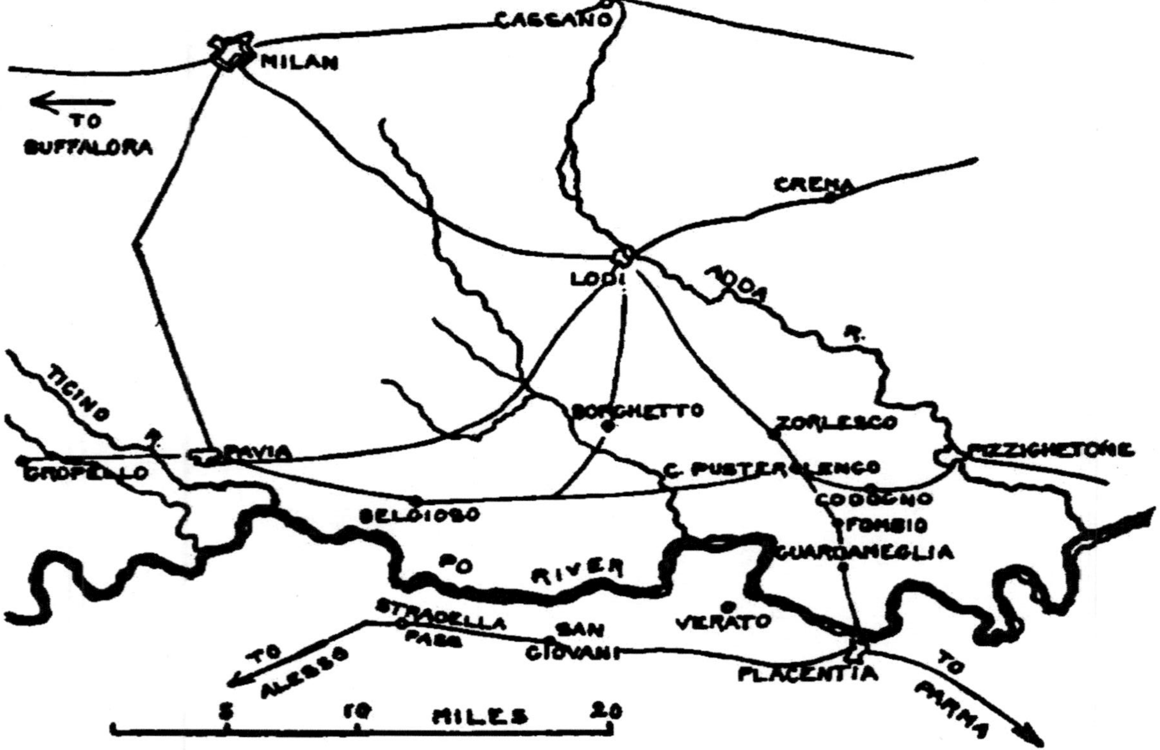

Placentia-Lodi Country

tachment, sent by Beaulieu from Belgiogoso, and coming from Casalpusterlengo, fell on Laharpe's outposts in the dark and came close to pushing them in. As ill fortune would have it, Laharpe, "a grenadier in height and heart," was killed by the fire of some of his own men, narrates the Order of the Day of May 9; and Menard received his division. Beaulieu had not only unduly spread out his main force, but had even divided the small body he had sent out to check the French crossing. When Bonaparte saw Beaulieu's awkward effort to arrest his advance, he was well satisfied that he would be able to concentrate on the north bank and meet the enemy on his own terms.

Curiously, Beaulieu had conceived the idea of a general engagement, and gave orders to this effect on May 8; but as the conditions gradually developed, he saw that he was not sufficiently concentrated to permit a battle, while the French were so; and during the night he changed the orders to his several divisions to such as would effect a withdrawal behind the Adda; and to protect this operation he stationed a force at Lodi, where there was an excellent bridge. His right under Colli, which had come down part way to Pavia, was compelled to make a detour; and it would scarcely have reached Cassano had Bonaparte been able to effect a quick passage of the Po. It consumed the 8th and up to the evening of the 9th for Massena and Augereau to complete the crossing (the latter, indeed, had to pass at Veratto, a few miles above), and they were then pushed forward on Lodi. Augereau reached Borghetto, Massena Casalpusterlengo, Dallemagne, who was now placed under Massena, got to Zorlesco, Menard to near Pizzighetone. On the 10th, at 3 a. m., Bonaparte reached Massena's division, pushed Dallemagne on Lodi, and on its being reported that the place was occupied, himself headed Augereau and Massena thither.

Beaulieu kept his main column on the march in retreat towards Cremona, where he hoped to establish a *point d'appui* on the Po below the point where Bonaparte had crossed; and he left Sebottendorf and ten thousand men as rearguard to hold Lodi until the main column could file past.

Having meanwhile masked Pizzighetone, and sent Serurier to Pavia to threaten Milan, and if possible to seize the Austrian magazines, and having thus protected his right and left, Bonaparte pushed on, and before noon on May 10 the French van reached Lodi, "with four pieces of light artillery which had just arrived, and which were drawn by the carriage horses of the lords of Placentia," as Bonaparte reported; and here they found the Austrian rearguard still on the right bank and holding the bridge, which Sebottendorf believed he could maintain or else destroy. Most of the Austrian force was at the end of the bridge on the farther bank. A detachment was at Corte del Palasio, where the stream was fordable, lest the French should attempt a passage there, and the cavalry was at Cadella Fontana, to protect the retreat of the rearguard, which it was expected might occur next day. Fourteen guns were trained on the bridge, supported by nine battalions. Curiously, Bonoparte, making the same error as at Jena, imagined that he had Beaulieu's main army in his front,—"Beaulieu with all his army was drawn up in line of battle,"—and determining to show his men that there were no obstacles for the Army of Italy, especially as he ran no strategic risk by failure, he at once prepared to seize Lodi out of hand and to force the passage, instead of turning the position. Throwing Dallemagne and his grenadiers upon the place, it was quickly ceded. Massena was coming up in his rear with six thousand men from Pusterlengo, Augereau with an equal number from Borghetto. The Austrians stationed in Lodi retired across the bridge, but the French so energetically followed them up that preparations for destroying the structure could not be completed. Bonaparte occupied the front of the town, and placed his artillery, as it arrived, on the overhanging right bank on the road along the river. Opening a cannonade which he kept up until the evening to gain time, and to enable the other divisions to come up, the French guns drove the Austrian batteries away from their post at the other end of the bridge. Beaumont with two thousand horse was sent upstream to cross at a ford near Montaraso and ride down on the Austrian right flank.

The young leader had already impressed himself on the Army of Italy in a wonderful fashion, but he concluded to storm the bridge as a further means of encouraging the troops. He " needed a stroke of vigour to affix the seal of individuality on his conduct; the occasion was good, and he seized it." The grenadiers were deployed into a deep column behind the Lodi walls, and at 7 p. m., with a battalion of *carbineers* at the head, debouched at a double-quick, and were hurled upon the bridge, which was dsome three hundred feet long, shouting "*Vive la Republique!*"

Met by a fire of grape and canister from the Austrian guns, which had been again brought up and well posted to command the bridge, the entire head of the column was swept away, and the brave grenadiers were brought to a pause; but they were instantly rallied by the valour of their general officers. Dallemagne was still at their head, Massena was close at hand; Berthier, Lannes, Cervoni rushed to the scene, and, filled with Gallic fury, led them on in their perilous task;

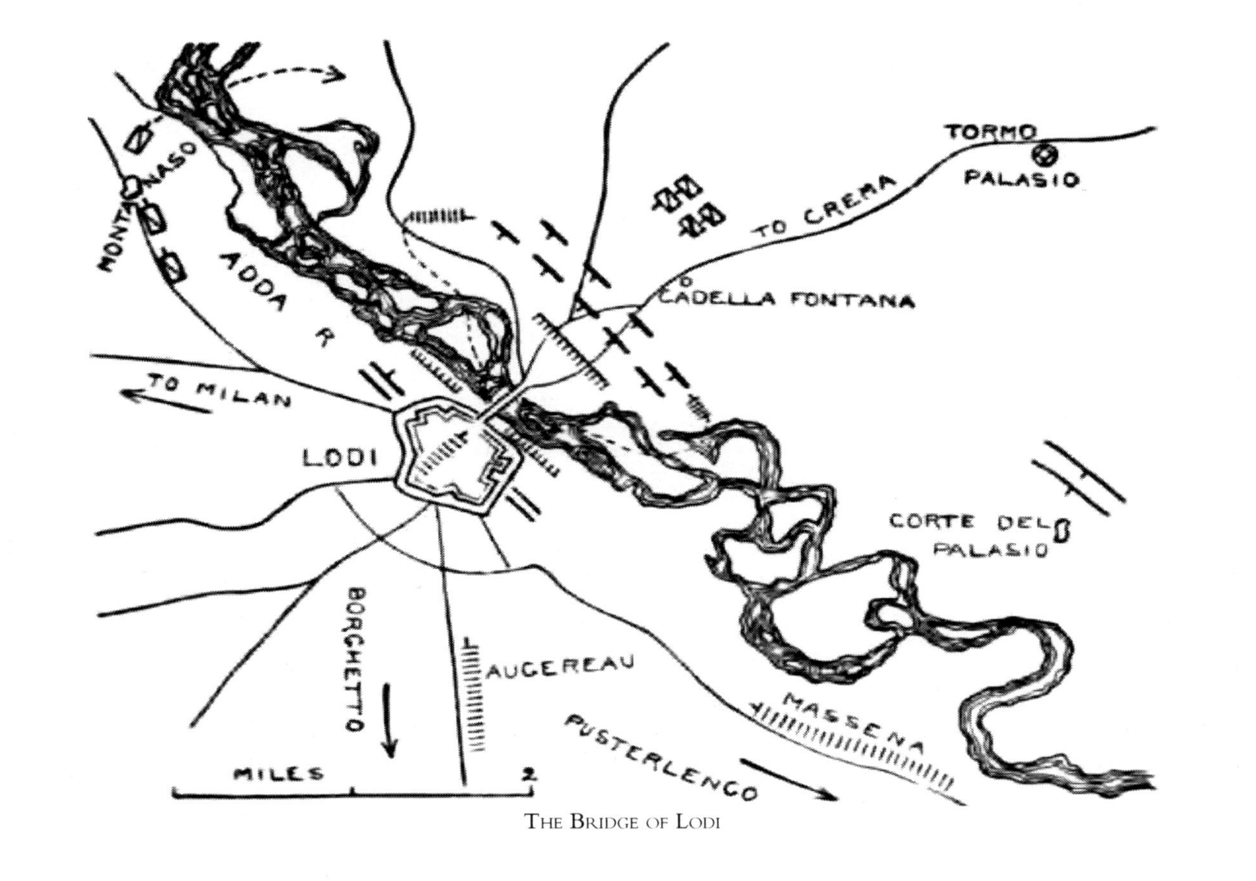

The Bridge of Lodi

when, promptly recovering their ardour, and making their way over the piles of dead and wounded men, these splendid battalions fell with rage upon the Austrian guns, bayoneted the artillerymen, and captured every piece. They were in their assault markedly aided by the diversion of a portion of their comrades, who, seeking a less murderous footing, had dropped from the timbers of the bridge upon islands in midstream up and down river, and then, finding they could wade to the farther bank, had formed as skirmishers, and, under cover of the bank, had taken the Austrians in reverse by a lively fire. The first Austrian line having been broken, the grenadiers pushed in without a moment's delay; Massena crossed and deployed on their right and left; and at the point of the bayonet the French fell upon the second line; the Austrian position was carried, and in addition to the fourteen guns, thirty munition-carts were taken. After uselessly putting in his cavalry, Sebottendorf retired with the loss of two thousand men. The French loss is not given. It was probably more. The combat had been only an affair of the rearguard, but a brilliant one. The French advanced to Tormo Palasio and camped, the cavalry, which arrived too late to take part in the battle, protecting their front.

As Beaulieu had already anticipated the French on the road to Brescia and Mantua, any gain there might have been made in the fight at the bridge of Lodi was forfeited.

In the Army of Italy there had grown up a habit among the old grenadiers to hold daily a little council of their own, to discuss events, and to promote from time to time their young leaders. It was on Bonaparte's return to camp after the battle of Lodi, when he rode around among the regiments, that the old grenadiers saluted him as "*P'tit Caporal!*"

It appears that the storming of the bridge of Lodi was what first gave Bonaparte the idea that he was cut out for great things. Though a handsome affair, it was one which has been many times equalled by other troops; but the young general's vast imagination had been set at work; and later, at St. Helena, the emperor said:

> Vendémiaire and Montenotte had not warranted me in considering myself an exceptional man. Only after Lodi did the idea come to me that henceforth I should be a decisive player on the political boards; then arose the first sparks of high ambition.

This seems to exhibit a somewhat curious limitation of judgment; for while Lodi was a bold, it was not a great feat of arms.

Bonaparte had imagined that Beaulieu in force stood beyond the river to defend the position of Lodi; and even on the evening of the fight he clung to the idea that he had beaten the whole Austrian army. His resolve under these circumstances to carry the bridge was an act of excessive hardihood, if not rashness, to be gauged by history as many other rash assaults have been,—as Gustavus' assault on the Alte Veste, or Sherman's on Kenesaw, have been alternately praised or blamed. Good fortune seconded the courage of his grenadiers. As the obstacle could have been readily turned; and as, had the entire Austrian force actually been present, the assault would almost to a certainty have failed, it can scarcely be called an act of wisdom. But if Bonaparte merely desired to give a lesson in daring to his opponents, he certainly gave it in good style. Moreover, it must be remembered that time was essential to him, and like Gneisenau he could say:

"Strategy is the science of how to use time and space. I am less miserly of this than that. We may recover space, lost time never again."

Bonaparte, "in his nightly rounds" after the battle of Lodi, "met a bivouac of prisoners, where was a talkative old Hungarian officer, of whom he asked how their affairs were going. The old captain could not help admitting that they went very ill: 'But,' he added, 'there is no longer means of understanding anything about it; we have to do with a young general, who is sometimes before us, sometimes on our rear, then again on our flanks; we never know how we ought to place ourselves. This way of making war is insupportable, and violates every usage!'" He did not know who his interrogator was.

For a month the French troops had known no rest, night or day. They needed a respite. But it was short. On May 11 Bonaparte remained near Lodi, sending a detachment across to Crema, and one to Milan. His first idea was to "follow up Beaulieu, and to draw some use from his stupor, so as to again beat him." When he learned that the Austrians had moved on Pizzighetone, he started thither at early morning of the 12th; Massena and Dallemagne marched on the left bank of the Adda; Menard was to attack on the right bank; Serurier, yet at Placentia, to move up and support him, if pressed. Augereau was ordered during the 12th to march on Pizzighetone by way of Crema. But the prey had escaped. Beaulieu had concentrated his forces during that day at Cremona and retired thence across the Oglio. He was more rapid in retreat than in advance. Pizzighetone, attacked by Massena, with Menard and Serurier on the other side, had no chance, but surrendered after half an hour's bombardment. "This last affair, by yielding the whole course of the Adda to the Republicans, assures them the Milanese, conquered by the winning of the battle of Lodi," says the *Relation* of May 14.

Bonaparte was now convinced that Beaulieu proposed to retire behind the Mincio to Mantua, and that neither could he be caught, nor was any danger to be apprehended from him. Only the semblance of a pursuit by Augereau was undertaken. It seemed and was wiser to complete the conquest of what had already been overrun. Sending Massena to Milan, and Augereau to Pavia, while Serurier remained at Cremona and Placentia, Menard at Codogno and Pizzighetone, and detachments held the Adda, Bonaparte prepared to make secure his footing in Lombardy by military occupation, for he could conclude no treaty with the Austrians as he had with the Piedmontese.

In seventeen days the Army of Italy, under its new commander, had conquered all Lombardy. Bonaparte made a triumphal entry into Milan May 15. The National Guard, formed on either side of the streets with the colours of Lombardy, and under command of the Duke of Serbelloni, received the conqueror. His coming was hailed by many as the advent of Italian liberty. A triumph in Paris would scarcely have shown greater elation on the part of the populace, he tells us. But there were many regrettable French excesses.

Bonaparte was instant in his demands for more and good material and men.

> Since the death of Steingel I have no superior officer of cavalry who will fight. Send me some who have fire, and who do not know how to make learned retreats.

Lambert was chief commissary of the army, and while Bonaparte could give him orders as to where to send rations, he could not control his methods. On April 28 he asks for an able commissary.

> I have only pigmies, who make me die of hunger in the midst of abundance.

With the commissary department beyond military control, and a commissioner of the Directory to interfere with manoeuvres, the French successes were to be wondered at. But Bonaparte was lucky in having Saliceti as chief commissioner. At this time Bonaparte wrote to a commissary of the Directory who was mixing too far in the operations of the army: "The requisition you have made on General Vaubois is contrary to the instructions given me by the government. I desire that you shall restrict yourself from now on within the bounds of the functions prescribed to you by the Executive Directory, without which, I shall be obliged to forbid in army orders the filling of your requisitions. We exist all of us only by the law. Whoso desires to command and usurp functions which it does not accord him is not a Republican."

While at Lodi, in answer to his repeated suggestions that Kellermann's idle forces be placed under his command, Bonaparte, to whom there was some opposition from jealousy of his brilliant successes, received from the Directory the absurd proposition to consolidate the Army of Italy and the Army of the Alps, placing Kellermann in command of half of the joint forces on the Mincio, while he himself, with twenty-five thousand men, to be known as the Army of the South, should march on Rome and Naples. Too intelligent to be compromised by impossible conditions at a moment when the French had to encounter all the forces of Austria, Bonaparte resigned his command; but while awaiting the action of the Directory, he made preparations to push Beaulieu still farther back towards the Tyrol. His answer to the Directory, dated May 14, contained the following:

> I think it very impolitic to divide the Army of Italy in two; it is equally contrary to the interests of the Republic to put over it two different generals. The expedition on Leghorn, Rome and Naples is a small affair. . . .
>
> For that (the main operation) is needed not only a single general, but also that nothing should disturb him in his march and his operations. I have made the campaign without consulting any one; I should have done nothing good had I been obliged to reconcile my views with another's. I have obtained some advantages over very superior forces, and this while lacking everything, because, persuaded that your confidence was reposed in me, my march was as prompt as my thought.
>
> If you impose on me impediments of all kinds; if I am to refer all my steps to the commissioners of the government; if they have the right to change my movements, to take from me or send me troops, expect nothing more that is good. If you weaken your means by dividing your forces, if you break in Italy the unity of the military thought, I tell you with sorrow, you will have lost the finest occasion of imposing laws on Italy.
>
> It is indispensable that you should have a general who possesses your confidence entirely. If it were not I, I should not complain, but I should make efforts to redouble my zeal to merit your esteem in the post you confided to me. Everyone

> has his method of conducting war. General Kellermann has more experience, and will conduct it better than I; we two together will conduct it very ill.
>
> It requires much courage to write this letter . . . but I owe you the expression of all my sentiments.

The above letter to the Directory was sent to Carnot, to deliver or not, as he saw fit. In his letter, a confidential one, to Carnot, Bonaparte said:

> Kellermann will command the army as well as I; for no one is more convinced than I that the victories are due to the courage and audacity of the army; but I believe that to join Kellermann and me in Italy would be to lose all. I cannot serve willingly with a man who believes himself the first general in Europe, and besides, I believe that one poor general is better than two good ones. War is like government, it is a matter of tact. . . . Whether I make war here or elsewhere is indifferent to me . . . but I have it much at heart not to lose in eight days two months of fatigue, pains and dangers.

Let us remember our motto, that the great captain is the product of exceptional intellect, exceptional force of character and exceptional opportunity. Given the two first, without the last factor, no general can do his best. History shows us many splendid commanders, like Turenne and Marlborough, who have been so hampered by the authorities behind them as to have accomplished far less than they might have done With full power to act. Bonaparte believed that opportunity would come to him if he waited. He was conscious of the brain and the moral force which impelled him; and he was wise to refuse to conduct an army on terms so unsuited to what he had already accomplished. Upon this subject he once said:

> Every commander-in-chief who undertakes to carry out a plan which he holds to be bad and ruinous, is at fault; he should make representations, insist on changes, and in the end rather demand to be relieved, than be the cause of disaster to his people.

From whatever motive, such was now his action.

What Bonaparte had done had more than settled him in command. From the moment of his arrival in the Army of Italy he had, in his own manner, secured implicit obedience to all his orders, and had shown the army who was master—of troops and situation alike.

Infantryman on the march, 1796

He had demonstrated to the rank and file, and to every officer, high and low, that he had not only the commission of the Directory, but possessed the inborn right to supreme command. In his case, in order to command, it was not necessary to know how to obey. This lesson Bonaparte had never fully learned.

In a certain sense it is the lieutenants of a commanding general who win his battles. Without good ones no captain can succeed. But the great captain makes good lieutenants: that he can make them is one proof of his power. In the Army of Italy, when Bonaparte took command, there were excellent lieutenants, young, ambitious, enterprising, and yet well trained. There was Massena, the miserly, reckless, but high-strung and unsurpassed leader of men; "he was never discouraged; . . . if vanquished, he began over again as if he had been victor." There was Augereau, the severe disciplinarian, whom still his soldiers loved; the excellent battle commander, intrepid and yet careful; the talkative, quick-witted, sound. There were Serurier, the veteran in service, severe and hard-working; Laharpe, the simple-minded but able; Steingel, the tireless pattern of a cavalryman. They were all older in years and war than Bonaparte, and they looked askance at him—but not for long. Not once during the entire campaign, in which Bonaparte made the severest demands on his lieutenants, was there ever a sign of anything but quick obedience—a great tribute to a commanding general of twenty-seven.

The amount of hard work which Bonaparte did is well measured by the numberless political papers he wrote, the orders he issued, and the amount of ground these all covered. The perusal of a volume of his *Correspondence* is as interesting as it is instructive. The orders for the march were coupled with instructions to the commissaries for bread, to be delivered to the troops at various places; and the mayors of towns and officials of provinces were often held personally responsible to see the bread baked and delivered. Entire populations of a district were set to work to repair bridges broken by the enemy. Officers and diplomatic agents were sent ahead of the army to study the country, ascertain the sentiment of the people, and to foster good feeling. The train of the army was carefully inspected, officers were forbidden to have carriages or carts, or more horses than regulations allowed; private horses seized were ordered to be turned in to the provost; women were forbidden and ordered out of camp. In no department was the leader's eye or the proper order wanting. Moreover, he was keen in his appreciation of every fact, and saw its significance when others did not. Detail was plain to him without his losing sight of the whole.

Another thing is worth noting in Bonaparte's reports. All the officers who distinguished themselves were cordially mentioned and unstintingly praised, and in all he did the chief, while not underrating himself, ascribed his successes to the courage and willing help of his officers and men. "Since the beginning of the campaign," he wrote the Directory, May 6, "General Berthier has always passed the day beside me in the combats, and the night at his desk. It is impossible to join more activity, good-will, courage and knowledge. By just title, I have passed on to him one half of the flattering and honourable things that you express in your letters."

The action of the Directory was altered May 21. Bonaparte retained command of the undivided Army of Italy.

In less than a month the new leader had turned the line of the Alps, won a number of sharp combats and three well-contested engagements,—Montenotte, Millesimo, Lodi,—made twelve thousand prisoners, taken a number of fortresses and two capitals, detached Piedmont from the Coalition, opened the route into Italy through Savoy, and overrun Lombardy. "I believe," says Jomini, "that if Napoleon had commanded the most excellent troops, he would not have accomplished more, even as Frederick, in the reversed case, would not have accomplished less."

Chapter 10

On the Mincio

May 15-August 1, 1796

Bonaparte was starting for the Mincio when a revolt occurred in Milan and Pavia. He returned, and made a cruel but necessary example in both places. In the rich valley of the Po the troops were now well fed, and the Army of Italy was in the highest morale. The Austrians defended the Mincio on the cordon system, strung out from Lake Garda to Mantua. Operating from Brescia so as to make the Austrians fear for their communications with the Tyrol, Bonaparte broke through this line at Borghetto and hurried the enemy into retreat up the Adige. The Austrians still held Mantua in force, and based on Trent. Venice was aggrieved at an invasion of her territory. Naples and the Pope were antagonistic. The English held the sea. The line of the Mincio could only be maintained by fighting for it, and this Bonaparte prepared to do. He began the blockade of Mantua with thirteen thousand men. He had pacified the countries in his rear, and mulcted them heavily in money and works of art, thus making war support war, and presenting to Paris what would give the people cause to remember him. Wurmser was now put in command of the enemy. At the end of July he advanced down the Adige and on the west of Lake Garda. Bonaparte was placed in a dangerous situation, but as the enemy had divided his forces, he prepared to attack each body in turn. He threw up the siege of Mantua and advanced on the Austrians west of Lake Garda, recapturing Brescia, which they had temporarily taken.

While awaiting the decision of the Directory, Bonaparte called on the Gallic fervour of his troops, and addressed himself to the peoples of Italy in the following: proclamation

> Soldiers! You have precipitated yourselves like a torrent from the top of the Apennines; you have overturned, dispersed and scattered everything which opposed your march!
>
> Piedmont, delivered from Austrian tyranny, has yielded to her natural sentiments of peace and friendship for France.

Milan is yours, and the Republican standard floats over all Lombardy.

The dukes of Parma and Modena owe their political existence to your generosity alone.

The army which menaced you with so much pride now finds no barrier which can insure it against your courage. The Po, the Ticino, the Adda, have not been able to arrest you a single day; these vaunted *boulevards* of Italy have been insufficient; you have crossed them as rapidly as you did the Apennines.

So many successes have carried joy to the bosom of the country; your representatives have ordered a fete, dedicated to your victories, to be celebrated in all the communes of the Republic; there your fathers, your mothers, your wives, your sisters, your sweethearts, rejoice in your success, and boast with pride that they belong to you.

Yes, soldiers, you have done much; but yet, is there nothing left to do? Shall they say of us that we have known how to conquer, but that we have not known how to profit by victory? Shall posterity reproach us with having found a Capua in Lombardy? But I see you already run to arms; a cowardly repose wearies you; days lost for glory are lost for your happiness. Well, let us be gone! We yet have forced marches to make, enemies to suppress, laurels to gather, injuries to avenge.

Let those tremble who have sharpened the daggers of civil war in France, who have, like cowards, assassinated our ministers, and burned our ships in Toulon. The hour of vengeance has struck!

But let the people be without disquiet; we are friends of all peoples, and especially of the descendants of the Brutus, the Scipios, and of the great men whom we have taken as models. To re-establish the capital, to place there with honour the statues of the heroes who made themselves celebrated, awake the Roman people, benumbed with several centuries of slavery, such shall be the fruit of your victories. They will make an epoch in posterity. You will have the immortal glory of changing the face of the most beautiful part of Europe.

The French people, free, respected by the whole world, will give to Europe a glorious peace, which will indemnify it for the sacrifices of all kinds it has made in the past six years; you will then go back to your hearthstones, and your fellow citizens will say in pointing you out: "He was of the Army of Italy!"

Bonaparte knew his fellow soldiers; he knew the Latin heart of sunny Italy, and he trusted that the proclamation would arouse the same enthusiasm among the middle classes as a former one had done in the capital of Piedmont.

After the defeat at Lodi, Beaulieu had not dared to defend the lines of the Oglio or Chiese, but had retired for safely behind the Mincio, which he hoped he would be able to maintain. He took up a position with his left at Goito, his right at Peschiera and his centre at Valleggio.

That the Directory chose to suggest an inexpedient division of the French forces, and that Bonaparte saw fit to decline to serve in a campaign whose end he could in advance predict to be failure, was no reason why the commander-in-chief of the Army of Italy should not keep up his pressure on Beaulieu. During the few days' rest that he allowed his divisions, he made arrangements for future victual, adopted means to secure his communications with the rear (he now had a line through Savoy, as well as along the coast), planned the necessary measures for reducing the citadel of Milan, which had held out, and for the siege of which material was to be sent from Alessandria and Tortona, issued orders on May 19 for a further advance to the Adda, and four days later instructions to continue this advance to the Oglio. In command of the van of five grenadier and three carbineer battalions, with sixteen hundred horse, now stood Kilmaine; and this officer broke up at 4 a. m. on the 24th, and marched to Soncino, where he seized the bridge. The bulk of the army got afoot an hour later and moved, Augereau from Cassano to Fontanella, Massena from Lodi to Offanengo, Menard from Codogno to Soresina, Serurier from Cremona to Casalbuttano. Headquarters was transferred to Crema.

Onerous contributions had been levied on all the cities of Lombardy. This was not all Bonaparte's doing. He could not fail to see that to bring so-called liberty with one hand and to levy oppressive assessments with the other was not the best military or civil policy. But he was under the orders of the Directory to do this thing, and he did it in a magnificent way. At the same time, he was wise enough to place the members of the French government under obligations to himself, as when he sent a hundred of the finest horses he could find in Lombardy to Paris, "to replace the mediocre ones which had drawn their carriages." Bonaparte personally cared little for wealth except to influence others, or bribe them, if you will; but for this purpose he used the wealth his armies conquered with a superb profusion. All his favourite generals and marshals became wealthy.

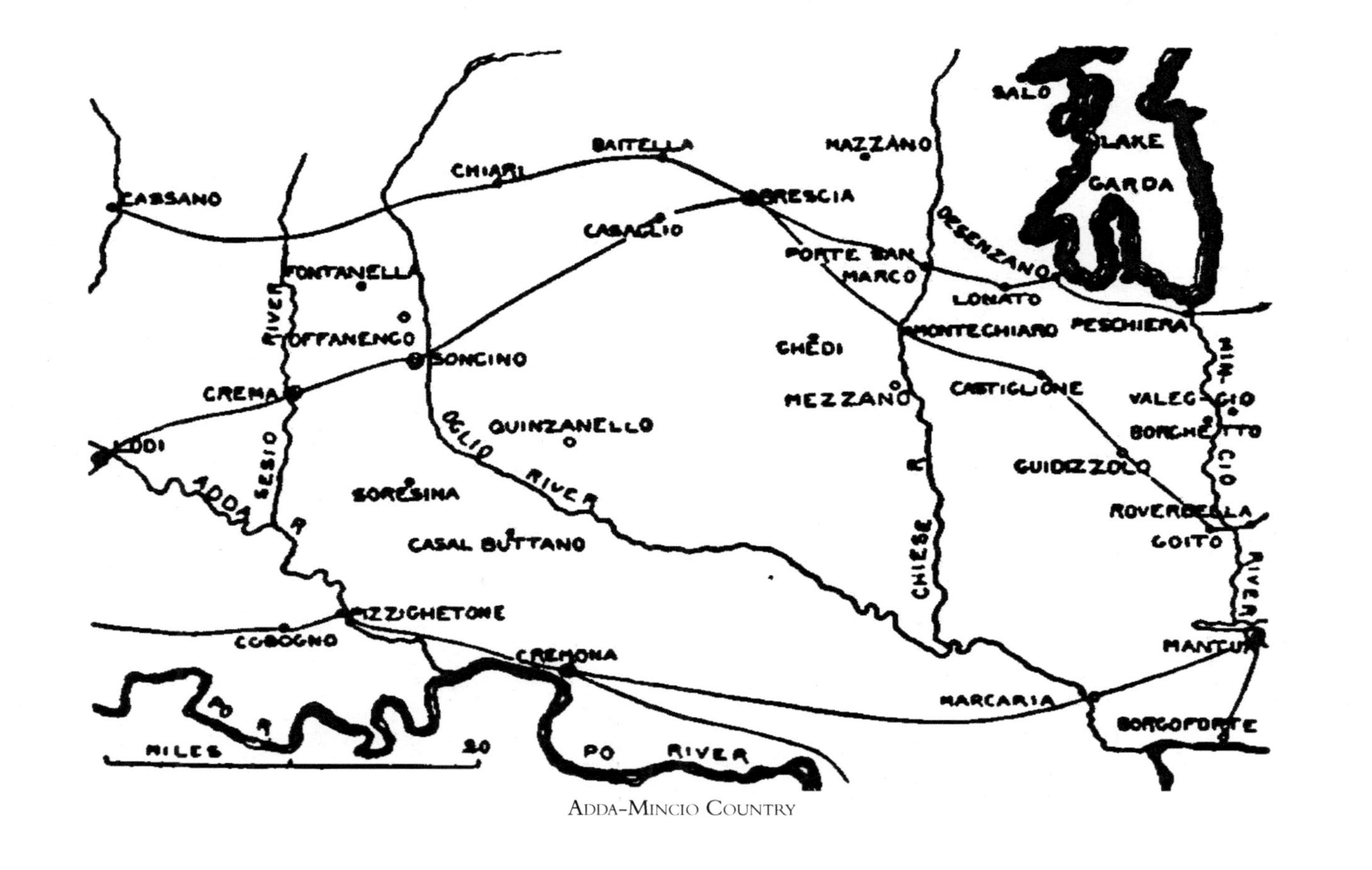

Adda-Mincio Country

His friend Saliceti accumulated a fortune by his connection with the army. And so with many others. No sooner was Bonaparte's back turned than trouble broke out in the rear. It could scarcely be expected that so sadden an upheaval as his coming had made in Lombardy should take place without leaving a mass of malcontents, and these had fostered serious uprisings in Milan and Pavia.

Convinced that in these uprisings half-way measures were suicidal, Bonaparte at once ordered Berthier to send to Milan three battalions, two regiments of cavalry and four guns, and he himself hurried thither to put down the revolt with a strong hand. This he did in Milan, holding a summary court there on May 25, and meting out quick military justice to those found guilty; and thence went straight to Pavia, where eight thousand armed peasants had broken in and captured the French garrison. His demand for admittance being refused, Bonaparte, on the 26th, forced an entrance into the city, cut down a number of the rebels in the streets, had the French commandant who surrendered the place shot by drumhead court-martial, and some of the municipal officers sentenced to death. The latter penalty was, however, commuted; and two hundred hostages were sent to Paris to ensure future good behaviour. Bonaparte was on the point of setting fire to the town, but he refrained from his purpose, and in lieu of this punishment gave it over to the troops for several hours' pillage. This cruelty—brutality if you will—has been much commented on; and indeed, within little more than a century it seems scarcely possible. Yet the lives sacrificed at Pavia saved multitudes that by any other treatment would have been elsewhere lost; an example was needed if the French were to hold Lombardy, which they had fairly conquered, and Bonaparte delayed not, neither shrank from extreme measures in giving it. The speedy vengeance was distinctly effective. Further risings there were none.

Discipline improved as the men were better fed. They had been on his arrival "without bread, without discipline, without subordination," and "the soldier without bread is driven to an excess of fury which makes one blush at being a man," he said. The leader now strove to seek excuses for the past.

> Discipline re-establishes itself every day, but we have frequently to shoot pillagers.
>
> From the moment that we can arrest our movements, we will clothe the army afresh. It is yet in a frightful condition, but the soldier is growing fat. He eats only Gonesse bread, good meat and in plenty, and has good wine.

All through the Italian campaign occasional orders against pillaging had to be issued, and instructions were given summarily to shoot men caught in the act, at the head of their battalions. A number were thus executed. But on the other hand, he had on June 14 to write to Lambert, chief commissary with the Army of Italy, about similar difficulties he could not personally control:

> From all sides. Citizen Ordonnator, arrive complaints to the general-in-chief about the vexations which the miserable inhabitants of the conquered country are made to suffer, from the requisition that the transport contractor exercises to procure horses and cattle. . . . The desolation is such among the poorest in the Mantuan country that they are getting ready to emigrate with all their beasts. Verify this . . . and stop the cupidity of the agents. . . . Bonaparte.

Meanwhile the French army had been advancing, under orders, towards the Mincio, where, according to the plan of the Directory, it was to await reinforcements from the Rhine, that were to come to it through the Tyrol. But wait Bonaparte could not. It was not in his nature to sit down and idle, especially as certain additional forces had come up from the rear, so that, not counting the troops left in Lombardy, he had some twenty-seven thousand men. Moreover, the reinforcements from the Rhine had been contingent on success there; and instead of success there had been failure. On May 25 the divisions had crossed the Oglio, and Kilmaine reached Brescia, Massena Casaglio, Augereau Baitella, Serurier Quinzanello, and in these several places they remained May 26. Next day Bonaparte rejoined the army at Soncino, and on the 28th pushed on to the Chiese, with van out beyond the river to Lonato. This movement, the collection of boats at Desenzano, and the advance of a half-brigade to Salo were intended to give the impression that Bonaparte was manoeuvring towards the Tyrol, to turn the Austrian right, join the Army of the Rhine by the roads west and north of the Lake of Garda, or at least to reach Beaulieu's line of communications far to the rear, and there to cut off his expected reinforcements. Serurier, by way of Ghedi, reached Mezzano, on the Chiese, May 29, and at the same time Augereau crossed and advanced to Desenzano, and Massena to Montechiaro, while Kilmaine moved forward towards Castiglione. At 2 a. m. of the 30th—there were no delays in Bonaparte's programme—the entire force broke up to cross the Mincio at Borghetto, Kilmaine in the van with Bonaparte in his company, and the other divisions *echeloned* a few miles in the rear.

It had been the plan of the Austrian commander-in-chief to defend the line of the Mincio. He now had nearly eleven thousand men in Mantua, twelve battalions near Roverbella, and the balance in various detachments, small and large, along the lake and the river. His ideas of defence were, however, scarcely abreast of Bonaparte's ideas of attack. Instead of remaining in one body, so placed on the left bank as to move rapidly on any threatened point, and of carefully scouting the right bank, towards which the French were pressing,—a proceeding which might have inspired even Bonaparte with some respect,—Beaulieu was frightened at the French diversion towards Salo and Lonato, and so completely thrown off his balance by the feeling of uncertainty as to what was to happen, that he again shifted his forces, and now placed Liptay at Peschiera, Hohenzollern at Valleggio with Sebottendorf below, and Colli at Goito, meanwhile keeping a big force in Mantua. Thus, not counting this latter fortress, Beaulieu had strung two thirds of his men along a stretch of fifteen miles from Peschiera to Goito; while Bonaparte, in one solid body, was ready to break through his line at any point he chose. A mere advance would do it, without serious fighting.

Beaulieu's conception of defending the Mincio was all wrong. Indeed, had he stood with all his forces at Gavardo, he would have prevented Bonaparte from moving beyond Brescia, lest the Austrians should fall upon the flank of the Army of Italy. Had he stood with the bulk of his forces near Mantua, Bonaparte could not have gone beyond the Mincio, for fear the French communications should be cut Nothing can be worse than the cordon system of defending a river which Beaulieu adopted.

"The art of strategy," says Jomini, "consists in leading upon the decisive points of a line of operations the greatest mass possible of your forces." Bonaparte had done just this, and at 7 a. m. on May 30 Kilmaine with the van appeared in front of Borghetto, which was on the right bank, and having pushed in the enemy's small body lying on guard there, was ready to force the river. An arch in the bridge had been burnt by the retreating Austrians, and while the repairs were going on to enable the heavy foot and guns to cross, a few enterprising grenadiers waded the river at a ford about four feet deep, holding aloft their pieces, and by their very audacity seized the farther bank. By noon Kilmaine had driven the few Austrian companies away from the left bank and beyond Valleggio. Beaulieu, with Hohenzollern, took up a position on the heights between Villafranca and Valleggio, but held it only a short while, and then fell

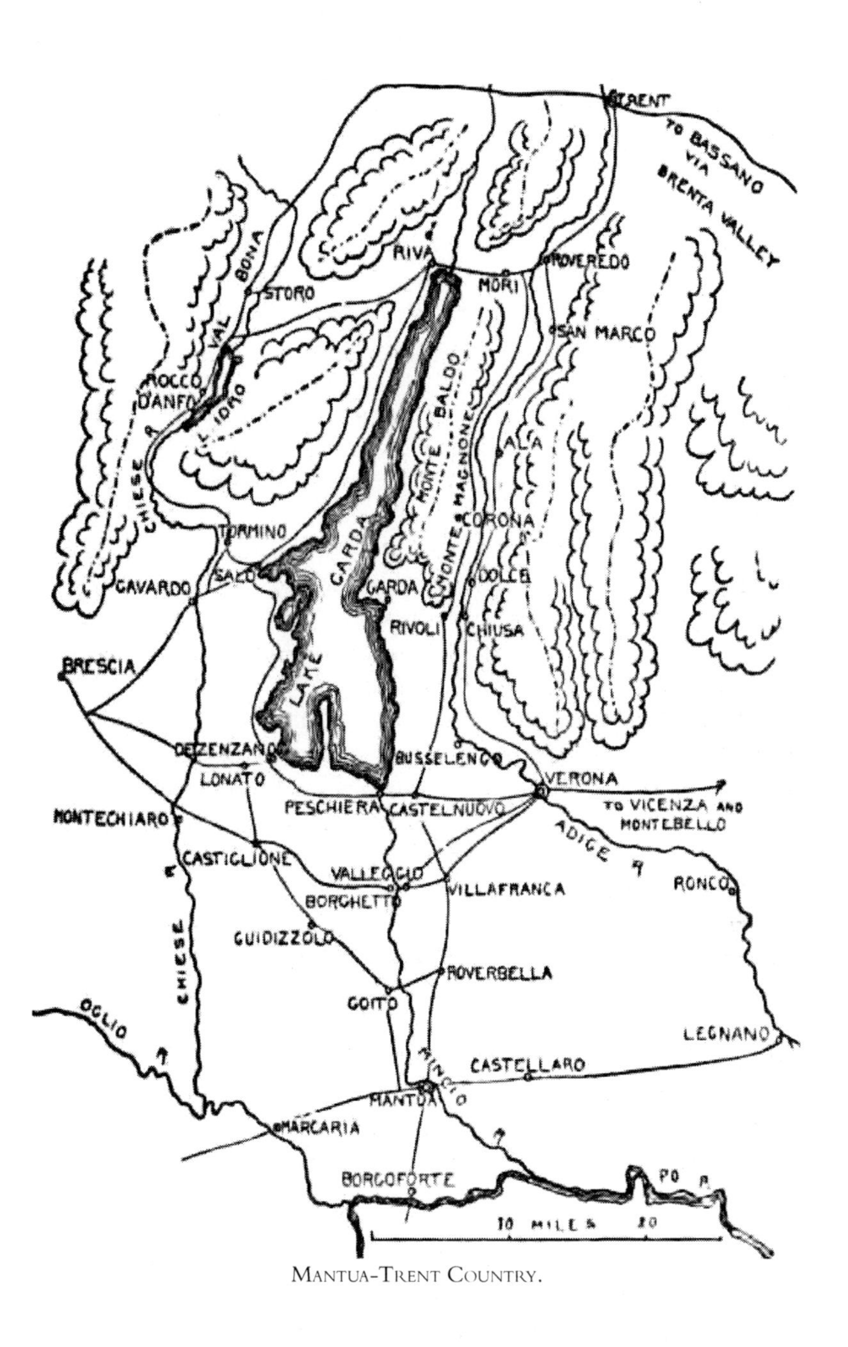

Mantua-Trent Country.

back to Castelnuovo, where he joined Liptay. The passage accomplished, Bonaparte at once determined to move against the right flank of Beaulieu's line, which was now collecting at Castelnuovo, so as if possible to turn it and to cut it off from the Tyrol. It is probable that he expected to find Beaulieu in force at that place.

While Kilmaine remained at Valleggio to cover Massena's crossing, Augereau, already across, advanced on Peschiera. Reaching it the same evening, the Austrians withdrew, and Augereau occupied the fortress, which belonged to Venice, but without being able to cut the enemy's road up the Adige, as he had hoped to do. As soon as Massena had crossed, Kilmaine followed along on the road to Castelnuovo. Serurier was yet on the right bank at Guidizzolo. Headquarters was established at Valleggio, and the complete task had been accomplished by early evening of May 30. In his report of the day's operations, Bonaparte says that "Murat with the cavalry did prodigies of valour."

Early next morning Kilmaine and Augereau advanced on Castelnuovo, hoping to find the enemy there and to attack him; Massena went to Villafranca to clear the country of what Austrians might still be there; Serurier crossed to Valleggio. But Beaulieu had got too much demoralized to attempt any further defence along the Mincio. By the shortest road he had fallen back behind the Adige, and had made Dolce the point of assembling of his scattered divisions. Sebottendorf marched on the same point *via* Villafranca and Bussolengo. Receiving no orders. Colli from the Roverbella region marched upstream, thinking to be able to attack the French right, and thus aid in the battle that he supposed would be fought near Valleggio to hold the river; but finding that Beaulieu had withdrawn and that his own road was cut, he sent his foot back to Mantua, raising that garrison to over thirteen thousand men, and with his horse skirted Villafranca and Castelnuovo, and crossing the Adige above Verona, marched to Dolce. Having thus collected his forces, Beaulieu retired towards Roveredo, having lost six hundred men and four guns in what could hardly be called a defence of the Mincio.

Thus in a week from leaving the Adda, Bonaparte could write to the Directory:

> The Austrians are entirely driven out of Italy. Our outposts are on the hills of Germany.

Proud words, but true, and uttered by the man who had earned the right to use them. He also added:

> I will not cite you the men who have distinguished themselves by traits of bravery. I should have to name all the grenadiers and *carbineers* of the vanguard. They play and laugh with death. . . . Nothing equals their intrepidity, unless it be the gayety with which they make the hardest forced marches,—they sing alternately *la patrie et l'amour.*

As Frederick had some narrow personal escapes during the Silesian wars, so here Bonaparte almost fell into the hands of the Austrians. A reconnoitring party of Sebottendorf's, marching along the Mincio to rejoin the main army, ran across the French headquarters at Valleggio, and quite took by surprise its all too feeble guard. The commanding general was occupying a palace, where he was indulging in the luxury of a bath, and it was only by a summary flight through some gardens in the rear—actually, as Mother Goose hath it, *one shoe off and one shoe on*—that Bonaparte managed to escape, and to reach Massena's column. This narrow chance was the origin of the formation of the "Guides," a body *d'élite,* each man in which had seen ten years' service, to do duty near the commanding officer's person. Its leader was Bessières, "an officer of reserve, full of vigour, but prudent and circumspect."

Bonaparte had done on the Mincio substantially what he had done on the Po. By his march through Brescia, and the pushing of a detachment up to Salo, he had created the impression in Beaulieu's mind that he might march to the Tyrol on the west of the Lake of Garda, just as his diversion at Valencia had kept Beaulieu from guessing that he would move down to Placentia to cross; and fearing for his communications, Beaulieu had left several passages of the river practically naked, and had reached out his right to save himself from an imaginary threat. Napoleon has said that he knew of but three things to do in war:

> . . . . march twelve leagues a day, fight, and then quietly go into cantonments.

It goes without saying that the leagues must be in the right direction, and that the fighting shall be for a proper object and in proper force, for—

> . . . the secret in war does not lie in the legs, it resides entirely in the brain that sets the legs in motion. An army may make forced marches all through the campaign; it will yet be lost if the direction of these marches is faulty.

Bonaparte's manoeuvres on the Po enabled him to take Beaulieu in reverse, and had he been able to cross the river rapidly, he might have forced battle on the Austrians to their great disadvantage. Here the Lake of Garda protected the strategic flank of the Austrians, and enabled them to preserve their line of retreat, as well as compelled Bonaparte to force his passage opposite their centre, or at least in their front Happily, this was not made difficult for him. So soon as he had crossed, he essayed an advance against the enemy's communications by his march on Peschiera and Castelnuovo; and Beaulieu by his retreat confessed his weakness and gave up the whole campaign.

Augereau effectively followed up the retiring enemy for a day, and Massena marched on Verona, and then turned on Dolce, out of which he drove the Austrian rearguard. Here the column stopped: it was idle to pursue farther; there were other things more important to be done to secure what the French had so quickly won. Bonaparte turned towards Mantua.

Trent, on the upper Adige, was the Austrian depot and place of assembly, their secondary base, as it were, from which was to start their line of operations, whose objective now was Mantua, a fortress essential to their holding northern Italy, and one that, if they would not confess to failure, they must relieve. And there was no question that they would soon undertake to do so. Mantua lies in a bend of the Mincio, and has about it a network of marshes and lakes, fed by the slow flowing river. There entered the fortress at this time two bridges and three causeways, the ends of the roads from Legnano, Verona, Brescia, Cremona and Borgoforte. The plain north of Mantua is not far from thirty miles wide, from the city to the foothills of the Alps; and to this plain there were from Trent down but three roads fit for artillery. The shortest was by the way of Roveredo and Dolce to Verona along the left bank of the Adige, with an occasional crossing to another road which ran down on the right bank. The longest way was through the Brenta valley to Vicenza, where the highway from Carinthia came in. The third lay through the Val Bona along the Chiese to Brescia. The Dolce and Brenta roads were not connected, except at the upper part by a few mountain paths. At the head of the Lake of Garda was a road from Roveredo to the Val Bona; but this could easily be closed at Rocca d'Anfo. The highway along the right bank of the Adige was at placed useless for artillery, and was commanded by the defile of La Corona, and by Monte Magnone and Monte Baldo, a pile of hills which dominate the country like a huge square fortress. South of these latter heights lies a large natural amphitheatre, from the middle of which rises the plateau of Rivoli, around which, in a plain, flows the Tasso stream. The plateau is of itself a species of natural bastion over a mile in length. The Adige and the Brenta are both torrential rivers. The former on reaching the plain is some four hundred feet wide, and its main bridges at that time were protected by Chiusa, Verona and Legnano. From the topographical conditions described, it appears that, starting from the mountain base of Trent, the Austrians would be compelled to march to the plain in one dangerously long column, or in several columns far apart; and the parts of the one long column would have to be as much separated by distance as the several columns would have to be by natural obstacles. On the other hand, the French divisions at Legnano, Verona, Rivoli, La Corona and Salo could easily concentrate on the open ground south of Garda. This was much in Bonaparte's favour. Still, should a superior Austrian army carefully debouch from the mountains, deploy and march in mass on Mantua, striking the French forces whenever met, it might by intelligent and energetic initiative overwhelm them. Wonderful as had been his gain so far, the French leader's task was far from completed.

As is not uncommon with success, Bonaparte's recent achievements had brought serious difficulties in their wake. The Austrian column was by its retreat nearing the large reinforcements which had been sent to it from the Rhine; while Bonaparte was growing weaker the farther he moved away from his base, and could not look for equal accessions to his army. The Italian princes were, to be sure, neutral; but feigned friendliness was not the best of guaranties. Rome and Naples in the south might do the French a mischief. Already annoyed at the French forced requisitions of bread, Venice had grown fairly wroth at Bonaparte's unwarranted invasion of her territory at Peschiera, though indeed she had laid herself open to this treatment by giving free passage through that fortress to the Austrians. An English division of ten thousand men, now in Corsica, might land at Livorno and incite opposition to the French arms. All these items, each small in itself, would make a great sum of strength when added to the efforts of the Austrian army already in the field. Bonaparte had but forty-five thousand men, part in garrison; the Austrians had thirty thousand impregnably posted on the Adige, and as many more said to be coming along as reinforcements. It has been suggested by some military critics that Bonaparte should have at once masked Mantua and followed up Beaulieu. But this is an extravagant view. Such a course would change what had so far been remarkable enterprise and courage into what would have been foolhardiness unworthy of even a Charles XII. And with all his boldness and enterprise, Bonaparte possessed a well-developed bump of caution.

Three things were most prominently essential.

First, Bonaparte must watch the avenues by which the enemy might approach, to learn the fact at once and use means to check their oncoming.

Second, he must take Mantua, as a part of his base for a further advance from the line of the Mincio.

Third, he must make terms with the Italian states to the south of him, lest at some inopportune moment they fall upon his rear. This last indeed was the idea of the Directory, with which, as we have seen, Bonaparte only in part agreed. The Directory saw, like "many good generals in Europe," altogether "too many things at once." Bonaparte kept his eye on one thing, the Austrian army, certain that so long as this was beaten or neutralized, he need not fear the others. Still, operations against the Austrian army depended on careful arrangements in his rear, and these he at once began to make. Although Bonaparte did not believe in an eccentric movement by a large force on Rome and Naples, he did propose to anticipate trouble from thence; and being moreover constrained to meet the views of his superiors, he redistributed his army.

Massena was given charge of Verona and its important bridges, as well as the country up the Adige, with orders to watch for and fend off any Austrian advance; and a small force of his was to be stationed west of the Lake of Garda at Salo, and an equal force at Monte Baldo, on the east of the lake. Serurier and Augereau were sent to Mantua to shut in the fortress, if this could be done. Vaubois' division was coming on from the Army of the Alps, and this with Dallemagne's three grenadier battalions, twelve thousand five hundred in all, remained free in Bonaparte's own hand for use as occasion demanded. A part of Augereau's force was dispatched to Legnano. The garrisons in Lombardy numbered nine thousand men. Inasmuch as in forty-eight hours the French divisions could assemble on either bank of the Mincio, the Army of Italy may be said to have been firmly established on that river; and all northern Italy was in its possession, save only the citadel of Milan and the fortress of Mantua. The works at Peschiera were ordered to be put in good condition with as great dispatch as possible; and after inspecting Verona, Bonaparte established his headquarters in Roverbella, a central point from whence he could watch the north, as well as carry on the siege of Mantua.

Bessières

Beaulieu

Lannes

Wurmser

Bonaparte

Situated with a semicircular lagoon on the north and marshes on the south, Mantua was exceptionally strong. The citadel on the north side of the Mincio was practically inexpugnable; but the south and the west of the fortress Were possible of approach. Augereau, on the right bank, seized the two causeway roads leading into the city on the west and south sides of the lagoon near the fortress; and Serurier, on the left bank, seized the two on the east side, and occupied the suburb of San Giorgio. Dallemagne, who was at first stationed at headquarters, later replaced Augereau.

The latter on June 12 was sent to Bologna, crossing the Po at Borgoforte, to further the enterprises ordered by the Directory, and which Bonaparte found it essential to inaugurate against Tuscany and Rome. These south Italian matters did not, however, long remain of military significance. By a lucky accident, such as all through life often subserved Napoleon's vigour and genius, Ferdinand of Naples treated for peace and withdrew his contingent from Beaulieu. And as, judging it wise to draw the temper of the divine pontiff, Bonaparte directed Augereau to march on Bologna, it was an agreeable surprise when this city received the French willingly, while a detachment captured Livorno with a large supply of English stores; whereupon His Holiness made haste to sue for peace, and signing an armistice, paid twelve and a half million *francs* indemnity, gave up a hundred of his best pictures, busts, vases and statues, selected by the French Commissioners from the Vatican collection, and five hundred manuscripts from its library, to enrich the galleries of Paris, and yielded up Ferrara, Ancona and Castel Urbino. The guns of these towns, added to those sent on from the Piedmont fortresses, made up an ample siege equipment at Mantua. The Grand Duke of Tuscany, who had broken neutrality, was also mulcted. In addition to the above good fortune, the citadel of Milan surrendered June 29, and the material there employed could also be sent on to be used in the siege of Mantua.

When Bonaparte visited Tuscany, where his family had originated, he was received by an Abbé Bonoparte, who treated him and his staff with great distinction. The general bade the *abbé* ask some favour, and after much pressing, the churchman desired that the victorious general should procure from the Pope the canonization of a certain Father Bonaventure Bonoparte, who had generations before been a Capuchin monk of Bologna. The general laughed heartily at his distant cousin's choice, but the latter persisted, saying that he desired to have in the family a great man on earth and a saint in heaven. Later, indeed, on his death, he left his considerable property to Napoleon, who created with it a charitable institution in Tuscany.

The siege was pressed vigorously from July 5 on. But news was constantly running in concerning heavy Austrian reinforcements on the way, and the force which Bonaparte figured out as the one he would shortly be called on to face summed up some sixty thousand men. So, at least, he announced to the Directory in asking for further accessions to his own force of forty-two thousand. This was perhaps an excessive estimate, but not far wrong if it included the garrison of Mantua, and far too low if any of the Italian states should join the Austrians. The Mantua garrison, which Bonaparte gauged at eight thousand men, was really thirteen thousand strong.

It was indeed important that Mantua should be taken at as early a day as possible, for Field-marshal Count Wurmser had been appointed to succeed Beaulieu, with instructions to relieve the fortress at all hazards; and this officer had left the Rhine with twenty-five thousand old and tried troops. He had served Austria fifty years, in the Seven Years' War and against the Turks; he had gallantly forced the Weissemburg lines in 1793, had beaten Pichegru at Heidelberg in 1795, and had invaded the Palatinate. A fine old cavalry officer he was; and yet he lacked much of being an army leader.

Until the new Austrian army got so close to the outlet of the mountains on the upper Adige as to be an immediate danger, Bonaparte would not give over the siege of Mantua, which seemed to be approaching its end. Massena at Verona and Rivoli had fifteen thousand men; Augereau's troops on the right at Legnano comprised six to eight thousand more; while on the left, west of the lake, stood Sauret at Salo with five thousand men, under Massena's orders. Despinoy's division of five thousand men had just arrived from Milan, and was set to watching the Adige from Verona to Ronco; Serurier, with eight thousand men, was operating against Mantua; while Kilmaine, with three thousand reserve cavalry, occupied Valese, subject to Bonaparte's quick call. As reserve there was a brigade at Peschiera, one at Verona, and one in camp between the Lake of Garda and the Adige. The numbers in the several divisions are stated with so much diversity in the various reports that now, as always in Napoleon's campaigns, it is impossible to arrive at accuracy. The effective given is, however, near enough the truth. The French leader watched operations from Verona and Roverbella alternately with eager eyes.

The siege of Mantua had been heartily pushed. As in the early weeks, however, the French were far from being well equipped for the operation, an attempt was made early in July to capture the fortress by surprise; but it failed, for as Bonaparte then said, "all undertakings of this kind depend absolutely on luck, on a dog or a goose." Upon the return of Augereau from the south, the first parallels were opened in the night of July 18-19, and completed the succeeding night. An attack was made on the outworks of the place July 19, but this also failed, and Bonaparte then resorted to a steady bombardment until the end of the month. But Mantua, with its three hundred and sixteen guns and ample garrison, though indeed out of the thirteen thousand men there were four thousand sick, fended off every attempt the French could make to break down her defence. The several towns captured during the preceding campaign had furnished one hundred and forty heavy guns, which were gradually put in place; and having given his personal attention to the inauguration of this work, Bonaparte returned to the front to watch the oncoming of the Austrian reinforced army.

He did not have to wait long. Wurmser, whose forces, nearly fifty thousand strong, had assembled at Trent by the end of July, made no great haste, but he came in touch with the French outlying forces on the 29th, and pushed in with energy. Acting in part on the controlling cordon idea, and in part as prescribed by the theatre of operations, he divided his army into halves, one to go around each bank of the Lake of Garda; and each of the halves was subdivided into two or more columns.

The part marching on the west bank under Quosdanovich, about eighteen thousand strong, had three columns: one to march on Brescia, one on Salo, one on Gavardo. It had orders to capture these places, and if the French should retire to the right bank of the Po, as Wurmser fondly imagined they might, to march on Placentia, and cut their line of communications. The part marching on the east side of the lake was divided into two columns, one on either bank of the Adige. These various columns were organized for the purpose of compelling the French to divide their forces. This they indeed accomplished, but Wurmser did not appreciate the difference between divided forces having interior lines, and divided forces operating eccentrically. He was to learn it now. The several Austrian columns all duly advanced on their respective errands, in high heart and excellently equipped.

During the Silesian wars and during the Bonapartist wars, the Austrians have so often fought the losing part that one might almost believe something to be lacking in the make-up of the Austrian army. But when you examine into the details associated with their frequent defeats, you arrive at a very high estimate of the fine qualities of the

Austrian soldier, of the devotion and intelligence of the Austrian officer, and frequently of the skill of the Austrian army leader. There was always plenty of fight in an Austrian army, and its good countenance under conditions fit to dull the keenest martial edge commands the admiration of the student of those campaigns which have, on the other hand, illustrated the irresistible genius of a Frederick and a Napoleon. Moreover, the Austrian army was always subject to that extraordinarily hide-bound body, the Aulic Council; and on many a day when Austrian courage rose to culminating fervour could it accomplish no result, because the patriarchs in Vienna had given it a task absolutely impossible of accomplishment. No praise can be too high for the gallant white-coats.

At Salo the head of one of Quosdanovich's columns struck and threw back the small detachment of Sauret's forces that held the place, pushed on to Gavardo, and sent a body to take and garrison Brescia. Sauret concentrated to the rear at Desenzano. The column on the right bank of the Adige, under the commanding general in person, and numbering twenty-four thousand men, turned the position of Massena's outlying force at La Corona, in advance of Rivoli, in the early dawn of the 29th; and this French force was also compelled to fall back on Castelnuovo with loss of sixteen hundred men. The Austrians occupied Rivoli. On the left bank of the Adige, the column under Davidovich was expected to seize Verona, at which place a rendezvous was given to all the forces, as there could be no doubt, thought the Austrians, that Bonaparte must fall back at once to the right bank of the Po. At the same time a flying column of five thousand men had been sent into the Brenta valley to mislead the French commander, as at first it did.

Bonaparte, who was in Montechiaro on the 29th, at once ordered the concentration of Massena, Despinoy and the reserve cavalry under Kilmaine at Castelnuovo, and instructed Augereau to collect his forces, cross the Adige to the left bank, march *via* Villanova to Montebello, and attack the enemy on the 30th; for he looked on the Brenta detachment as one of the main bodies of the enemy. Further intelligence shortly came in about the columns in the Adige valley, and Sauret likewise reported his unequal engagement with the enemy; whereupon Augereau, before he had gone too far, was withdrawn to Roverbella and Villafranca. News of the loss of Brescia came in on the afternoon of the 30th.

For once in his life Napoleon was not seized on the instant by the fighting fever. For a few hours he greatly feared that this sudden Austrian onslaught would compel his retreat from the Mincio. The baggage and trains in the rear of the Army of Italy were started back towards Milan, and the citadel there was ordered to be put into a state of perfect defence. On this same July 29 Bonaparte wrote to Serurier:

> Part of the division of General Massena has been obliged to fall back. I am going tonight to Castelnuovo with several half-brigades. Perhaps we will re-establish the business, but it meanwhile compels me to take serious precautions for retreat.

Then giving him orders what to do, he added:

> All that I tell you is only measure of precaution, for we have yet brave and numerous soldiers who have not been in action.

The siege lines at Mantua were not yet ordered to be evacuated, but Bonaparte wrote even next day to Augereau to abandon his position on the Adige.

> The moments are precious. I confide the execution of these measures to your wisdom and to your prudence. Following is the unfortunate position of the army: the enemy has pierced our lines at three points; he is master of La Corona and of Rivoli, important posts. Massena and Joubert have been obliged to cede to force. Sauret has abandoned Salo and has made his retreat on Desenzano. The enemy has seized Brescia and the bridge at San Marco. You see that our communications are cut with Milan and Verona. Await new orders at Roverbella. I shall go there in person.

All this sounds unlike the vibrating tones of the orders issued months ago; but it must be remembered that this was Bonaparte's first sample of the difficulties of the defensive. He had commanded an army in one series of offensive operations, when the briskness of the work carried him and everything before it. Now, for the moment, when struck at several points, though he had been carefully watching the enemy's manoeuvres, he seemed not immediately to collect himself. He had no precedents to follow: he had to create them. But the arrested combativeness was but temporary. Within a day and night he was himself again.

To some of his lieutenants, who saw the matter only from their own partial standpoint, the situation appeared less threatening. With reference to the Brenta column, Massena wrote from Pieverono, July 29:

I expect to see the number of troops which yesterday reached Vicenza diminish. You will see. Citizen General, that after all it will turn out only a reconnoissance.

And Sahaguet wrote from Milan, July 31:

Up till now nothing indicates, despite the usual exaggerations, that the enemy's force which marched to Brescia is worth notice.

This by no means indicates that Bonaparte's judgment on the general situation was not the more intelligent one. For any but a fighting leader, it would have been a sound conclusion. And any one of the division commanders who had served through the late campaign would have weakened under the situation, and have at once elected to leave the conduct of the entire defence to his present chief, so strongly had he already impressed himself upon them all. This had been shown when Bonaparte was absent from the front at the time of the revolts in Milan and Pavia: a feeling of uncertainty had reigned as the army approached the enemy, and Berthier from Crema, May 25, wrote him: "The army longs with impatience for you."

The whole incident is interesting as a study of Napoleon's character; but as his action, shortly undertaken, was coloured by all his own peculiar genius, his first idea has no other value. According to Jomini, Bonaparte assembled a council of war, in which Kilmaine and the educated soldiers voted for retreat; Augereau, in a fine fervour not usual with him, demanded to fight his division, as he gallantly did a few days later; others followed suit.

The entire incident reminds one of the equally curious mental attitude of Frederick at Mollwitz. After freely exposing, himself in the thick of the fight, he was persuaded by Schwerin to leave the field, though the battle was then not absolutely lost, as the sequel proved. To such weakness the king never again yielded. Neither did Napoleon.

So soon as the affair developed, the conviction seized Bonaparte that here lay another chance to operate against the separated halves of the Austrian army; and this soon fully possessed him. The report to the Directory of August 6 says:

The enemy, in descending from the Tyrol by way of Brescia and the Adige, put me in the middle; if my army was too feeble to make head to the two divisions of the enemy, it could beat each one of them separately. . .

With a view, then, to fall first on the column descending on the west bank, be-cause it was nearer to and threatened his communications, he galloped to Desenzano and ordered Sauret, whom Despinoy should follow, to march July 31 on Salo, and attack the Austrians afresh. In his march on Salo, Quosdanovich had cut off Guyeux, of Sauret's division; but this officer retired to a walled inclosure on the lake, "shut himself up in a great house in Salo," says the report, and desperately held himself; and three Austrian battalions were left to watch him. Part of Sauret's orders was to rescue his lieutenant. From Desenzano Bonaparte galloped over to Castelnuovo, to which point Massena had been forced to fall back, and instructed this general to evacuate Verona and to take position at Peschiera, into which he was to throw a sufficient garrison, and on the right bank, facing the Mincio, and to guard the bridge at Valeggio with a strong detachment. Augereau and Kilmaine had got back to Roverbella and Castellaro, where they were to stand for the moment to protect the siege operations at Mantua; but as it was evident that these could be no longer maintained, for every man who could carry a musket must march against the approaching Austrians, they soon ceased to be of value there. Though the work was nearing its end, Serurier was ordered to raise the siege, get the artillery away if possible, and march part of his division to the support of Augereau. If not able to save the material, he was to spike the guns, burn the carriages and caissons, destroy the emplacements, bury the projectiles, and throw the powder into the river. As a matter of fact, Serurier had little transportation, and was obliged to destroy the siege equipment, which he did in the night of July 31-August 1. Some of the guns were left intact to the enemy. In justifying this abandonment, Bonaparte said:

> . . . to save guns is a matter of honour to an officer of artillery; to accomplish results, with or without loss of guns, is the affair of the commanding general.

Late at night, Bonaparte, who scarcely left the saddle, reached Roverbella, and hurried Augereau, Kilmaine and that part of Serurier's division which had come up, by way of Goito and Guidizzolo, towards Montechiaro; while Serurier's siege troops on the right bank of the Mincio were headed to the bridge over the Oglio at Marcaria, to secure the line of retreat by the Cremona-Pizzighetone-Pavia road, should the army have to forfeit the line back to Milan; and a few hours later Massena was ordered to move to Lonato, whither Despinoy would also follow, and Kilmaine with the reserve cavalry.

The commander-in-chief had quite regained his equipoise; if he was to deal a blow, he meant that it should be a massed one; and thus retiring his whole force behind the Mincio, he prepared to crush Quosdanovich. Having without resistance occupied Brescia, this Austrian general had advanced July 30 on Montechiaro, and sent Ocskay to Lonato. On July 31 he ran across the French advance parties.

Bonaparte was omnipresent, and always found himself at the point most threatened. He proposed to have his plan executed in his own fashion; and during these few restless days he rode to a standstill five horses, and these of the best to be had, on his never ceasing gallops from place to place.

On the 31st, also, Sauret moved forward to Salo, and turning the left flank of the Austrian line, seized the place and released Guyeux from his peculiar position; "General Guyeux and the troops under his orders remained forty-eight hours with-out bread, constantly fighting against the enemy," reported Bonaparte; having done which, as the Austrian body nearby was reinforced to a point far superior to his own, and threatened to cut him off, Sauret again retired to Desenzano. Meanwhile Despinoy and Massena's head of column, advancing from Peschiera, threw the Austrian detachment under Ocskay out of Lonato. Quosdanovich now recognized that he had a superior force in his front; and beginning after the Salo surprise to fear for his line of retreat,—for the good road along the lake bank to Salo afforded the French an opportunity of throwing forward a large body,—he started back to Gavardo late at night, leaving only a small force at Montechiaro. During the same night Augereau and his division were making a forced march towards Brescia, which they reached August 1, driving the enemy out of Montechiaro on the way; and the possession of this city at once gave back to the French their direct line of communications to Milan, recovered the large stores of bread-stuffs and material there lying, which the Austrians had left in too much haste to destroy, and rendered the Pizzighetone-Pavia line that Bonaparte had seized at Marcaria superfluous. Sauret was again ordered forward to Salo in support of the general programme, but he did not advance far; while Massena assembled his arriving columns at Lonato, as the key-point of the region. Quosdanovich got to Gavardo, and here the Austrian forces which had been in Brescia, Lonato and Moutechiaro rallied on him August 1. In this place, and at Tormino, he took up his stand, feeling secure of his line of retreat, but having practically accomplished nothing in the general scheme for beating the French and recovering Mantua.

Chapter 11

Lonato and Castiglione, Bassano and Mantua

August & September, 1796

Bonaparte had lost Peschiera and Lonato, but had driven Quosdanovich back to Gavardo. Wurmser proposed to cross the Mincio and join his lieutenant. Bonaparte lay between the two. Wurmser was slow. Had he operated rapidly, the Army of Italy would have been crushed between superior bodies. On August 3 Quosdanovich advanced towards Lonato, which had been retaken, and from here Massena drove him back, while Augereau by handsome fighting checked Wurmser's van at Castiglione. On August 4 the French left advanced again on Quosdanovich, but found that he had retired up the lake. This enabled Massena to join in the battle of next day at Castiglione. Having rid himself of the Austrian right, Bonaparte now outnumbered the Austrian left near Castiglione. Augereau remained in place, Massena came up from Lonato, and Serurier's corps from Mantua; and the Brescia troops came along as reserve. Wurmser prepared to fight a defensive battle, and at the proper moment to turn Bonaparte's left. On his side Bonaparte proposed to turn Wurmser's left and cut him off from the Mincio. The French preparations were the better, and the attack was sharp. Augereau quickly broke through the Austrian line, and Wurmser was wise to retire and save his bridges. For six days the French had been marching and fighting, but they were enthused by their splendid success. The siege of Mantua was renewed. Wurmser began a fresh advance at the end of August down the Adige by way of Bassano. Bonaparte kept on with the siege of Mantua, held the lower Adige with small forces, and early in September marched up river, capturing Roveredo and Trent, and thus getting on the rear of the column in the Brenta valley. Holding the Austrians on the upper Adige, he followed Wurmser down the Brenta, beat him at Bassano, threw part of his forces back on the Piave, and followed the rest towards Mantua. A race ensued towards the fortress; the faster French almost trapped the enemy, but Wurmser eluded Bonaparte's van. In a sharp fight on August

16 the Austrians were defeated and hemmed up in Mantua. The place was again shut in. Wurmser' s army had been practically destroyed. The French marching has been rarely equalled. Bonaparte had again proved that speed was one of the great factors in war.

Having reached Valeggio the last day of July, and learning that Mantua was freed of the French, Wurmser determined to cross the Mincio, and fall on the rear of the army which was now manifestly opposing the oncoming of his lieutenant, Quosdanovich, of whose general whereabouts he knew, but from whom he received no news as to details. But the Austrian commander was much too deliberate; he felt that he must first visit the fortress he had relieved; and this he did, entering Mantua in state with two foot and one horse divisions; beseemed not to know that time is of the very essence of manoeuvres leading up to battle, and on August 1 he only sent a van forward to Goito, and a small party over at Borghetto to hold the crossing, while the bulk of this Austrian wing assembled at Roverbella. Next day, August 2, Liptay made a formal passage at Goito and moved on Castiglione, but advancing beyond this place, his van was met by some of Augereau's troops from Montechiaro, and hustled back. Bayalich, with more energy, crossed below Peschiera, and marching on Lonato, smartly attacked and drove out Massena, who retired to Ponte San Marco. Bonaparte had in person reached Brescia late on August 1, and while Liptay was crossing at Goito, Brescia now being out of danger, he established Augereau's division in Montechiaro, and ordered Guyeux, who commanded wounded Sauret's division, backed by Despinoy, to definitely push Quosdanovich out of Gavardo and Salo to the north. Massena received instructions to hold Ponte San Marco as a general central reserve, and Augereau to base on Montechiaro, in any advance he might make against Wurmser.

A detachment of Augereau's division, acting as rearguard, had retired fighting before Wurmser's advance across the Mincio, as far back as Castiglione; and here Bonaparte ordered its commanding officer, Valette, to maintain his ground. The task was a hard one, with less than two thousand men to "defend this important position and thus always keep the division of General Wurmser distant from" the forces under Bonaparte; but allowing himself again to be, as his chief declared, unnecessarily driven in by the much superior Austrian head of column under Liptay, Bonaparte at once cashiered him in the presence of his men. Liptay occupied Castiglione, but Wurmser did not reach Goito until August 2, nor cross until next day.

On August 3 came the real clash of arms, the French having to

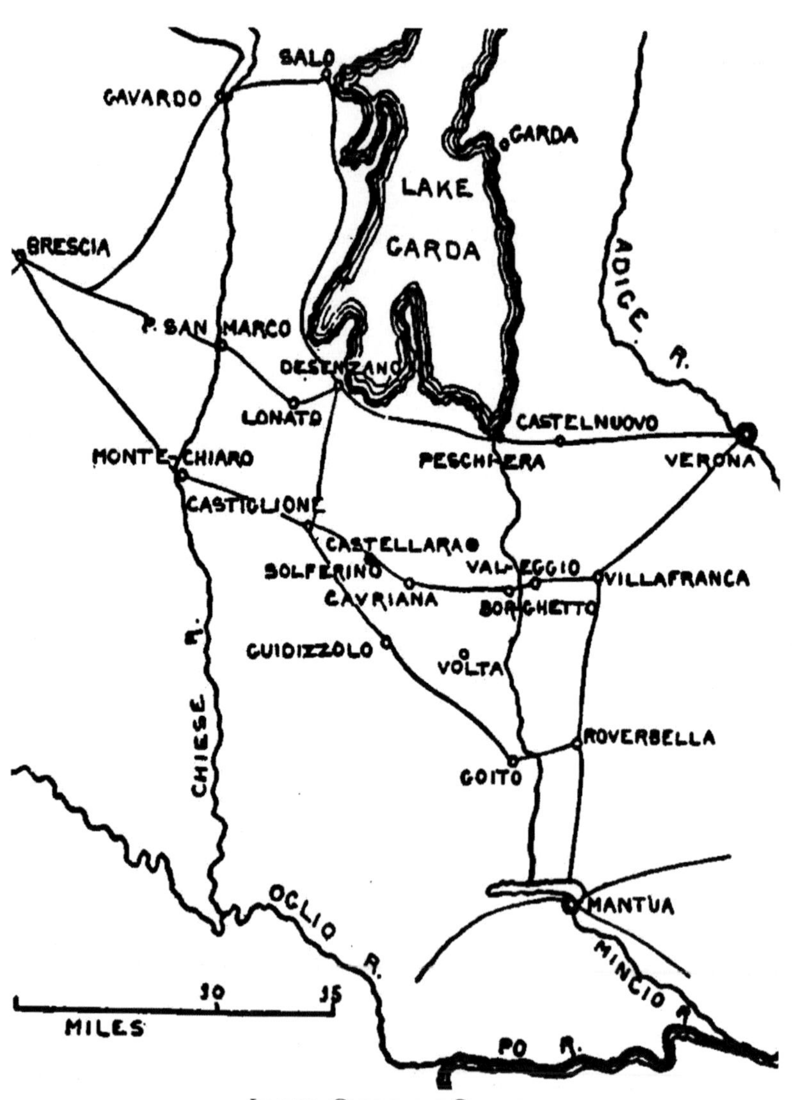

Lonato-Castiglione Country

fight to both front and rear. Bonaparte describes his position as a long line, with Guyeux on the left to attack Salo, Massena in the centre to attack Lonato, and Augereau on the right to attack Castiglione. This, in a sense, it may have been considered. Counting in Massena, Bonaparte could face Wurmser with twenty-five thousand men. He was now backing on the Chiese, as the Austrians were on the Mincio. Exact details of the operations of the day are difficult to exhume from the letters, reports, or contemporary accounts and histories, as the movements of the minor bodies are carelessly referred to, and the hours or even days of their manoeuvres are mostly slurred or omitted. Even Bonaparte's report to the Directory is blind reading. But the general work of each day is plain, and studied with the map, gives a reasonably clear idea of how oddly large bodies of both French and Austrians wandered and fought over the twenty-five miles long battlefield from Salo to Goito. Fortunately Wurmser's slowness enabled Bonaparte to keep his mass in action against Quosdanovich, and to reserve his heavier blow on Wurmser for a future hour. Had the Austrian commander saved one day by being a trifle more active, the French situation would have been far more dangerous.

Bonaparte's first problem was to hold Wurmser from advancing, and meanwhile permanently to drive Quosdanovich away from the vicinity of the French line of retreat. Bayalich was in Lonato, and him Bonaparte must force back in order to keep this Austrian officer from reaching out towards Quosdanovich and establishing connection. Heading Massena's division at San Marco, he advanced during the morning of the 3rd towards Lonato. Meanwhile one of Quosdanovich's columns under Ocskay had advanced, unopposed, from Gavardo on Desenzano, and thence made its way to Lonato, and taken place on the right of Bayalich. As the armies approached each other in front of Lonato, the French van was thrown back by a well-timed Austrian attack which anticipated Massena, and Bayalich strove to take advantage of the momentary gain by extending his wings so as to lap the French line, and with his right to get beyond its left in the direction of Quosdanovich. For this extension Bonaparte speedily punished the Austrian general. Throwing out lines of skirmishers to fend off the Austrian wings, which the clever French light troops succeeded for some time in doing by a sharp fire from cover, and forming two half-brigades in close battalion columns with a dragoon regiment in support, he launched the mass forward, and quickly broke through the enemy's centre. General Pijon and some guns, lost in the first rush, were recaptured. By following this blow up with a second line, before

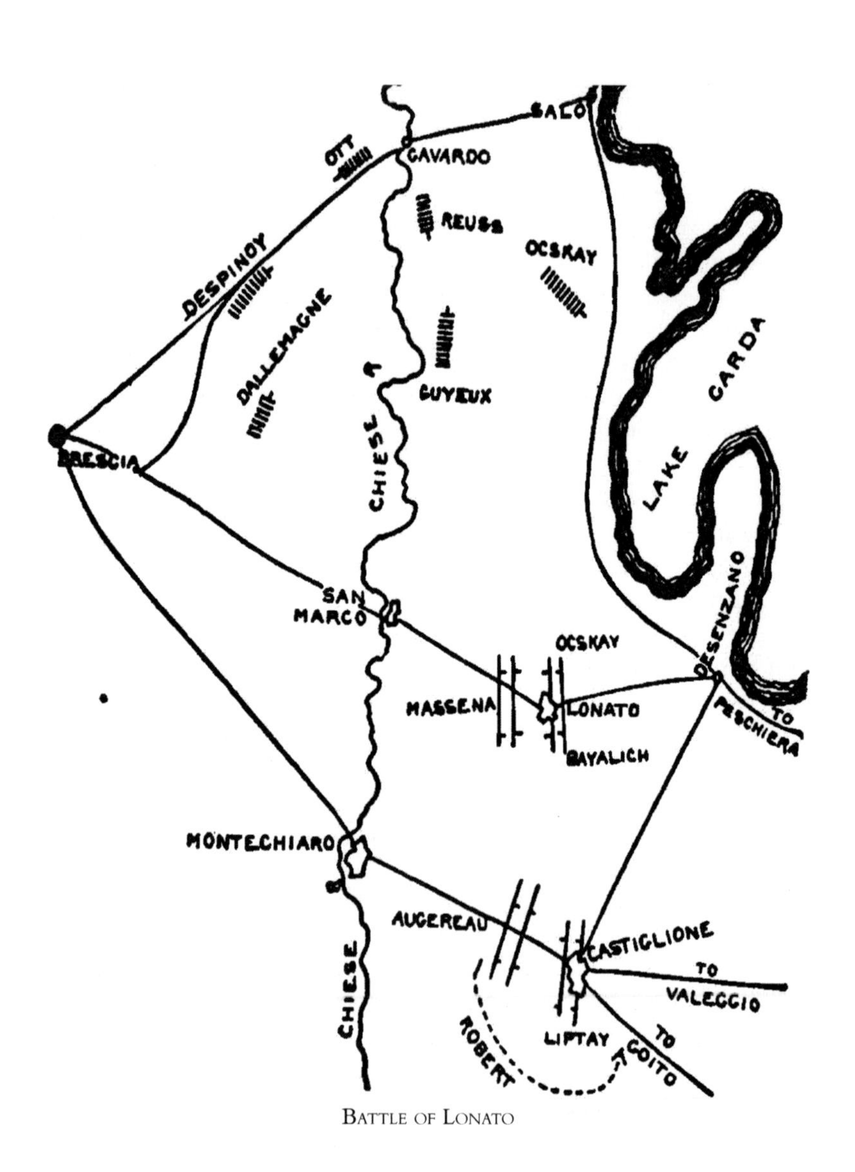

Battle of Lonato

the enemy recovered his equipoise, the victory was completed. Of the two Austrian wings thus separated, the left one under Bayalich naturally retired on the Mincio; the right one under Ocskay as naturally strove to march back whence it came, unaware that Guyeux by his advance now blocked its way. Massena reoccupied Lonato. Thus Quosdanovich was definitely cut off from his chief, and the French could turn upon either one at will.

Early on the 3rd, in addition to the others, Bonaparte had organized three columns, consisting of Guyeux and Despinoy, with Dallemagne's division in support between them, and sent them forward from Brescia and San Marco on Gavardo, relying on Massena, who as a central reserve should occupy Lonato, and on Augereau's column, which was to advance from Montechiaro on Castiglione, to fend off the main Austrian army until he himself could drive off Quosdanovich, this officer being under orders to make a fresh effort to join his chief. Wurmser's slowness was fortunate; but more fortunate still, instead of working in one body, Quosdanovich, while his chief was concentrating forward on Castiglione, had cut up his own force into several columns, under Ott on the right, Reuss in the centre, and Ocskay on the left, which, operating on diverging lines, could by no possibility act in unison. In their advance from Gavardo, the two Austrian columns under Ott and Reuss met the French under Guyeux and Despinoy, and after a smart exchange retired to Gavardo. The third column under Ocskay marched, as narrated, to Desenzano, and thence towards Lonato, where it joined Bayalich, and got defeated; and when Ocskay started back the way he came, he was not only pursued by Massena, but found himself intercepted by Guyeux.

This is how it occurred. Ott and Reuss had been followed by the French to Gavardo. Here Guyeux attacked the Austrian left, but by their hardy onslaught was cut off from Despinoy, and driven back to Salo, followed part way by the enemy. Meanwhile Despinoy and Dallemagne fell on the Austrian right, but with equal lack of success, and after a combat of some hours, they also were forced back towards Brescia. Matters began to look somewhat doubtful for the French left, despite excellent conduct on the part of both officers and men. But again fortune favoured Bonaparte's energy and determination. Though Guyeux was marching in retreat, he was yet in good order, and when, moving south from Salo, he met Ocskay retiring from Lonato and pursued by Massena's troops, he at once set heartily to work to aid his brother officer. Between the two, Ocskay was in evil case, and after a smart resistance saw that to avoid losing his last man, he must lay down his arms. This he did. A small part only of his brigade managed to escape and rejoin Reuss, who had advanced on the road to Desenzano, but on hearing of Ocskay's disaster, had retired. Quosdanovich had thus won a handsome but partial victory against two of Bonaparte's columns. Yet he was so disheartened by the loss of Ocskay's division, and so thoroughly puzzled by the report of a few men who escaped from the disaster as to the numbers of the French, that he determined on retreat, and at once issued orders accordingly. With plenty of physical, he lacked that moral courage which bids defiance to disaster.

Though perhaps at times prejudiced for or against his lieutenants, Bonaparte was not slow to spread the praises of his favourites. In his report to the Directory of August 6 he says:

> I ordered my aide-de-camp, Chief of Brigade Junot, to place himself at the head of my company of guides and to follow the enemy, to catch him by his speed at Desenzano, and to oblige him to retire on Salo. Arrived at Desenzano, he encountered Colonel Bender with a part of his regiment of lancers, which he charged; but Junot, not wanting to amuse himself by charging the rear of the column, made a detour by the right, took the regiment in front, and had wounded the colonel, whom he wished to take prisoner, when he was himself surrounded, and after having killed six men with his own hand, he was overturned, tumbled into a ditch, and wounded with six sabre cuts, none of which, they lead me to hope, will be mortal.

The Battle of Lonato was thus .a series of isolated marches and combats. The main reserve body under Massena, in fighting towards the east, had recaptured Lonato. The body under Guyeux, Despinoy and Dallemagne had started as a whole towards the north, but had been cut in two, and then, after operating on the Austrian flank, had been forced to withdraw. Ocskay had marched south, past Guyeux's right, on Lonato, and on retiring after his defeat, had been caught between Massena and Guyeux, and captured. Augereau was holding head to Liptay by superb fighting near Castiglione. This to-and-fro almost hap-hazard battle-manoeuvring had, however, resulted in cutting Quosdanovich from his chief, and in throwing him back up the lake—which was the end aimed at.

While all this was going on at and north of Lonato, Augereau, in order to hold back Wurmser, had been equally busy. He had started early on the 3rd from Montechiaro towards Castiglione, to contain the main Austrian column under Wurmser. Liptay had also received orders from Wurmser to advance on Montechiaro, and no sooner out of Castiglione than, as stated, he ran against the much superior forces of Augereau. Hoping to be sustained, Liptay fell back to a position on the right and left of Castiglione, and here accepted the French attack that Augereau delayed not to deliver. Beyrand fell on Liptay's left; Verdier and the grenadiers attacked the castle at the south of the town, while Pelletier indulged in a feint against his right. Robert had made a long circuit in the early hours of the day around Liptay's left, and lay in ambush in his rear; and Augereau kept a reserve well in hand behind his line. Liptay held his position with distinct tenacity despite the French superior forces, and yielded no ground to the repeated attacks until Robert broke out of ambush and fell upon him unawares. He then retired in good order to the heights behind Castiglione, where he threw back several further assaults by Augereau. He had done himself vast credit in resisting the masterful onsets of the French general. Late in the day Wurmser's column began to reach the ground. These reinforcements might have enabled the Austrians to push Augereau back, but they contented themselves with holding their ground, and at night retired to the heights behind Castiglione and near Solferino, where during the 4th Wurmser collected twenty thousand men. Augereau had done his work bravely and skilfully. But the report exaggerates in saying that "all the day he delivered and sustained fierce combats against forces double his own." The Austrian loss at Lonato is stated as three thousand men killed and wounded, four thousand prisoners and twenty guns; at Castiglione on the 3rd, four thousand killed, wounded and missing. The French casualties were less, as they lost no prisoners on that day, though during the campaign Bonaparte acknowledges thirteen hundred captured. Towards evening the leader came up and inspected the work of "intrepid Augereau," as he calls him in the report, gave instructions for the morrow, and returned to his headquarters, then at Lonato, to supervise the whole scheme of action.

When, according to orders, on August 4 Despinoy, reinforced by three thousand men from the Army of the Alps, and Guyeux, reinforced by a brigade of Massena's, again sallied out respectively from Brescia and Salo, determined to drive Quosdanovich out of Gavardo, as they had the day before failed to do, they found to their surprise that the Austrians were in full retreat up river on Riva. All they could do was to fall on the Austrian rear, which they did with effect. Quosdanovich had made up his mind that he could not effect a junction with his chief by this route, and had concluded to march around the north of the lake to the Adige. A small party had been left behind. This rearguard got cut off by the French advance under Guyeux. Part of it, however, made its way to the main column. The other part essayed to cut its way through to Wurmser south of the lake. Quosdanovich's retreat was a lucky termination to what might have been a situation beyond even Bonaparte's resourcefulness; but it was well earned by the French leader's energy and defiance of danger.

While Massena on the 4th was marching towards Castiglione and the expected battle there, Bonaparte had returned to headquarters at Lonato, which he deemed to be sufficiently protected with a guard of twelve hundred men. But that part of Quosdanovich's rearguard which had marched south had lost its way in seeking to join Wurmser, and suddenly appearing at Lonato, boldly summoned the headquarters guard to surrender. Only by a feat of audacity, and at marked personal risk, could Bonaparte face the matter out; but he succeeded in bluffing the Austrian officer in command, and after some show of resistance the party of two thousand men (four thousand he calls it), with four guns, gave in and surrendered. Bonaparte's narration of this affair is interesting:

> I myself went to Lonato to look at the troops that I was to draw from thence; but what was my surprise on entering the place to receive a parliamentary who summoned the commandant to surrender, because, said he, you are surrounded on all sides! In effect, the different cavalry videttes announced to me that several columns were in touch with our grand guard, and that already the road from Brescia to Lonato was intercepted at the bridge of San Marco. I then felt that it could only be the debris of the division that had been cut off, which, after having wandered around and assembled, was striving to make a passage for itself. The circumstance was rather embarrassing. I had at Lonato only about twelve hundred men. I had the parliamentary come before me, and caused his eyes to be unbandaged. I told him that if his general had the presumption to capture the general-in-chief of the Army of Italy, he had only to come forward to do it; that he ought to know that I was at Lonato, because all the world knew that my army was there; that all the general officers and superior officers of his division should be held responsible for the personal insult he had been guilty of. I declared to him that if, in eight minutes, his division had not

> laid down its arms, I would not pardon a single one. The parliamentary appeared much astonished to find me there, and an instant afterwards the whole column laid down its arms.

This occurrence, and what he learned by cross-examining the officers captured, proved to Bonaparte that he had definitely got rid of Quosdanovich, and that he was now safe to turn with his entire force on the main Austrian army. Guyeux and Despinoy were ordered to follow up Quosdanovich, and this a part of their force did until he reached Lake Idro and the Rocca d'Anfo defile.

Wurmser meanwhile had been making some changes in his position behind Castiglione, but had done little either in the way of concentration, or to help Quosdanovich in his efforts to come on to his assistance. He had detached one force on a useless errand down the Po, and another equally useless one to blockade Peschiera on the east bank of the Mincio. Bonaparte, on the contrary, prepared during the 4th to put in his last man against the Austrian main army, and in reality, on the field itself, secured the preponderance of numbers. Wurmser had, however, drawn up his line with care, leaning the right on Solferino and the left on Medolano, and here he cheerfully awaited the French onset. Serurier had fallen ill, but his division, under General Fiorella, by 8 a. m. on August 5 arrived from Marcaria; on the disappearance of Quosdanovich, Guyeux and Despinoy, so far as not engaged in his pursuit, were ordered down by rapid marches, and Massena was placed on the left of Augereau, who still continued to face Wurmser. The French line thus ran: Massena on the left, Augereau in the centre, Fiorella on the right, Despinoy and Guyeux coming up in reserve. Bonaparte was massing his forces according to what Jomini enunciates as this great captain's general rule, as it had been Frederick's:

> When you want to deliver battle, assemble all your forces; neglect none of them; a battalion sometimes decides a day.

And moreover the blow was to be aimed in such a way as to compromise Wurmser, should he defeat him. For the Austrian retreat across the river must be at or near Valeggio, and his left was his strategic flank.

Before daylight of August 5 Bonaparte was at Castiglione, marshalling his troops for the battle which was to decide the fate of Italy. Each army leaned on the hills which lie south of Garda and up to the Mincio, the French left and the Austrian right being strongly posted there; and Wurmser had well entrenched his left at Medolano. His twenty battalions and ten squadrons were deployed in two lines, and he had made ready to fight a defensive battle. Moreover, his tactics played into Bonaparte's hands. He essayed to extend his right so as to turn the French left, and at the same time to enable him to reach out towards Quosdanovich, of whose retreat beyond Lake Idro, to be sure, he did not know, but on whom he had no right to believe he could any longer rely. Augereau, in two lines, stood on the right of the road to Valeggio, with Kilmaine and the reserve cavalry echeloned in his right and rear. Massena in one line, with a second line of columns in support, stood on the left of the road. Fiorella came up at Birbisi, and was ordered under cover of the accentuations of the ground, via Guidizzolo on Cavriana, to turn the Austrian left, and roll the enemy up and away from the bridges at Borghetto. Jomini says:

> One must not deliver battle only to win it; one should aim at the destruction of the enemy's organized body.

In the prosecution of his plan, and to allow Fiorella ample time to gain Wurmser's left, Bonaparte made several simple demonstrations during the early part of the day on Wurmser's front. In fact, he made a slight feint of a retrograde movement with the whole army to tempt Wurmser forward from his position, so that Serurier's division might get in his rear. Wurmser replied by extending his right to outflank Massena, but without the careful preparation of the French commander. Bonaparte slowly extended his own right; and as soon as Fiorella had reached his position in advance of Guidizzolo, this whole French wing was ordered forward on the Austrian left flank. Augereau assaulted the centre at the tower of Solferino, Massena contained the right Wurmser's left centre was protected by a strong redoubt he had built in the plain. This, cannonaded by twenty pieces assembled under Bonaparte's orders by Marmont, and attacked by General Verdier with three grenadier battalions, could not hold long. While the placing of the troops does not appear to have been in Frederick's echeloned oblique order, yet the general advance of the French has often been said to suggest Leuthen, which in a sense it does, though there the gallant king was attacking thrice his force, and with a tactical precision not elsewhere seen in modern days.

The lines went forward with a will. Verdier rushed the redoubt and captured Medolano; and Wurmser from his second line threw a crotchet back on his left, to fend off the threat and protect his position from the French reserve cavalry, which had ridden out towards the Austrian left and was heading for San Cassiano. Other battalions from his second line moved on Cavriano, which Fiorella could now be seen to be fast

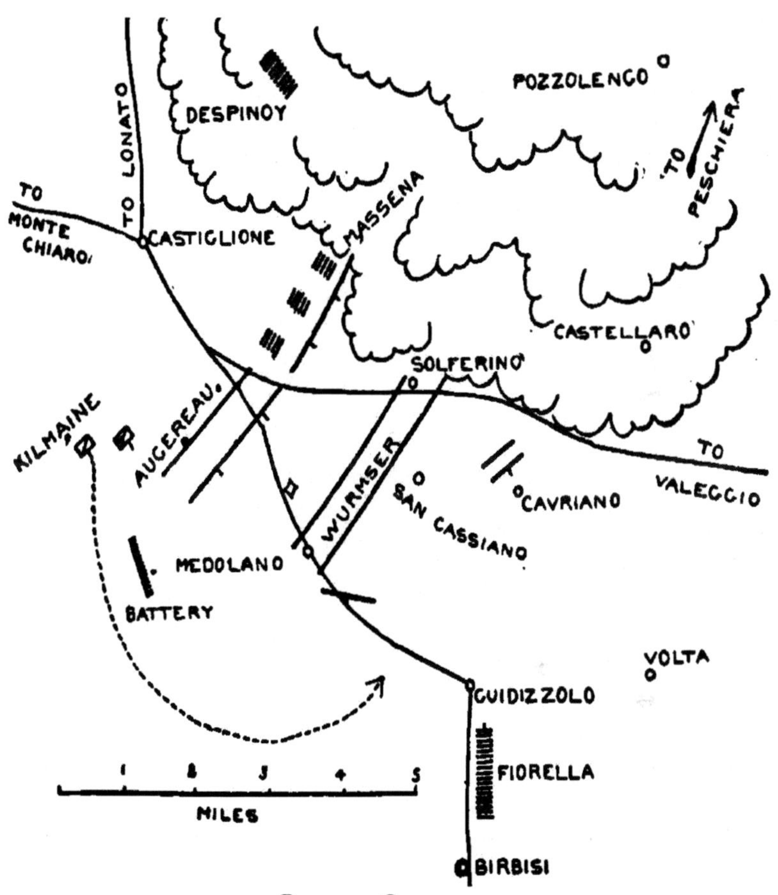

Battle of Castiglione

approaching. Bonaparte ordered forward his centre and left. Augereau with a stout onset broke through the Austrian weakened line. Owing to Wurmser's manoeuvre towards the right, Massena had harder work in his front, but Despinoy now came up, a fresh advance was undertaken, and by a strong joint effort the victory was made secure. Wurmser was not slow to recognize his defeat, and before his army was quite broken, retired straight towards the Mincio; but he was hard put to it to retain his bridges at Borghetto. This, however, he eventually, though with heavy losses, succeeded in doing. The French followed on, and produced grave disorder in his divisions. The Mincio was crossed with a decimated and disorganized army, leaving behind, as the tale for this day, two thousand men killed and wounded, and twenty guns.

The French were quite exhausted by their long marches and their full week's fighting, but gloriously happy at their wonderful success. Augereau camped under arms at Castellaro, Massena at Pozzolengo, Fiorella at Volta.

On August 6 Bonaparte could write to the Directory:

> Here, then, in five days is another campaign finished. Wurmser has lost in these five days seventy field-guns, all his infantry wagons, twelve to fifteen thousand prisoners, six thousand men killed and wounded, and nearly all these troops coming from the Rhine. We lost on our side thirteen hundred prisoners and two thousand men killed or wounded. All the soldiers, officers and generals displayed in this difficult circumstance a great character for bravery.

As a sample of Bonaparte's summary methods, the following order is interesting:

> Headquarters
> Castiglione
> 19 *Thermidor*, Year IV (August 6)
> The municipality of Castiglione will immediately cause to be buried the dead who are found in its territory; the horses will be likewise buried. For this operation all the inhabitants are requisitioned. The municipality of Castiglione will notify all the neighbouring communes which have any dead on their territory to cause them immediately to be buried. The municipal officers are personally responsible for the execution of the present order, and if, this evening by ten o'clock, there remains a single corpse which has not been buried, they shall be punished by martial law.

By many authors, all the combats from July 29 to August 5 are included in the title. Battle of Castiglione.

To prevent Wurmser from holding the Mincio, Augereau, early on the 6th, was ordered to demonstrate for a crossing at Valeggio, while Massena, to turn the Austrian right, moved by way of Peschiera, the garrison of which had managed to hold out against Wurmser. He reached Peschiera by 9 a. m., Augereau meanwhile cannonading Wurmser to attract his attention. Massena crossed the Mincio, and threw back the Austrian force he there met, which was entrenched along the heights on the southeast of the fortress. Bonaparte, deeming this now the place to give the *coup de graces* shortly sustained him with Fiorella and Augereau. But Wurmser had already issued orders to retire up the Adige valley towards the Tyrol, and could not be caught. The road by way of Bussolengo having been closed by the French, the Austrians moved through Verona, sending the cavalry along the Brenta valley, where it could better forage.

Serurier's division reached Verona at ten o'clock in the evening. The official report says:

> The rearguard of the enemy was still in Verona; the gates were shut and the drawbridges up. The Proveditor of the Republic of Venice, summoned to open them, declared that he could not do it short of two hours. I ordered at once that the gates should be opened by cannon-balls, which General Dommartin executed in less than quarter of an hour. . . . At Castelnuovo, on Venetian territory, a volunteer was assassinated. I had the house where this was done burned, and on its ashes I put up a sign, 'Here a Frenchman was assassinated.'

In due time Quosdanovich and Wurmser again assembled at Trent their beaten forces. All they had accomplished for their heavy losses was to leave seven fresh battalions in Mantua. The French had lost some five thousand men, and at Mantua had abandoned one hundred and eighty-seven guns.

The French pursuit was neither active nor long continued. The troops were absolutely exhausted, and Bonaparte gave them their well-earned rest. Massena went into the old positions he had held in July, Sauret did the same, Augereau took post at Verona, Fiorella led his troops back to Mantua and resumed the siege. The loss of the siege material was heavily felt, and only a slow blockade could be resorted to.

One marked effect of these victories was the signing of a new treaty, offensive and defensive, between France and Spain.

Works of art were not the only things which were collected in the French campaigns. From Brescia, August 13, 1796, Bonaparte wrote:

> The jewellery and diamonds. Citizen Directors, that the army has sent to Genoa, which since then were on the way to Paris, and which have been started back to Genoa, ought to be worth at least two or three millions; yet there has been offered for them only four hundred thousand *francs*. I believe that it is the interest of the Republic that these precious objects should be transported to Paris. The great number of strangers who are in this capital will make the sale of these objects more fruitful. Moreover, I understand that the Flaschat Company is to take them for four hundred thousand *francs*; that would be a ruinous transaction for the Republic.

During this "Campaign of Five Days" Napoleon reported to the Directory:

> You would believe, that when we arrive in the bivouac our soldiers would at least go to sleep. Not at all. Each one makes up his reckoning, or his plan of operations for the morrow, and many of the latter are very true. The other day I was watching a half-brigade file before me. A *chasseur* approached my horse. 'General,' said he, 'you ought to do this.' 'Wretch,' said I, 'wilt thou hold thy tongue!' He disappeared instantly, and I sought him in vain. What he had said to me was just what I had ordered to be done.

This will appear natural enough to all old soldiers. During our Civil War the veterans were often able to prognosticate what the conditions demanded.

Whenever an army pushes rapidly into the enemy's country, it by and by reaches a point where its initial force has been exhausted, when it must stop and either act on the defensive, or else create a strong secondary base for a fresh advance. Bonaparte had long before pointed out to the Directory the Adige as the limit of possible operations from Piedmont as the only base. The Alps, between him and the Austrian Tyrol, were too serious an obstacle to overcome with what force was left him; and the Mincio, flanked by Peschiera and Mantua, was the proper secondary base. Both the mountains as a natural obstacle and Mantua in the enemy's hands as an artificial obstacle were factors altogether too much in his opponent's favour, and Bonaparte's offensive campaign had to come to a legitimate strategical pause. To pave the way for further offensive work, he re-established as far as possible the siege of Mantua, and placed an observation army to watch the Alps.,

It has been said that on reaching the Mincio Bonaparte should at once have used his entire force to insure the early capture of Mantua. But suppose, as was probable, that Mantua had made a long defence. This would have left him at the mercy of the oncoming reinforced Austrian army, which he knew to be much larger than his own, and which, unopposed, would have first cut him off from Milan by way of Peschiera or Brescia, and then have turned on his isolated army at Mantua. In what a trap, then, with communications cut and with only forty thousand men, would the French commander have been! He would have had to face an army of relief of fifty thousand men, plus the thirteen thousand men in Mantua; he himself would have been besieged in his own siege-lines, and if he had broken out from them, he would have even then had to undertake just what he now chose to undertake of his own free will—a renewed offensive against the oncoming Austrian army. It is not frequent in history that armies have been able to cut their way out of a besieged fortress. Besiegers have now and then driven away relief armies and still held on to the siege of a fortress, but rarely, and under exceptional conditions as to communications, force and character of ground. Bonaparte with his food cut off would have been in ill case. Whether he remained before Mantua or not, he must eventually choose either to retire to Piedmont, or to fight for his holding on the Mincio; and it was unquestionably his wiser policy to undertake the offensive at first, rather than be forced into a series of defensive battles.

Having come to this conclusion, Bonaparte would have been more than unwise to throw away his theory of masses, leave a substantial part of his forces before Mantua, and fight an enemy already superior with a still more diminished body. His main task was to hold the Mincio and thus hold Lombardy; to take Mantua was, to be sure, the immediate task, but it was a subsidiary one. He showed his grasp of the whole problem and a strong sense of perspective by selecting the course he did, by throwing up the operation against Mantua as of secondary importance, and by directing his whole mass with the utmost rapidity on the enemy; and especially was this so because Wurmser had divided his forces. "The strength of an army, like that of a body in motion in mechanics, is expressed by the mass multiplied by the velocity." This the French general proved true along the Mincio.

When Frederick had shut in Prague in 1757, he had before him much the same problem. Daun was approaching with a large army. Had Frederick decided as Bonaparte did; had he thrown up the siege of Prague, or left only a few regiments there as an observation party to contain the enemy or delay him; had he concentrated his whole force and marched rapidly against Daun, is there any reason to doubt that he would have crushed him—as, indeed, with his thirty-four thousand men to Daun's fifty-three thousand, he came near to doing,—and then have returned and marched with flying colours into Prague? But Frederick, in his estimate of masses, had been taught a careless lesson by his extraordinary victories with inferior numbers. On this occasion "he saw too many things at once," and forgot his own rule, "Whoever seeks to conserve everything will lose everything;" and as a result he lost Kolin, lost Prague, and lost the campaign of 1757.

Wurmser had been thrown back into the mountains, but this was by no means to be the last of the energetic old soldier, who, moreover, had received stringent orders from Vienna to advance once more against the enemy. Bonaparte anticipated a further movement, and finding that the late operations had somewhat disorganized not only the troops, but the supply department, and that some time should be devoted to this end, he set vigorously to work on reorganization. It would have been a thrust in the air to follow the Austrians into the Tyrol until he had some knowledge of the advance into Germany of the Army of the Rhine. Instead of blindly pushing on, irrespective of difficulties, and relying solely on his destiny, as he is often carelessly represented to have done, we see him devoting his days and weeks to the smallest details of the commissariat and ordnance, while neglecting no factor in the broad strategic scheme. Again, if he was to advance with the Mincio as a secondary base, he must have fresh accessions of troops, for the rule of numbers was the constant basis of his calculations; and for these reinforcements he never ceased to press in his dispatches to the Directory. Yet, despite all difficulties, Bonaparte knew that the safest way of countering the blow he felt sure Wurmser would again deliver was himself at the proper moment to assume the offensive.

The equipment of the army at this time was lacking. Bonaparte wrote to the chief commissary from Brescia, August 18:

> In four or five days. Citizen Ordinator, a new campaign will be opened by the invincible Army of Italy. The barriers of the

Tyrol will be forced, and the theatre of war will extend to Germany. The army is partly naked, and the nights are very cold. The mountains demand that the soldiers should have shoes, and many are with naked feet.... Gather all your means, and let me know on what we can count. . . . Have we got capes? Finally, what can I announce to the division generals?

Some changes were now made in the troops, stations and commands; and at the end of August the army lay as follows: Sahuguet's division of eight thousand men blockaded Mantua, now held by seventeen thousand men, of whom a quarter were sick; Augereau's nine thousand men stood at Verona; Massena with thirteen thousand men occupied Rivoli and vicinity; and Vaubois with eleven thousand men lay at Storo on the Chiese, near the head of the Lake of Garda.

The following letter of August 14 to the Directory is of interest:

Headquarters
Brescia
27 Thermidor, Year IV
I think it is useful, Citizen Directors, to give you my opinion as to the generals employed in this army; you will see that there are very few who can serve me.

Berthier: Talents, activity, courage, character. He deserves everything.

Augereau: Much character, courage, firmness, activity, has the habit of war, is loved by the soldier, lucky in his operations.

Massena: Active, indefatigable, has audacity, *coup deceit* and promptness in decision.

Serurier: Fights like a soldier; will not accept responsibility; firm, has not confidence enough in his soldiers; is a sick man.

Despinoy: Soft, without activity, without audacity; has not the feeling for war, is not liked by the men, does not fight at their head; moreover, he is haughty; has brains and sound political views; good to command in the interior.

Sauret: Good, very good soldier, not clever enough to be a general; little lucky.

Abatucci: Not good to command fifty men.

Garnier, Meunier, Casabianca: Incapable; not good to command a battalion in a war as active and as serious as this one.

Macquart: brave man; no talents; lively.

Gaultier: Good for an office; has never made war.

Vaubois and Sahuguet: . . . I shall learn to gauge them. So

> far they have acquitted themselves very well of what I have confided to them; but the example of General Despinoy, who was very good in Milan and very bad at the head of his division, obliges me to judge men by their actions.
> *Bonaparte*

The war commissaries frequently gave much trouble.. On August 26, 1796, Bonaparte wrote the Directory about a commissary named Salva, who had fled from the army in a panic fright.

> Nothing equals this cowardice except the bravery of the soldiers. Many of the commissaries of war have not been more courageous. Such, Citizen Directors, is the inconvenience of the law, which directs that the commissaries of war shall be only civil agents, while they need more courage and military usage than the officers themselves. The courage they need has to be entirely moral. It is never the fruit of anything but the custom of danger.

On the last day of August Bonaparte wrote Moreau that he was ready to cooperate with him, and should, two days thence, move on Trent, now Wurmser's headquarters. Despite initial success, however, the Army of the Rhine and the Army of the Sambre and Mouse, respectively under Moreau and Jourdan, were not destined to cooperate with the Army of Italy; and shortly after the time when Bonaparte stood ready to reach out towards these associates, join, and with them march on Vienna, both (as will be later detailed) were to be compromised by the able strategy of young Archduke Charles, and to beat a retreat to the Rhine; while Bonaparte on the Mincio was to be left to rely on his own unaided efforts for whatever success France was to obtain in the general campaign of 1796.

When, at the end of August, Moreau in his initial success had crossed the Lech, the authorities in Vienna, fearing the capture of Innsbruck and the invasion of the Tyrol, drew up a new plan to drive back Bonaparte, or at least to forestall his advance up the Adige. Accordingly Wurmser began his preparations for a fresh advance from Trent, this time to attack the line of the Mincio from the east. After being reinforced, he had some forty-five thousand men, and these he was to divide into two parts, of which one was to close the Tyrol to Bonaparte by holding the Adige valley at its upper waters, while with the other he would himself march down the Brenta valley on Bassano, whence he would turn to Verona or Legnano, and make his way to Mantua. He had small doubt that he should thus take Bonaparte unawares, and succeed in raising the siege of the great fortress, with the numerous troops in which, added to his own, he would be able to inflict a severe blow on the French.

To Davidovich he gave command of twenty thousand men, of which six thousand were at Roveredo, seven thousand behind them at Trent, and the rest at various good defensive posts in the mountains in the rear, observing the entrances from the valley of the Po; and with twenty-five thousand the chief started out on his offensive thrust. His three divisions were under Mezaros, Sebottendorf and Quosdanovich, and he had a fine large body of reserve cavalry. On August 81 sixteen thousand men had got to Bassano, four thousand were in Pergine, and six thousand still in Trent. In a week he purposed to have them all in Bassano.

Wurmser was beset by a notion that a demonstration down the Brenta valley against Bonaparte's flank would drive him back beyond the Mincio. It never appeared to enter his calculations that the French commander could meanwhile do some fairly intelligent manoeuvring on his own account. It is curious that any general of experience should thus continue to divide his forces; but such was the habit of the day, and the requirement of the universal cordon system. His late campaign had taught him nothing. He calculated that, should Bonaparte turn on his column near Verona or Legnano, Davidovich would debouch on his rear; while he himself would do the same should the French march up the Adige. If, as was probable, Bonaparte retired behind the Mincio, the Austrians would have gained that much territory, and he would pursue the enemy and recover Lombardy. Should Bonaparte, however, defend the Oglio or the Adda, the Austrians, having relieved Mantua, would cross the Po and march on Tortona. Wurmser failed to consider that, if he was to fight Bonaparte, his division of forces would be fatal. In war you are constantly called on to divide your forces; but it behooves you to see to it that you can assemble them more rapidly than the enemy—in other words, that you control the interior lines.

Although Bonaparte was ready to move at the same moment as his opponent, neither had as yet guessed the other's intentions. On September 1 orders issued from the Verona headquarters were to the effect that Massena should start next day up the road which ran on the right bank of the Adige towards Ala, while Augereau, keeping touch with him, was to follow in his right rear on the road along the left bank, so as to sustain his associate at need. Both started about noon, leaving Kilmaine with three thousand men in Verona, from which place he was to patrol down the river to Legnano. Vaubois had already been ordered to start on the same day up the Chiese and around the head of the Lake of Garda to Riva and Mori. This gave Bonaparte somewhat under thirty thousand men for his marching army.

Sahuguet, with his eight thousand men at Mantua, was merely notified of the forward movement and warned to be on the alert. That a small detachment of the enemy had been in Bassano, Bonaparte already knew; but he believed the bulk of the Austrians to be still in Trent, and had no idea of Wurmser's intended operation through the Brenta valley on Mantua. But, like Frederick, Bonaparte always provided for even remote probabilities. "Should the enemy, however, commit such a piece of stupidity," said he, referring to just this manoeuvre, Kilmaine was to retire behind the Mincio, and Sahuguet to give up the siege of Mantua, and withdraw behind the Oglio. But Peschiera was to be garrisoned and held at all hazards, to keep open the line of retreat of the main army.

The above movements were made September 2 and 3, and a few Austrian outposts were driven out of Ala and vicinity. The joint concentration was to be made the next day by all three divisions near Mori, before reaching the immediate presence of the enemy, and the march on Roveredo was to follow.

Every great captain has recognized the value of the offensive,—of the initiative. He cannot bring himself to accept the enemy's directions, to act in accordance with the enemy's plan. He prefers to prescribe the plan himself. To Napoleon the offensive implied concentrated masses hurled at the right spot; and from the start he acted on the idea of concentration. Division of forces, concentric columns, he will none of. To command success, concentric columns require a clever and exceptionally pushing leader at the head of each one; no one man can direct several such; any minor interruption of one of them may be fatal to all. Yet despite their disadvantages, there is something about concentric manoeuvres which has always fascinated the average general. To surround an enemy on all sides sounds and looks well; but this can rarely be accomplished in the face of a clever adversary; and the latter nearly always has a superiority of forces at whatever point in the chain he chooses to attack. Napoleon wrote in 1807 to Jerome:

> I see that you are on a false military road; I see that you think that two columns which shall seize the enemy between them

are an advantage; but this does not occur in war, because the two columns never act in unison, and the enemy can beat one after the other. Of course you must turn the enemy, *but concentrate first.*

Napoleon sought so to operate that his plans should not fail because the leader of one of his separate columns did not or could not carry out his part of the united plan. So scrupulous was he as to concentrating before he met the enemy that, with regard to the very movement now in progress, he doubted if the columns had not gone too near the enemy before uniting. And we remember how careful he was to concentrate on his right before beginning the campaign in April. In this particular instance, while Bonaparte had organized three columns, Vaubois, Massena and Augereau, they were so to march as to be able to concentrate before they should reach the enemy. The Austrian commander, on the contrary, separated his two columns so that neither would be able to aid the other.

Reuss had been stationed and had entrenched himself at Mori to stop Vaubois' advance; and Wukassovich had been ordered to defend "the inexpugnable defile," as Bonaparte calls it, at San Marco, where the mountains come down near the Adige, against Massena and Augereau; the reserve held the equally strong defile at Caliano. The situation of the Austrian force was good. Would they be stout enough to hold their ground?

On September 3 the leading brigades of Massena's column drove in the enemy's outposts, and next day Massena in force fell on Wukassovich at San Marco, while Vaubois forced the Sarca, stormed the Austrian works at Mori, and then advancing on Roveredo, threatened to turn the Austrian right flank. Wukassovich had placed the bulk of his forces in this position. Bonaparte made use of the common tactics of mountain warfare. By heavy artillery fire on the front battalion, followed up by a smart infantry attack, he succeeded in unsettling the Austrian troops in the rear, that could take no part in the struggle. At the same time strong parties of riflemen under Pijon were sent up along the mountain sides to take the Austrians in flank. Soon he launched Victor with a close column at the double-quick along the highway, on the troops holding the defile, and the fighting came to close quarters. This was followed by a charge of Dubois and his hussars. The Austrians, outnumbered and overwhelmed, turned, after two hours' fighting, from the defence they had handsomely maintained; and between this attack and Vaubois' flank march, the French forced

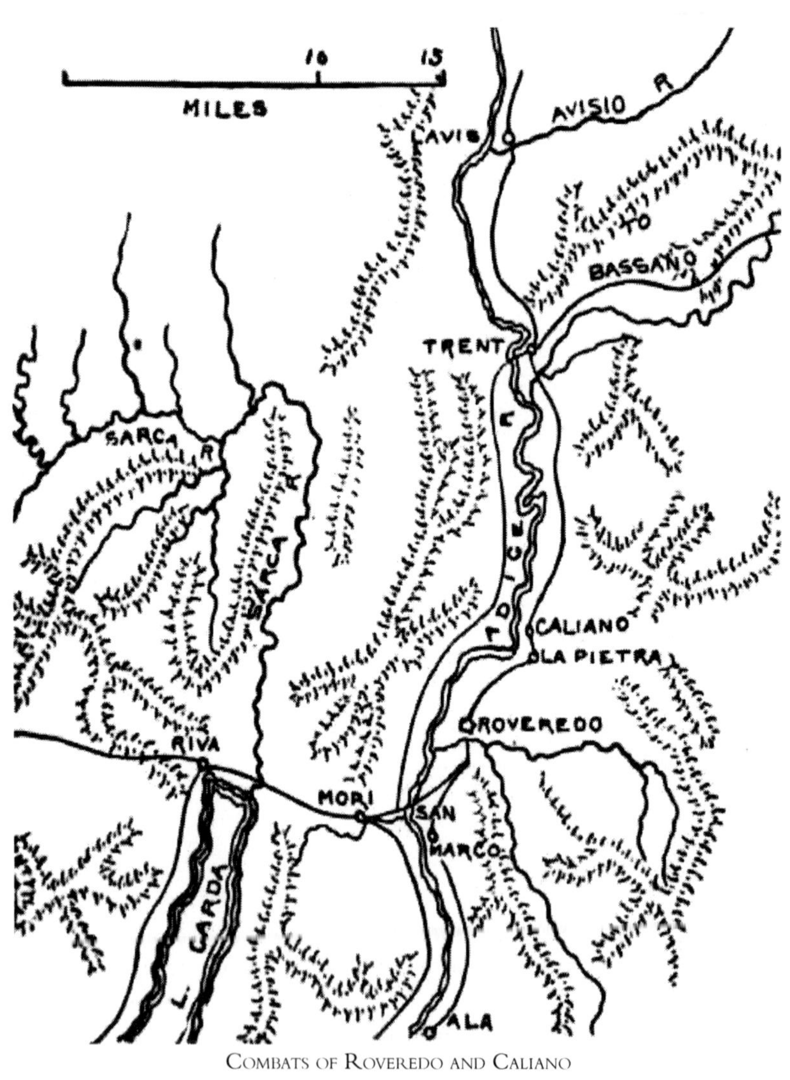

Combats of Roveredo and Caliano

Davidovich back with heavy casualties on Roveredo. For the possession of this town there was another stubborn contest on the same day. Victor again at the double-quick followed the Austrians along the main road, while Rampon was sent through the open ground between Roveredo and the river, and Vaubois arrived from Mori. The place being made untenable, the Austrian forces gradually fell back towards Caliano, and the French took breath at Roveredo and prepared to advance farther. It was one o'clock. Bonaparte reported:

> We had yet taken only three guns and made about one thousand prisoners. This was not to win a victory.

Somewhat to the south of Caliano runs a narrow defile,—some two hundred feet wide,—between river and perpendicular rocks. This is dominated by the castle of La Pietra and closed by a good wall; and Davidovich thought the position to be sufficiently held by a few battalions, especially as the castle was well equipped with guns that could be trained on an assaulting party. Bonaparte repeated his tactics of San Marco. Sending bodies of riflemen under Pijon to climb the heights on the right, and other bodies to make their way along the river on the left, and posting some artillery on a projecting rocky eminence, he vigorously bombarded the castle, and this then fell at the first assault. Thereupon three half-brigades were thrown into the defile in close column. There was no space to fight, except hand to hand, and the contest was fierce. A small party of French horse strove to get around and cut the Austrians off at the upper end; other cavalry followed, and after a short but deadly struggle the defile was taken with its twenty-five guns, and three thousand Austrians laid down their arms. The defile having thus suddenly yielded to the vigorous thrust, the French column pushed on through it, and Davidovich's main body, which had deemed itself secure in its camp at Caliano, was forced into disorderly retreat on Trent. Bonaparte reported to the Directory:

> The Citizen Bessières, captain of my company of guides, saw two guns on the point of escape; he rushed forward with five or six guides, and despite the efforts of the enemy, stopped these pieces.

Thus was the road to the Tyrol opened by the brilliant fighting of the French advance. Davidovich cannot be said to have acted with as much discretion or vigour as his opponent.

Had he recognized the meaning of this occurrence, it would have much disturbed Wurmser, whose columns were systematically pursuing their march down the Brenta valley, the rear having already reached Borgo. But though, during the same afternoon, he heard of the Roveredo combat at his headquarters, which was still at Trent, Wurmser not only made no change of plan, but himself set out to join the field force at Bassano, leaving Davidovich behind with orders to defend Trent to the last man. He held fast to the impression, now that Bonaparte had adventured so far up the Adige, that the moment was all the more auspicious to seize the lower Adige, while his lieutenant should hold the key to the Tyrol, and thus catch the French, as it were, in a trap. He forgot that his method would necessitate a battle, that in this battle he would be outnumbered, and that this was just the scheme, slightly varied, in which he had failed before. That Trent, which had excellent means of defence, could be held seemed certain; but the irresistible flood of French brigades speedily swamped the Austrian resistance, and his task immediately proving impossible, Davidovich retired behind the Avisio, and Massena entered the famous City of Councils on the morning of September 5, followed by Vaubois at noon, with Augereau still coming up.

When he found that he could not hold head to the French, Davidovich had made a fatal error in not leaving the defence of the Tyrol to his lieutenant, Laudon, and a small force, to which could have been added much Tyrolese militia, and marching down the Brenta valley to join his chief. This would have given Wurmser considerably over thirty thousand men with which to oppose the twenty thousand of Massena and Augereau. But Davidovich, like all the Austrian generals, was hampered by his orders from Vienna, which were to the effect that the passage through the Tyrol was to be held in force and kept closed to the French at all hazards. He had no independence of action.

By the possession of Trent the French were established on the rear of Wurmser's column. Bonaparte, though still knowing nothing about the operation of Moreau, saw that here was a better game to play than to adventure into the Tyrol in an attempt to join the Army of the Rhine, even had he believed it to be approaching. Moreover, he was clearly holden, first of all, to protect his own rear, and not to expose the troops he had left behind. But Wurmser's manoeuvre itself Bonaparte did not at first correctly interpret. He believed that his own forward movement had been at the root of the Austrian's eccentric march, and he prepared at once to do two things to meet the conditions: dispose of Davidovich, so as to have his own rear protected, and then follow Wurmser, fall on his rear wherever he should reach him, and force him to a battle. He had no idea that Wurmser was aiming to relieve Mantua, but imagined that he was seeking to cut the French communications, while Davidovich should fend the French off from the Tyrol by holding on to Trent. This scheme Bonaparte proposed to render nugatory.

Davidovich recognized the gravity of the situation, and essayed to defend the bridge over the Avisio River at Lavis. Vaubois strove in vain to seize it. Bonaparte found his presence essential. Riding to Lavis, Vaubois was again pushed forward, and by evening, under the chiefs eye, the French had driven Davidovich out of Lavis and up the Adige on Salurn and Neumarkt. Meanwhile Massena was hurried towards the Brenta valley to Pergine, which he reached late on the 6th; and Augereau, by a short cut, on the same day moved over the mountains to Levico, to follow up Wurmser's manoeuvre, whatever it might portend. On the 6th Wurmser was at Bassano, with a rearguard of three battalions at Primolano.

Bonaparte was now sure of victory. He again had before him an enemy divided in two parts, between which he had thrust himself; and he had beaten the right wing and turned the flank of the left. The march in pursuit was continued on the 6th, Vaubois' division being left behind at Lavis to protect the rear of the marching column from the direction of the Tyrol; but all the grenadiers accompanied the commanding general. Augereau and headquarters got to Borgo and pushed out a van to Ospedaletto; Massena marched to Levico, out of which place Augereau's van had previously driven the last of the Austrian rear. Next day another Austrian detachment of three battalions was pushed out of Primolano, where they were holding the Brenta defile, which here, too, was defended by a castle. The attack was made with a line of skirmishers and the light infantry, followed by a close column under cover of the artillery fire; and a regiment of French dragoons having got in the rear of the position and seized the defile, the party laid down their arms. Bonaparte says:

> The ardour of the soldier is equal to that of the generals and the officers. There are, however, traits of courage which merit to be gathered by the historians, and that I will let you know at my first leisure.

On the same day the headquarters reached Cismone. On the 8th, in a start at 2 a. m., Massena was put across the Brenta to the right bank, along which ran a fairly good road, while the main column advanced to Bassano, and during the forenoon struck the enemy, who

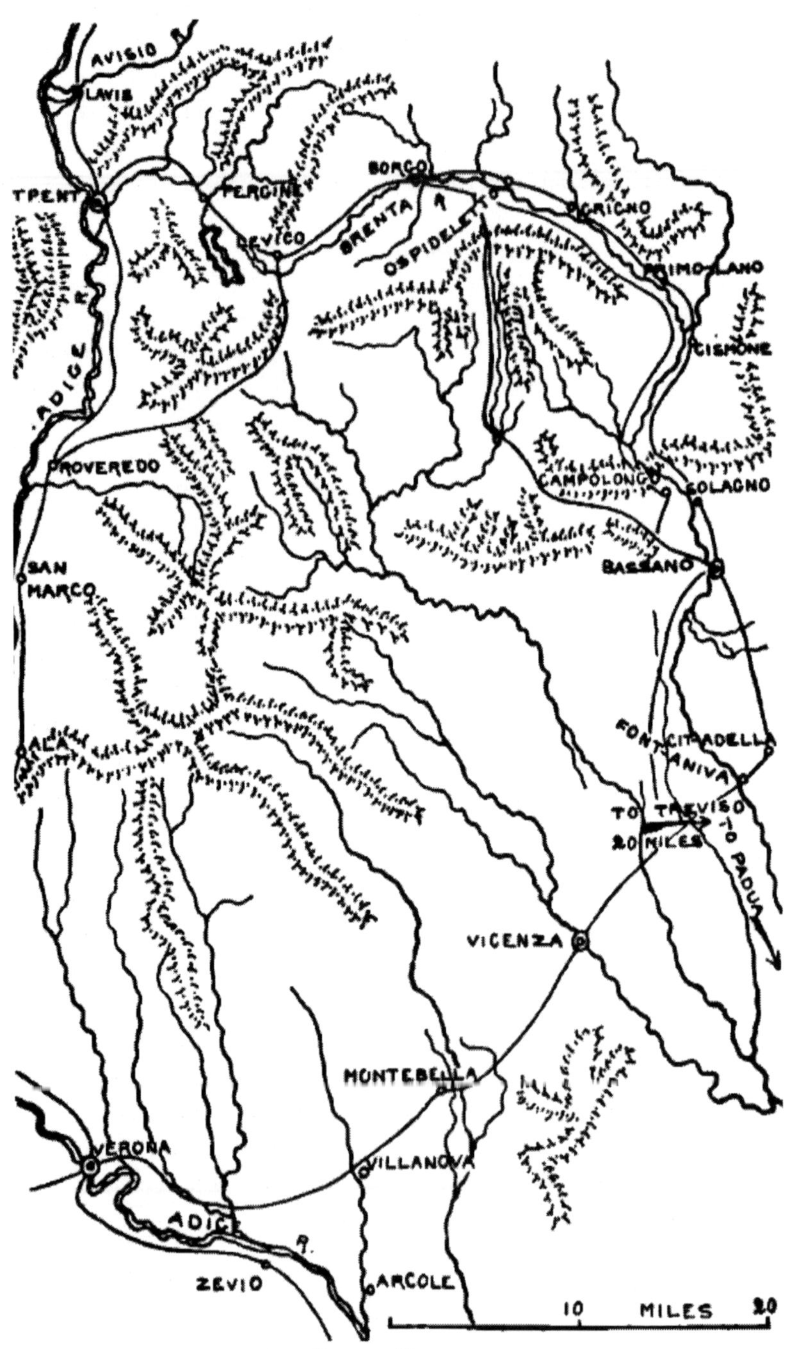

Bassano Country

had drawn up on the heights in front of the town, with a van of six battalions holding the long defile at Solagno, and Campo Lungo, on the other bank, being also held in force.

Bassano is on the left bank of the Brenta, connected with the right bank by a bridge. Quosdanovich lay before the town with his left on the river. Sebottendorf was drawn up on the farther bank to protect the bridge.

Wurmser had been of a mind to march by way of Vicenza and Verona to Mantua, and a third of his force under Mezaros was already at Montebello. He was utterly taken aback by the sudden appearance of the French in force. He had expected that Bonaparte would head for Innsbruck, and that his own march on Verona would call him back down the Adige roads. He could scarcely have got himself in a worse dilemma; and now, instead of listening to his discretion, leaving a rearguard of good troops under a plucky officer to delay Bonaparte's pursuit, and striving to rejoin his other division at Montebello by a forced march, he hearkened to his courage and stood to fight a superior enemy, sending a hurried dispatch to Mezaros to come back to help in the approaching battle—for which operation there was no more time. The defile between rocks and river at Solagno was taken by Augereau's eager brigades at the first rush; Massena, with equal ardour, pushed on through Campo Lungo, seized the bridge, though defended by guns and the Austrian grenadiers *d'élite,* and entered the town pell-mell with the retiring Austrians; while Augereau, following along from Solagno, had equal fortune against his opponent, whom his brigades, certain of victory, drove from their defence in a couple of hours. The two Austrian divisions were thus cut apart, and Quosdanovich, finding his road suddenly blocked, was compelled to retire to the Piave. Wurmser barely escaped with his headquarters guard. With pardonable exaggeration as to captured men Bonaparte reports:

> In this day we took five thousand prisoners, thirty-five guns all harnessed with their *caissons*, two pontoon equipages of thirty-two boats, all harnessed, more than two hundred wagons, all equally harnessed, carrying a part of the enemy's baggage. We took five flags. Chief of Brigade Lannes took two with his own hands. General Wurmser and the treasury of the army were missed by only a minute. . . . I beg of you to accord the grade of general of brigade to the Chief of Brigade Lannes. He is the first who put the enemy into rout at Dego, who passed the Po, the bridge of Lodi, and who entered Bassano.

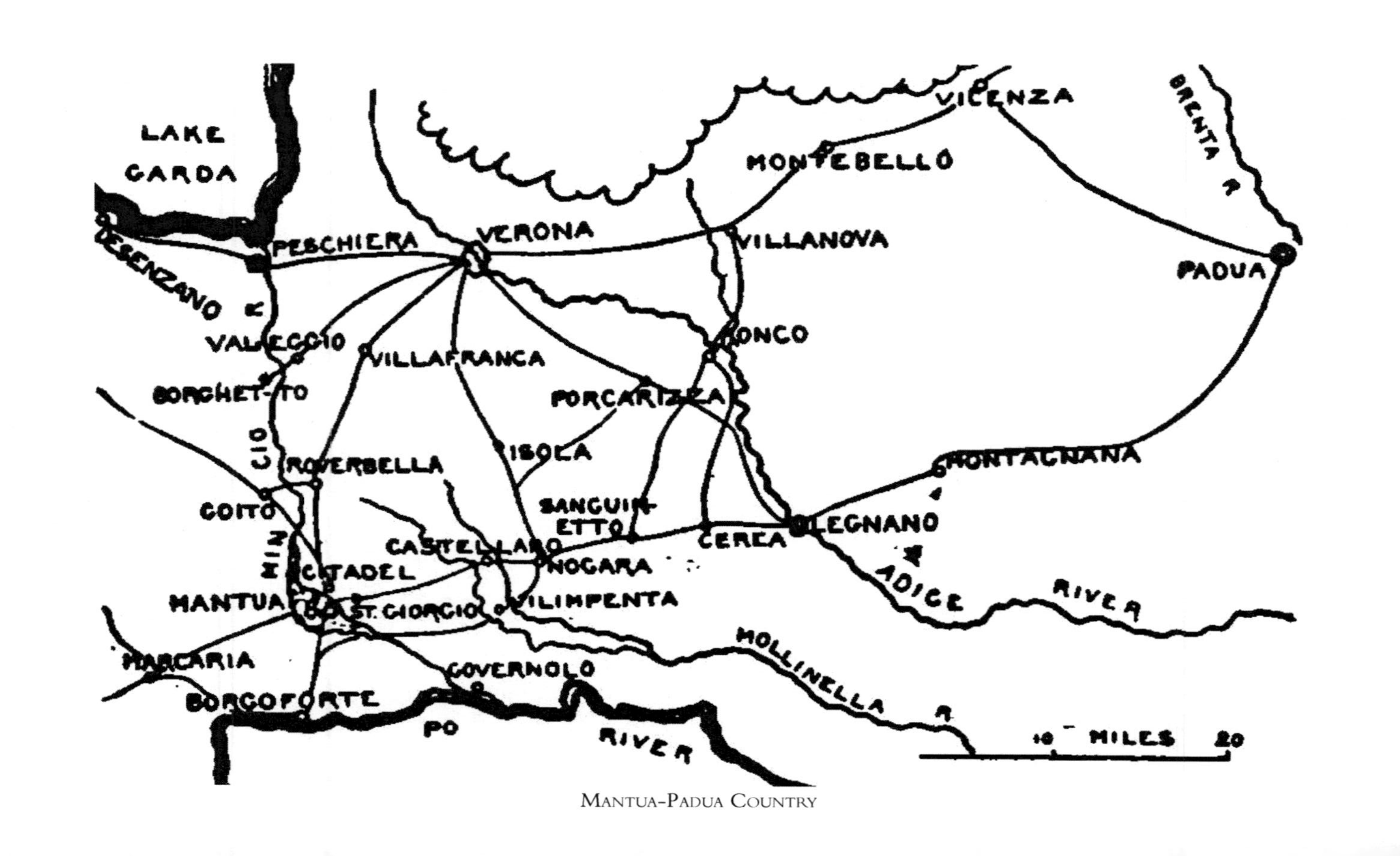

Mantua-Padua Country

The Austrian leader now had but sixteen thousand men left, of whom, however, six thousand was a body of excellent horse. He made a hasty and irregular retreat with Sebottendorf on Fontaniva, where he crossed the Brenta to join Mezaros, who was on the way from Montebello, losing many men by desertion and by being driven off the main road. The French gathered in at least four thousand prisoners, half of them at the battle of Bassano. The other casualties were not severe on either side, for the Austrians had made no marked resistance; but they abandoned a vast amount of material. Reaching the vicinity of Montebello, Wurmser joined his advance division, and hurried *via* Villanova and Arcole towards Legnano, off his projected line, and on arrival there, numbered a bare twelve thousand men. With this small wreck of his fine army he crossed the Adige and, protected by a bridge-head, gave his troops some rest.

The Austrian commander could scarcely have manoeuvred or fought with more pluck or less common sense. There was now an excellent chance that Bonaparte might surround and capture the entire Austrian force, and he lost no time in ordering his troops accordingly. Wurmser no longer had front, rear, or communications. As speedily as he was able, Bonaparte made arrangements to pursue, and yet on the 8th headed Augereau down the Brenta towards Padua, to cut the Austrians off from retreat to the Frioul and Trieste, while with Massena's division he marched on Vicenza, which place he reached next day. Here he received intelligence which enabled him to guess that Wurmser's intention was to make for Mantua, and he at once ordered Augereau to push on Legnano, and himself with Massena marched on Montebello. He intended to use the ground between the Adige and Mincio, which is much cut up by streams and canals, to head off Wurmser at the Tidone or Molinella Rivers. By the evening of the 10th Massena, who had come on *via* Villanova, began to cross the Adige at Ronco,—which he did by great exertion, owing to lack of boats,—and Augereau reached Montagnana, while Wurmser on the 10th dallied at Legnano to rest his men, vainly imagining that the French would march no faster than he did. Learning Wurmser's whereabouts, Bonaparte, true to the mass idea, drew his forces together so as to deliver battle if he could reach the Austrians with his main army. Kilmaine, with the garrison of Verona, was ordered to Isola della Scala; Sahuguet was to cross at Goito, with orders to use the difficult country between Mantua and Legnano to delay Wurmser's advance; and on the 11th, while these two joined at Castellaro, and took position on either side of the road behind the

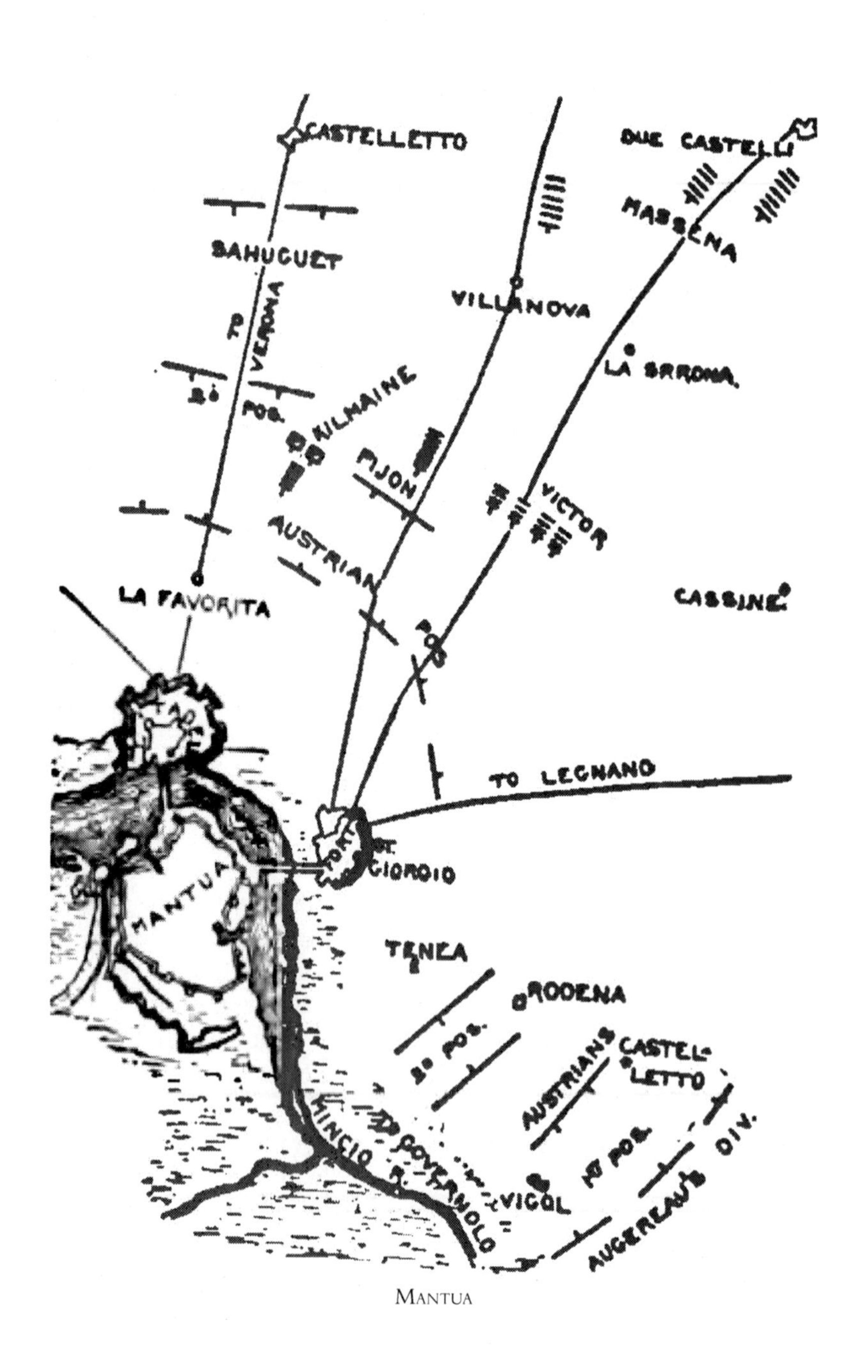
CASTELLETTO
DUE CASTELLI
SAHUGUET
TO VERONA
MASSENA
VILLANOVA
LA SRRONA
2D POS.
KILMAINE
PIJON
VICTOR
AUSTRIAN
CASSINE
LA FAVORITA
TO LEGNANO
FORT
ST. GIORGIO
MANTUA
TENCA
RODENA
2D POS.
AUSTRIANS
CASTEL-LETTO
1ST POS.
MINCIO R.
GOVERNOLO
VIGOL
AUGEREAU'S DIV.

MANTUA

Molinella, and while Augereau's van reached Legnano, and Massena a point near Porcarizza, Wurmser kept leisurely on towards Mantua. From the position he had reached Massena, by a vigorous push forward, might have out off Wurmser from Nogara; but a stupid guide, instead of taking the road to Sanguinetto, led his column to Cerea. This point Wurmser reached about the same time, and man-aging to cut a passage through Massena's van commanded by Murat and Pijon, got safely to Nogara. Had Massena marched to Sanguinetto, he could have occupied the road in force before Wurmser's arrival. But this was not to be the only accident.

Sahuguet had been given positive orders to cut the bridges of the Molinella, and to stop the Austrians on that line, but he forgot the bridge at Villimpenta. After a short rest, Wurmser continued his march early on the 12th, and hearing of Sahuguet at Castellaro, he made a detour to the left *via* Villimpenta, where a French detachment sent from the Mantua besiegers was met and cut to pieces. Crossing here, the Austrian general reached Mantua during the afternoon. Bonaparte thus lost his prey, and he never forgave Sahuguet.

"One must make for the flying enemy a bridge of gold or oppose to him a barrier of steel," said Bonaparte. Here neither had been done. Legnano, held between Augereau and Massena as in a vice, capitulated on the 12th with seventeen hundred men.

Wurmser had expected to reach Mantua with twenty thousand men, fresh and cheered by success. He arrived with not much over ten thousand men, beaten, tired, pursued. Instead of raising the siege, he was himself destined to be besieged in the fortress, which had, to be sure, an enormous garrison, but of this a third were on the sick list, the Mantuan marshes making the city liable to fevers and dysentery. At first he camped outside the place, between San Giorgio, and the citadel, whence he could readily forage. Bonaparte determined to drive him inside, and ordered on Mantua the bulk of the army. On the 13th Augereau, advancing on the place from Governolo, by which circuit he had come, cut Wurmser off from the lower Po, while Sahuguet, with the blockade corps, came in touch with the enemy on the right, north of La Favorita; and Massena, in the centre, marched from Castellaro as far as Due Castelli, on the way to San Giorgio. But, lacking not courage, Wurmser held his own. On the 14th Massena advanced on a body of thirteen battalions and twenty-four squadrons, which had camped outside the fortress walls, but though at first successful, a body of Austrian horse returning from foraging upset his calculations, and he withdrew. On the 15th nearly the entire garrison sallied out to forage in force, covered by the cavalry, which took up a position in front of San Giorgio, and extending to the left to cover La Favorita, holding both the Verona and Legnano roads. The same day had been chosen by Bonaparte for an attack in force. Sahuguet was on the right astride the Verona road in front of Castelletto; Massena, in the centre, was kept massed at Due Castelli and hidden by rolling ground, so that Wurmser only saw Sahuguet in his front; Augereau's division, this day commanded by Bon, was advancing on the left. When the word was given, Sahuguet moved towards La Favorita; Augereau, who had marched on San Giorgio, forced back the Austrian outposts on Vigol and the Castelletto which is east of Mantua, with so much energy that Wurmser, assuming this to be the main attack, drew forces from his centre and hurried them through Tenea to hold it back. These troops deployed between Vigol and Castelletto, and held head to Bon, who had drawn up in face of them. Massena remained at Due Castelli until he heard the firing on the left, which was his signal to advance on San Giorgio; and this he did in two columns, by way of Villanova and La Sprona, so as to cut the Austrian connection between La Favorita and San Giorgio. At the same time that Sahuguet advanced on La Favorita, Massena fell on the weakened Austrian line with vigour, Victor in battalion column forcing the right half of the centre back into San Giorgio at the point of the bayonet. The fire in its rear alarmed the Austrian right, which fell back on Rodena heights, followed by Bon, who cut off several companies and took them prisoners. While Victor was following on the heels of the defeated Austrians, and forcing his way into San Giorgio, Pijon, sustained by Kilmaine, was striving to cut off this fort from La Favorita; but Sahuguet failed to help them by a stanch attack on the latter place, only advancing a short distance, when he paused. Had he pressed in as hard as Massena and Bon, Wurmser might have been captured in a body. His weak conduct enabled the enemy to hold himself for a time in front of the citadel, and then by the left to retire through it into Mantua, the French following hard upon. The battle had cost each side twenty-five hundred men, and the Austrians had lost eleven guns.

This day's result prevented Wurmser from again debouching on the left bank of the Mincio, and the various sorties he attempted in October were easily driven back.

The news now ran in that Jourdan had been forced back to the Rhine, and that this had enabled Archduke Charles to turn in force on Moreau. It was well that the commander of the Army of Italy had not striven to join his associates through the Tyrol.

Bonaparte had not compelled a surrender of Wurmser's army, but he had followed the Austrians up closely and forced them to enter the fortress, which he now again shut in with Kilmaine's, late Serurier's, division of nine thousand men. Kilmaine made good use of his position, erecting works on the left bank. On the right bank there was only a blockade, but Wurmser was gradually narrowed down to a small territory in which to forage. Vaubois was still at Trent with ten thousand men; Massena was dispatched to Bassano and Treviso with nine thousand men, and Augereau with an equal number to Verona. For a reserve Macquart was ordered to Villafranca with three thousand men, and Bonaparte returned to Milan. By October 1 these stations were occupied, and despite the severe campaign just passed, reinforcements enough had come in to level the divisions up to the numbers specified. Wurmser was now in Mantua with twenty-eight thousand men, about twenty thousand being duty fit. Davidovich was in the Tyrol with fourteen thousand men. Three thousand stood in Voralberg. On the Isonzo was a goodly force guarding the passes to Carinthia.

On October 1 Bonaparte wrote to the Directory that he had less than nineteen thousand men in the army of observation, and nine thousand in the army of siege, and that the enemy would have fifty thousand in six weeks. This was his usual method of procuring reinforcements. He insisted that he must have over fifty thousand men all told, and specified troops that might be sent him. He needed twenty thousand muskets, for those he had captured were Austrian, much too heavy, "and our soldiers cannot use them. . . . If the conservation of Italy is dear to you. Citizen Directors, send me all this aid."

He also addressed the following letter, October 2:

Quarters General
Milan
11 Vendémiaire, Year V
To His Majesty the Emperor of Germany
Your Majesty, Europe desires peace. This disastrous war has lasted too long. I have the honour to notify Your Majesty, that if you do not send plenipotentiaries to Paris to open negotiations of peace, the Executive Directory has ordered me to fill up the port of Trieste, and to destroy all the establishments of Your Majesty on the Adriatic. Until now I have been restrained in the execution of this plan by the hope of not increasing the

number of innocent victims of this war. I trust that Your Majesty may be moved by the distress which menaces your subjects, and may restore to the world repose and tranquillity.

I am, with respect. Your Majesty's etc., etc.

Bonaparte

From anyone else this would have been mere *brutum fulmen*. In a sense it was no more from him.

The success of this campaign had depended on the French capacity to march, which had proved exceptional. In 1805 the French soldier used to say, "The emperor has discovered a new way to make war: he uses our legs and not our bayonets." He had already begun to use their legs and their bayonets, too. From the afternoon of September 5 to the early morning of the 8th, sixty hours, the French had marched over fifty miles down the Brenta valley to Bassano, with two combats at Levico and Primolano. Having beaten Wurmser at Bassano, Massena reached Vicenza on the 9th, thus fighting a battle and marching twenty-one miles in thirty-six hours; and in the succeeding twenty-four hours, Massena marched another twenty-one miles to the Adige, which his men at once began to cross. From the morning of the 8th, in eighty-four hours, Augereau fought a battle and marched sixty miles. In sum, from the 6th to the 11th of September, or six days, Bonaparte's army had marched, Massena over one hundred and Augereau one hundred and ten miles, and fought two combats and one battle. The pursuit of Wurmser had been brilliant.

To say pursue is easy; actually to pursue is the rarest thing in war. Out of a dozen battles won by bravery and intelligence, barely one has the results which proper pursuit would yield it. Men who have won a victory feel that this is all they should be called on to perform, and yet, if the enemy has strength to flee, the victor has surely strength to follow. But it has always required a great man to compel this to be done.

In one sense the army in Mantua afforded a prospect of many trophies and much glory when the place should be taken; but now that the French armies had been driven out of Germany, there was a probability of a fresh Austrian reinforcement for the forces on the Adige, and these would again attempt the rescue of their penned-up comrades. In case another army had to be met by Bonaparte, twenty thousand men issuing from this fortress in his rear might well turn the scale. Moreover, the French army had been much used up, in its late campaign, and the feverish marshes of Mantua were far from favourable for its re-establishment. The campaign had been glorious, but there was much yet to anticipate.

Chapter 12

Archduke Charles v. Moreau and Jourdan

May to October, 1796

Although Bonaparte was showing the world how to make war, yet on the Rhine Moreau was expected to do the brilliant work of the year. Opposed to him stood young Archduke Charles, who, when troops were sent to reinforce the Italian army, was reduced to the defensive. In June Jourdan crossed the Rhine at Düsseldorf, and as this enabled Moreau to pass at Strasburg, Jourdan retired, and Charles moved up to face Moreau. This general pushed the Austrians out of the Neckar valley by a victory at Malsch, and early in August advanced on them at Neresheim. Determined to cross the Danube, Charles fought here so as to prevent interference. The battle was indecisive, and Charles made his crossing. Moreau followed, and then remained south of the Danube, instead of cooperating with Jourdan, who meanwhile had forced Charles' lieutenant back to the Bamberg region. Charles now conceived an operation worthy of a great soldier. Leaving Latour to contain Moreau, he crossed the Danube, joined his lieutenant, and falling sharply on Jourdan, drove him back. This afforded Moreau a chance of crushing Latour, but he did not improve it. Meanwhile Charles advanced to Würzburg, where he beat Jourdan in a hearty battle, and threw him back into the mountains. Carnot's plan of attacking both flanks of the enemy by separate columns had thus proved an error; for, so soon as Charles had pushed Jourdan back across the Rhine, he moved up river to take Moreau in rear. Anticipating this, Moreau was obliged summarily to retire, and Latour followed him up. Moreau fought at Biberach to save his retreat, and having defeated Latour, retired through the Höllenthal on Freiburg. Here Charles had already arrived, and Moreau was compelled to fight at Emmendingen and Schliegen to effectuate his retreat, and cross the Rhine at Hüningen. Charles had covered himself with glory. He grew to be one of the best soldiers of his time. As Bonaparte had advanced to the Adige, and Moreau and Jourdan had been driven back across the Rhine, all idea of their cooperation had vanished.

In order to keep before us the general plan of the French operations, as well as to enable us to gauge the value of the other French generals, it is essential to cast a hasty glance at the campaign in Germany, which was going on while Bonaparte by such transcendent ability fought his way from the Var to the Mincio.

At the opening of 1796, neither allies nor French had imagined that Italy would be the great field on which the future fortunes of France were to be decided. It was along the Rhine that the bulk of the forces and the supposed ablest leaders had been stationed. The allies had two armies in the Rhine country. The Army of the Upper Rhine was under Wurmser, eighty thousand strong; its left wing, under Sztarray, Fröhlich and Condé, stretched along the right bank from the Neckar mouth to the Swiss frontier, and as right wing a considerable force was on the left bank, opposite Mannheim and at Kaiserslautern. The Army of the Lower Rhine, under Archduke Charles, then but twenty-five years old, numbered ninety thousand men. Its left wing of seventy thousand men lay on the Nahe, and its right wing of twenty thousand, under the Duke of Wurtemberg and Kienmayer, was on the Sieg and Lahn, watching the debouches of Düsseldorf and Coblenz. Ten thousand men garrisoned Mainz and Ehrenbreitstein. Later, when, in consequence of Bonaparte's victories in Italy, Wurmser was ordered to the Tyrol with twenty-five thousand veterans to take command there, Charles was given control of both armies, and this lent him a certain advantage over the French commanders, each of whom was probably bound, by hard and fast instructions, to a previously settled and not cooperative plan of campaign.

The Army of the Rhine and Moselle was under Moreau. He had succeeded Pichegru, who, suspected of treachery, though no evidence was forthcoming, had retired to his estates. It had eighty thousand men, and leaned its right on Hüningen, while its centre lay behind the Queich, and its left was near Saarbrück. The Army of the Sambre and Meuse under Jourdan, equally strong, had its centre and right along the left bank of the Rhine from Cologne to St. Wendel in the Nahe country; and its left wing, under Kleber, of twenty-two thousand men, lay in a fortified camp at Düsseldorf.

There are numerous crossings of the Rhine, of which the principal ones are Hüningen, Breisach, Strasburg, Selz near Rastadt, Lauterburg, Germersheim near Philipsburg, Speyer, Mannheim, Worms, Mainz. At many other places the river can be spanned by pontoon-bridges. The only fortified bridge held by the French was the one at Düsseldorf; the Austrians had one at Mainz, and one at Mannheim.

The first Austrian plan was to push on Trèves, and having thus secured a foothold on the Moselle, to file up and down the left bank of the Rhine, taking each French army in reverse. But when Wurmser was withdrawn with his veteran divisions to meet the Italian danger, the archduke was instructed by the Vienna Council to act on the defensive. The forces facing each other were of about equal strength; but the allies had much more and better cavalry. The French planned to push the Army of the Sambre and Meuse, pivoting on its right on the Hundsrück mountains, forward *via* Düsseldorf, to attract the allied attention, so that the Army of the Rhine and Moselle could the easier cross the river to operate against the allied left wing. The advance by Jourdan would at the same time threaten the Austrian communications, and tend, it was believed, to induce Charles to withdraw all the Austrian troops to the right bank. But as Jourdan, counting out garrisons and detachments, had only forty thousand men for the field, his advance became something of a problem, and moreover the question of food and equipment worked much delay, for French finances were at a low ebb. The general idea of the campaign, though on a larger scale than heretofore, was in Carnot's usual style: to advance a force against each flank of the enemy. This method lay at the root of the French failure in this campaign. Great as Carnot was as an organizer, his strategic views were far from sound. But at that day no one's military views were sound—except Bonaparte's. Carnot was truly a great man, even if not a perfect strategist. He had been brought up as an officer of engineers. Napoleon said of him that:

> . . . . he had no experience of war, his ideas were false on every part of the military art; . . . he has published works on the attack and defence of places, and on the principles of fortification, which can be acknowledged only by a man who has no practice in war.

Yet Carnot honestly earned his title as "Organizer of Victory" during the wars of the Revolution.

At the end of 1795 there had been a truce made between the opposing armies along the Rhine, and this truce lasted until May 81, 1796, when Austria chose to end it. Still, as the detaching of Wurmser to Italy had arrested the proposed Austrian offensive, the French were enabled to take the initiative. Kleber, twenty thousand strong, was ordered to drive Wurtemberg behind the Lahn, whereupon Jourdan would cross the Rhine. This Kleber accomplished early in June; the Army of the Sambre and Meuse was put over June 10 at Neuwied, and masking Ehrenbreitstein with a considerable force, took possession of the Lahn right bank. Endangered by this operation, the allied troops near Kaiserslautern had to be withdrawn to the right bank at Mannheim; and they were followed to the river by a part of Moreau's force. Twelve thousand Austrians occupied the Mannheim bridge-head, while the rest reinforced the two allied armies. Latour took command of what was left of Wurmser's troops, and Archduke Charles was made *generalissimo*, while Wurtemberg was succeeded by Wartensleben. This initial French manoeuvre had, as it was expected, swept the left bank of the Rhine clear of the enemy, and would now enable Jourdan and Moreau to carry the war into Germany.

The Austrians on the Lahn were spread along a distance of fifty miles. Jourdan had an opportunity to break through this cordon, but being too deliberate, he gave Charles time to come to the aid of his overmatched divisions. The archduke too might have operated to advantage against the French right flank, and cut Jourdan off from the Rhine. But he deemed it wiser to attack the left and beat it in detail; and in fact he did defeat the French left under Lefebvre at Wetzlar, and crossed the Lahn at Leun, June 16. Jourdan, whose immediate duty was limited by the Directory to engaging the. enemy's attention, which he had done, retired to Neuwied and recrossed to the left bank of the Rhine. Charles followed awhile, and then retraced his steps, so as to be near Latour, now seriously threatened by Moreau.

The latter had been meanwhile demonstrating with his left near the Mannheim bridge-head to lead Charles to expect operations at that point, and secretly preparing means of crossing the Rhine at Strasburg. The long cordon of the allies from Hüningen to Philipsburg made this easy. In the night of June 23-24 Desaix seized Kehl by a *coup de main*. Moreau put over his divisions June 26 and 27, and advanced against the Austrians, who could at the moment concentrate but eighteen thousand men to oppose the thirty thousand he had got across. Laborde remained on the left bank between Breisach and Hüningen. The French general speedily drove the allies towards the Murg, and took up a defensive position with Desaix and St. Cyr, until he could secure his right in the Black Forest. Cut off from the Austrian right and centre, the left wing under Condé and Fröhlich retired up the Rhine and Kinzig; the Swabian troops fell back into the mountains at Freudenstadt, and the Saxons joined Sztarray, who retired in the same direction. By this advance Moreau had drawn the pressure from Jourdan, but the specific duty prescribed him was to carry the war away from the Rhine, and as a first step he purposed to

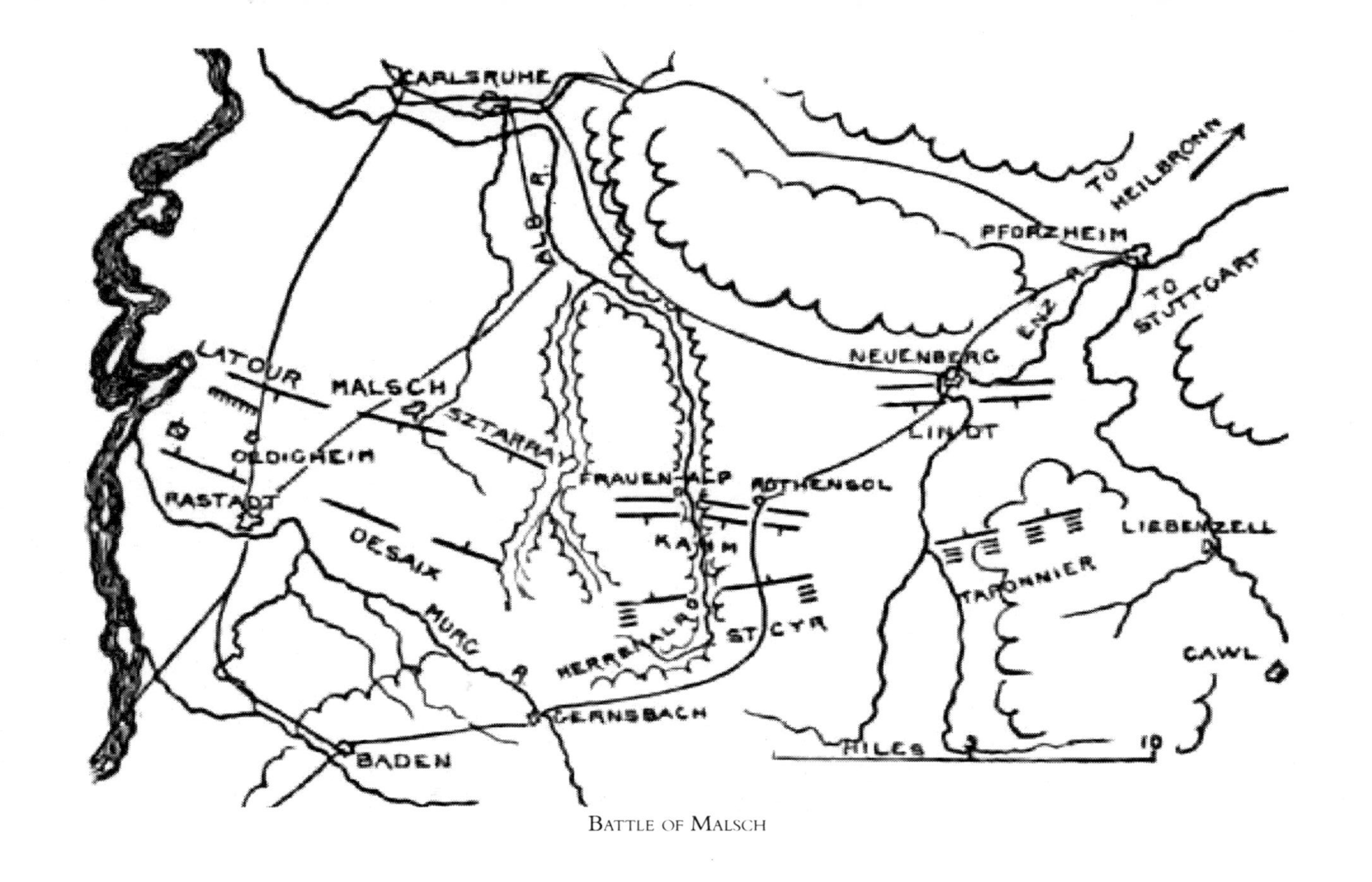

Battle of Malsch

push the archduke across the mountains to the valley of the Neckar. Ferino followed Condé and Fröhlich, and occupied the Freiburg country; St. Cyr pushed the Swabians out of the Freudenstadt country, and a detachment got as far as the Neckar. Latour and Sztarray sought to defend the Murg, but Desaix attacked them at Rastadt and drove them back to the Alb, where they joined the archduke.

These interesting manoeuvres can be afforded no great space. Charles came rapidly up in the early days of July, with twenty thousand men, leaving his main force of forty thousand men under Wartensleben along the Main to face Jourdan. As the role of Wartensleben was only to delay Jourdan's advance, Charles, as he himself acknowledges, would have been wiser to leave but twenty thousand men on the Lahn, and to march up river with sufficient force to defeat Moreau and drive him back across the Rhine. Wartensleben could have accomplished all he did do with half his force, used with energy. Charles made preparations to attack Moreau July 10. But the alert French commander anticipated him July 9 at Malsch. His plan was to contain the Austrian right near Rastadt in the plain at the foot of the hills, and to turn its left in the direction of Pforzheim, on the hills at Herrenalp and Frauenalp. Meanwhile Charles was aiming to force Gernsbach on the Murg, and to turn the French left wing at Rastadt.

In pursuance of Moreau's plan, early on the 9th, St. Cyr sharply pushed his way about the allied left at Rothensohl, though Kaim so heartily defended his position that it took five successive assaults to accomplish the result. At the same time Taponnier threw back Lindt near Neuenburg. Desaix made an equally good showing against Sztarray at Malsch; but Latour at Oedigheim, by using his artillery against the superior French horse, which he had not sufficient squadrons to match, enabled Charles to hold the plain. Malsch was taken and retaken twice; but finally Sztarray held it and drove Desaix back to near Rastadt, Latour also forcing his way close to the town. Charles, though he had held his own with good countenance, in fact, been victorious on his right, lest by the French turning manoeuvre he should be cut off from Stuttgart, and anxious to protect his magazines at Heilbronn, was fain to retire by his left to Pforzheim; and on July 18 he crossed to the right bank of the Neckar at Cannstadt, and marched on Gmund, leaving a small force on the left bank to watch the French. Victorious Moreau was now enabled to bring his left wing across the Rhine at Speyer; but he pursued the Austrians much too slowly. St. Cyr took Stuttgart. The allied left, which had been early sundered from the centre and right, retired to Villingen and beyond, followed by the French

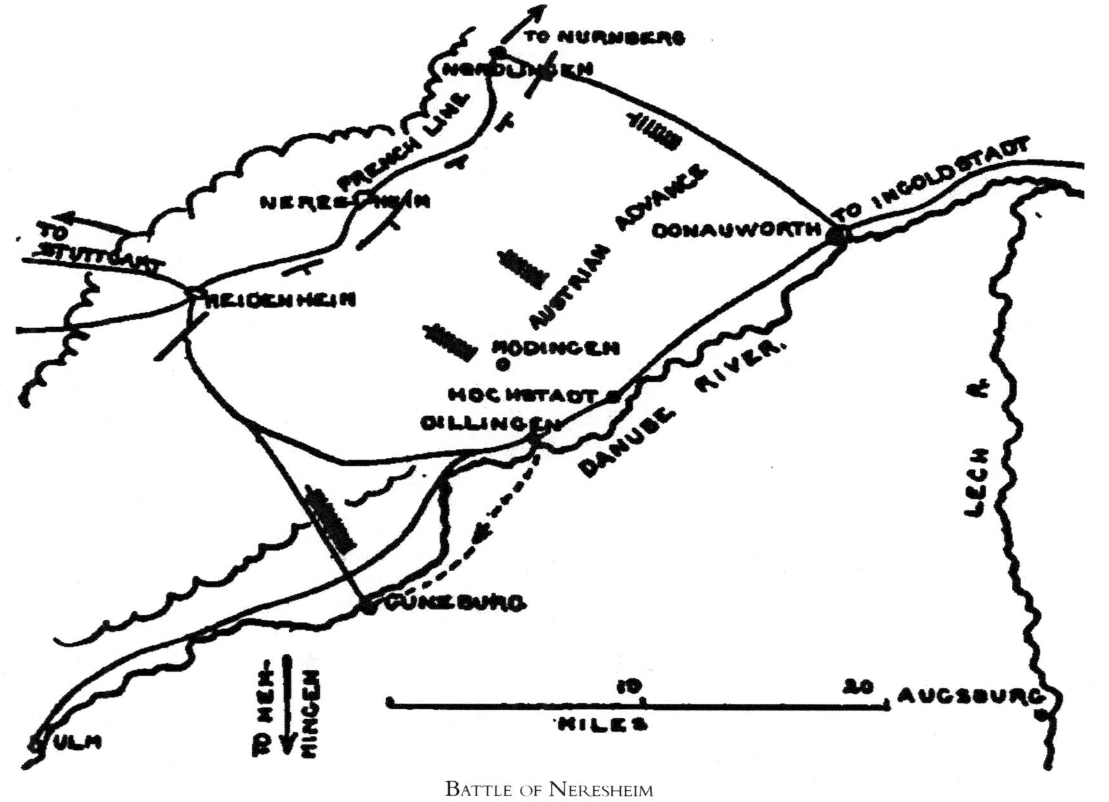

Battle of Neresheim

under Ferino, with whom Moreau strove, but uselessly, to keep in touch. The Swabians and Bavarians entered into negotiations with the French, and Charles, by so much weaker, retired towards the Danube. The French opening of the campaign had been brilliant, and they now much outnumbered the enemy.

On July 22 the archduke began his retreat from the Neckar, the Saxon troops joining Wartensleben. He had been compelled to deplete his forces by placing garrisons in Mainz, Ehrenbreitstein, Philipsburg, Mannheim and Königstein, the sum total of which was thirty thousand men. And the defection of his allies, added to these drafts, forced him to adopt a cautious policy; for the French had a third more men in line than he. Yet again, Moreau was over-cautious in following up the enemy. He had no maps, and knew the rugged country ill. On August 2 he reached the Austrians near Geislingen, but Charles continued his retreat down the Danube, his rear sharply skirmishing with the French van every day for a full week. On August 10 the Austrian army stood on the line Nördlingen-Hochstädt-Dillingen, while the French advanced to Neresheim, Ferino, far away on the right, having followed up the enemy's left to Memmingen. It was now the intention of the archduke to retire to the right bank of the Danube, to lure Moreau away from Jourdan, and to take advantage of the many affluents on the south side, the defence of which was easy; but in order to do this with safety, he deemed it necessary first to neutralize Moreau, who with his forty-five thousand men, in the Neresheim region, was altogether too near to make the crossing of the river safe. Moreover Jourdan was fast approaching the Danube country, and if Moreau could be defeated and driven well back, the two French armies would not be able to make a junction. Only battle would accomplish this double end, and despite his inferiority, Charles made ready to attack the French on August 11. The archduke backed up against the Danube; the French had the mountain ravines in their rear, and Moreau, marching by his left, had his forty-five thousand men extended over a front of twenty-five miles, from Heidenheim through Neresheim to a point near Nördlingen.

The Austrian troops were ready to start shortly after midnight, but a heavy rain made the progress of the several columns slow. A corps was sent across the Danube, to recross at Gunzburg above and take the French right in reverse; but the distance was excessive, and this part of the operation proved a failure. Part of Charles' left wing won a distinct success in advance of Mödingen, driving the French well back, and turning their centre and cutting it from their right at Heidenheim;

another of the Austrian columns likewise made a good deal of headway towards taking the French right in reverse; but not being in touch with the rest of the army, the French concentrated, and stopped its onset before any serious harm was done, though the headquarters and artillery park had to make a lively retreat. The battle, which was fought over a wide area, in detached columns not mutually sustaining each other, though heartily contested, degenerated at the last into a mere cannonade at a number of points, and was at nightfall undecided. It had been a fair sample of one of those cordon engagements in which, on both sides, the forces were ill in hand, and no such manoeuvring as leads up to great results could possibly be undertaken. The losses in this battle of Neresheim were about three thousand on each side.

Inasmuch as Charles had Ulm on which to retire, as well as several bridges over the Danube, he would have done better to attack by his left and cut Moreau's communications. As it was, the column there operating did the best work; and such an attack, well driven home, would probably have been fatal to the French army, which was stretched over a long line with both flanks in the air.

Moreau was not in good case. To contrast his work with Bonaparte's is fruitful. He had orders, it is said, under the Carnot theory of turning both the enemy's flanks, to advance down the right bank of the Danube; his forces were all strung out; his artillery park had moved beyond reach; and his right was still threatened. He had, nevertheless, the courage to prepare to attack the Austrians next day; but when at 6 a. m. he advanced on the enemy, he found that Charles, in accordance with his prearranged plan, had retired. The battle had no result, except to enable the Austrians, uninterrupted, to cross the Danube. At Dillingen and Donauwörth the Austrian divisions were put over the river, and destroyed the bridges. Reinforcements soon came up which increased the archduke's effective to sixty thousand men; he was once more abreast of the situation; and of these thirty-five thousand men were stationed on the Lech under Latour, with orders to contain Moreau. The latter had been afforded a brilliant opportunity of utilizing the drawn battle of Neresheim, by marching up towards Nürnberg to join Jourdan, who about mid-August was advancing to this vicinity; and between the two they could have crushed the Austrians. But under the orders of the Directory he may not have felt authorized to undertake this manoeuvre. In the *St. Helena Memoirs* Napoleon assumes that he had no such specific directions. "General Moreau remained several days on the battlefield of Neresheim . . . without even sending a party of cavalry to

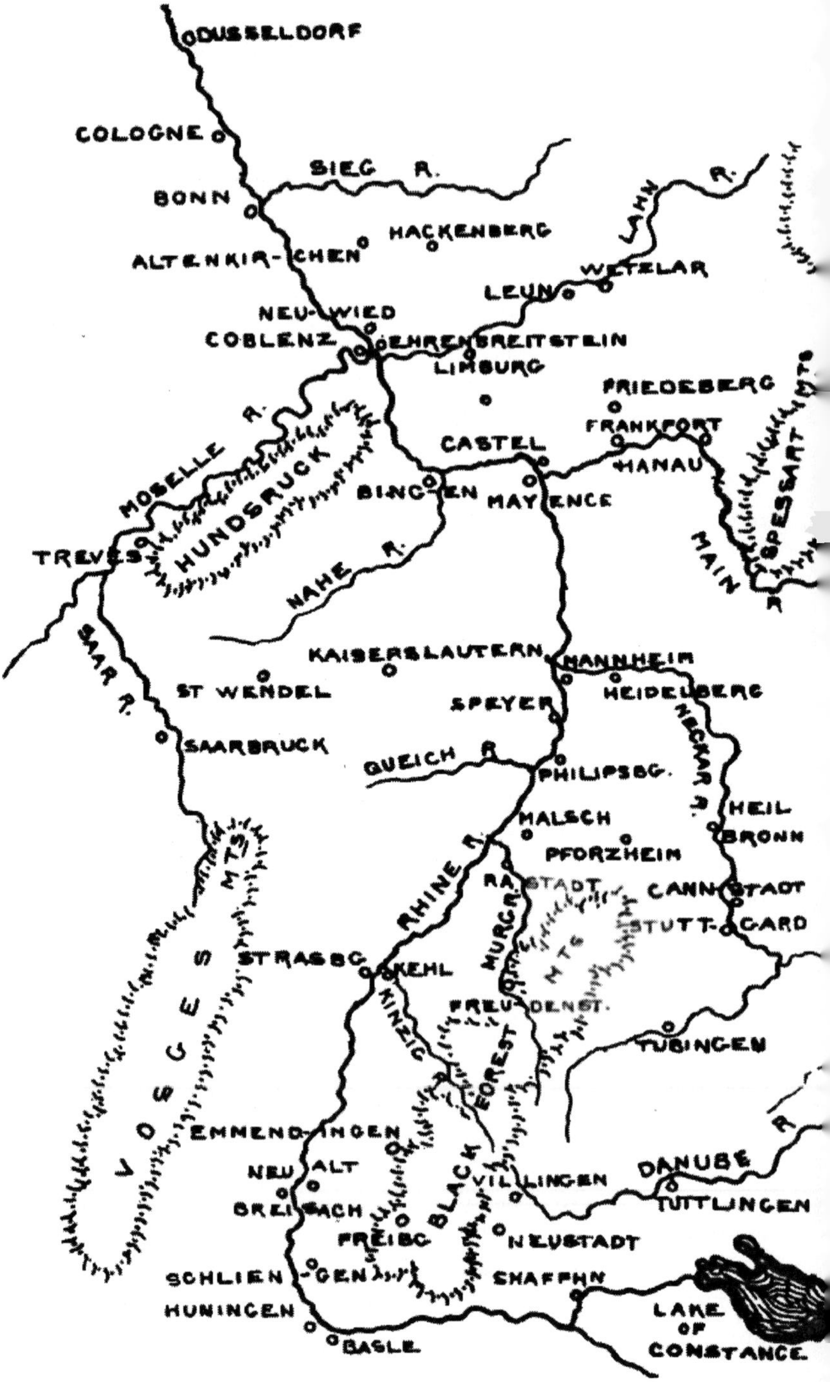

DUSSELDORF
COLOGNE
SIEG R.
BONN
HACKENBERG
ALTENKIR-CHEN
LAHN R.
WETZLAR
LEUN
NEU-WIED
COBLENZ
EHRENBREITSTEIN
LIMBURG
FRIEDEBERG
FRANKFORT
MOSELLE R.
CASTEL
HANAU
SPESSART MTS
HUNDSRUCK
BINGEN
MAYENCE
MAIN R.
TREVES
NAHE R.
SAAR R.
KAISERSLAUTERN
MANNHEIM
ST WENDEL
HEIDELBERG
SPEYER
NECKAR R.
SAARBRUCK
GUEICH R.
PHILIPSBG.
MALSCH
HEIL BRONN
PFORZHEIM
VOSGES MTS
RHINE R.
RASTADT
MURG R.
CANNSTADT
STUTT-GARD
MTS
STRASBG
KEHL
KINZIG
FREUDENST.
TUBINGEN
BLACK FOREST
EMMENDINGEN
NEU ALT
BREISACH
VILLINGEN
DANUBE R.
TUTTLINGEN
FREIBG
NEUSTADT
SCHLIENGEN
SHAFFHN
HUNINGEN
LAKE OF CONSTANCE
BASLE

GEMUNDEN
WURZBURG
SCHWEINFORT
HASFORT
MAIN R.
BAYREUTH
WIESENT R.
KITZINGEN
BAMBERG
FORSCHEIM
NURNBERG
REGNITZ R.
SULZBACH
NAABURG
ALTDORF
AMBERG
NEUMARKT
SCHWANDORF
NAAB R.
RATISBON
NORDLINGEN
NERESHEIM
DONAUWORTH
EICHSTADT
HEIDENHEIM
HOCHST.
INGOLDST
GEISENFELD
ISAR R.
NEUBURG
DILLINGEN
LANDSHUT
ULM
AUGSBURG
FRIEDEBURG
FREISING
BIBERACH
MUNICH
ILLER R.
LECH R.
FEDERSEE
MEMMINGEN
50
100
MILES

the Altmühl to seek to operate his junction." Immediately after the battle, the *Memoirs* go on to say, Moreau should have reached out to Jourdan, and with him marched on and seized Ratisbon and fortified it, an operation which would have decided the campaign. But his delays played into Charles' hands. "One would have said that he was ignorant that a French army existed on his left."

While Moreau had been pushing back Charles, the Army of the Sambre and Meuse, towards the end of June, had again crossed the Rhine, and Wartensleben had retired behind the Lahn July 6. Jourdan then advanced, defeated the Austrians July 13 at Friedeberg, and after some further exchanges Wartensleben retreated back of the Main at Frankfort, where, drawing in the bulk of the Mainz garrison, he prepared to defend the river. Jourdan bombarded Frankfort and took it July 16, and the Austrians fell back to Würzburg. Leaving Marceau with twenty-eight thousand men to hold his communications and mask Ehrenbreitstein and Mainz, Jourdan with forty-five thousand marched up the Main, and through Gemünden advanced on the enemy July 18. His front covered altogether too wide an area, but as his advance, in accordance with Carnot's orders to operate against the outer Austrian flank, constantly threatened the Austrian right, Wartensleben again fell back on Kitzingen, and the French entered Würzburg August 4. The Austrian forces had dwindled down to twenty-five thousand men by sickness and desertion; while the French, who had captured much victual and munition in Frankfort and along the line of advance, were encouraged by success and in fine fettle. Jourdan was nearing Moreau and he determined to keep on, operating constantly against the enemy's flank; and within a few days Wartensleben still farther retired to Bamberg. It is asserted that Jourdan sent a number of couriers to Moreau, to invite cooperation; but it is also claimed that none of these dispatches got through the lines. Jourdan falling sick, Kleber replaced him for a week or two, kept up the pursuit with diligence, and the Austrian commander still farther fell back behind the Wisent, a small affluent of the Regnitz. Following him up, Kleber attacked Wartensleben August 7 at Forschheim, and beat him with loss; and the latter, instead of retiring to Nürnberg, on the road towards Archduke Charles, fell back on Amberg as if to protect Bohemia. Jourdan soon resumed command, and still pressing the Austrian flank, Wartensleben retired behind the Naab August 18.

Jourdan followed to the Sulzbach-Amberg country, and then took up a position on the hither bank of the Naab, between Naaburg and

Schwandorf. The Austrians lay where they could not easily be attacked, and Jourdan held his position, sending Bernadotte to Neumarkt to observe the archduke's army.

Charles now matured his plan. It was worthy of a great soldier. Leaving Latour on the Lech to contain Moreau, he determined to join Wartensleben with twenty-five thousand men, mostly his veterans, fall on Jourdan with force enough to crush his army and, driving it back to the Rhine, again turn on Moreau, who, for every mile he advanced beyond the Lech, would be the worse compromised. Scarce one of Bonaparte's operations is superior to this; and Charles proceeded at once to put it into execution. His general idea, similar to Bonaparte's, had been to operate on the enemy's centre, and keep in touch with Wartensleben. Carnot's plan of turning both allied flanks played into his hands. His lieutenant's retreat had prevented the execution of his truly fine conception until now; and still he had to be cautious lest, by turning Jourdan's right, he should open to him a road to the Danube to join Moreau by the rear of the Austrian army. Yet Charles did not believe Jourdan to be capable of so bold a manoeuvre; nor, indeed, did Jourdan know where Moreau was.

Sending word to Wartensleben to refuse battle, with twenty-five thousand men Charles crossed to the left bank of the Danube at Ratisbon, and on August 22 reached the vicinity of his lieutenant's army. Sharply attacking Bernadotte at Neumarkt, he sent the French corps spinning back through Altdorf to the Peguitz, and then masking him with Hotze's division, he turned on Jourdan, who, with Wartensleben in his front and Charles on his right, at once retired to Amberg, where on the 24th the Austrians dealt a heavy blow to his rearguard, in which two French battalions were destroyed to the last man. Charles had effectively cut the two Republican armies apart. Jourdan had expected Moreau at least to hold the archduke in his own front, if he himself could not come over to his assistance; or, failing to keep him south of the Danube, to follow him up so as to equalize the bodies. But Jourdan now had to fight his battles alone and against superior forces. Wartensleben pushed on the heels of Jourdan's main army, while Charles advanced from Neumarkt; and Jourdan fell back to Sulzbach August 24. Hotze marched on and entered Nürnberg. Only by most rapid marching around the head of Charles' column could Bernadotte rejoin his chief behind the Wiesent, August 28.

Though his army was spread over too much territory in a number of columns from Hochstädt north, the archduke came close to cutting off Jourdan's retreat. He was in his way doing as distinguished work as Bonaparte in Italy. In the Memoirs Napoleon taxes him with slowness; and measuring his operations by Bonaparte's rapidity in Italy, he was indeed so. But no one at that day knew what speed meant; and much of what the emperor says savours of hypercriticism. His columns were expertly placed, though being too much on the cordon system Jourdan broke through the net, and seeking to make his way to Würzburg, he actually did reach Schweinfurt, and crossed to the right bank of the Main. His army, no longer upborne by success, had shrunk to forty thousand men, hungry and footsore. Bad discipline was rampant, which Jourdan ascribed to the requisition system, and the consequent inevitable marauding, despite which the French soldiers had been ill-fed for weeks, and were in bad health and heart. It takes but little success or failure to affect the morale of troops. Jourdan had heard a rumour that Moreau had beaten Latour on the Lech, and his present idea was to await the enemy in the great bend of the Main in which Würzburg is situated, and there deliver a general battle, so as if possible to resume Carnot's strategic scheme of a double advance on the Austrian flanks. He marched thither *via* Schweinfurt.

Charles now saw his chance. He could assemble a superior force, and *via* Kitzingen could reach Würzburg before the Army of the Rhine and Meuse could do so, thus shunting the French off the main and good post-road to the Rhine, and back into the hill country, where it was difficult to march or subsist an army. To this task he at once addressed himself, and we now see both commanders, intent on battle, heading for the one point which would lend either a marked advantage. An Austrian detachment was sent by way of Bamberg and Hasfurt to observe Jourdan's manoeuvres, while Lichtenstein crossed the Main at Kitzingen, and pushing on Würzburg, captured and garrisoned it September 1, shut in the citadel on the left bank, and took possession of the Galgenberg in front of the city. Sztarray, in his rear, reached Reperndorf, and deploying in its front, slowly moved forward; and the main Austrian army got on to Schwarzach early September 2, ready to cross on a bridge there to be thrown.

Hearing of the archduke's march on September 1, Jourdan left Lefebvre with ten thousand men to hold Schweinfurt, which was essential to him in case of disaster, and hurried on the reserve cavalry to Würzburg, followed successively by the divisions of Simon, Championnet and Grenier, thirty thousand effective. The cavalry reached Würzburg at noon on the 2nd, and seized the Steinberg. Simon shortly came up, and pushing the Austrians across the brooks, took position between Estenfeld and Lengfeld; while Championnet, who arrived an

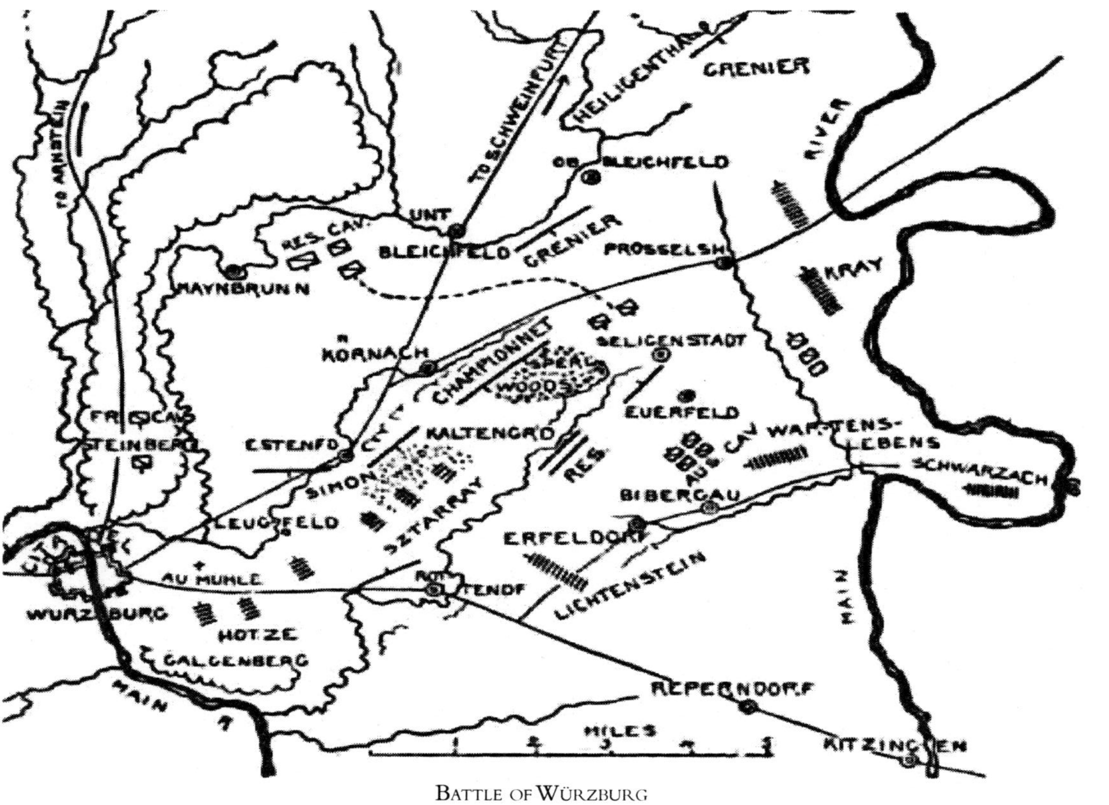

Battle of Würzburg

hour later, after a hard fight drove a division of Lichtenstein out of the Körnach and Sperl meadows, lying between the two brooks. The Austrians fell back to Euerfeld, where they barely held themselves. The French had begun well; and this easy success led Jourdan to believe that Charles had sent most of his forces to meet Moreau, and that here was an auspicious moment for battle: but as a fact, Charles was only manoeuvring to allow his main force to come up to the field. Grenier, arriving last, was posted between the two Bleichfeld villages, with the reserve cavalry in the rear of the centre at Maynbrunn. Sztarray now marched forward to the battlefield, held the wood south of Estenfeld, and posted forces in Euerfeld and on the heights of Rottendorf, with a reserve near the Kaltengrund. The Austrian left wing thus had an excellent position; but the right wing was ill-placed, for if the French could turn and push it back on Euerfeld, the Austrian hold on the Main crossings would be imperilled.

On the lifting of the fog, about 9 a. m. of September 8, Sztarray, who had his columns all formed, moved forward on Lengfeld, and after a sharp resistance, drove out Simon, while Hotze forced the French divisions out of the Aumühle valley, along which for some hours there was a lively clash of arms, and the rival lines again and again held the field. Simon and Championnet, however, not only remained in possession of the valley, but the latter forged on and gained possession of the Estenfeld woods, after a long sustained effort, pushing the Austrian foot back to Erfeldorf, and the cavalry to Euerfeld. This latter place now became the critical point Should the French win and hold it, Charles would be compelled to fall back to save his bridges. The archduke failed not to appreciate the fact, but he was also aware that he had considerable forces still coming up, and on these he was quietly counting, while Jourdan, ignorant of this fact, was over-confident that he should yet win the day; and Grenier's division, with the reserve cavalry, was ordered to sustain Championnet at Erfeldorf and Euerfeld. This order, however, was but partially executed. Grenier deemed it essential to station a considerable force at Heiligenthal to contain an Austrian column that he saw advancing from Prosselsheim in a direction to turn the French left,—it was indeed Kray's van,—and ordered only the reserve cavalry to Seligenstadt and the Sperl woods, holding the rest at Bleichfeld. Charles had expected his rearward column under Kray to cross the Main at Schwarzach early in the day; but owing to difficulty with the bridges, it was noon before Kray's head of column was able to come up. Then Wartensleben advanced on Bibergau, while Kray pushed rapidly on Prosselsheim, in an attempt to turn the extreme French left. Despite tenacious resistance, the Austrians shortly won back the Sperl woods and the Kaltengrund; and an artillery duel in the centre of both armies ensued, while each was awaiting the oncoming of fresh troops to sustain the tired ones in line. Charles had reserved his critical blow until Kray's arrival with the bulk of his men. About 8 p. m. the fight recommenced. As the Austrian *cuirassier* squadron came up, Lichtenstein headed it also on the French left wing. The French reserve of horse made a handsome bid to keep the Sperl woods; but it was driven out, and ranged itself behind the line of foot, while the Austrians again forced Championnet out of the Estenfeld woods. Kray overwhelmed Grenier at Heiligenthal, and his cavalry completed the rout of Championnet. The French had no reserve to call upon, while fresh Austrian troops were still coming up. Jourdan recognized that he had lost the battle, and retired on Arnstein, where at night he reassembled his divisions, Championnet with the cavalry having covered Simon's retreat by a brilliant fight on Kornach heights.

Charles organized four columns to follow up the French; but the formal method of their marshalling and the poor ground prevented a vigorous pursuit. Yet Simon's rear was badly cut up. If the Austrian loss of about fifteen hundred men out of over forty-four thousand, and the French loss of two thousand out of thirty thousand men, is accurately stated, neither the casualties nor the fighting can be said to have been heavy; but Charles had won the innings. The French lost seven guns.

Thus pushed off his main line of retreat, Jourdan was compelled to retire through the Spessart mountains, which he did in two columns towards Giessen on the Lahn. It was of the highest importance that he should reach the Mainz country, and there hold head to the Austrian advance, but he was unable to do so. He actually reached the Lahn September 9, where Marceau joined him, and with other incoming detachments, he got together over fifty thousand men. With these he held the line of the river, but covering too much front. And while Moreau was advancing to the Isar, Charles continued his march along the highway, and took Hanau and Frankfort September 8; whence moving forward, he crossed the Lahn and attacked the French at Altenkirchen September 16, with some success. The French line fell back, and with greater speed Charles could have compromised Jourdan, and cut him off from the Rhine. But he was over-cautious. In his turn Jourdan neglected near Hof a chance of retrieving the campaign. He fell back behind the Sieg, resigned his command, and was succeeded by Beurnonville, who shortly withdrew behind the Rhine at Bonn, Lefebvre occupying Düsseldorf. Charles followed; but satisfied that the Army of the Sambre and Meuse would undertake no more active work this season, he headed a detachment up the Rhine to get in Moreau's rear. This body captured Kehl, but shortly again lost the fortress. Napoleon points out that Charles would have accomplished more, so soon as the French had crossed the Rhine, by moving with forty thousand men on Ulm, and calling in Latour to join him *via* Ratisbon and the left bank of the Danube. Moreau would then have truly been in evil case. Charles left too many men on the Lower Rhine.

After the battle of Neresheim, it had looked as if the issue of the campaign lay in the hands of Moreau, and indeed, had the commander of the Army of the Rhine and Moselle marched up to join his associate, instead of following Latour, the archduke's brilliant plan would have been shattered; for the Austrian army, caught between two French armies vastly outnumbering it, could not have successfully manoeuvred. How much of this failure was due to Moreau, and how much to the orders of Carnot and the Directory, there seems to be no record to disclose. In retiring August 12 to the right bank of the Danube, Charles had guessed aright that Moreau would follow him, and as the Austrians destroyed all the bridges, the French were compelled to seek crossings well up the stream. On August 20 Moreau concentrated on the Lech, and here Ferino joined him. With his sixty thousand men he proposed to take Augsburg. Latour's thirty-five thousand men were too much spread out to be effective; and when Moreau advanced on him August 24, he was compelled to fall back after a lively fight at Friedeberg, in which he lost fifteen hundred men and seventeen guns, and to take up the Isar line for defence, occupying the river from Munich down to Landshut.

Charles' manoeuvre, like all such operations, practically opened the road to Vienna to Moreau. But, though the arch-duke's instructions to Latour were to resist the French onset to the utmost, he could well afford the risk, aware that he himself had Bohemia in his rear as a base, and that after defeating Jourdan he could turn to the left and cut Moreau's sole line of retreat. His entire plan was of the highest value.

As he gained these advantages, Moreau grew more cautious, and followed too slowly to impress his operation on Charles, who was just beginning to push hard on Jourdan. St. Cyr seized the Isar crossing at Freisingen on September 3, and Latour assembled at Landshut, where reinforcements sent him by Charles were met. It is clear that the best military policy had demanded that Moreau should weeks before have marched to a junction with Jourdan. But though St. Cyr testifies that Moreau knew Jourdan to be hard pressed, yet this was at a date when a junction could no longer be effected. Moreover, Moreau was negotiating with Bavaria for peace, and cared not to leave the Isar; and his orders no doubt also limited his action. Finally he did what might have earlier turned the scales: Desaix was ordered across the Danube and towards Nürnberg, September 10, to interfere with Charles' communications. As the archduke paid no heed to this threat, Moreau put his centre over the river at Neuburg. This was an extra-hazardous manoeuvre, which placed the French army in a critical position astride a great river, rather than interfered with Charles' operations. Moreau's left was at Eichstadt; the centre at Ingolstadt; the right at Geisenfeld. The object to be attained is not apparent. Had Charles not been intent on better game, or had Latour been more enterprising, Moreau might have found himself in evil case. As it was, after four or five days he recognized the weakness of his situation, and reassembled on the right bank. But Charles' brilliant operation was now bearing fruit. Jourdan was painfully making his way towards the Rhine, and Moreau, on learning of his associate's defeat, was forced to recognize that Carnot's plan of two lines of operation, one against each of the allied flanks, had failed. The whole history of war is full of such failures, but it needed a Charles to take advantage of the error, and a Bonaparte to evolve a new maxim out of the failures. It was manifest that Moreau could no longer remain in Bavaria, with Charles so near the Rhine and the French line of retreat; it required small intelligence to guess that so soon as Charles had forced Jourdan across the Rhine, he would turn towards the Neckar country, to cut the communications of the Army of the Rhine and Moselle; and he determined to retire to Ulm, where he could defend the line of the Iller, and by holding the great fortress, operate on either bank of the Danube at will. Indeed, retreat was imperative, for as couriers between the two French armies, except by a long detour, had during the entire campaign been irregular, and were of late quite interrupted, and as Moreau knew not how far Charles had forced back Jourdan, it was quite within the possibilities that the Austrian *generalissimo* might cross the Danube and cut him off from France. Indeed, a rumour that part of the Mannheim garrison had marched up river and attacked the Kehl bridge added to his disquietude.

Moreau, accordingly, with his sixty thousand men, retired from the Isar in three columns, with the artillery and train in the advance,

Latour following him up step by step. On September 21 he reached the Iller, about the time when the Army of the Sambre and Meuse was seeking refuge beyond the Rhine; and Desaix crossed the Danube and took up a position behind the Blau. Yet even here Moreau did not deem himself secure from an allied column which might advance up the Rhine right bank, or indeed up the Neckar valley; and in the last days of September he again retired, this time towards the Upper Rhine. But he deployed his forces over so large an area in the Biberach and Federsee region that he retained but twenty-six thousand men under his own eye. The splendid successes of the Austrian archduke now encouraged Latour and his lieutenants to a marked degree, and they followed up and harassed Moreau with energy and skill. Nauendorf threatened the French left by crossing over into the Neckar valley to Tübingen; Latour kept on his heels; a third corps was getting between him and Lake Constance, and Petrasch was advancing up the Rhine from Charles' forces, and would soon seize the Black Forest debouches. The unexpected retreat and the want of regular issues of rations had caused as much deterioration in the French ranks in this army as in Jourdan's. Superb as is the gallantry of the Gallic soldier,—and there is no denying him a brilliant record in history,—yet he weakens under failure faster than the Anglo-Saxon. The three-o'clock-in-the-morning courage, the cold persistence in fighting against fate, is peculiarly the birthright of the latter. The French army was quite out of heart, and Moreau was soon fain to acknowledge that he could not expect to hold himself on the right bank of the Shine. He must fray his path by way of the rugged ravines of the Black Forest, through what is called the Höllenthal, Hell Valley, to Freiburg; and in order to accomplish this retreat without losing his train, he deemed it essential to neutralize Latour's army by a battle, just as Charles had done at Neresheim, so that it could not pursue him with too much vigour . In two weeks Moreau's handsome achievement had been turned into dire disaster by the archduke's masterly operation against Jourdan.

The country near the Federsee is hilly, wooded and full of ravines. The position which, on his arrival, Latour had taken up on the hills along the Biss, with that stream in his rear, was a bad one, and his several corps were much too isolated. So indeed were Moreau's. Desaix with sixteen thousand men was north of the Federsee from Alschausen to Wittenweiler; St. Cyr with ten thousand men was on the south of the lake from Buchau to Schussenried; and Ferino was at Ravensburg between the Waldsee and the Lake of Constance, more than a day's march away, where he could scarcely be of use in the pro-

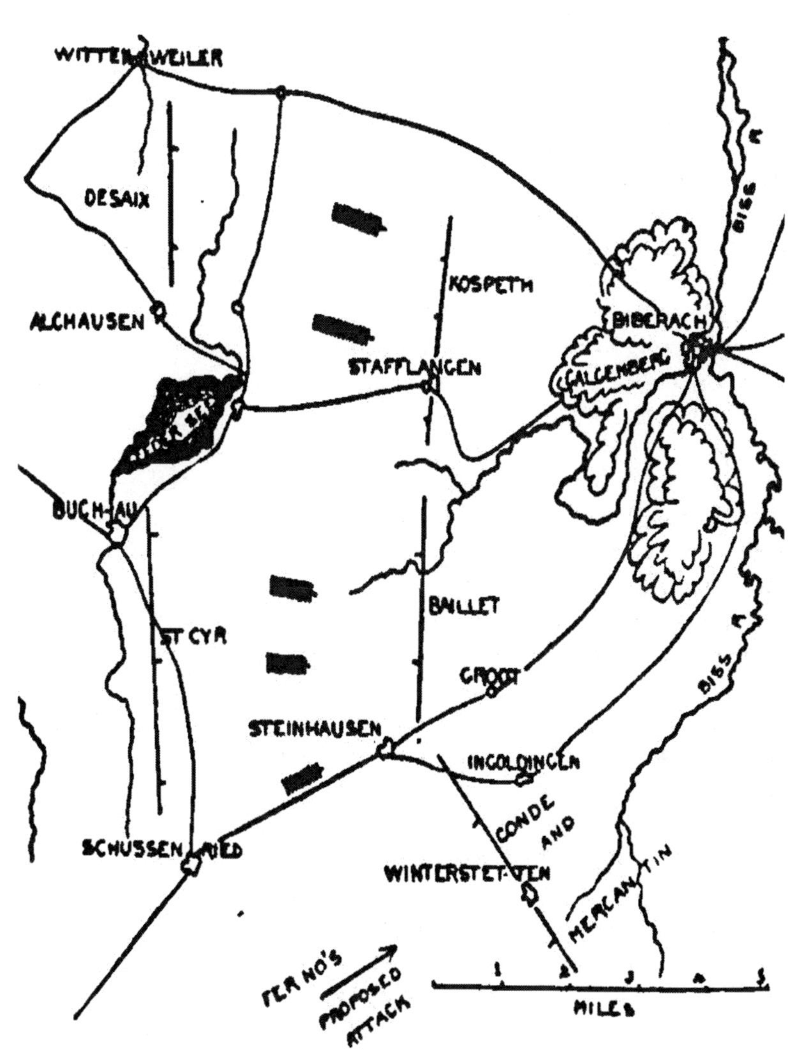

Battle of Biberach

posed battle. Moreau planned that on October 2 Desaix should attack the Austrian right under Kospeth at Stafflangen; that St. Cyr should advance against Latour at Steinhausen in the centre; and to Ferino were sent orders to march on Winterstetten, and turn the enemy's left under Condé and Mercantin.

This plan was only partially carried out; Ferino did not receive his orders in season. Desaix drove the enemy's right almost back to Biberach, and deployed in their front St. Cyr, in three columns, attacked the Austrian centre at Steinhausen, and on the right front of the village, and after much to-and-fro fighting, forced it back to Grodt. Latour disputed the ground with tenacity, but the French onset was too hearty, and the Austrian divisions finally fell back to Ingoldingen and Winterstetten, and thence towards Biberach. Instead of following up his success, St. Cyr obliqued to the left and captured Grodt. The French outdid themselves, but they had to pay a heavy price for every step. Unable to force the Austrians from the Galgenberg in front of Biberach, Desaix sent turning columns around the right and left of the hill, and seized the enemy's communications back of Biberach, whereupon the town fell to the French. Latour's defeat was complete, with a loss of four thousand men, eighteen guns and two flags; and he was glad to retire in any kind of order on Ulm, unpursued. Moreau had won the battle without Ferino's aid, who had not had time to come up. He did not follow beyond the Biss.

But the French commander still had the task of retiring through a bad mountain country, with Nauendorf and Petrasch to dispute his advance or fall upon his flanks. Had he possessed Bonaparte's activity, he could have marched on Rothweil, where they stood, brushed them aside, and then turned on Charles on the Rench. As it was, had the Austrians not been seriously checked by their defeat at Biberach, the indecisive and deliberate French retreat might have been converted into a rout. Latour had missed his chance of compromising the Army of the Rhine and Moselle before it reached its base. Moreau would have preferred to march through the Kinzig valley on Kehl, and in fact made an attempt so to do; but Nauendorf had already headed him off. The only route he could pursue was through the pass which bisects the Black Forest—the Höllenthal. This he set out to accomplish, sending his train down the, Wiese towards Hüningen. St. Cyr in the advance was to open the way through Neustadt, occupied by the Austrians. Desaix held his own for a day to fend off Latour, and then fell in at his rear. Ferino closed the column. By skilful work Moreau made his way through manifold difficulties

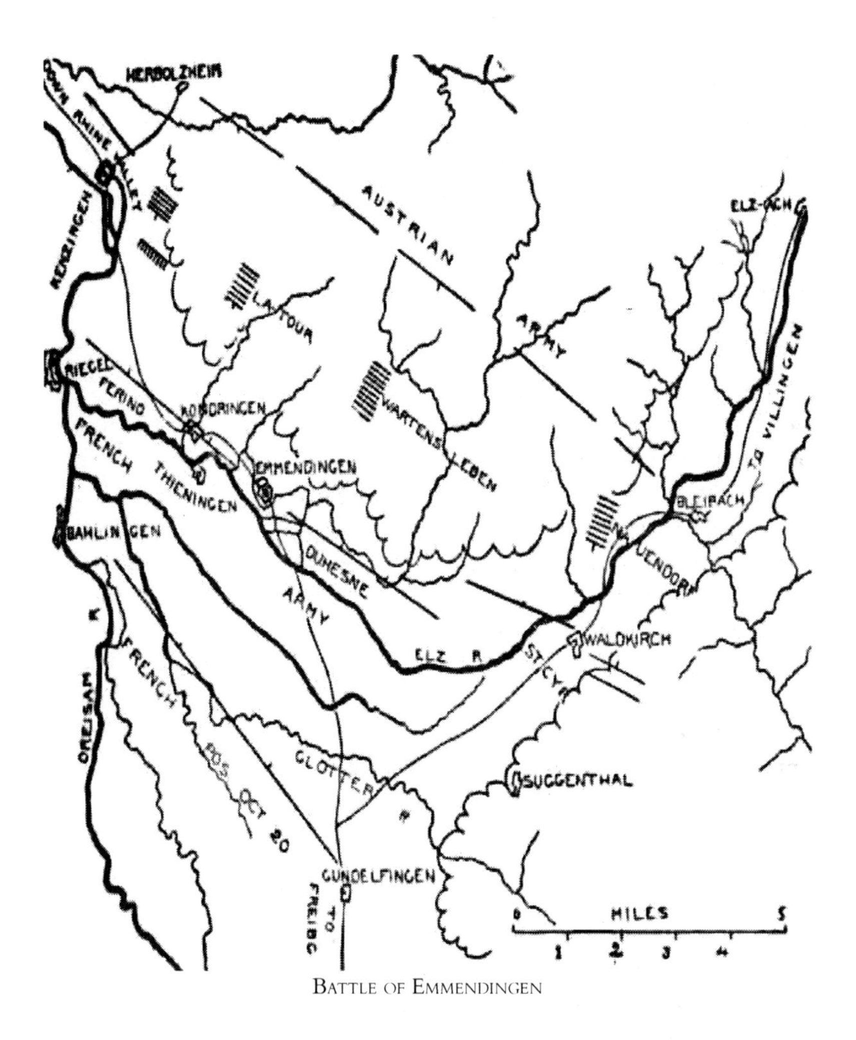

Battle of Emmendingen

to Freiburg by October 12. He had still hoped to be able to move downstream to Kehl; but by this time Charles with a small corps had himself come up the river, and drawing in Latour and other detachments, to all of which the road was now open, stood with thirty-five thousand men athwart his path to that fortress, and was preparing to advance upon him.

On October 19 Charles had taken up a line from Herbolzheim to Bleibach and beyond. The French went into position to cover Freiburg, from Riegel through Emmendingen to Waldkirch. Moreau had here the same problem to face that he had had against Latour: he must defeat Charles in order to retire deliberately on Hüningen and give his train time to get to a place of safety. The archduke advanced on him in several columns October 19, though at a few points the French sallied out and made the first attack. Nauendorf took Waldkirch from St. Cyr after several hours' fighting, and occupied Suggenthal; Wartensleben drove Duhesne across the Elz and captured Emmendingen; Latour's column after hearty opposition drove the French out of Kondringen and Thieningen; while a fourth column, headed against Riegel, only cannonaded the French position, though this in a way contributed to the Austrian success. Thus Ferino alone held head to the enemy; but Moreau had to withdraw his right to the woodland about Gundelfingen, with his left extending down towards Bahlingen. Next day Charles again attacked the French in the villages they held in front of the Dreisam, but they succeeded in holding themselves. Moreau decided to put Desaix with the left wing across the Rhine at Alt Breisach, and to retire with the rest to Hüningen; for as the roads were narrow and the bridge accommodation was limited, . he feared that these might become congested. Moreover, he gave Desaix instructions, if feasible, to march down river to Strasburg, cross to Kehl, and fall on Charles' communications with the Main. This did not get done, however.

When Charles was ready for attack on the third day, he found that Moreau had retired. The French commander had assembled the centre and right at Freiburg during the night of October 20-21, and had retired up river to Schliengen, at the entrance to the mountains. Charles rapidly followed him up, and he found that he must again turn and face the Austrians if he would not be driven in disorder back on Hüningen. Numbering in all over thirty thousand men, he formed line with his left wing under St. Cyr leaning on the Rhine at Steinstadt, and thence through Schliengen to Liel and out to Eckenen, holding the villages in front, and the heights right and left of

BATTLE OF SCHLIENGEN

Mauchen, with strong parties. Ferino on the right was thrown back as a crotchet from Eckenen to Kandern, with outposts in the villages in his front. The cavalry stood between Holzen and Riedlingen.

Charles reconnoitred the position October 23, and determined to attack next day in four columns. He designed to turn Moreau's right, and by cutting him off from Hüningen, compromise his army. He launched the columns forward with vigour . Condé on the right captured Steinstadt; Fürstenberg, next him, took Mauchen, and both held the enemy in place. But the French centre and right were too strong. A first gain by Latour at Eckenen was not followed by further success, as he was unable to cross a ravine protecting the French line, nor indeed to bring up his artillery. Nauendorf drove the French out of Sitzenkirch, but they took up a position behind the Kandern ravine and held him off. It was not until nightfall that Kandern, after a hard day's fight, fell to Nauendorf. The Austrians had been checked by Moreau's determined stand, and the French army in three columns followed the train. On the 25th a halt was made at Haltingen, and next day the Army of the Rhine and Moselle, heartsick and footsore, was glad to file within the bridge-head, and to cross safely at Hüningen to its protecting base.

Blame was cast by many on Moreau's conduct of this campaign; and indeed he had not aided Jourdan as much as he might have done at the auspicious moment. His friends, on the other hand, foolishly likened his retreat through the Black Forest to Xenophon's march to the sea. The simple fact is that Charles outmanoeuvred both him and Jourdan. The *Memoirs* say:

> Thus, after having nourished the war four months in Germany, disarmed and detached from the cause of the emperor the Margrave of Baden, the Duke of Wurtemberg and the Elector of Bavaria, and having accorded them forces, and imposed on them contributions which it had not the time to collect, having carried off several victories without having suffered an important defeat, the French army repassed the Rhine.

Napoleon shows in his incisive way how Moreau could have retrieved the campaign, even at the last; but he tries him by his own rapid standard—a scarcely equitable test.

So soon as Moreau had reached the left bank of the Rhine, he assigned the defence of Kehl to Desaix, and to Ferino that of Hüningen. Charles masked the latter place and turned on Kehl, fearing a fresh crossing by the Army of the Rhine and Moselle. He was indeed ordered by the Vienna authorities to capture both Kehl and Hüningen; and in consequence of these instructions, Latour closed in Kehl with thirty-five thousand men, early in November. The place surrendered January 19. The bridge-head of Hüningen was captured in February. The Austrians went into winter quarters on the right bank, the French on the left bank.

The campaign in Germany in 1796, which, for lack of space, has been but baldly sketched, almost equals in interest that of Bonaparte in Italy, and its hero is the twenty-five-year-old Archduke Charles. The operations of the French armies were all in the hands of one man, the able war minister, Carnot, who, more rich in theory than practice, still lay under the weight of the old cordon system, and of his own false scheme of concentrating the bulk of the operating forces at the ends of his own cordon, so as to turn the flanks of the enemy's cordon. How mistaken this theory was, it needed only Bonaparte in Italy in this same year to demonstrate. Yet it was much in favour of the French arms that to Carnot was given the sole power, while the Austrian arms were subject to the whims of the Vienna Council, whose pedantic methods often came close to wrecking what would have been excellent operations, if let alone.

Carnot's general plan was to have Moreau and Jourdan advance, each on either bank of the Danube, and join hands with Bonaparte at the gates of Vienna. The plan was magnificent, but like all concentric operations, it possessed the distinct element of failure. The Austrian general plan was to gain a strong foothold on the left bank of the middle or lower Rhine, and thence reconquer the Netherlands. With the forces Austria placed on the Rhine ployed into one body, a determined and able leader might have marched on Paris; but when Bonaparte reached the Mincio, the wiseacres in Vienna withdrew Wurmser and the best of the veterans from the Rhine, and assumed a defensive role where they had purposed to deliver their heartiest blow. It was merely by a piece of good luck that the field operations were placed under one man—and he the Archduke Charles.

The scheme of Carnot was perhaps superior to that of the Austrians; but its details were less well managed. The principal operations were confided to Moreau, whether because his army lay on the straight road to Vienna, or from the idea that he was more able than Jourdan, cannot be said. Jourdan's entire army was to begin by making a mere demonstration to aid Moreau's. The two were later to operate, each limited to his own line; and yet they were supposed to be in cooperation. This is not, however, the sort of cooperation which produces results. The falsity of this gigantic plan stands out in marked contrast to Bonaparte's success in Italy, in his beautifully simple manoeuvres against the centre of the Austro-Sardinian armies. Had Carnot placed both Rhine armies in one body to operate down the Danube, what might not, in connection with the Army of Italy, have been the result? The same reasoning applies to the two Austrian armies. Would not Archduke Charles have been better equipped, if both these armies had at the outset been in one body, which could push in between Jourdan and Moreau and destroy each singly? This was in fact what Charles eventually, but only in part did, and it was this which brought to so brilliant an end this memorable campaign.

Why Charles retired so constantly at the opening of the campaign, when he had practically the same opportunity as in the latter half, unless he was controlled by the Vienna Council, has been often asked. The answer is that the garrisons left on the Rhine, and the defection of allied contingents, reduced him to an inferiority; and being inexperienced, he needed to prove his weapons. He himself says that his object was, so soon as he should reach the Danube, to dispute the advance of the enemy foot by foot, without risking a general engagement; to draw in his left wing, which had been cut off; to rejoin Wartensleben farther to the rear; and to seek a chance of falling with superior forces on one or the other French army. And from the moment he decided to operate against Jourdan, while holding Moreau in check with Latour, he showed marked capacity for war. The inevitable happened. Moreau was compelled to retire when his associate was forced back, and both were glad to seek refuge behind the Rhine. Even gauging Moreau's retreat at its highest value, and it was boldly and skilfully conducted, yet he was fortunate, in view of Charles' prompt march up the Rhine, after he had disposed of the Army of the Sambre and Meuse, to effectuate his escape as he did. The object of the German campaign, say the Memoirs, was to prevent forces being detached to Italy; take from the emperor his allies; feed the army in Germany, and seize horses and material there; capture Ehrenbreitstein, Mainz, Mannheim and Philipsburg; to secure the Rhine as a frontier for France; take winter quarters on the Danube, so as to be ready in 1797, after Mantua should have been captured, to advance on Vienna in concord with the Army of Italy. To accomplish this, the above places should have been besieged, and all the French forces disposable should have been consolidated into one army of one hundred and fifty thousand men to move into the heart of Germany.

Moreau can scarcely be said to have exhibited more than ordinary talent in this campaign. Jourdan showed even less. The *Memoirs* say:

> He was very brave on the day of battle, in face of the enemy and in the midst of fire; but he had not the courage of the head in the middle of the calm of night, at two o'clock in the morning. He lacked not penetration or intellectual faculties, but he was without resolution, and imbued with false principles of war."

Wartensleben and Latour were on a common plane. Despite some minor miscalculations, the operations of Archduke Charles on the Rhine and Danube were masterful to a high degree.

There is, however, this marked difference. In Germany the results were naught; in Italy the results were immense. In Germany, each opponent ended where he began; Bonaparte won all northern Italy by his new method of conducting war. Not only this, but Bonaparte created a new art; Charles remained under the influence of the cordon system; and when later he encountered Bonaparte, he found that he had met more than his match.

CHAPTER 13

Arcole

October & November, 1796

Bonaparte foresaw that he would again have to fight for Mantua, and his position was far from sound. Still by every means, political and military, he strove to better his position. The Austrians were largely reinforced from the successful armies on the Danube, and Alvinzi in October was sent to relieve Mantua. As usual, the Austrians divided their army, proposing to move from Trent and from Bassano on Verona, and there join hands. To meet this double threat Bonaparte left Vaubois to hold the upper Adige while he attacked Alvinzi; but Davidovich drove back Vaubois, and Alvinzi held his own against Bonaparte on the Brenta. Thus both French columns early in November fell back, and Bonaparte saw that if he lost Verona he must retire behind the Mincio. He had never yet been in such danger. At Caldiero, November 11, Bonaparte attacked Alvinzi, but, unable to make any impression on the superior Austrians, retired to Verona. Had Alvinzi, Davidovich and Wurmser now advanced promptly on Bonaparte, the French would have been in ill case. Some new plan must be devised, or Bonaparte could not hold himself. Leaving a small force in Verona, he marched down the Adige, crossed at Ronco, and attempted to turn Alvinzi's left and reach his rear. But the French were stopped at Arcole by the marshy ground, over which they could only advance along causeways, and here for three days was fought a bloody battle. On each evening the French retired to the west bank of the river. The Army of Italy was saved by Davidovich's slowness, who during all this time did not attack Vaubois, and finally on the 17th Alvinzi weakened, and the Battle of Arcole was won. This enabled Bonaparte to drive Davidovich back up the Adige, which he could now do with superior numbers. Wurmser made an ill-timed sortie from Mantua, which in nowise aided Alvinzi.

The lost campaign in Germany had seriously affected the position of the Army of Italy, and the Directory had no means wherewith to help it. Efforts had been made to open negotiations between the contending powers, but until Austria could recover Lombardy, she would listen to no overtures from whatever source. Despite all Bonaparte's victories, his situation continued dangerous. He had lost twenty thousand men by battle and disease, and had not over thirty-six thousand men left. And yet he must have reinforcements. Repeatedly he warned the Directory, "Troops, or Italy goes lost." And while France did naught to sustain her one successful general, Austria put fresh hosts into the field.

On October 1, 1796, Bonaparte wrote to the Directory:

> In January the emperor will have a powerful army in the Tyrol and in Friuli. . . . Nothing equals the activity that there is in the empire to recruit the Italian army. Here is the force of our army: Vaubois with eight thousand men covers Trent; Massena with fifty-five hundred men and Augereau with fifty-four hundred men are on the march to the Brenta; Sahuguet and Dallemagne with forty-five hundred men are before Mantua. In Lombardy, at Coni, at Alessandria, at Tortona, at Ceva, at Cherasco, are four thousand. Sick, fourteen thousand; wounded, four thousand. Thus I have eighteen thousand nine hundred men in the army of observation, nine thousand men in the army of siege. I leave it to you to judge, if I receive no help, whether it is possible that I can this winter resist the emperor, who will have fifty thousand men here in six weeks. . . . Reflect that you should have here in Italy, to be able to sustain yourselves during the winter, thirty-five thousand men of infantry in the army of observation, and eighteen thousand men of infantry in the army of siege, to make face to the emperor.

During the two months which the French forces spent in the fever-stricken lowlands about Mantua, Bonaparte was kept busy in working daylight out of the conflicting shadows of Italian politics. His desire was, while respecting and taking advantage of the aristocratic and ecclesiastical sentiments of both classes and masses, to make republics out of the principalities of northern Italy, the population of which had taken kindly to the republican ideas, and was wavering between love of their religion and hatred of domestic oppression. After much negotiation and canvassing, Bologna and Ferrara were actually erected into a Transpadane Republic; Modena and Reggio into a Cispadane, the former town having been occupied by French troops.

But there were many awkward questions staring Bonaparte in the face. Venice might at any time declare for Austria, and she could put twenty thousand men into the field. The Pope had broken the terms of his armistice, and had made overtures to Vienna. Naples had delayed signing the treaty with France, whose terms had been agreed to. By the death of the king of Sardinia, the attitude of Piedmont again became questionable; and without this base as a positive factor, the French forces on the Mincio were absolutely in the air. Some of Bonaparte's fears, however, came to an early end by the final execution by the Directory of a very liberal treaty with Naples on October 10; and this treaty likewise settled the Roman question, for the Pope was apt to attempt nothing, unless sure of the countenance of Naples.

As Bonaparte had long desired to create for the Republic in Italy a strong place upon which he could rely, he renewed certain of his demands on Genoa, and these eventually resulted in that city paying a tribute, excluding the English fleet, and the great port being transformed into a French armed place. About the same time the English occupied Porto Ferajo, and Corsica having become troublesome, they left that island, which was thereupon promptly seized by a French expedition, October 21.

There was sufficient reason why Bonaparte, whose troops were still before Mantua, and in the Brenta and Adige valleys watching the enemy, had not initiated active operations. In addition to the political work, which always consumed much of his time, for Bonaparte was as apt to rely on what he could accomplish by statesmanship as by war, his army demanded much time; for it had suffered severely from epidemic fevers, which had depleted the ranks and filled the hospitals, and reinforcements came in all too slowly. Yet he must keep it in good fighting trim, which was no easy task with its then half-civil, half-military organization. In a long dispatch to the Directory, dated October 12, 1796, Bonaparte made formal complaint by name against many of the civil employees of the army as being villains of the first water.

> Since I am in Milan, Citizen Directors, I occupy myself with making war against rogues. I have had several tried and punished. I myself denounce others to you. In making an open war against them, it is clear that I arouse against myself a thousand voices, which will seek to pervert the (public) opinion. I understand that, if 'two months ago I wanted to be Duke of Milan, today I would like to be King of Italy.' But as long as my force and your confidence last, I shall make a pitiless war against the rogues and the Austrians.

He then goes on to state that the evidence proves that the contractors and commissaries pocketed a large part of the money furnished them, that they delivered poor goods, that they demanded fifteen and twenty *per cent*, rebate on government orders, that they corrupted the military storekeepers and forged vouchers.

> They steal in a manner so ridiculous and so impudent that if I had a month of leisure, there would not be one of them who might not be shot.

A number of these men are identified by name in this dispatch; and among them, to their credit, a number of honest men are also mentioned. This trouble was ever recurring. In writing Berthier January 1, 1797, about three citizens who had stolen and made false vouchers, Bonaparte wrote:

> I demand in consequence that these three employees shall be condemned to death. They should not be considered as common thieves, but as men who every day diminish the means of the army, and cause the best concerted operations to fail, or at least only allow their success after the spilling of much French blood.

While Bonaparte waged war on plunderers of the army supplies, he consistently upheld the arts and sciences. On October 25 he wrote:

> It seems, Citizens Directors, by your letter of the 14 Vendémiaire, that the savants and the artists have complained of not having what they need. It would be very ungrateful on our part not to give them all that is necessary, for they serve the Republic with as much zeal as success, and I beg you to believe that on my side I appreciate more than anybody the real service which arts and sciences render to the state, and that I shall always be anxious to second with all my zeal your intentions on this subject.

Turning from the civil to the military side of his duties, on October 16 Bonaparte wrote to Wurmser, stating the fact that Mantua was beyond being saved, offering to let him personally see what the existing conditions were, and suggesting that he had better yield up the fortress. This diplomatic attempt had, however, no result. On October 25 he wrote the Directory:

> Wurmser is in the last extremity, he has no wine, meat or forage. He is eating his horses, and has fifteen thousand sick. He found means of getting the proposition I made him to Vienna.

For all that, the fortress continued to hold out. Wurmser had pluck, if not ability.

Meanwhile the defeat of Jourdan enabled the Voralberg troops to march to the Adige, and Davidovich, who had been put in command with orders to take Trent, received accessions which ran his army up to nearly twenty thousand men; and the army of Quosdanovich, which after the defeat of Bassano had retired to Gorice on the Isonzo, was also increased to thirty thousand, partly Croats, recently organized into regiments, partly men from the Rhine armies to act as a leaven and partly recruits from the interior.

Bonaparte's political operations were interrupted by the arrival at the end of October of a fresh Austrian army under Alvinzi, who, like his predecessor, was charged with the relief of Mantua, which Austria was determined to keep at any price. The force which had been assembling in the Friuli under Alvinzi had concentrated October 22 at Pordenone, reached Conegliano October 30, and crossed the Piave on November 2, on the way to Bassano, while Davidovich with eighteen thousand men recaptured Trent. Each of these two columns proposed to push its advance, Davidovich down the Adige, Alvinzi towards Verona, until they could join hands at the latter city; and meanwhile Wurmser would debouch in force from Mantua. This intention, which shortly became manifest, prevented Bonaparte from advancing on Alvinzi on the Brenta or the Piave, lest he should, by his absence, enable Davidovich to beat Vaubois, march down and join Wurmser at Mantua, and establish a large body on the French communications. Nor could he well advance to Roveredo, lest he open to Alvinzi the road to Mantua, with the same results. And should he remain massed at Verona, the two Austrian commanders might join hands by the Brenta valley. The one thing in his favour was that the two armies were again to operate on concentric lines, so that either could be attacked separately, so long as the other kept quiet, or could be neutralized. The late defeat of Wurmser seemed not to have taught the Austrians any military wisdom. But the superior numbers of the enemy were most disquieting.

Of Alvinzi's movement towards the Brenta valley Bonaparte had received news by October 25, and he proposed, as a first step, to have Vaubois push the Tyrolese troops back on Neumarkt, so that he could draw from his division a goodly detachment to reinforce the main body; and he sent Berthier thither to see the work done as directed. Should a heavy force move on Bassano, Massena, who was on the Brenta, was ordered to withdraw to Vicenza, and when the enemy had got tired out by his long marches over bad roads, Bonaparte's time of attack would have come. The French general's calculations were, however, as we shall see, much upset by Vaubois' inability even to hold his own.

On October 29 Massena made a reconnoissance towards the Piave, and ascertaining the presence of Austrians on the farther side, concentrated at Bassano the troops with which he had been protecting the Brenta valley and watched for the enemy. That Alvinzi had crossed the Piave November 2 was soon reported to Bonaparte at headquarters in Verona; and next day the Austrian army was in the Treviso-Asolo region. Upon the approach of Quosdanovich with the right wing to Bassano on November 4, Massena vacated the town early in the morning, and withdrew towards Vicenza; while Augereau, under previous orders, approached Montebello, and Bonaparte came thither to take command. On the 15th Massena and Augereau concentrated at Vicenza. Provera and the left wing marched to the Brenta in front of Citadella.

While this was going on opposite the Austrian lower Adige army, Vaubois advanced on the upper Adige army under Davidovich according to orders; and though attacking with vigour on November 2, at early dawn, the position of the Austrians near San Michele above the Avisio, was unable to carry the place; and his right having been turned, he retired by evening to Lavis. Next day Davidovich, who had twice the force of Vaubois, led the attack on the French right at Segonzano, and fearing to be turned, Vaubois withdrew his left to Trent. On the 4th Davidovich, encouraged by success, pushed sharply in on Trent, and by nightfall Vaubois was fain to leave this town also, and take up the next available position, in the defile of Caliano. Again Davidovich advanced, and on the 5th attacked the defile, sending at the same time a turning force of Tyrolese riflemen under Laudon, by way of Mori and Torbole on the other side of the river, to reach the French rear. He was playing the same role, in the opposite direction, that Bonaparte had played two months before.

On November 5, 1796, Joubert, in whom Bonaparte had recognized the true quality of the soldier, was ordered to turn over his command of Legnano to another officer, and to report to Vaubois to help him in his campaign. It was here that Joubert learned the Adige country, as a preparation to his future brilliant services there.

Why Alvinzi did not essay to join Davidovich by the Brenta, or at least organize a line of couriers between the armies, so as to work in some sort in concert with his lieutenant, or at all events with knowl-

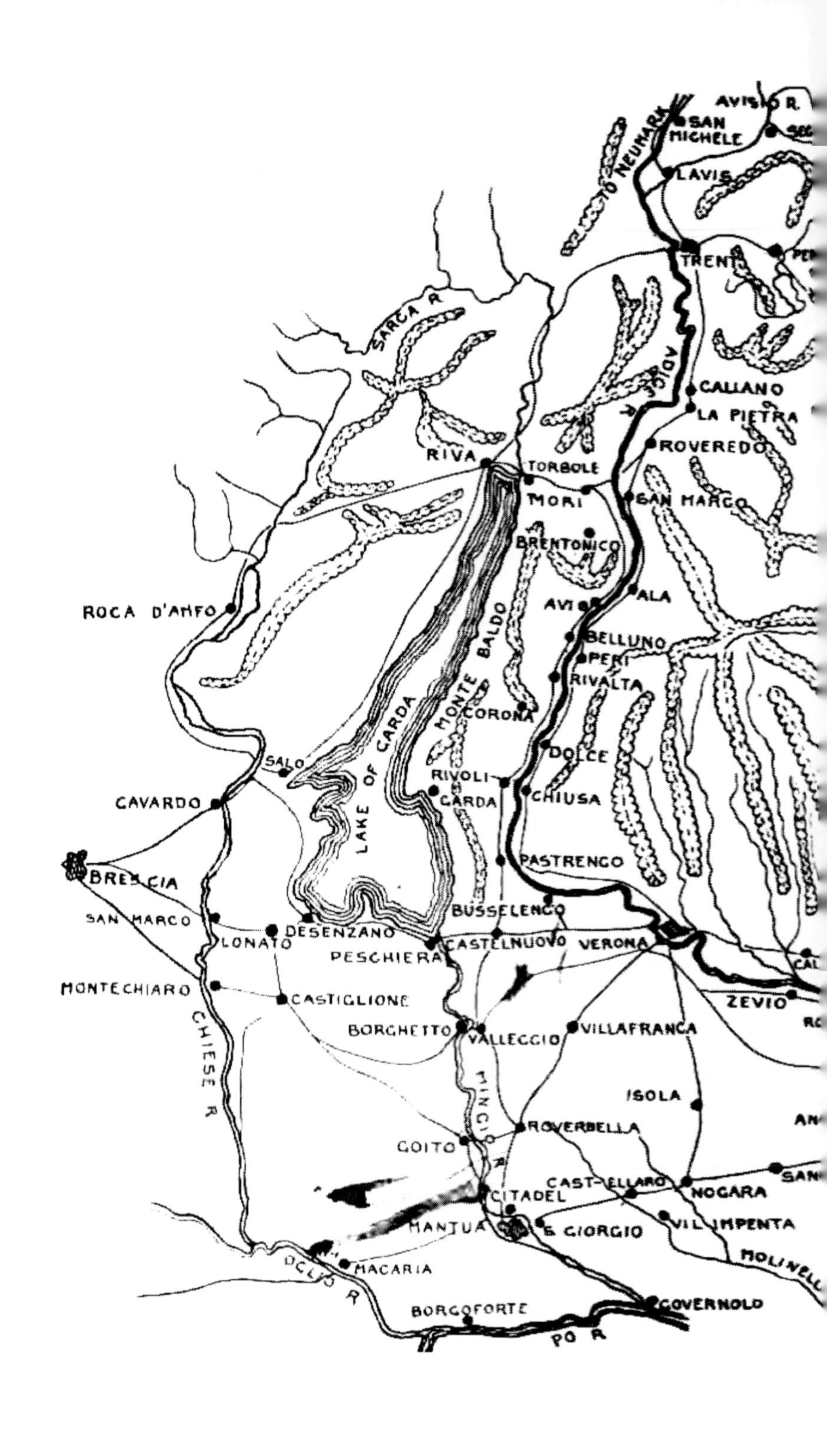

AVISIO R.
SAN MICHELE
TO NEUMARK
LAVIS
TRENT
SARCA R.
ADIGE
CALIANO
LA PIETRA
ROVEREDO
RIVA
TORBOLE
MORI
SAN MARCO
BRENTONICO
ALA
ROCA D'AMFO
AVIO
BELLUNO
PERI
RIVALTA
MONTE BALDO
CORONA
LAKE OF GARDA
DOLCE
SALO
RIVOLI
GARDA
CHIUSA
CAVARDO
PASTRENGO
BRESCIA
BUSSELENGO
SAN MARCO
DESENZANO
LONATO
CASTELNUOVO
VERONA
PESCHIERA
MONTECHIARO
CASTIGLIONE
ZEVIO
CHIESE R.
BORGHETTO
VALLEGGIO
VILLAFRANCA
MINCIO R.
ISOLA
GOITO
ROVERBELLA
CAST-ELLARO
NOGARA
CITADEL
MANTUA
S. GIORGIO
VILIMPENTA
MACARIA
OGLIO R.
BORGOFORTE
GOVERNOLO
PO R.

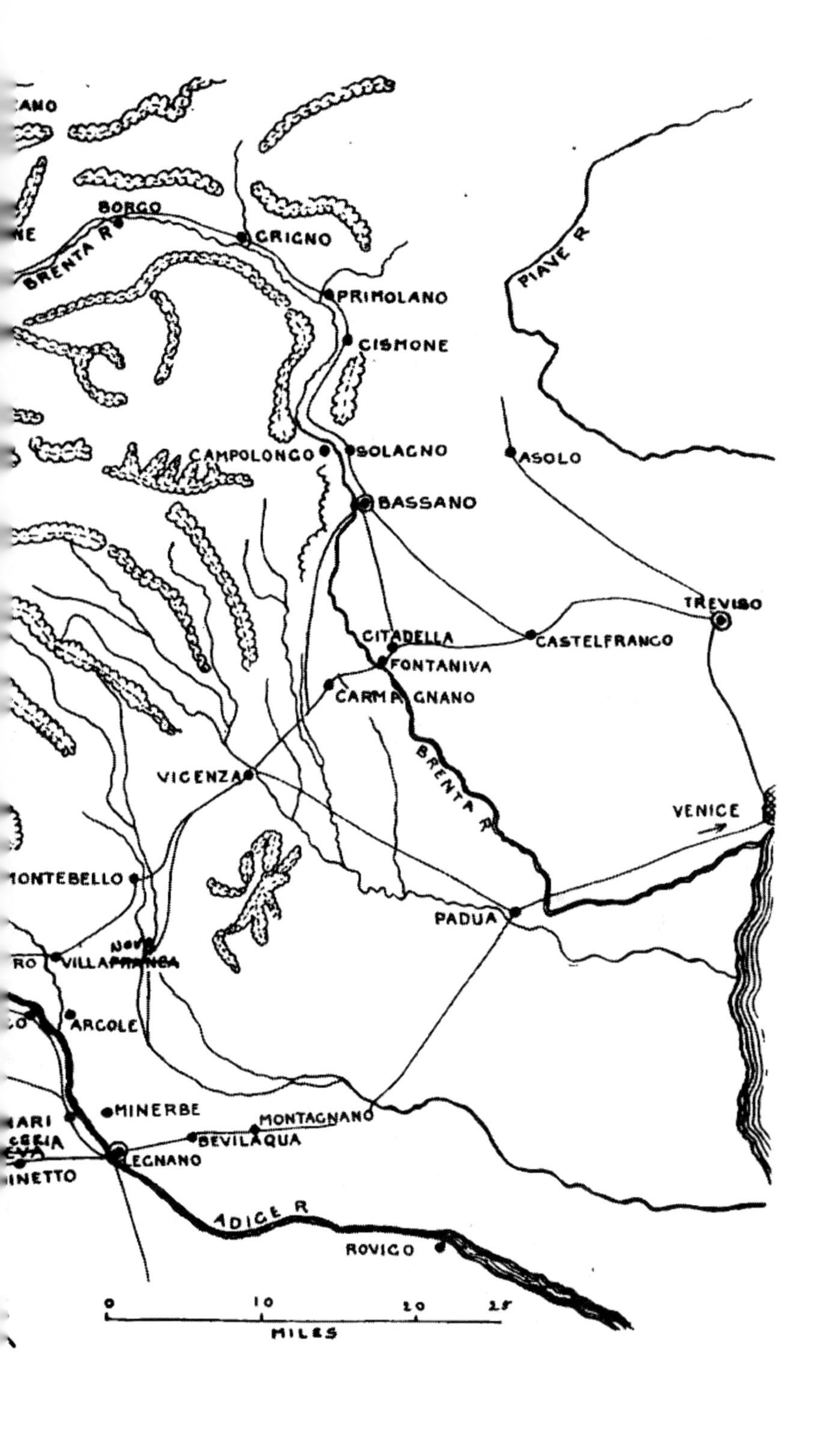

BORGO
BRENTA R
GRIGNO
PRIMOLANO
CISMONE
PIAVE R
CAMPOLONGO
SOLAGNO
ASOLO
BASSANO
TREVISO
CITADELLA
CASTELFRANCO
FONTANIVA
CARMAGNANO
BRENTA R
VICENZA
VENICE
MONTEBELLO
PADUA
VILLAFRANCA
ARCOLE
MINERBE
MONTAGNANO
BEVILAQUA
LEGNANO
INETTO
ADICE R
ROVIGO
0
10
20
25
MILES

edge of each other's manoeuvres, it is hard to comprehend. But a division of forces at that day was not deemed an error. In fact, it is yet the common resort of all incompetent strategists.

In the Brenta valley, on November 6, the armies also clashed. Early in the morning Bonaparte had moved Augereau forward on Alvinzi's right under Quosdanovich at Bassano, and Massena on his left under Liptay and Provera, who stood at Carmagnano and Fontaniva, and had striven all day long by repeated attacks to win the crossings of the Brenta held by the enemy; but though, on the whole, the French were successful, and Alvinzi retired most of his troops across the river, yet the Austrians, by bringing up their reserves, held fast to the crossings, and the day was without gainful result. The loss was fortunately not great. Having in mind the Wurmser campaign, Bonaparte was surprised at the good countenance of the Austrian troops. They appeared to be quite equal to his own in action. He proposed to renew the attack next day; but bad news from Vaubois held him back. While the commander-in-chief was thus forfeiting the chance he had hoped for, of throwing Alvinzi permanently towards the Piave, and then of marching up the Brenta valley and taking Davidovich in the rear, the latter had attacked La Pietra in force, and had failed by a frontal attack to take the defile. But a turning column had proved more successful, and on learning of its presence, Vaubois was again smitten with the fever of retreat, and wrote his chief that he feared he should probably be forced still farther back by dint of numbers. This forward movement of Davidovich, if carried too far, threatened to take Verona in reverse, and Bonaparte concluded that he must defer his operations against Alvinzi, and turn his attention to the Adige valley. Augereau and Massena were ordered back to Vicenza, which they reached November 7, and after a short respite, withdrew to Verona by the forenoon of the 8th. This rearward movement markedly encouraged Alvinzi and his Austrians.

Davidovich had not a clever soldier in his front. On the 7th he repeated his attack on Vaubois at Caliano, captured the place by 4 p. m., and the French were forced back to the La Corona-Rivoli line. This operation was getting to be so dangerous that Bonaparte himself went up to Rivoli to encourage the troops. Two half-brigades had specially shown lack of endurance in the fight of the 7th; and the commanding general issued an "Allocution to the Division Vaubois."

Rivoli
17 Brumaire, Year V
Soldiers! I am not satisfied with you; you have shown neither

> discipline, nor constancy, nor bravery; in no position could you be rallied; you abandoned yourselves to a panic terror; you have allowed yourselves to be driven from positions where a handful of brave men should stop an army. Soldiers of the 39th and of the 85th, you are not French soldiers. General, Chief of Staff, cause to be written on the flags:
> "*They are no longer of the Army of Italy!*"
> *Bonaparte*

This punishment bit deep; the men, with true Gallic fervour, vowed to conquer or die; and when they thereafter kept their word, the stigma was removed. Bonaparte had a way with him which commanded the respect and won the hearts of his soldiers.

In his dispatches to the Directory November 13, the general-in-chief was fain to apologize for some of these troops. Speaking of this fight at La Pietra, "At the beginning of the night a panic terror seized our troops, the rout became general, we abandoned six guns," he reports, and he wrote November 24:

> General of Division Vaubois is a brave man, fit to sustain a siege in a place but in no sense fit to command a division in an army as active, and in a kind of war as decisive. I have sent him to command in Leghorn; he might be sent to command in Corsica. I ask of you the grade of division general for the General of Brigade Joubert, a young man of greatest merit.

Bonaparte was ever ready to recognize and reward good service.

On the same day, the 7th of November, that had seen Vaubois' defeat, Alvinzi moved within five miles of Vicenza. On the 8th he kept on and reached the city, while Davidovich got as far down the Adige as Roveredo—each with his main body. Matters were coming to a crisis. It began to look as if Alvinzi's eccentric advance was about to succeed against Bonaparte's interior lines.

One thing is worthy of special remark in these days, and that is how little favoured by fortune Bonaparte was. Despite work twice as hard as any done by his opponent, despite marches twice as long, despite courage equal to that of any troops, yet Bonaparte and his men frequently fell far short of success. It has generally been said that he was the constant favourite of the fickle goddess; but it should rather be said that when she did smile on him, he quickly seized his opportunity; and that when she withdrew her favours, he worked all the harder to win back her smiles. In this particular case Bonaparte had set himself a task with marked risk. As has been pointed out, he wanted to reverse the manoeuvre he had used against Wurmser, and having thrown Alvinzi back beyond the Brenta, to march up the valley, and fall on the rear of Davidovich. After a fashion, this was laying his own communications open to interruption, for unless he beat Alvinzi so thoroughly as to neutralize him for many days, he could not expect to prevent his again advancing towards the Mincio before the French could crush Davidovich and reach the danger-zone by the long detour up the Brenta and down the Adige.

Now, when Vaubois was beaten, and he himself had failed to beat Alvinzi,—in other words, when Dame Fortune frowned upon him,—Bonaparte saw that he must woo her by some other means; and he changed his plan at once and radically. That he was ready to do so, that he was speedily prepared with another plan, shows that, like Frederick, he was always studying the situation. "A great captain must ask himself daily a number of times: 'If the enemy's army should appear in my front, on my right flank, on my left, what should I do?' If this question puzzles him, he is badly placed, he is not well ordered, he must rectify things." From this study came Bonaparte's readiness, his alertness.

In these quotations from Napoleon's utterances, there is so much which is, idea for idea, the same which we find in Frederick's writings, that one must conclude not only that Napoleon knew these writings, but that they had sunk deep into his mind. He can scarcely have failed to read or ponder what had already become public property, by translation and publication in many places outside of Prussia; and though he nowhere refers to inspiration from Frederick's pages,—this would not in any case have been the way of this self-sufficient man,—the internal evidence would show that he was indebted to the great king for much of what he knew of war. Frederick's seed fell on fertile soil.

On November 8, then, Bonaparte was at Verona with twenty-one thousand men, and Vaubois at La Corona with eight thousand; and in their front Alvinzi lay with twenty-seven thousand men at Vicenza, and Davidovich with sixteen thousand at Roveredo,—an active field force of twenty-nine thousand French to forty-three thousand Austrians. Next day Alvinzi moved forward to Montebello; but Davidovich, hearing that Vaubois had received reinforcements, remained inactive. On the 10th Alvinzi sent a detachment out to Caldiero, and the following day he marched his main column to Villanova. Bonaparte had meanwhile sent Massena in person to gauge the situation in the Adige valley, and himself closely watched Alvinzi. Should Davidovich advance farther, Bonaparte determined to fall on him and destroy him at any cost; else his line of retreat *via* Peschiera and across the Mincio might be compromised. But Massena came back with the reassuring news that Davidovich showed no immediate sign of moving; and Bonaparte, instead of sending Massena's division to sustain Vaubois, as he had feared he must, determined to keep him for an attack on Alvinzi. He was to need his every man. The French army, then, had rest on the 9th and 10th; and not until the 11th did Bonaparte hear any definite news of Alvinzi's advance towards Verona.

If we can imagine Alvinzi's advancing rapidly on Verona, which city he could turn by crossing the Adige below, Davidovich continuing to press Vaubois day by day, and Wurmser making a hearty sortie from Mantua with twenty thousand men, it would seem as if this Austrian total of sixty-seven thousand men, although advancing in a faulty manner, ought to have overwhelmed Bonaparte's total of forty-five thousand men, relieved Mantua, and driven the Army of Italy behind the Mincio. But Alvinzi's slowness was matched by that of both Davidovich and Wurmser.

Before marching out to meet the enemy, Bonaparte, on the 11th of November, issued his usual proclamation:

> When the drum of battle shall have beaten, and when we march straight at the enemy, with fixed bayonets and in the dull silence which guarantees victory, Soldiers! be worthy of yourselves. I say to you but two words, they suffice for Frenchmen: 'Italy! Mantua!' The peace of Europe, the happiness of your parents, will be the result of your courage. Let us do once more what we have done so often, and Europe will not contest us the title of the bravest and most powerful nation in the world.

On the afternoon of the 11th, having heard that Alvinzi was marching towards him from Vicenza, Bonaparte determined on an offensive counter. Rapidly assembling some troops, he marched out about three o'clock, struck the Austrian van at San Martino, and by dark, at no great cost, drove it back on Caldiero. The heights of Caldiero come down to, indeed, cross the post-road which runs through Vicenza to Verona; and, covered by vines, walls and gardens, and flanked by river and mountains, make an exceptionally favourable position for troops to defend. During the night of November 11-12 the Austrian van had entrenched itself at this place, and, to forestall the arrival of the main body, Bonaparte attacked it by 8 a. m. of the 12th, Augereau going in along the road, while he threw Massena around the enemy's right flank at Colognola, which appeared to him to be less strongly

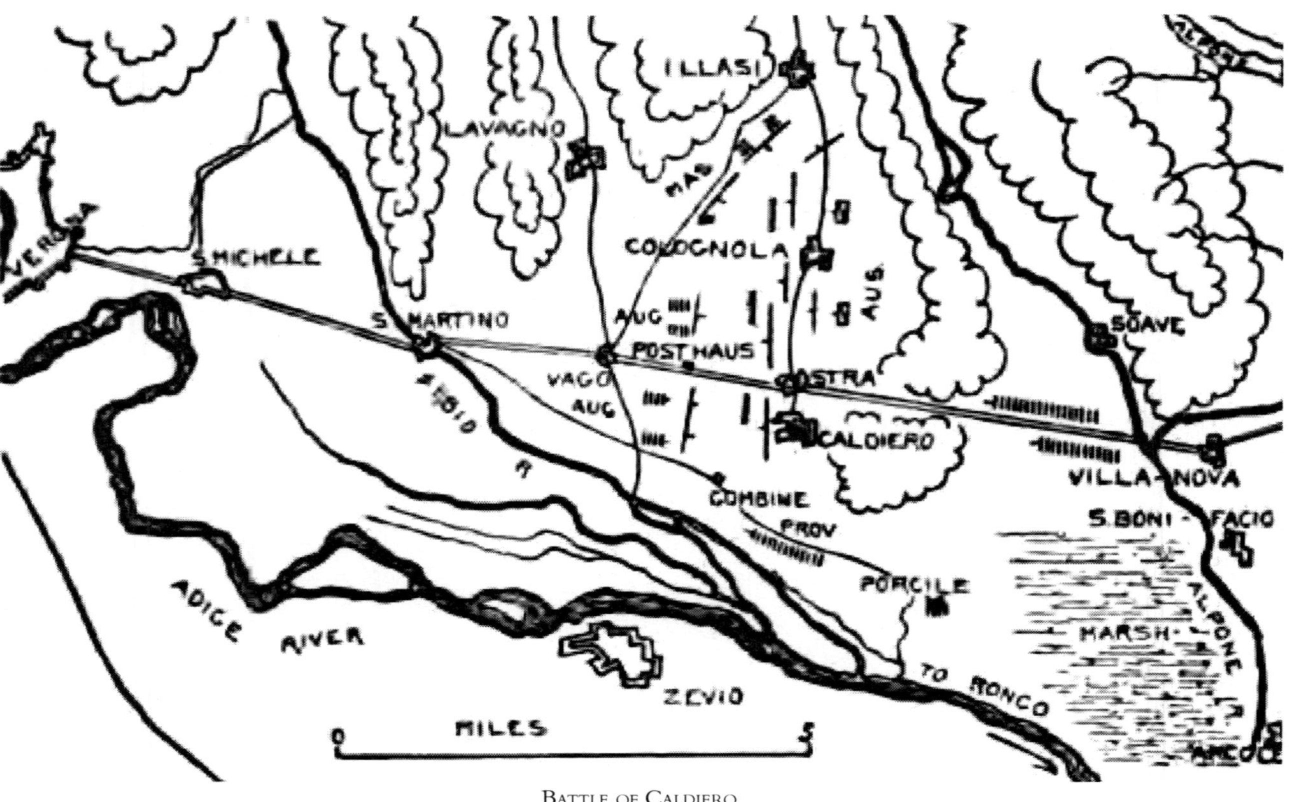

Battle of Caldiero

held. The Austrians had two battalions at Caldiero; three battalions and three squadrons on the Colognola heights; two battalions and six squadrons between the two villages; one battalion stood in front of Stra; and twenty-six guns covered the line. The battle in front of Stra; and Caldiero was of the heartiest description, these villages being taken and retaken time and again. It was raining hard, the side roads were almost impassable, the Austrian guns had all been got into place, while many of the French guns were stalled in the muddy fields and could not be put in position to do effective work, and Augereau was accomplishing little. Meanwhile Massena, by way of Lavagno and Illasi, had reached the Colognola heights, and opened his attack. But by 4 p. m., before he had made a marked impression, Alvinzi's main body began to arrive; the rain turned to sleet and hail, a northeast wind blew the freezing gusts into the faces of the French troops; Massena not only made no further gain, but when Alvinzi put in his oncoming reserves, he was thrown back from Colognola heights; and the turning manoeuvre being forfeited, Bonaparte deemed it best to retire from the unequal contest. At the same time Caldiero and Stra were definitely ceded by Augereau, who had to fall back to the post-house on the road, to save his right from an attack by Provera's column advancing by way of Gombine. Night was coming on, the battle was lost, and under these untoward circumstances the troops were gradually withdrawn by Bonaparte to Verona, while next day the Austrians advanced to Vago, the cavalry swept as far as the gates of the fortress, and ladders were collected for the assault it was proposed soon to make.

After Caldiero, November 13, 1796, Bonaparte, who keenly felt his defeat, wrote the Directory:

> The wounded are the élite of the army. All our superior officers, all our best generals, are *hors de combat* . . . The Army of Italy, reduced to a handful of men, is exhausted. The heroes of Lodi, of Millesimo, of Castiglione, of Bassano, have died for the fatherland, or are in the hospital. There is naught left the corps but their reputation and their pride. Joubert, Lannes, Lanusse, Victor, Murat, Chabot, Dupuy, Rampon, Pijon, Chabran, St. Hilaire are wounded, as well as Mesnard. . . . We are abandoned at the end of Italy. . . . I have lost in this war few men, but they are all men *d'élite*, impossible to replace. The brave who remain flee inevitable death, in the midst of continual risks and with forces too small. Perhaps the hour of brave Augereau, of intrepid Massena, of Berthier, my own, is ready to strike. Then,

> then, what shall become of these brave men? This idea holds me back; I no longer dare brave a death which would be a subject of discouragement and misfortune for those who are the object of my solicitude.

As this jeremiad was, however, part of a dispatch leading up to prayers for reinforcements, we must construe it accordingly. He added, "In a few days we shall essay a last effort."

Though Davidovich was making no further sign of immediate operations, the French position was becoming critical in a high degree. Verona was at the apex of an angle, an excellent place for successful offensive operations; but so soon as Bonaparte retired from this apex, the two bodies of the Austrians would join bands, and, added to the Mantua garrison, might readily overwhelm him. Verona was within easy reach of three heavy columns, Alvinzi's, Davidovich's, Wurmser's. Man for man, the enemy had so far fought as well as the French; the wonderful work which Frederick's grenadiers used to exhibit against double or treble their numbers is not here apparent; and Bonaparte was right in feeling that he must so manoeuvre as to be able to outnumber the Austrians whenever contact came. With troops of equal value, the mass theory was all the more essential.

The chance of retrieving the disaster appeared small. Vaubois and the left wing had been beaten by Davidovich, and had a bare eight thousand men left; Bonaparte and the right wing had been beaten by Alvinzi, and could place in line scarcely above seventeen thousand men; Kilmaine's nine thousand men at Mantua might easily be driven back by a sortie from the fortress, whose garrison was thrice as big. There was no general in the Army of Italy, there are few at any time, who under these conditions would not have retired to the right bank of the Mincio. Not so Bonaparte. His keen eye could still see an outlet to the maze, and so long as there was one left, it was no time to weaken. He had in the past benefited by good fortune, should he not now be able to face the ill? Moreover, the Citizen Bonaparte knew that all his future depended on the success of these few coming months. If he lost the game at this stage, good-by to his growth, political or military. Once shelved by the Directory, in which he had as many enemies as friends, would he have another chance? It was evident that he must hold his own against even the heavy odds he had now to meet. There could be no turning back; win he must. And Fortune favoured his courage by casting her cloak of stupor over both Davidovich and Wurmser.

Bonaparte devised a new plan. So long as Alvinzi's force immediately before him was superior to his own in numbers, rather than again to chance an attack on him in front, the French general determined to turn the Austrian left flank and fall on its rear at Villanova, where he might seize the artillery park and train. Such a manoeuvre demanded prompt and secret execution, and it also required quite new arrangements that consumed many hours. A body of three thousand men was called from the Mantua besiegers, and under Kilmaine ordered at all hazards to hold Verona, the one thing needful to prevent Alvinzi and Davidovich from joining hands; while Bonaparte proposed on the evening of November 14 to start downstream on his new manoeuvre.

The 14th was spent in unusual quiet in Verona. An army is a barometer of success or failure, and the troops were hourly wondering what their chief would do. Yet not a man doubted that the best would be done. As night fell, the divisions were ordered under arms, to form three columns, and to march in silence. Surprise seized on all when, instead of debouching from Verona by the gate opposite the enemy, the head of column filed out of the Milan gate and headed towards the west. Was it a retreat? Were all the battles won at such cost of blood to be forfeited at this late day? "*Non, camarade,*" quoth the old French grenadier. "*Tu verras! Le p'tit caporal leur flanquera un bon!*" The question was soon answered. Not far from Verona the head of column filed to the left, and the Army of Italy headed rapidly and silently down the Adige towards Ronco. Here Bonaparte had already ordered a bridge to be built, and on the morning of the 15th the French army crossed the Adige, leaving the reserve cavalry under Beaurevoir on the west bank.

Just below Ronco the Alpone flows into the larger river from the northeast, and between the two lies a triangular stretch of marsh land over four miles from apex to base, and crossed by a number of drainage canals, and by two principal roads on built-up meandering causeways: one leading to Arcole by a circuit to the right, and a long one on the left running northerly to Porcile, which had branches to La Bona and Serena. At places the marsh land would bear men; at others it was soft; clumps of bushes and willow-trees grew at intervals. Skirmishers might here and there find a footing; but infantry in line could nowhere deploy. Along these causeways Augereau was in the early forenoon of the 16th sent forward to Arcole, to capture the town as an exit, and Massena was ordered to Porcile to protect the French left against the Austrians at Caldiero, and to engage their attention while Augereau should debouch upon the plain beyond.

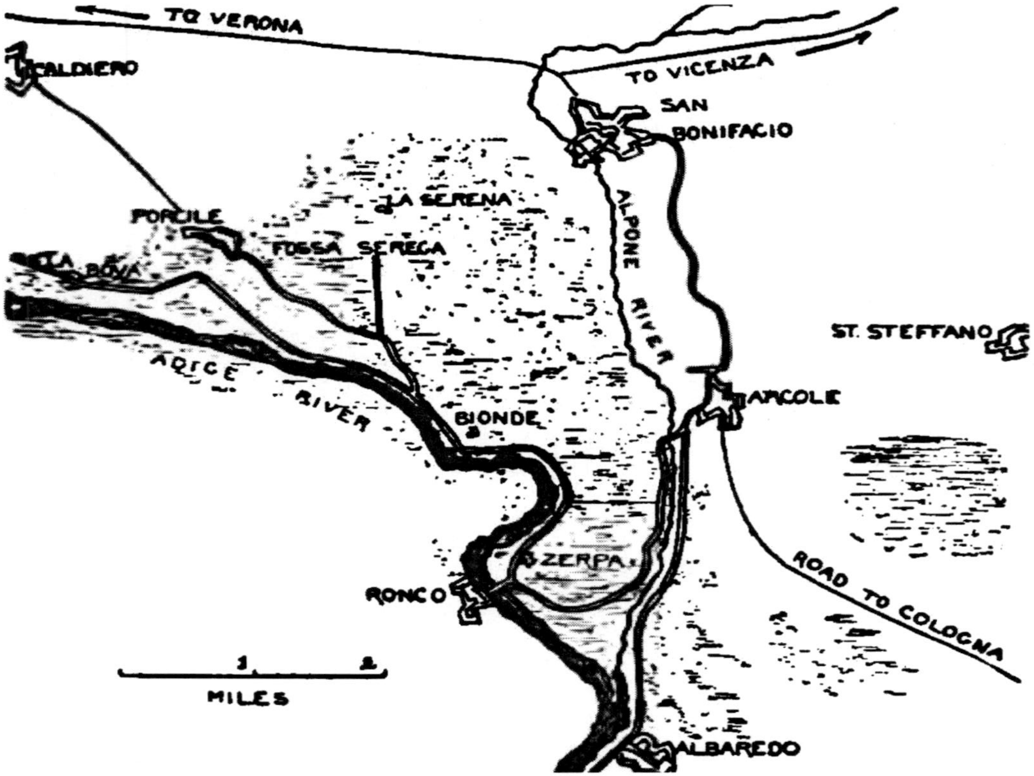

Battle of Arcole

As he stood before Verona coming along the post-road from Vicenza, Alvinzi leaned his right on the foothills of the Alps, down which at this point all the streams run south into the Adige, and the ravines are such that only mountain paths had been cut along their sides. Two roads ran into Verona from west and northwest, one on either side of the river; but only the post-road ran into the city from the east. Around the city by the north there was practically no route for an army. On Alvinzi's left ran the Adige, and in his front, in an angle between hills and rivers, lay the fortified city, which he could not capture out of hand; while in his rear was the defile of Villanova, between mountain and marsh. This was not a good situation for an army, and if Bonaparte could promptly reach the enemy's left rear by way of Ronco, the Austrian superiority disappeared in a measure, as the fighting had to be done either along the causeway over the Alpone marshes, where only so many men could stand, and only the head of column could fight, or else, on the part of the Austrians, in line faced to the rear, with their communications cut,—a condition which would lend superior morale to the French.

Some critics have suggested that Bonaparte should have thrown his bridge at Albaredo below the confluence, and have then gone around the marshes. There is some value in this suggestion, and later in his career Bonaparte might have done so. But it was just this open country he now desired to avoid, especially in view of the superior Austrian cavalry, and of the recent excellent fighting of the Austrian foot. Bonaparte never possessed Frederick's contempt of numbers, neither had he the marvellous men Friedrich Wilhelm and the Old Dessauer had drilled. He had no idea of blocking Alvinzi up in a *cul-de-sac*, and forcing him to fight to the death; he preferred to beat him and then offer him a bridge of gold, so that he might retire, for a week at least, and enable the French to drive back Davidovich, and again turn on him; and moreover it was important to be as near as possible to his communications with Vaubois, Verona and Mantua. With Massena, Augereau and the reserve cavalry, the French numbered about eighteen thousand men; Alvinzi five or six thousand more.

While Bonaparte was engaged in this turning manoeuvre, the Austrian outposts were all but on the glacis of Verona; the main body lay along the post-road or upon the heights to the north of it, with the reserves and train in Villanova; and Alvinzi was preparing one body to move on Verona, and another body at the same time to pass the Adige at Zevio to turn the French flank. It does not appear that Alvinzi had conceived any danger of a flank attack in force by the French; but in view of his own crossing at Zevio, he had taken the precaution to occupy Arcole by two battalions, a squadron and two guns under Colonel Brigido. This was a small force, to be sure, but enough under a determined officer to hold the causeway until reinforcements could reach him, and Brigido proved to be the man. The Austrian commander expected Davidovich to do his share in netting Bonaparte; but the manoeuvre was a concentric one, and as is usual with concentric movements, the clever general was not on hand to be trapped; so that Alvinzi woke up to find his opponent turning the tables on him by debouching at an entirely unexpected point. Yet though the Austrian commander found his bearings with uncommon rapidity, it was noon before any number of troops could be got where they could protect the threatened flank. Luckily for Alvinzi, the terrain was in favour of his defence, as a small body could temporarily hold each end of the causeways, and, owing to the complicated operation, the French were necessarily slow. Provera had some troops on hand to meet Massena when he reached Porcile, and Alvinzi promptly fell back from Verona on San Bonifacio, and extended his left towards San Stefano, throwing Mitrowsky's Croats into Arcole to sustain Brigido. In Bonaparte's report to the Directory, November 19, he states that a regiment of Croats and several Hungarian regiments had been stationed in Arcole.

Like the battle of Caesar at Alexandria, the fighting was begun along the causeways. Massena took Bionde and pushed on; but despite a vigorous onset, he was arrested at Porcile, and Augereau, though he made several stout attacks on the little stone bridge over the Alpone at Arcole, which was held by Mitrowsky and Brigido, was unable to cross. Watching the operations from Ronco, Bonaparte could see Massena checked, and Augereau, into whose right flank the Austrian sharpshooters stationed along the Alpone were pouring a deadly fire, pause and waver. But Arcole must be had. Even though Bonaparte might manage to advance by way of Porcile on Alvinzi's line of retreat, he could not leave behind such a tactical threat to his own rear of column. It seemed as if his first plan to debouch through Arcole on Villanova was to be wrecked. The enemy's small force was doing famous work. Several French generals had been shot in leading the column and striving to take the bridge; and yet this must be captured.

> It was in vain that all the generals, feeling the importance of the moment, threw themselves at the head to oblige our columns to cross the little bridge of Arcole," says the dispatch. Too much

> courage was harmful, and nearly all were wounded. Generals Verdier, Bon, Verne and Lannes were put *hors de combat.* Augereau seized a flag, carried it to the end of the bridge: 'Cowards,' he cried to his troops, 'do you fear death so much?' and he stayed there several minutes, but without any effect. . . . I went there myself; I demanded of the soldiers if they were still the victors of Lodi. My presence produced on the troops a movement which decided me to try the passage again.

The commander-in-chief indeed did gallop from Ronco over the causeway, and recklessly put himself at the head of another storming column against the Arcole bridge. Yet even Bonaparte's personal example in heading his men did not accomplish the desired result; and in fact he came near capture, if he escaped death. As the fresh column charged the bridge, it was met by a counter-charge delivered with true Slavic fury. The French column was forced back, and Bonaparte and a number of the grenadiers at the head were hustled off the causeway, and fell into the marsh, where they sank up to the middle. The Croats rushed on with loud cries, and actually all but passed the place where the commanding general was floundering in the mud, when Belliard, one of Bonaparte's aides, gathering a few men devoted to their chief, with a desperate rush stopped the Croats, who were unaware of the accident, long enough for Bonaparte and his men to climb up on the causeway. The chief then mounted his horse and rode back whence he came. The assault had failed.

All is not glory in war. The commonplace—the ridiculous—is ever and anon mixed with the heroic, as all old soldiers know. The gallantry on both sides was far from inconsistent with the prosaic accident to the commanding general. Nor does this in any sense detract from the performance in history. It did not with the grenadiers. They remembered that *Le P'tit Caporal* feared not death, and was ready to lend a hand beside them. The rest was forgotten.

Meanwhile Massena had made a fresh attack, which Provera met upon the causeway. As happens often in war, one of the Austrian rear battalions fired into its own leading battalion and threw it into confusion; the whole column fell back, and in the *mêlée* Massena reached Porcile. In addition to the two main attacks, a small detachment under Guyeux had been sent by Bonaparte by way of Alvaredo to turn the Arcole force; but though this body late in the afternoon actually drove the Austrians into the town (Napoleon said at St. Helena that they captured it, though this is denied) and created a diversion which a few hours before would have been of marked benefit, yet at 7 p. m., when the result was obtained, the attack was too much isolated to be of value; and as the main body had withdrawn, not only had Guyeux to retire, but the general plan of a surprise on Alvinzi's flank and a march by way of Arcole to Villanova on his rear—and this was the essence—had utterly failed. In ignorance of what Vaubois might be doing, and lest a night march might be necessary to join his lieutenant on the Mincio, Bonaparte thought best to withdraw all the forces and recross the Adige. Alvinzi's van camped at Caldiero; Provera at La Bona, Porcile and Bionde; Mitrowski on the plain from San Bonifacio to San Stefano. The French camped back of Ronco.

The day had been lost, but if Bonaparte had not surprised Alvinzi, he had at all events arrested his manoeuvre against Verona, and he had taken some prisoners. To save the situation, however, and enable the main army to turn against Davidovich, Alvinzi must be thrown back on the Brenta. This was now the only chance, and gauging the contending forces equal in effective striking power, the result depended on the situation and the commanders, with the chances decidedly against Bonaparte.

News from Vaubois, showing that Davidovich had not moved on the 15th, ran in during the night. This was cheering information. Bonaparte determined to renew his attack on the 16th; and Augereau and Massena went in again, each as on November 15. On this day Alvinzi had grasped the situation. He reinforced both Porcile and Arcole, and determined to take the initiative, Provera from Bionde and Mitrowsky from Arcole advancing at daybreak along the causeways, in the hope to force their way to Ronco and attack the French on their own ground. But Provera's force, which was in the lead, was met by Massena in front of Zerpa and lustily attacked. The French riflemen along the shore also plied the Austrian column with a demoralizing fire, as Augereau had been served the day before; and shortly the loss of officers became so great that the column dissolved into flight, and was scarcely rallied until it had reached Caldiero. Following up this success, Massena advanced along the causeway towards Porcile, and gave way to Augereau, who sharply threw back Mitrowsky's column at the point of the bayonet, and would have entered Arcole with him, had not an Austrian battalion along the edge of the Alpone again taken him in flank with a murderous fire and forced him back. All day long this fighting went on at intervals and with alternate success, but the French gained little. Bonaparte strove to make an artificial ford at the confluence of the Alpone and Adige by the use of fascines, and sent Vial down river to seek a crossing and join the garrison of Legnano, which had been ordered up river to turn Arcole; but the work at the artificial ford proved too long, and Vial found no crossing. Massena once more got possession of Porcile; but without Arcole it could advantage nothing to the French. Fresh troops succeeded the tired ones, but the fighting had to be in detail, and the Croats continued, in a manner quite beyond praise, to bold the bridge of Arcole. The fighting was sometimes by musketry at a distance, sometimes with the bayonet close at hand, with the intervals between clashes usual in such fighting; but the French could not force their way across the bridge; and again Bonaparte, for the same reason as yesterday's, felt it wise to recross the river at night. The Davidovich column gave him great uneasiness, and the Austrians were fighting be-yond expectation well. The news from Vaubois still indicated that another day could be risked at Arcole; for though Davidovich had taken La Corona and Rivoli on the 16th, Vaubois was holding Bussolengo and Castelnuovo. It was still evident that Alvinzi must be neutralized; and Bonaparte was in a mood to perish with his men rather than retire from the contest, with all that the defeat implied. With his characteristic self-confidence, moreover, he believed that the enemy had lost more men than he had, and was in a condition of morale far less satisfactory; and now that he felt sure that the real superiority was on his side,—for despite their severe handling his men were in good heart,—he determined to move out on the plain, where at first, and so soon after the defeat at Caldiero, he had not been ready to adventure his inferior forces.

On the 17th, then, with a persistency which is truly admirable, Bonaparte for the third time crossed the Adige at Ronco,—though there was nearly a fatal delay by a break in the bridge, brought on by the sinking of a boat,—and on this day sent a half-brigade of Massena's under Robert against Arcole, while Massena with another half-brigade marched on Porcile, and the rest of the division remained in reserve near the bridge. It was arranged for Augereau to move down and cross the Alpone on a trestle-bridge constructed at the mouth of the stream during the night, and not perceived by the enemy, and then turn the Austrian left. Massena's column met the enemy on the causeway as before, and the same to-and-fro fighting, but of a less tenacious character, occurred as on the previous days. Robert made a gallant attempt on the bridge at Arcole, where the Austrians had been reinforced, but failed; and a Croat column, pursuing his retiring regiments back towards the Ronco bridge, came so close to taking this and obtaining a foothold on the mainland that at the last moment Bonaparte ordered it broken. But anticipating such a possibility, as the French columns were small, he had concealed a half-brigade in a willow copse which extended on the right along the causeway; the Croats were there taken in flank by so sudden and close a salvo, followed by an immediate attack with the bayonet, that, surrounded by the reserves of Massena's division and by some of Augereau's troops, they were completely broken; a large number were killed; and three thousand men were captured. By noon Augereau had crossed the new bridge and smartly attacked Miloradovich, who now commanded the line which defended Arcole, and whose right leaned on the Alpone and left on low land near the confluence; but still the bravery of the enemy held him off, despite their exhaustion from the long defence. A small body of eight hundred men from Legnano had been expected even yesterday to turn this marsh; but they were beyond reason delayed in their advance. Neither would Austrian retire, nor could Frenchman make a further step forward. After three days' fighting over the same ground, it had become, outside interference apart, a question of endurance, not of the men, but of the moral courage of the army commanders. Alvinzi was ready to quit on short notice; Bonaparte might be called off by Davidovich.

On the evening of the 17th Alvinzi had written to his lieutenant that while he might resist another attack, to undertake the offensive was out of the question. He had, in fact, sent his train well to the rear. Why, when Alvinzi saw that he must fight at or near Verona, he had not urged Davidovich to advance on the 16th or 17th as a diversion to aid himself and annoy the French, it is hard to say. But that he did not do so was Bonaparte's salvation. As a matter of fact, the turning-point had been reached. Napoleon says:

> The fate of a battle is the happening of an instant, of a thought, . . . the decisive moment arrives, a moral spark flares up, and the smallest reserve carries it out. . . . In battle there is a moment when the smallest manoeuvre decides and gives the superiority; it is the drop of water which causes the overflow.

It had grown to be evident where the moral spark lay, and it was not in Alvinzi's soul. He had become morally exhausted. The decisive moment arrived, and a mere make-believe attack by a handful of men flashed the spark and carried the French forward to victory. About 3 p. m., when Massena and Augereau were pushed in for the last time, Beaurevoir's head of column came up, and the small garrison from Legnano finally arrived and advanced on the enemy by way of Albaredo, threatening to turn his left flank, there were signs of weaker resistance, and all that seemed needed was one more thrust to disturb the enemy's equipoise. The Austrians had grown benumbed with constant fighting, and were ready to dissolve. Now came the needed flurry. A small group of horsemen (twenty-five guides under an officer nicknamed Hercules, with four trumpeters, say the Memoirs) had been dispatched by Bonaparte on a circuit around the marsh to fall from ambush on the Austrian left and rear with as much noise as they could make, to simulate the arrival of a column of cavalry. This raw device, used at the proper moment, drew the last grain of resistance from the Austrians defending Arcole. About 5 p. m. this handful of horsemen rode in on the enemy's left with loud outcries and strident blare of trumpets, a few Austrian companies gave way, a regiment followed, and the heart-sick, worn-out soldiers under Miloradovich ceased resistance and sullenly fell back. The troops in Arcole did the like; and the entire Austrian force, which for three days had so pluckily held the bridge against the repeated French attacks, withdrew along the road to Cologna, leaving Arcole to the French. The combined attack along both banks of the Alpone had succeeded, and the battle of Arcole was won. Massena meanwhile, having driven the enemy out of Porcile, left a half-brigade there, and was withdrawn to Arcole to strengthen the main column. There being no good ground for defence along the Alpone flats, Alvinzi retired by way of San Bonifacio and Villanova. The troops which had stood at Verona on the 15th and 16th without undertaking any operation, and had then retired to Caldiero, summarily withdrew. A slight French attack on San Bonifacio was repulsed, and this ended the battle. The troops of both armies, utterly exhausted, slept on their arms.

From the battlefield of Arcole, Bonaparte wrote General Clarke:

> Your nephew, Elliot, has been killed on the battlefield. This young man had become familiar with arms. He has several times marched at the head of column. He would have been one day an estimable officer. He died with glory and in the face of the enemy. He did not suffer an instant. Where is the reasonable man who would not envy such a death?

On November 18 Alvinzi, reduced to fifteen thousand men under the colours, withdrew by way of Montebello to the Brenta valley. Bonaparte wrote, November 19, from Verona:

Quarters General
Verona
20 Brumaire, Year V
To the Citizen Carnot
. . . Never was battlefield disputed like that of Arcole. I scarcely have any generals left; their devotion and their courage are without example. The General of Brigade Lannes came to the battlefield not yet healed of the wound he received at Governolo. He was wounded twice during the first day of the battle; he was, at three in the afternoon, stretched on his bed and suffering, when he learnt that I myself was going to the head of the column. He jumped from his bed, mounted his horse, and came to join me. As he could not stay afoot, he was obliged to remain on horseback; he received at the head of the bridge of Arcole a wound which stretched him lifeless. I assure you it needed all that to win. . . . Send us succour promptly, for we cannot do again what we have done. You know the character of the Frenchman, a little inconstant.
Bonaparte

But at Arcole the Frenchman had not been inconstant.

Bonaparte had not defeated Alvinzi; he had lost nearly as many men; but he had forced back the Austrians by superior morale, and could now turn on Davidovich. There was no more fight left in Alvinzi for a number of days.

The Austrian losses at Arcole were sixty-three hundred men, eleven guns and ten munition wagons. The French lost, as quoted, forty-five hundred men; but nearly every French general was wounded, among them Lannes, Verne, Bon and Verdier, Robert and Gardanne.

The pursuit of Alvinzi was intrusted to the cavalry.

With regard to the conduct of the soldiers at Arcole, Bonaparte wrote the Directory, November 19:

I must not conceal from you that I have not found in the soldiers my phalanxes of Lodi, of Millesimo, of Castiglione; fatigue and the absence of the brave men" (who have been lost) "took from them that impetuosity with which I had the right to hope to capture Alvinzi and the larger part of his array.

Nor was this all. His complaints against the contractors never ceased. He wrote Garrau, November 19:

The army is without shoes, without money, without clothes,

> the hospitals lack everything, our wounded are on the floors, and in the most horrible distress; all that comes from want of money, and this at the moment when we have just acquired four millions of francs at Leghorn.

The brave little French soldier had to exercise a deal of patience. But victory warmed his heart.

The salvation of the French had hinged on the temporary lack of enterprise of Davidovic, and this was in a way due to good fortune. This general could scarcely have better played the French game. Satisfied with forcing Vaubois back to Rivoli, he sat down to contemplate his work, regardless of what was happening to his chief. Finally, when it was too late to be of any solid service, and Alvinzi had retired because his lieutenant did not appear, Davidovich undertook to advance on Vaubois at Rivoli. For a week he had amused himself by tapping with a small vanguard at the French earthworks at La Corona; on the 16th he made a feint at an attack. Early on the 17th, when Bonaparte was for the third time crossing the Adige on his perilous undertaking,—what might not a smart Austrian attack have accomplished two days before?—Davidovich broke up with his corps from Roveredo, and started on his too long delayed manoeuvre against the French left flank. He had three columns: a brigade marching *via* Riva on Rocca d'Anfo, and one on each side of the Adige, that on the left bank being intended as a turning manoeuvre. He was two to one of his opponent; there was no question of his success (though indeed one's mind cannot, during this battle, but recur again and again to the days when the Last of the Kings hurled his little masses at the thrice greater body of Austrians, and beat them), and by 2 p. m., after a fairly stubborn resistance to the Austrian attack on front and flank, Vaubois, having lost twelve hundred men, was in full retreat from Rivoli along the Adige road. The French division paused for a rest not far from Bussolengo, continued its retreat on Castelnuovo during the night, and on the 18th, in the forenoon, withdrew beyond the Mincio at Peschiera. What a chance for Davidovich, had he but pressed Vaubois back on the 15th or 16th I But the Austrians remained on the battlefield even on the night of the 17th, and next day advanced only to Pastrengo.

Exhausted though the French troops were, victory gave them back good cheer, and with the alacrity all soldiers show towards the man who wins success, they turned their backs on the bloody marshes of Arcole and marched towards the Mincio. No sooner had the news run in that Vaubois had crossed that river than Bonaparte recognized that one more hearty blow would win the day for good. He soon ascertained that Alvinzi would not stand at Villanova; and deeming the cavalry sufficient for the moment, he headed Augereau for Verona on the left bank of the Adige, and Massena on the right bank for Villafranca. He would now punish Davidovich for his temerity. To see a French column re-enter Verona on the 18th in triumph by the gate of Venice, when apparently in retreat it had left the city on the 15th by the gate of Milan, puzzled and enthused the population of Verona, and added to the French fervour. On the 19th Davidovich received news of Alvinzi's defeat and withdrawal. He was much taken aback, and not caring to face the divisions which had won at Arcole, he turned in his tracks and retired, November 20, to Rivoli. Bonaparte joined Massena's division to Vaubois, who recrossed the Mincio at Borghetto and advanced to Villafranca, and sent them on the 21st on the track of the Austrians retiring up the Adige, while Augereau was ordered from Verona by the left-bank roads to Dolce, hoping to get up the river faster than they and to cut off their retreat.

The loss by Davidovich of the 16th and 17th had borne ill fruit to the Austrian scheme. When Alvinzi saw that he was not being pursued by any heavy force, he resolved to about face and return to the attack on Verona, so as to disengage Davidovich, if perchance he were in difficulties. He would have been wiser to move up the Brenta to join him at Trent, so as now to operate in one body, as he should have begun by doing; but unaware that Davidovich had retired to Rivoli, he advanced to Villanova on the 20th, and next day to Caldiero, easily pushing before him the small French detachments on the road. Just at that moment, as, learning of the advance of Massena and Vaubois, Davidovich was retiring from Rivoli, he heard from Alvinzi that the latter proposed to renew the effort to join him, and gave orders to return to the Rivoli position. But no sooner were these orders issued than the difficulties of the situation began to oppress him, and he again countermanded them. Such indecision worked ill on the troops, with the result that when Massena and Vaubois attacked the Austrian position at Rivoli, Davidovich, with but half a fight, fell back; and on learning of Augereau's march on Dolce, he made haste to retire to Ala. Augereau had, however, made excellent speed, and part of his troops had reached Peri. Davidovich had to cut his way through the French advance regiments, which he did in truth, but reached safety beyond Augereau only with an army utterly disorganized, a loss of eighteen hundred men and his pontoon-train.

Between the two Austrian armies there was such poor means of communication that not until the 23rd did Alvinzi ascertain the utter rout of Davidovich. Upon hearing this, however, he saw that there was no further chance for him (though had he been energetic, the road was well open to Mantua with its enormous garrison), and on the night of the 24th he started definitely to retire behind the Brenta. Wurmser, hoping to accomplish some good end, made, on the 23rd, according to previous arrangement with Alvinzi, who had notified him that he could reach Mantua on that day, a sortie which a week before would have been of distinct value. With eight thousand men he drove back the French blockading troops, and seized San Antonio and La Favorita. But finding no sign of Davidovich or Alvinzi, and as the regiments detailed to help at Arcole had already returned to the blockading force, the sortie was driven back with ease. Alvinzi's army retired behind the Brenta; the Tyrolese army held itself in Riva and Roveredo. Communication was maintained through the Brenta valley.

The campaign was closed. Bonaparte, by a bold offensive against two concentrically advancing armies, had again maintained his defensive position on the Mincio. There are few short struggles which better illustrate the strength of interior lines coupled to vigorous offense, as well as exhibit the weakness of operations conducted by divided or concentrically operating forces. When you add the numbers of Alvinzi and Davidovich to the big garrison of Mantua, it seems as if worse use could hardly have been made of this superiority.

The Austrians during the campaign had lost twenty thousand men. The French army had also lost heavily, but some reinforcements came in to fill the gaps, and after the divisions had been given their new stations, they reached before the end of the year a respectable figure. Kilmaine, who had fallen sick in the Mantuan marshes, was replaced by Serurier, convalescent, and he continued the blockade with nine thousand men. Massena held Verona with the same effective. Joubert took Vaubois' place at Rivoli with ten thousand men. Augereau was posted with nine thousand men at and near Legnano. A new division under Rey was on the Chiese, watching the left bank of Lake Garda, four thousand men being between Salo and Brescia, while Victor, with two thousand reserves, lay on the Mincio, at Castelnuovo and Goito. In garrison in Lombardy were six thousand men. For the nonce, field operations ceased—on the French side to give time to capture Mantua, and on the Austrian side to repair damages and reorganize for a fresh advance.

The Directory sent Clarke to Vienna to treat for peace, and Austrian plenipotentiaries came to Vicenza for a similar purpose; but neither attempt resulted favourably. Venice and the Pope were ready for war. In fact, His Holiness proposed to send troops to Bologna, on which Wurmser from Mantua might in case of need retire. Sardinia was untrustworthy. French military affairs in Germany were in a bad way, and Bonaparte kept on the defensive. By January, 1797, Alvinzi, reinforced up to forty-five thousand men, was ready for another campaign. The Tyrolese army, with which Alvinzi had his headquarters, was in the Adige valley at Ala, Roveredo and San Marco, with detachments at Mori and Riva. The Friuli army was behind the Brenta, with communication established with the Tyrolese, Mitrowski in Borgo, Quosdanovich in Bassano, Provera in Padua.

Chapter 14

Rivoli

November, 1796-February, 1797

The Austrian determination to hold Mantua and the Mincio was admirable. With the opening of 1797 Alvinzi was reinforced and began a winter campaign. Haying learned nothing from previous failures, he advanced from three directions. Provera was to capture Legnano, Bayalich Verona, and Alvinzi was to march down the Adige. Meanwhile Wurmser should operate by a sortie. Bonaparte, guessing which of the columns was the strongest, made ready to hold the Rivoli plateau, leaving a small force to contain the others. The topography compelled the enemy to advance in several tactical columns. Bonaparte reached Rivoli only in time to prevent Joubert from vacating it, and on January 14 the Austrians attacked the plateau. Bonaparte's divisions had not all reached the field, but he opened the day by driving back the troops in his front and taking up a position along the Trombalora heights. Here three of the columns attacked him vigorously, and at one time the French left weakened; but Bonaparte re-established it in season to turn to a very heavy attack on his right, where two Austrian columns advanced up a narrow defile to reach the plateau. At its month Bonaparte met them with horse, foot and artillery, and breaking down their head, drove them back in disorder. Meanwhile a last column, which was to get in the French rear, was cut off and captured or dispersed, and a second assault by the Austrian centre was driven back. The Battle of Rivoli was won. Leaving Joubert to follow Alvinzi, Bonaparte hurried back to meet Provera. Joubert accomplished the task with some fighting. Bonaparte reached Provera at the gates of Mantua, closed him in, and captured his army. The French marching had again won the campaign. It has rarely been equalled. Mantua surrendered February 2. The three campaigns on the Mincio had cost the Austrians sixty thousand men. Bonaparte now imposed harsh terms on the Pope, and the Army of Italy was reinforced.

During this cessation of hostilities Bonaparte had his hands full to do justice to the varying phases of the political situation. Venice had rejected a French alliance, and this antagonism he met by sedulously cultivating the Cispadane and Transpadane Republics, and by disseminating democratic principles among the various populations neighbour to Venice; while to secure the left of his army against any advance from the Alps, and give it a further *point d'appui*, he directed the seizure of the castle of Bergamo, in northern Lombardy, and there placed a suitable garrison.

It was well that Bonaparte had not relied on cooperation from the Army of the Rhine. The French armies which had so lustily invaded Germany in the spring had been forced back to their bases at Hüningen and Düsseldorf. Archduke Charles was at his task of capturing Kehl, ably defended by Desaix, while Beurnonville on the lower Rhine, though reinforced up to eighty thousand men, sat still for months opposite an Austrian force of twenty-five thousand, when any advance whatever would have relieved the pressure on both Moreau on the upper Rhine and Bonaparte in Italy.

So far, the Directory had sent the Army of Italy few troops except the six thousand men under Rey, and now a descent on Ireland by Hoche threatened to divert all further reinforcements from the Mincio. The Irish expedition came to naught in December, when a tempest dispersed the French squadron, and the vessels were lucky in that, for the most part, they were able to reach home ports. Negotiations were had with England, looking, among other things, to a formal cession by Austria of her title to Belgium, that country being already in French hands; but it was Austria that should first have been treated with, and the successes against Moreau and Jourdan had made Vienna equally difficult to approach or to convince. Catherine of Russia died in November; and it was possible that the great Slavic nation, under her successor, Paul I., might seriously change the trend of European affairs. The result of all these events was that the Directory was embarrassed, and that Bonaparte was denied the reinforcements he needed and, as the one successful captain, had a right to demand. After much deliberation, however, it was finally determined to keep up the forces of the armies at Strasburg and Düsseldorf by accessions from other sources, and Bonaparte was promised the fine divisions of Bernadotte and Delmas, which were to traverse the Alps in the winter season and join the Army of Italy. This promised to raise its force to seventy-five thousand men. But though his army grew, Bonaparte still had his trials, as his letter to the Executive Directory of January 6, 1797, proves:

Milan
17 Nivose, Year V
. . . The accountability of the army, in the paymaster's office, is in striking disorder; nothing can be accounted for, and to the reputation for cheating of the controller is joined the foolishness of the employees. Everything is purchasable. The army consumes five times what is necessary, because the storekeepers make false receipts, and go halves with the war commissaries. The principal actresses of Italy are entertained by the employees of the French army; luxury, depravity and embezzlement are at their height. . . . The only remedy is a temporary court with the right to shoot any army administrator. . . . Marshal Brunswick had the army intendant hung because he was short of victual, and we, in the middle of Italy, having everything in abundance, and disbursing in a month five times what we need, are often in want. . . . Do not think that I am weak and that I betray the country in this essential part of my functions. I have employees arrested every day, I have their papers examined, I visit their strong boxes; but I am seconded by nobody, and the laws do not allow sufficient authority to the general to impress a salutary terror on this cloud of rogues. Still, the evil is diminishing by means of scoldings, of punishments and of getting angry. Things I hope will be got done with a little more decency.

Then follow observations on various good and bad commissaries, by name. Nor was discipline by any means perfect, as the following extract from orders of February 4, 1797, at Forli, seems to show:

Art. 1. Every soldier who shall be convicted of having struck or assaulted in any manner any person, or taken any property of the vanquished people, or who shall have in his haversack pillaged articles, shall be shot at the head of his battalion.

In this the leader was sustained by the better element in the army, which did not approve of pillaging. A sub-lieutenant named Rey, as an instance, had despoiled an Austrian officer whom he had made prisoner, and his brother officers met and unanimously demanded his cashiering. But while Bonaparte ordered this done October 5, 1796, he vigorously defended the army against outside accusations. In a letter to the General Proveditor of Venice, dated December 8, answering one from that official, he exculpates the French army from charges of misconduct.

I formally give the lie to whoso shall dare assert that there has been in the states of Venice a single woman violated by French troops. Would not one think, in reading the ridiculous note which has been sent me, that all properties have been lost, that there is not a church left, nor a woman respected in the Veronese and the Brescian?'

When the new year of 1797 was about to open. Field-marshal Alvinzi found himself again at the head of an excellent army of over forty thousand men, and ready for a fourth attempt to relieve beleaguered Mantua. He had not yet learned wisdom enough to advance in one body, but again drew up, or else the Vienna Council did it for him, an elaborate plan which divided his forces into three parts. Provera at Padua had nine thousand men, with which body he was to break up January 7, on the 9th to attack and capture Legnano, and from thence to push on to Mantua. Bayalich at Bassano was also to advance January 7 with his six thousand men, and on the 12th was to attack and capture Verona. In case of success, these two columns were to act with Wurmser in Mantua, and with his army to join the papal contingent and operate on the south of the Po. Alvinzi reserved to himself a working column of twenty-eight thousand men, with which he proposed to move from the Tyrol on Rivoli, and after taking this on January 13, to march down and join his lieutenants at Mantua. The plan was exact and carefully worked out; but in effect the two smaller columns were about as good as thrown away. Campaigning armies do not often march like clockwork.

Though reinforcements were on the way, Bonaparte had at this moment but four divisions of eight thousand to ten thousand men each, and one small one: Serurier in front of Mantua; Augereau on the Adige from Verona to Legnano; Massena at Verona; Joubert at Rivoli, with van out at La Corona, a small village with a big nunnery and a valuable strategic defile in the mountains. Looking upon the division under Rey at Salo and Desenzano as a species of reserve, the Austrian advance was thus to be pushed against each French wing, and the centre at Verona.

In accordance with Alvinzi's plan, on the 9th Bayalich reached Villanova; and Provera, after a fight at Bevilacqua on the 8th with some of Augereau's outlying troops, in which the French lost two guns and several hundred prisoners, got the mass of his corps as far as Montagnana. Bonaparte was anxious to make no move until he was sure which column contained the mass of the Austrian army. On the 9th

Augereau reported Provera's advance, but deeming no serious attempt probable on Legnano, he left Guyeux at Ronco with part of his division. On the 10th Bonaparte, in Bologna, received dispatches from his several lieutenants, and foreseeing what was to come, he headed the two thousand men he there had under Lannes on Rovigo to Augereau's succour, while he himself joined Serurier at Mantua. On the same day Bayalich's van reached Caldiero; Provera did not move this day or the next; Alvinzi was still up the Adige getting his divisions in prime order for an advance. On January 11 Bayalich reached Verona, and Alvinzi's head of column advanced as far as the upper slopes of Monte Baldo. Though uncertain what the operations of the campaign would develop, yet in the certainty of active work all French troops both on the upper and lower Adige were now kept under arms; but there was no substantial change in any of their positions. Along which of the three lines—Rivoli, Verona, Legnano—would come the main Austrian attack was as yet a matter of conjecture.

Alvinzi had depleted Bayalich of a portion of his troops, which are said to have marched to join the main column by one of the minor valleys between the Brenta and the Adige; and on reaching Verona on January 12, Massena sallied out and easily drove him back, Bayalich retiring to Caldiero. He had accomplished his task of diverting the attention of the French commander. Reinforced by Bayalich's detachment, Alvinzi's van began shortly to move forward into touch with Joubert's forces in the vicinity of La Corona. On the 10th the several columns had assembled at their starting-points. Lusignan was at Brentonico, Liptay at Avio, Köblös at Belluno, Ocskay and Quosdanovich lay between Ala and Roveredo. As contemplated by the plan, Lusignan was to cross Monte Baldo, and by January 12 reach the rear of the French position at La Corona, while Liptay and Köblös were to co-operate in front. The other two columns, with which were to march the train and artillery, headed for Belluno to act in second line. Lusignan was delayed by deep snow, and Liptay and Köblös reached the front of La Corona long before he could reach its rear. The French party here was but three thousand strong. Köblös wanted to attack, as the Austrians were superior in numbers, but Liptay held to the letter of his orders, which were to let the French vacate the position when Lusignan should have turned it. Only a slight demonstration was made, against which the French held themselves, during the 12th, but at night, under Joubert's orders, they retired from their untenable position, and fell back on the main body at Rivoli. Provera for the moment did nothing.

In order to study the situation from a central standpoint, Bonaparte now came on to Verona. From the first message of Augereau and his own first summary of all that he heard, he was led to believe that the Austrian mass was aiming at Mantua by way of the lower Adige; and to anticipate this, from Roverbella he dispatched orders to Massena to hold himself in readiness on the right bank to march from Verona to Legnano. But arrived in Verona, especially after Bayalich's feeble attack, the chief modified his view, and left Massena in that fortress, in light marching order. He was yet by no means sure of his ground. So soon as Joubert's report of the Austrian advance on La Corona reached him, however, he began to feel as if here might after all be the knot of the problem. It looked opposite Augereau, according to this general's reports, less like a large body than it had a day or two since; he concluded, from his own observation, that he had but a small force in front ofVerona; he could see why the enemy at Rivoli might well be the mass; and believing the issue would again be one of working from interior lines against successive oncoming columns of the enemy from the three directions indicated, he held himself in readiness personally to hurry to any threatened point At the same time he kept his eye keenly fixed on Rivoli. No signs of the enemy were apparent on the Chiese.

Alvinzi's van had revealed some strength in its attack on La Corona; and as Joubert saw that with his one division he could not long retain his hold on a position which was liable to be turned at any moment, he had been justified in withdrawing his forces from that outlying post, so as to concentrate all the men he had in one body on the Rivoli *plateau*. The Austrian van, finding no further opposition at La Corona, soon passed the place, and debouching from the hills during the afternoon of the 13th, threatened also to turn the French position at Rivoli. The dispatches of Joubert to Bonaparte were the clear and precise reports of a good soldier, and the French commander-in-chief quickly recognized, from what they told, that Alvinzi had in reality massed his army at Roveredo for an advance down the Adige.

No sooner assured as to where the enemy's mass lay than Bonaparte, true to his constant theory, began to assemble his own mass with which to overwhelm Alvinzi, regardless for the moment of the other two columns, whose feeble efforts so far gave apprehension of no great danger. To Augereau's force was added a small equipment of cavalry, and he was ordered to defend the Adige, but to refrain from a general engagement. Serurier was to keep up the blockade of Mantua, but move what troops he could spare as a reserve up to Villafranca. Orders were issued on the afternoon of the 18th for Victor to march to Villafranca; for Rey to move from Salo to Castelnuovo as a central reserve, whence he was later dispatched to Rivoli; and for Massena to leave one foot and one horse regiment, something over two thousand men, in Verona, and moving up to Rivoli, to go in on Joubert's left. The commander-in-chief himself started out for the front, Joubert having previously been instructed to hold on to the Rivoli *plateau* at all hazards.

The French brigades tramped cheerfully through the night of January 13-14. Bonaparte reached Joubert about 2 a. m.

Having heretofore fully gauged Alvinzi, and quite familiar with the country, it was not difficult for Bonaparte to guess that not only had the Austrian leader divided his mass into three strategic parts, but that he would almost certainly subdivide his own part into several tactical columns, which he could not, on the hilly terrain, assemble for battle before he struck the Rivoli *plateau*. This *plateau* was the "crossroads" of the open plain, where the many mountain paths and roads meet, and its possessor could readily debouch in any direction on forces coming from the surrounding hills.

As you stand on the irregular-shaped *plateau* of Rivoli on a winter day, looking north, you see immediately before you the bold snow-clad height of Monte Baldo, and in the northwest, with a gap between, the less marked Monte Gazo. On your right, at the east foot of the *plateau*, runs the Adige, which has just emerged from the Tyrolese Alps, and continues its rapid course down to the plains of the Po, with hills and defiles on both hands. A road practicable for all arms meanders along the left bank, a less good one along the right; and east of the village of Rivoli on the farther bank is the defile of Chiusa, between precipice and stream. To the west is the broad expanse of Lake Garda, of which glimpses may be caught, and through the plain which surrounds the *plateau*, from the north around by the west to the south, runs a swift stream called the Tasso, usually bridged or fordable at a number of places. Parallel to the Adige comes down toward the *plateau* the long narrow ridge of Monte Magnone, terminating near Incanale in the heights of San Marco.

The rear or south of the Rivoli *plateau* is closed in by an east and west ridge called Monte Pipolo; and the *plateau* is accessible from the plain on the north, west and south by a number of roads, while at most points troops can mount the slopes across country from the plain.

It will be remembered that of the two roads down the Adige, the one on the left bank is the better. That on the right bank, when it strikes Monte Baldo, follows the river some distance, but at Incanale, midway between Dolce and Rivoli, where by a westerly sweep the Adige strikes Monte Magnone, and there is scant place for a road, this turns up over the hills and later debouches through a difficult zigzag defile on the Rivoli *plateau*. Near this defile, at the foot of the hill, was a cluster of houses around a well-known inn, or Osteria; at the mouth of the defile was a custom-house building, or Dogana. Well up the river several mountain roads branch out from the main one, and run southerly by long circuits around or across Monte Baldo, to tap the upland villages, and thence rejoin the Rivoli cross-roads. These mountain ways are only available for infantry. One of them, on which La Corona is situated, runs between Monte Baldo and Monte Magnone. The Corona heights command the roads on either side of the Adige; and artillery posted at available places could play havoc with a column filing by.

The Rivoli *plateau* is peculiarly suited to defence.

As it happened, Joubert had, about 10 p. m. of the 13th, begun to leave his Rivoli position, intending to retire to Castelnuovo, lest the Austrians, coming on in great numbers and from several directions, should surround and overwhelm his one division. Luckily, his chief's orders reached him in season for him to turn back and reoccupy a position on the *plateau* just in front of Rivoli, leaning on Campana and Monte Castello, with van in Zoane. Had the Austrians anticipated him, the Battle of Rivoli might not have been a French victory. Bonaparte's message also informed him that his chief was on the way with reinforcements. He prepared for a hard fight to carry out his orders.

It was the topography that constrained Alvinzi either to move down upon Rivoli along several roads, or else to consume more time than in the presence of an active foe was wise, in a march on one or two; and the Austrian army was actually coming on in six columns. Counting from the Austrian right, the second, third and fourth of these columns, forming the centre, the first two composed of five battalions and the last one of four, respectively under Liptay, Köblös and Ocskay, had come on after the capture of La Corona, and had on the evening of the 18th reached the plain out of which rises the Rivoli *plateau*; the first and right flank column under Lusignan also of five battalions, was still skirting the west slope of Monte Baldo. The fifth under Quosdanovich, of nine battalions and twelve squadrons, and the sixth under Wukassovich, of three battalions, were approaching along both banks of the Adige.

The Austrians, during this night, were camped, Liptay and Köblös on a line in front of Caprino and San Giovanni, with Ocskay in front of Gambaron in prolongation of their line; Lusignan at Lumini, away back over the Monte Baldo western slope. Wukassovich had not yet reached Dolce; Quosdanovich was still near Rivalta. And, while this was going on at the theatre of an approaching great battle, to keep the whole strategical situation in view, Bayalich had been driven back to Villanova by Massena's troops left in Verona, and Provera, as a feint, had moved forward to Minerbe, three miles from Legnano, but actually was making dispositions to cross the river at Anghiari.

The falling weather had ceased, and it was fortunately a clear, cold, moonlight night when Bonaparte reached Joubert's headquarters at Rivoli; and knowing the country well, "he ascended the different heights and observed the lines of the enemy's camp-fires;" and could easily recognize the array of Austrian divisions threatening to close in around his lieutenant's position. "The atmosphere was aflame with them," He gauged the enemy at forty-five thousand men,—much too high an estimate of any troops he could possibly see,—and recognized that here, on the heights of Rivoli, was the one place to meet him; for here only could he keep the several Austrian columns, now far apart, from joining hands. The infantry, marching alone, he would receive with salvos of artillery; and the cavalry would not be able to deploy on the zigzag roads for any big manoeuvre. Lusignan and Wukassovich were for some hours practically harmless.

No one was better aware than Bonaparte that a sharp offense is the best defensive operation; and his first orders were given to Joubert to move his division forward before daylight to a position with left in front of Zoane, and right extending out north-easterly, so as to recapture San Marco Chapel which he had once held and abandoned, and thus prevent the forces he could see in his front (Liptay-Köblös-Ocskay) from joining hands by way of the Dogana defile with those coming down the Adige. Though it made a long thin line, this was promptly done; by four o'clock Vial had driven some Croats out of San Marco and taken it; and somewhat later three half-brigades were ordered on La Presa and Lubiana; still another half-brigade was sent forward by way of Zovo; and Joubert's left moved forward to the edge of the *plateau*. When this advance was completed, the French left, consisting of two half-brigades, stood along the heights of Trombalora, the centre of four half-brigades was well to the front, while on the right another half-brigade, in a separate position, held the entrenched defile by which, near the Dogana, the road leads up from Osteria. At the latter place a small French force had entrenched itself. Quosdanovich,

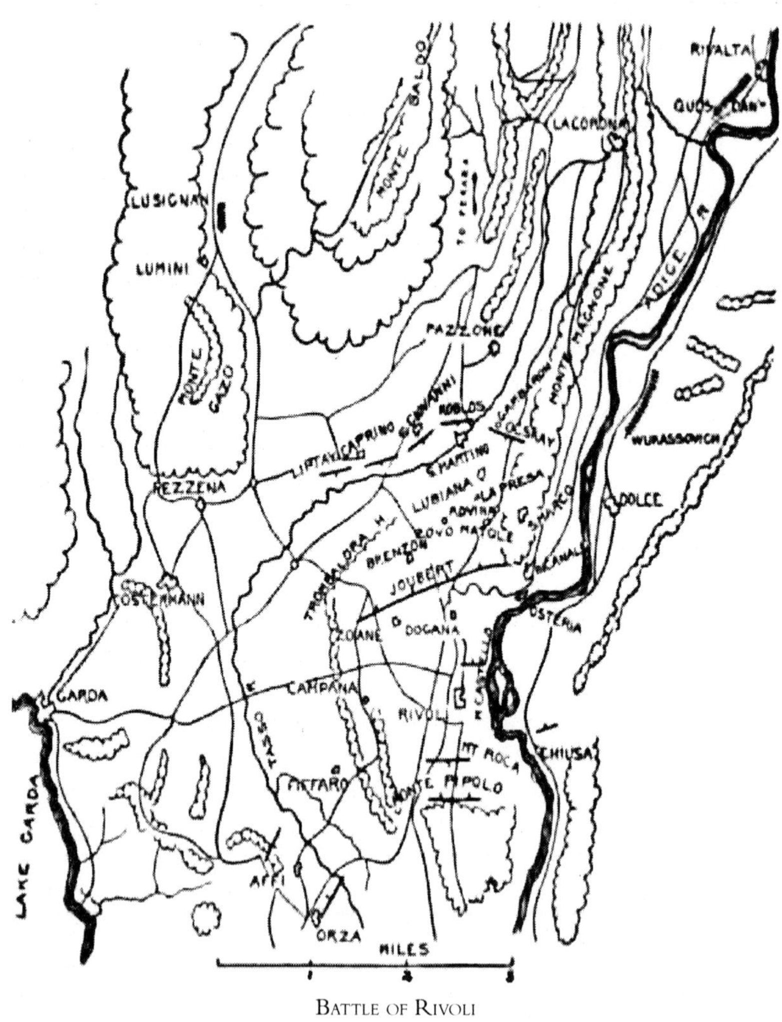

Battle of Rivoli

recognizing the value of San Marco heights, as a means of joining the Austrian central columns, attempted to regain possession of them; but they were fiercely held by the French.

Small detachments were at Chiusa on the left bank, and at Monte Roca and Monte Castello on the right bank.

At daylight the Austrian columns were also set in motion. The right column under Lusignan had early got to Pezzena and Costerman. Four thousand strong, it was under orders to make a complete circuit of the Rivoli *plateau* by way of Affi, and to fall on the French rear from the slopes of Monte Pipolo. At a very early hour Massena came up to Rivoli with two half-brigades and two cavalry regiments, the van of his division. One of these, as soon as his manoeuvre was discovered, was directed *via* Garda to fend off Lusignan, and couriers were sent back to Rey to speed his march on Orza, for the same purpose. The left Austrian column, three thousand strong under Wukassovich, was still at Dolce at daylight, and was to march down river and to seize the Chiusa defile; and if it could get into position, to use its artillery against the French right flank. Columns two, three and four in the centre, some twelve thousand strong, under Liptay, Köblös and Ocskay, were to assault the Rivoli position in front. A column of eight thousand men under Quosdanovich had marched down the right or hither Adige bank, and was to wait behind Incanale for the result of the central attack, and then to assault the height from Osteria. The artillery train and cavalry followed this column, not being able to pass on the mountain roads without undue delay. This arrangement of columns dispersed the Austrian army all too much. As Lusignan's column was separated from all the rest by Monte Baldo and later by the Rivoli *plateau*, and the three central columns were separated from Quosdanovich by the San Marco hills, and Wukassovich was separated from all the other columns by the Adige, it was manifest that, good fortune apart, they could be handled by the French, one set at a time. Moreover, the Austrian columns were none of them, except those of Quosdanovich and Wukassovich, accompanied by even light artillery, while Napoleon, from the Rivoli *plateau*, could use his twelve-pounders and field-guns, of which he had a goodly number, to marked advantage. This, was much in his favour.

In the expectation that both Massena and Rey would shortly reach the field, Bonaparte had disgarnished both his left flank, thrown back along the heights of Trombolora, and his right, thrown back at the Osteria defile, and by his first advance had massed nearly all the forces which were present so as to receive the three central Austrian columns in the position beyond Zovo and La Presa, and out towards Lubiana, which Joubert had taken up. This action he took because it was evident that theirs was to be the initial attack. Bonaparte proposed to meet the Austrian advance by a counter, and if he could thus break through the Austrian centre, he would have the wings at his mercy. So far good fortune had accompanied his central operations; and here the conditions also led up to such a manoeuvre.

But the Austrian columns were in motion before Bonaparte could advance far; and Joubert alone was not strong enough. Instinct with ardour, Liptay and Köblös pushed in on the left centre of the French advanced line with uncommon speed, taking one of the half-brigades in flank, and driving it and the one on its left, after no long opposition, back in confusion. But though a veteran half-brigade, posted nearby, was headed by Berthier and threw itself crotchet-wise against the enemy, stood its ground and saved the guns, the Austrian line, stronger here than the French, broke through, and with the vigour of apparent victory pressed forward as far as Matole. Bonaparte hurried up Massena's leading half-brigade, and put it in to rally the two broken ones. This succeeded, and after a lively contest, lasting some three hours, Massena managed to re-establish the French line in a half-circle on the *plateau*, from Rovina through Zovo to Brenzon; and as the body of Massena's and Rey's divisions now began to arrive on the field, the French left was soon beyond danger, firmly established just back of the Trombalora hills. But the forenoon was slipping away.

None the less, although the Austrians had not maintained their initial gain on the French left, they had made a marked impression; and they were at this point superior in numbers. San Marco height was occupied by Ocskay, whose column threatened to get in the rear of the French works at Osteria, and Quosdanovich had come on and got ready to force his way up the defile from Incanale, which the defenders had pains to hold. Lusignan too was arriving at Affi on his way to the French rear. By noon the Austrian army had met success in the centre, had turned the French position on the left, and was ready to assault the right, where only one half-brigade held the defile. Alvinzi appeared to be on the eve of a handsome victory.

But it was in appearance only. Bonaparte knew that he could hold his ground for the moment, and that when Rey should have fully arrived, he would outnumber the enemy at every point of contact; and he calmly surveyed the field, conscious of both physical and moral preponderance. He saw that Lusignan's column was not dangerous, as Massena could easily neutralize it; and meanwhile

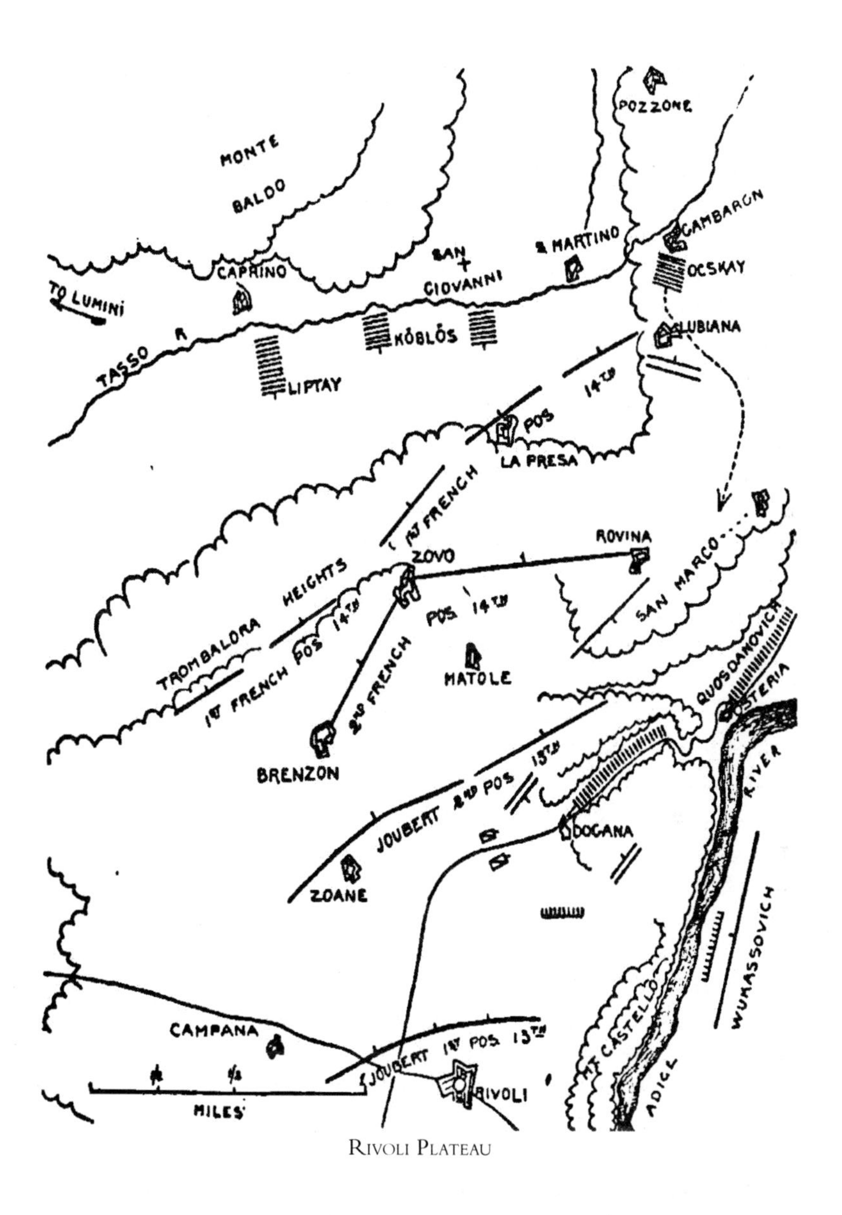

Rivoli Plateau

another half-brigade was sent to Tifaro to meet this division. He was likewise fully aware that the Dogana defile must be held at all hazards, lest Quosdanovich should be able to throw his heavy force up into the *plateau*, and by taking the French right in reverse, compromise the centre and left. Happily the defile was deep, and was enfiladed by a French battery. To this defence, then, he addressed himself, nor had he quite completed his preparations when the onset came. Alvinzi could also see that the Dogana defile was the key of the field; and, determined to take it, the Austrians, after ousting the Osteria party from its works, in a splendid exhibition of gallantry made their way without check up nearly to the top. The grenadiers of Quosdanovich had thrown back the half-brigade which held the mouth of the defile, while Wukassovich, who had reached Chiusa opposite, and driven out the small French detachment, shelled the troops across the river, who were already barely holding their own. The situation was for the moment critical. A flurry here might throw the whole line back.

But Bonaparte never for an instant lost his self-confidence or aplomb. His left was already well-secured by two half-brigades, and was in no danger. His right alone needed his presence. The balance of Massena's division was now at hand, and was speedily deployed so as to fend off Ocskay, or take in flank any troops emerging from the defile, while his cavalry under Lasalle was held in reserve back of its outlet. Some of Joubert's troops on the right flank were faced to the rear with the same purpose.

On came the Austrian grenadiers, already shouting victory, for had they not heard the sound of Lusignan's fire in the French rear? But their gallantry was vain. As they emerged from the deep zigzag cut upon the level, and before they could get a chance to deploy, the French foot, which Bonaparte had gathered, took the head of column on both flanks; the battery established nearby swept through their ranks with canister; and Lasalle struck the leading regiment in front with his column of hussars. The effect of the triple blow was immense. Brave as the Austrian onset had been, the head of column, torn almost to shreds, was stopped at the mouth of the defile, and the impetus of the entire column ceased. Thus summarily checked, Quosdanovich was falling back in more or less confusion, when the explosion of an Austrian caisson, accidentally hit by a French shell, shattered a body of the troops crowded in deep masses in the defile, and drove front and rear of column in wild flight down the rocky path. This disaster prevented any further effort. The Austrians fell back to Incanale.

The plateau was freed. But the Austrian centre, which was still in good order, had again to be met, for notwithstanding the recent checks, Alvinzi ordered Liptay, Köblös and Ocskay to assault afresh the Trombalora height. The brave Austrian battalions again pressed forward, and Vial, on the right of the French centre, after a stout fight, gave way and fell back some distance. The position of the French line was, however, a good one; the tactics of the Austrians seemed not to be directed by any one head, and of the two contestants the enemy was the more exhausted. Vial was supported by Joubert's light foot, and an advance of the French line between Matole and San Marco was ordered at the same time; Bonaparte pushed in Lasalle with his small body of dragoons to charge the enemy. Though few in numbers, their timely use produced the marked effect which cavalry alone can do, and horse and foot together, hurled on the Austrian line, which haply was in part composed of fresh levies, and had neither artillery nor cavalry to sustain it, drove it back with a shock which soon produced disorder; whereupon Joubert and Massena, pivoting on the left flank, made a quarter-wheel to the left, and dashed forward on the enemy. The Austrian line at this point had got disorganized by its own initial success, its power of resistance had been broken, the regiments fell back in complete wreck behind the Tasso, and could not be again assembled until they reached the Pozzone hills. It was 5 p. m.

This manoeuvre also resulted in cutting off from the rest of the army the column of Lusignan, which had so confidently started out to encircle the French left flank. Lusignan had got as far as Monte Pipolo, and was actually in line in Bonaparte's rear, astride the Verona road, expecting to catch the French troops in a trap, when Alvinzi should have driven them from the Rivoli *plateau*. But Bonaparte had faced two half-brigades of Massena's division to the rear to hold Lusignan in check, should he advance. And, already isolated, this column was soon further threatened by Rey with still another half-brigade, who came up from Orza in good season, when, though it strove gamely to cut its way through to Garda, it was utterly worsted and dispersed; and before the next noon, the entire body, wandering about in squads and companies, had been gathered in. A few hundred only got back to Monte Baldo.

Alvinzi had twenty-six thousand men in line at the battle of Rivoli; Bonaparte about four thousand less. The loss in killed and wounded does not appear to be determined; but the Austrians lost more heavily than the French. Especially in prisoners were their casualties serious. Quosdanovich retired in part by way of Rivalta, and in part by Dolce; Wukassovich, unable to assist his comrades, fell back up river; Liptay, Köblös and Ocskay held the foot of Monte Baldo, where they slept on their arms.

The battle of Rivoli is ill described in his reports by Bonaparte; the less important fights in front of Mantua are very carefully detailed. Time and fatigue explain this.

Just as Bonaparte was preparing, despite the late hour, to finish the day by moving on Osteria and annihilating Quosdanovich, he received word that Provera had crossed the Adige during the night of January 13-14. "Augereau had made bad dispositions." The importance of immediate action at that point, lest Mantua should be relieved out of hand, was plain; and placing Rey under Joubert's orders, he left the pursuit of Alvinzi's army to the latter. Withdrawing Massena from Rivoli, he ordered him to march on Roverbella at daylight of the 15th. Rey was to follow him as soon as Joubert could spare him. This gave Massena, who had gone into battle and fought all day on his arrival from Verona, but a short respite before he was again afoot. But it was just this tremendous activity of mind and body, infused by Bonaparte into his troops, which, like the divine fervour of Frederick, ran down through the officers to every private in the ranks.

From his position at Minerbe, where he had faced Augereau, and having fruitlessly paused, hoping to induce the inhabitants of Legnano to play into his hands, Provera had, as he designed, crossed the Adige at Anghiari on the 14th, unknown to Augereau, though Guyeux with the troops from Ronco offered his flankers some opposition; and leaving twenty-five hundred men in the Anghiari bridge-head, and Hohenzollern to fend off Augereau, he pushed on to Nogara, hoping to reach Mantua without a battle. Augereau, though he had allowed the Austrians to steal a passage, marched to Anghiari, surrounded and captured the enemy's bridge-head party, broke the bridge, and headed for Cerea. Lannes had reported to Augereau on the 18th, and these two, together with Guyeux, advanced on Provera, each from his own direction. They did not indeed succeed in heading him off, but they did considerably delay his progress; and at Cerea they cut off and captured his rearguard. He had been altogether too slow. On the day after the battle of Rivoli there was still a further passage of arms between the rival forces there. Disturbed at the cutting off of Lusignan, Alvinzi believed not only that he could help his lieutenant out of the net into which he had fallen, but as he heard that Bonaparte had turned against Provera, he deemed it his duty to make one more essay to save this officer and the campaign, by breaking through Joubert's line and pressing on to Mantua. At the same time Joubert, under the orders left by his chief, was himself advancing to disrupt whatever might be left of the Austrian army. At this moment Quosdanovich had retired on Rivalta; Lusignan had been captured, and Alvinzi's centre was left without support. Joubert gauged the situation with skill. Holding back his own centre, he extended his wings, and by a turning movement on both Austrian flanks. Vial moving along the slopes of Monte Magnone on La Corona, and Vaux along those of Monte Baldo on Ferrara, the enemy was thus taken in a trap. Murat had come up from Salo to Garda across the lake in boats, hoping to fall on the rear of the enemy. Him Vaux joined to his own force, and sent his fresh troops ahead to turn the Austrian flank, whereupon be fell on their front, as did also Vial. The enemy was absolutely at a disadvantage. Under these evil conditions there could be but one result. The Austrian soldiers had been roughly handled the day before; Alvinzi, though a good soldier, was not the man to revive their enthusiasm; they had for days been short of rations, their ammunition was running low, and they fought feebly. So soon as Joubert felt the weakness of the resistance to his onset, he pushed in with all the more vigour . The result speedily came: the Austrians fell into disorder and retired in confusion, some reaching Rivalta, some rallying on Quosdanovich, some getting caught at La Corona. The enemy left five thousand prisoners in the hands of the French, and this number, added to those taken on the 14th, made a tale of thirteen thousand men. By 9 a. m. the Austrian army had definitely retired, and out of the twenty-six thousand who had so gallantly struck the French on yestermorn, Alvinzi could barely call the roll of ten thousand men.

On this same January 15 Provera, with his ten thousand men, marched on towards Mantua, and by noon arrived at San Giorgio, which was held and entrenched by Miollio and fifteen hundred French. Demanding surrender, he was met with a salvo of artillery; and on turning towards the citadel, he ran into Serurier's troops. He then took up a position near La Favorita Palace, and managed to send a message across the lake in a boat to Wurmser, in which he prayed this officer to join him in an attack on the French on the morning of the 16th. The points of assault were to be La Favorita, on which Provera would fall, and San Antonio, just south of it, which Wurmser was to sally out and assault.

With regard to means by which the Mantua garrison managed to communicate with the outside world, in his dispatch to the Directory of December 28 Bonaparte says:

> Mantua is closed in with the greatest care. The 2nd of this month General Dumas surprised a spy who was entering the town. It was an Austrian cadet, who had been sent from Trent by Alvinzi. After a good deal of pretence, he confessed that he was the bearer of dispatches, and effectively he threw up twenty-four hours afterwards (*allant à la garde-robe*) a little cylinder, in which was enclosed a letter from the emperor, hereto appended. . . . If this method of having dispatches swallowed was not entirely known, I would give you the details, so that they might be sent to our generals, because the Austrians often make use of this method. Generally the spies keep it in the body for several days. If their stomach becomes upset, they take care to save the little cylinder, to soak it in elixir, and to swallow it again. This cylinder is soaked in Spanish wax dissolved in vinegar.

But in their attempt to overwhelm the small blockading force at Mantua, the Austrian generals failed to reckon on the wonderful speed of the French troops that had fought at Rivoli. Massena and Victor had arrived at Roverbella by the evening of the 15th, the latter having been picked up *en route* at Villafranca. They had but a short rest on the succeeding night. At Roverbella Bonaparte, ascertaining that his lieutenant still held San Giorgio, ordered Augereau to push in on Provera's rear; Serurier, in command of the blockading corps, was to take post at La Favorita to meet any sally Wurmser might make, which he judged rightly would fall on this spot; and he himself proposed to move down from Roverbella, and with Massena and Victor shut Provera in by an overwhelming circle of troops. Though Augereau had not followed up the Austrian column, he had been busy in arrangements to cut it off from the Adige, having burned the bridge at Anghiari and blocked the roads. He was, however, not so far away but what he could obey his orders in season to join in the attack at La Favorita.

Accordingly when, at 6 a. m. on the morning of the 16th, Provera's onset on La Favorita occurred, he soon ascertained that he had substantially the whole French army closing him in. He none the less began his attack, while Wurmser debouched on San Antonio. Serurier, who occupied both these places, replied with vigour and, aided by reinforcements sent him by Bonaparte, held on firmly. Wurmser was wise enough to discover the impossibility of his task, and to retire within walls; but Provera did not so easily escape. Though attacked in front by Serurier, on his left by the San Giorgio garrison, and on his right by Massena's and Victor's troops under Bonaparte in person, for a while he held his own; but when Augereau appeared in his rear, there was nothing left for him to do. He became convinced of the futility of resistance; and learning of the disaster at Rivoli, by noon, with his nine thousand men left, he concluded to lay down his arms. Bonaparte had tactically used a concentric manoeuvre which he always condemned strategically, but his troops were all within supporting distance, and he was present in overwhelming numbers.

The last trick was taken. The Austrians had made a fourth gallant attempt to relieve sore-beset Mantua, but the genius of Bonaparte in nine days had brought all their efforts to naught. Alvinzi had advanced on the Mincio with forty-three thousand men; he carried back less than twenty-five thousand with which to defend the frontiers of Austria.

In this campaign of Rivoli the French with thirty thousand men made nearly twenty thousand prisoners.

The rapidity of the marches made by the French was astonishing. The same troops which fought east of Verona on the 13th marched fourteen miles during the night to Rivoli, fought all day on the 14th, marched back to Roverbella, thirty-one miles, on the 15th, and on the 16th compelled the surrender of Provera, who believed them beaten on the plain of Rivoli. Few efforts equal this record.

Bonaparte reported to the Directory, January 18:

> All the half-brigades covered themselves with glory, and especially the 32nd, 57th and 18th of the line, which General Massena commanded, and which in three days beat the enemy at St. Michel, at Rivoli and at Roverbella. The Roman legions made, they say, twenty-four miles a day; our brigades made thirty, and fought in the intervals.

For gallantry in the next campaign it was ordered, March 21, 1797, to inscribe on the colours of the 57th, "The terrible 57th half-brigade, which nothing can stop."

Leaving Laudon with eight thousand men to defend the Tyrol, Alvinzi retreated behind the Piave, and at the opening of February the French forces were again in their old places. Joubert pushed the Tyrol army back *via* Avio, Mori, Caliano and Trent, to behind the Avisio, and took post at Lavis. Augereau's division went to Padua, and later to Castelfranco. Massena followed up the small Austrian force to the Brenta, where he destroyed its rearguard. Alvinzi thought to hold Bassano by intrenching it, but retired on the approach of the French. From Bassano, where his division was posted, Massena kept up communication with Joubert by way of the Brenta. The Tyrolese army kept in touch *via* Belluno with the Piave, behind which river the Austrians finally withdrew. Alvinzi resigned his command, and was succeeded by Archduke Charles.

Mantua was doomed. The garrison was at the last stage, had eaten its horses, and was dying of pestilence. On February 2, after a seven months' siege, the famous fortress surrendered to the French commander, with the enormous garrison of twenty thousand men, of whom over a third were invalided, as prisoners of war, and multitude of stores, including the guns Bonaparte had been forced to abandon when he first threw over the siege in the Castiglione days, plus three hundred and fifty pieces on the walls and in the arsenal. On the 3rd the French made a formal entry. In the absence of Bonaparte in the Romagna, Serurier received the formal surrender. Count Wurmser and his staff, together with a convoy of seven hundred men, were liberated; the prisoners were sent to Trieste to be exchanged.

"I took pains," said Bonaparte, "to show French generosity with regard to Wurmser, a general seventy years old, towards whom fortune has been in this campaign very cruel, but who has not ceased to show a constancy and a courage which history will take note of."

This magnanimity was not lost on the brave old Austrian general:

> A few days after he sent an aide-de-camp to Bologna to inform him of a project of poisoning which was to be carried out in the Romagna, and gave him instructions essential to hold himself harmless. The notice was useful.

The several expeditions sent to save Mantua had cost the Austrians sixty thousand men.

This result was a great reward for the eight months during which Bonaparte had so splendidly fought to capture the place and maintain himself on the Mincio. During this time he had met and defeated four armies, in each case inflicting an almost fatal blow. He had definitely won his secondary base on the Mincio; he was about to receive accessions of old troops, which would give him an army such as he had now the right to command, and he had made his own future secure.

During the Rivoli campaign the Pope saw fit to break the armistice made in June, and began to raise troops to be commanded by the Austrian general, Colli, whom Vienna had sent to Rome for the purpose. To meet this threat, though it had not much significance, Victor, with forty-six hundred French and four thousand Italians, was dispatched to Bologna and Imola on February 2, Bonaparte in person accompanying the column. The French took Faenza and followed

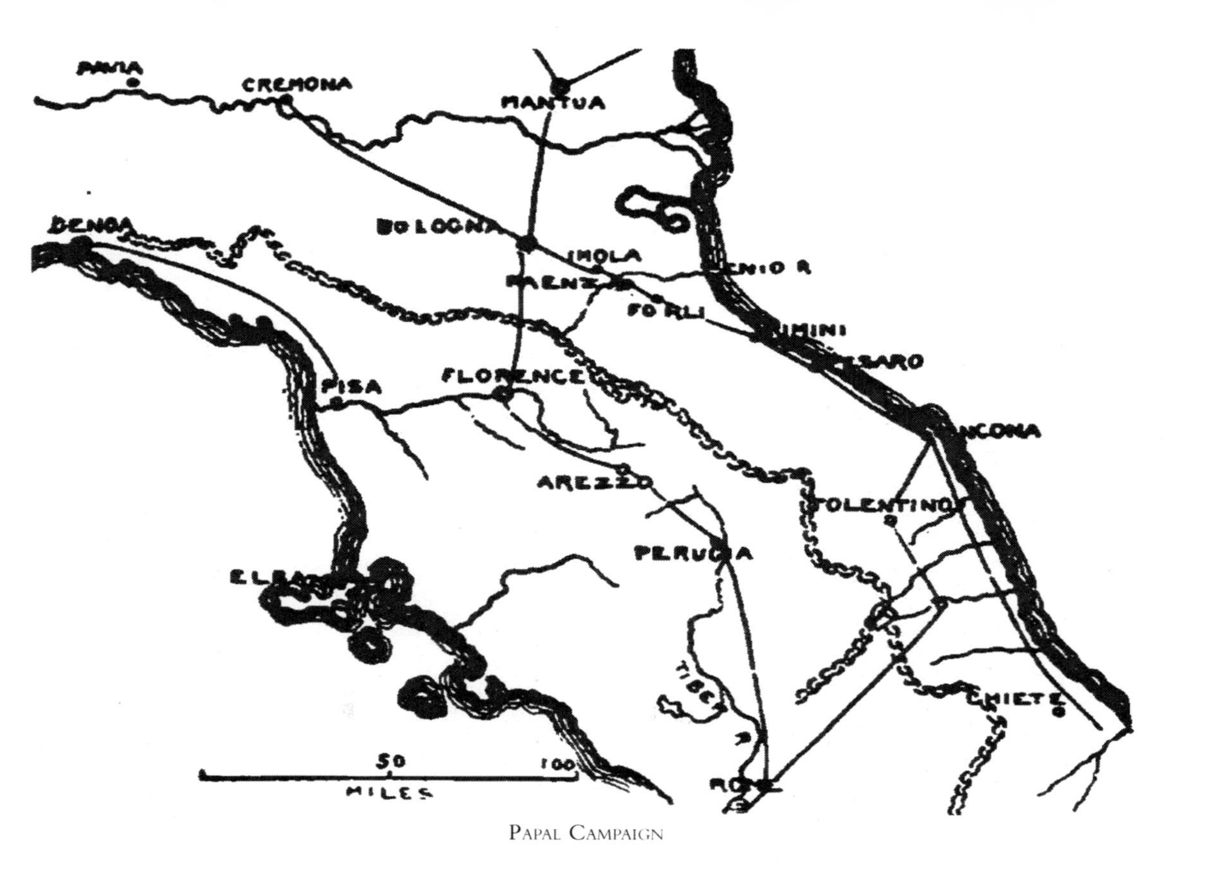

Papal Campaign

via Forli, Rimini and Pesaro towards Ancona, the papal troops having been defeated on the Senio and mostly captured. Victor reached Ancona the 9th, and by the 18th was at Tolentino, where His Holiness sued for peace. This was made February 19 at Bonaparte's dictation. The terms were not such as to crush the papal power, but they were sufficiently harsh to make of the Pope an implacable foe. He was to have no dealings with the enemies of France, and to keep his ports open to her ships. He was to yield up Avignon and Venaissin, Bologna, Ferrara and the Romagna. Ancona was to be garrisoned by the French until universal peace was made. He paid thirty million *francs* indemnity, and gave to France many of the best pictures and statues in the Vatican. The galleries of Paris had thus been enriched from Rome, Milan, Bologna, Parma, Modena and Placentia. The peace of Tolentino secured northern Italy and the line of the Mincio.

The French army was now increased to eighty thousand men. Massena at Bassano had eleven thousand five hundred men; Serurier at Castelfranco had ten thousand five hundred; Bernadotte, and Guyeux in command of Augereau's old division, each with an equal number, were at Padua and Treviso; Joubert lay in and about Trent with nineteen thousand five hundred men; Victor was on the Adige with six thousand five hundred; there was a cavalry reserve of eleven hundred men, and nine thousand men in garrison. In his St. Helena Memorial, Napoleon understates his army at fifty-three thousand foot, five thousand horse and three thousand artillery, with one hundred and twenty guns.

The Austrian army, over which Archduke Charles was now placed, had barely twenty thousand of the old forces, and reserve battalions of not over fifteen thousand men. These were stationed at great distances apart, to hold the mountain defiles on all the roads to Vienna.

It must have been with pride that Bonaparte sent Augereau to Paris with the Mantua standards; and he paid a marked compliment to his gallant lieutenant, in a letter to the Directory from Tolentino, dated February 18:

"General Augereau has left. Citizen Directors, with sixty flags coming from the garrison of Mantua. You will see in this brave general, to whom the Republic owes for marked services, a citizen extremely zealous,"

Nor were the others forgotten, for on March 6, 1797, the general-in-chief issued an order giving substantial rewards in the shape of gratuities to many officers, varying from one hundred and fifty *francs* to a brave trumpeter who was wounded, and two hundred and fifty *francs* each to the two soldiers who helped him out of the marsh at Arcole, up to twenty thousand *francs* to Joubert. Most of the items are ten thousand *francs* each to general officers, among them Rampon, Menard, St. Hilaire, Gardanne, Bessières and others. And to "every one bearing a sword "was given a pension of one hundred *francs*, to be levied on the Mantuan country.

Joubert had been educated for the bar, but the Revolution led him into the army. He had risen in the Army of Italy to be general of brigade. Tall, thin, apparently feeble by nature, he yet possessed great endurance. "He was intrepid, vigilant, active." He later was placed in command of the Army of Italy, but fell at Novi. He had the making of a grand soldier.

Chapter 15

On to Vienna

March, 1797

Italy was transformed, and the French holding there was strong. Charles succeeded Alvinzi, and Bonaparte was fairly reinforced. Though Austria had lost northern Italy, the gain on the Rhine was so marked that she was not discouraged. Bonaparte proposed to push on, and yet it required great courage to move into the heart of Austria, with the Mincio for a base. He left Joubert to hold the Adige, and a sufficient number in garrison in Lombardy; and feeling that a strong offense was his better plan, he advanced upon the Austrians on the Piave, sending Massena around the Austrian right Bonaparte's operation looks like a division of forces, but Joubert was really only protecting his base, with orders, in case of eventual success, to push forward and join the main army. Early in March the advance began. Prince Charles, whose reinforcements were mostly militia, retired slowly, offering slight resistance at the Tagliamento. He divided his forces into two columns, one to move towards the Tarvis defile, and the other by a circuit east by way of Laybach. Bonaparte hoped that he could pen the Austrians up in the Isonzo valley, and Massena was pushed towards the Tarvis pass, while Bernadotte followed the Laybach column. Charles was falling back on his reinforcements at Villach, and sent his train up the Isonzo. Massena pushed hard to reach the Tarvis defile, and by March 20 he did so; and by speedy pursuit Bonaparte managed to catch the Austrian train in the Predil pass, and captured it, with its escort. Meanwhile Joubert had pushed back the Austrians across the watershed of the Tyrol, and had marched towards his chief through the valley of the Drave.

The entire aspect of affairs in Italy had been changed by Bonaparte's work—by the peace with Naples and Rome, the evacuation of Corsica by the English, the capture of Mantua and the brilliant victory of Rivoli. Restless at delay and satisfied with the fresh reinforcements he had received, every man in which believed in his leader's ability to accomplish any task, he was ready to advance from his secondary base at Mantua, and to march into the heart of the Austrian empire. To guard this base and other essential points, twenty thousand men would suffice; and with over fifty thousand fighting effective, he could now make a serious thrust on Vienna, to aid which the Directory promised that Moreau should promptly cross at Kehl with the Army of the Rhine, and Hoche should move towards the Main with the Army of the Sambre and Meuse.

Yet by the brilliant outcome of the recent Italian campaigns, France was by no means freed from her troubles, external or internal, in which there was a mixture of good and evil. The ashes of the Vendée were still alive; the Royalists were active in the cities of the south; the finances were worse than ever before. More encouraged by Charles' gain in Germany than disheartened by Bonaparte's advance to the Mincio, Austria was again raising troops in vast numbers, still confident that she could reconquer the Netherlands and northern Italy. Fearing another French descent on Ireland, England markedly increased her regular army, created a militia of sixty thousand foot and twenty thousand horse, and added largely to her already gigantic navy. In Russia, Paul I. had come to the throne in November, 1796; the reinforcements promised by Catherine to Austria and England were arrested; and a treaty was made with Prussia. Sweden had also crowned a new monarch, Gustavus IV., who protected the *émigrés*, and became the tool of England. Denmark and Prussia remained neutral. All Italy, save Venice, which continued antagonistic, had come under the influence of France, though Naples was ripe for treachery. Sardinia's new king, Charles Emmanuel, soon concluded a treaty with France, and stood ready to furnish troops. Though willing to mediate between France and Austria, Turkey did nothing important; and true to her treaty with France, Spain furnished a small squadron in the Channel. Holland was fast becoming a French colony.

The descent on Ireland under Hoche at the end of 1796 had failed, and the troops detailed for the work were sent to Italy and the Rhine. Hoche took command of seventy thousand men on the Lower Rhine; and the forces on the Upper Rhine, still under Moreau, grew to sixty thousand men. Hoche stood on the left bank from Coblenz and the bridge-head at Neuwied to Düsseldorf; Moreau along the Middle Rhine and back of the Vosges at Zweibrücken. On receipt of the divisions of Bernadotte and Delmas, Bonaparte could number under his standard seventy thousand men between the Mincio and Piave, on the borders of the Tyrol and in northern Italy. On succeeding Alvinzi, Charles was given twenty-five thousand reinforcements. In Germany the Austrians had forty thousand men on the Upper Rhine and down to Mannheim, under Latour; on the Lower Rhine twenty-five thousand men under Werneck on the Lahn; and a similar number in reserve. It was plain that the French military problem could be best solved by a defence along the Rhine, and by giving Bonaparte one hundred thousand men wherewith to complete his work; but some members of the Directory feared to help him to over-much success, and it was decided to make the main effort in Germany. Moreau and Hoche were respectively to advance into Swabia and Franconia; and it was on the programme that the Army of Italy was merely to sustain them by threatening Carinthia. This proved not to be a wise plan, for the Rhine operations opened so late that Charles might have been enabled to crush Bonaparte by drawing in reinforcements from Germany. But the Aulic Council was ever slow and pedantic: advantage was not taken of the opportunity, and no harm ensued.

Despite their failure in Italy, the Austrians could not consider the year of 1796 entirely wasted. It had begun by the threat of three French armies to invade Austrian territory; and while of these three the smallest had wrung Lombardy from the Austrian sceptre, yet the two other and larger ones had been thrown back on the Rhine after two handsome imperial victories. Archduke Charles had shown signs of a true talent for arms, much was expected of him in the future, and it was the feeling in Vienna that all the fortunes of war had not been against them. The Aulic Council had, however, gained a hearty respect for the new commander of the Army of Italy, and made no sign of present intention to recover Lombardy. Neither had this august body the least idea that Bonaparte would attempt any further advance. France must surely be satisfied with what he had won. For the moment, at least, a defensive role was to be pursued here; and instead of pressing on to the plain of the Po, the Austrian armies were only so far reinforced that a sufficient body could be left to protect the Tyrol inlets, and a larger corps could be stationed on the Brenta.

In Bonaparte's mind there had been room for nothing but a further offensive advance as soon as he should have received such sufficient reinforcements as the crossing of a mountainous country and a march into the heart of Austria would demand. It was a bold operation, this advance across the Noric and Julie Alps, with the Tyrol army threatening his left flank, or, worse still, his communications, through the Adige valley, and with Venice lying sullenly on his right; and it needed the qualities of a great captain to undertake it. Until the accessions came in, however, Bonaparte had contented himself with pushing Massena out to Bassano, and Guyeux, commanding the division of Augereau, towards Treviso—which operation was followed by the withdrawal of the Austrian army from the Brenta valley to a new position behind the Piave; and with ordering Joubert up the Adige, to get in touch with the enemy, who shortly retired to above Lavis. It was in the pause brought on by the retrograde movement of the Austrians that occurred the operation on Rome, already narrated, and the peace of Tolentino of February 19.

Bonaparte was not satisfied to be long away from the Army of Italy. From Tolentino, February 17, he wrote to Joubert: "In a few days I shall be back with the army, where I feel my presence becomes necessary;" and one of the reasons he gave the Directory for speedy conclusion of peace with the Pope was, "because my presence is indispensable to the army." But this was not all. That Archduke Charles, with his reputation freshly won against Jourdan and Moreau, had been put in command in the place of Alvinzi was a still more potent factor in this desire again to grasp the helm. By March 10 the new Austrian commander was on the Piave, where Lusignan with the Austrian centre of ten thousand men was stationed, with right at Feltre, keeping touch with the Tyrol, while the relics of Alvinzi's army, seventeen thou-sand strong, held the Tagliamento from Gemona down, as the left wing, and in the Tyrol, as a right wing of the entire line of defence, fourteen thousand regular troops under Kerpen and Laudon, and ten thousand Tyrolese militia stood at Salurn and in the valleys of the Nos and Avisio. There were awaited three divisions from the Rhine, but these were still on the march through Bavaria. Altogether, Archduke Charles had a force variously estimated from thirty-five to forty-five thousand men under the colours, not counting militia. The quality of the force was far from high.

On this same March 10 Napoleon had returned to the Army of Italy and was at Bassano. His divisions were now stationed as follows: in Mantua and Verona were garrisons of fifteen hundred men under Miollio, and two thousand under Belland, respectively; in the Tyrol, along the Adige, Joubert had under his command his own division of ten thousand men, together with those of Baraguay d'Hilliers, numbering six thousand men, and Delmas, numbering five thousand men; Guyeux's (late Augereau's) division of ten thousand men was in the Citadella-Castelfranco country; Massena lay at Bassano with twelve thousand men; Serurier with nine thousand men at Asolo; and Bernadotte with ten thousand men held Padua. Victor with six thousand men from Ancona and Ferrara, where he had been watching the Pope and Naples, was ordered back to the Adige to protect the base along the Mincio. Lasalle with three thousand men held Lombardy; and Vaubois with twenty-five hundred, Leghorn. There is such vast discrepancy in the authorities as to the effective strength of both contestants that, added to Bonaparte's habit of exaggerating so as to produce a favourable impression, and of understating so as to get reinforcements, no numbers can be quite relied on; but the above figures are not far from accurate. Of this apparently large total a bare half would be able to move against the archduke; for the base on the Mincio could under no circumstances be denuded. But the French were largely veterans, elate with repeated victory and ready for immediate action; whereas the troops under Charles had included many fresh levies before the recent disastrous campaigns, and were dispirited by failure and unreliable.

From the Mincio there were two general lines of advance towards Austria proper: one up the Adige and through the Tyrol, and one through the Venetian states and the Austrian provinces of Illyria and Styria. These lines ran at right angles to one another, the apex being Verona. The first descends to the Danube by way of Salzburg; and from it to the second are five transverse roads, of which, however, only the Puster valley road came within the scope of Bonaparte's own movement. The others might come into play to enable the enemy to take his line of advance in flank, or to afford the Rhine armies a means of cooperation. The one through the mountains of the Tyrol was easy for the Austrians to defend, and gave small chance for the French to employ large bodies. The one to the east at first crossed the plains of the Po and Adige, skirting the foothills of the Alps, following the single great highway or stage-road by way of Vicenza, Treviso and Udine, and thence by a tortuous route through the mountains and many defiles to Villach, Klagenfurt and Bruck, and on to Vienna. In the first part, over the plains, the line had this advantage to the aggressor, that in attempting to successively defend the Piave, the Tagliamento and the Isonzo, the Austrians would be keeping their line of retreat in rear of their right flank, and liable to a turning movement which might throw them away from their base towards the Adriatic. From the Isonzo another post-road ran farther south by way of Gorizia, Prewald and Laybach to Klagenfurt. This was the high-road from Trieste to Vienna. Over the plain flowed numerous streams, all bridged or fordable; through the mountains the streams were torrential; and if bridges had been destroyed, they were difficult to pass. Other and less good roads there were, up all the riv-

Archduke Charles

Alvinzi

Kray

Desaix

Bernadotte

Bonaparte

ers, and skirting the foothills to the north of the stage-road; but these were practicable for foot and light horse only. After marching up the Adige, and its affluent the Eisach, to the top of the water-shed, several valleys, but especially that of the Drave,—the Pusterthal,—led down to the main line of advance to the east, the latter striking it at Villach. As the crow flies, it is a hundred and sixty miles from Verona to Villach, a hundred and ten from Verona to the headwaters of the Eisach, and a hundred from there to Villach; but the constant windings of the mountain roads add largely to these distances.

Charles would have protected the Austrian hereditary states to better advantage if he had occupied the Tyrol in force, and left a smaller army on the Piave. One need not stand astride a road in order to hold it. With a large force ready to debouch down the Adige, there was scant danger of the Army of Italy adventuring itself beyond the Isonzo. But no sooner had Bonaparte discovered the Austrian plan of protecting the Tyrol by one detached army, and the straight road to Vienna by another far removed from the first, than he formulated his own plan of campaign. Upon the forces on the Piave and Tagliamento, say twenty-seven thousand men, he would move with some forty thousand from such a direction that he would interpose between them and the forces in the Tyrol, and thus prevent help coming to them from the latter. Lying as they did, between the Noric Alps and the sea, with their communications back of their right flank, the Austrians were vulnerable; and Bonaparte proceeded to take advantage of this weakness. To accomplish his end Massena was to move *via* Feltre and Belluno, and thus around the archduke's right, while Bonaparte, with the divisions of Bernadotte, Guyeux and Serurier, would advance along the stage-road *via* Treviso. Pushing back the lesser forces of the archduke, he would then move straight towards the defile of Tarvis, at the summit of the Noric Alps, which was the key-obstacle along the Vienna highway. But as the Tyrolese army had still to be reckoned with during this march, Baraguay was sent up the Avisio and across the hills to Primiero to protect Massena's left flank. As to Joubert, on the upper Adige, if he was attacked by forces which he could not overcome, he had general orders to retire slowly down the river, fighting in every good position, as far as Castelnuovo. But as it was probable that Joubert would be able to push the Austrians back, it was understood that when he reached Brixen, Bonaparte might call him to join the main army by the Puster valley down the Drave; whereupon the joint forces would march on Vienna in one body.

The plan at first blush looks much like the division of forces which has been so much condemned in the Austrian manoeuvre of 1796. But inasmuch as Bonaparte, with the force he led against the Piave, considerably outnumbered his opponent and had better troops, and as so large a body of the enemy as that on the Tyrol border could not well be left to march down the Adige and cut the French communications, what Bonaparte really did was to leave the care of his communications with Joubert; but instead of his remaining quiet on the Mincio, he gave him an offensive role, and one which might render him useful to the main army, should his preliminary advance prove successful enough to neutralize the Tyrol troops and put them beyond danger of coping with Victor, who remained stationary at the base. As a whole the operation was not only conceived in the highest strategic sense, it was one of magnitude and marked difficulty.

Having conceived his plan, Bonaparte was not long in putting it into execution, and on March 10 issued a proclamation to the soldiers of the Army of Italy.

> Headquarters
> Bassano
> 20 Ventose, Year V
> The capture of Mantua has finished a campaign which has given you eternal title to the gratitude of the country.
>
> You have borne off the victory in fourteen pitched battles and in seventy combats; you have made more than a hundred thousand prisoners, taken from the enemy five hundred pieces of field artillery, two thousand of heavy calibre, four pontoon equipages.
>
> The contributions laid upon the countries which you have conquered have fed, clothed, paid the army throughout the campaign; you have, besides, sent thirty millions to the minister of finances, to ease the public treasury.
>
> You have enriched the Museum of Paris with more than three hundred objects, masterpieces of ancient and modern Italy, and which have taken thirty centuries to produce.
>
> You have conquered for the Republic the most beautiful countries of Europe; the Lombardy and Cispadane Republics owe you their liberty; the French colours float for the first time on the shores of the Adriatic, opposite and within twenty-four hours' sail of ancient Macedonia. . . .
>
> But you have not finished all. A great destiny is reserved to you. . . . You will continue to be worthy of it.

> . . . The emperor alone remains in our front. Degrading himself from the rank of a great power, this prince has placed himself in the pay of the merchants of London. He has no more will but that of these perfidious islanders.
>
> The Directory has spared no pains to give peace to Europe. It has not been heeded. . . . There is no hope of peace but by seeking it in the heart of the hereditary lands of the House of Austria. There you will find a brave people, bowed down with the war . . . and believing that English gold has corrupted the ministers of the emperor. You will respect their religion and customs, you will respect their properties. It is liberty you will bring to the brave Hungarian nation.
>
> The House of Austria . . . will descend to the rank of secondary powers, where she has already been placed by putting herself in the pay and at the disposition of England.
>
> *Bonaparte*

On March 10 Massena was headed for Feltre on the upper Piave, with instructions to strike Lusignan, cut the Austrian right wing in the Tyrol from its left wing on the plains of Venice, and threaten the right of the archduke's army. So soon as Charles became aware of Bonaparte's offensive manoeuvre, he withdrew his troops, which had been lying some ten thousand strong along the Piave, back behind the Livenza, observation parties alone being left on the Piave. The rivers at this season are wont to be full and rapid, and the roads heavy, so that the marching was far from easy. Lusignan being withdrawn up the river on the French approach, Massena on March 11 passed Feltre, and meanwhile Guyeux and Serurier approached the Piave; and next day the cavalry reserve crossed to the north of Montello forest near Vidor, and Guyeux to the south of it at Spesiano, reaching Conegliano. Serurier was not far behind the cavalry reserve. Massena advanced to Belluno; Bernadotte, who was in reserve, reached Castelfranco. The Austrian observation parties all fell back without crossing swords. Baraguay, somewhat belated by the mountain roads, finally reached Primiero. The Austrian line of retreat was along the main road and the parallel country roads towards Udine, and on March 18 the archduke was nearing the Tagliamento, Guyeux having, after a hearty fight, pushed Hohenzollern and the Austrian rearguard out of Sacile, and sent a force to follow it to Pordenone.

Massena on the 18th had not moved from Belluno, but he seized the defile of La Fossa upriver, cut out Lusignan's rearguard at Longaro, and threw this Austrian column back to Cadore, a town on the Piave and near the headwaters of the Tagliamento. Lusignan was taken prisoner. "M. de Lusignan covered himself with opprobrium by the conduct he held in Brescia towards our sick. I have ordered that he should be sent to France without right to exchange," Bonaparte wrote to Paris. Serurier and Bernadotte got respectively to Conegliano and Treviso. Bonaparte began to believe that the Austrians would stand at the Tagliamento and accept battle; but as he was unwilling to deliver one, even though superior in force, until Massena had joined the main column, he now ordered this general to march towards the army by way of Aviano, or if this, owing to the snows or bad roads, was not practicable, to join it at Sacile. From Conegliano, on the evening of March 13, Berthier wrote Massena:

> Though the general-in-chief deems the forces which he has at this moment sufficient to determine victory, he would decide to retard his attack by one day, so that the brave Massena division might be of the party.

Massena had practically accomplished his task by driving back Lusignan and severing the Austrian centre from the right in the Tyrol; and on receipt of his orders he set out for Serravalle on the 14th, while Serurier marched on Porto Buffole, Guyeux and headquarters assembled at Sacile, and Bernadotte got to Conegliano.

Bonaparte was thus concentrating his divisions so as to mass them for a heavy blow when the time should come, and this he did long before he reached the vicinity of the enemy, who he was convinced would not stand until he got to the Tagliamento. The Austrian rearguard reached the river on the 14th of March, the main body having already crossed and been posted on the line San Daniele-Codroipo-Latisana, with headquarters back in Udine. Anxious to have Massena join, Bonaparte sent him orders to Serravalle to march rapidly *via* Sacile and Pordenone, and be in Cordemons by the 16th. The bulk of the army advanced little: Guyeux and headquarters to Pordenone, Serurier across the Livenza, and Bernadotte to Sacile. The Austrian rearguard was then withdrawn across the Tagliamento.

From Sacile, on March 15, Bonaparte wrote Joubert two letters of military instruction, and one for civil conduct in the Tyrol, which contain so much excellent matter that some items in them may well be quoted. They first recite the general scheme. To operate the junction of the Tyrolese and Friuli divisions, the latter (his own

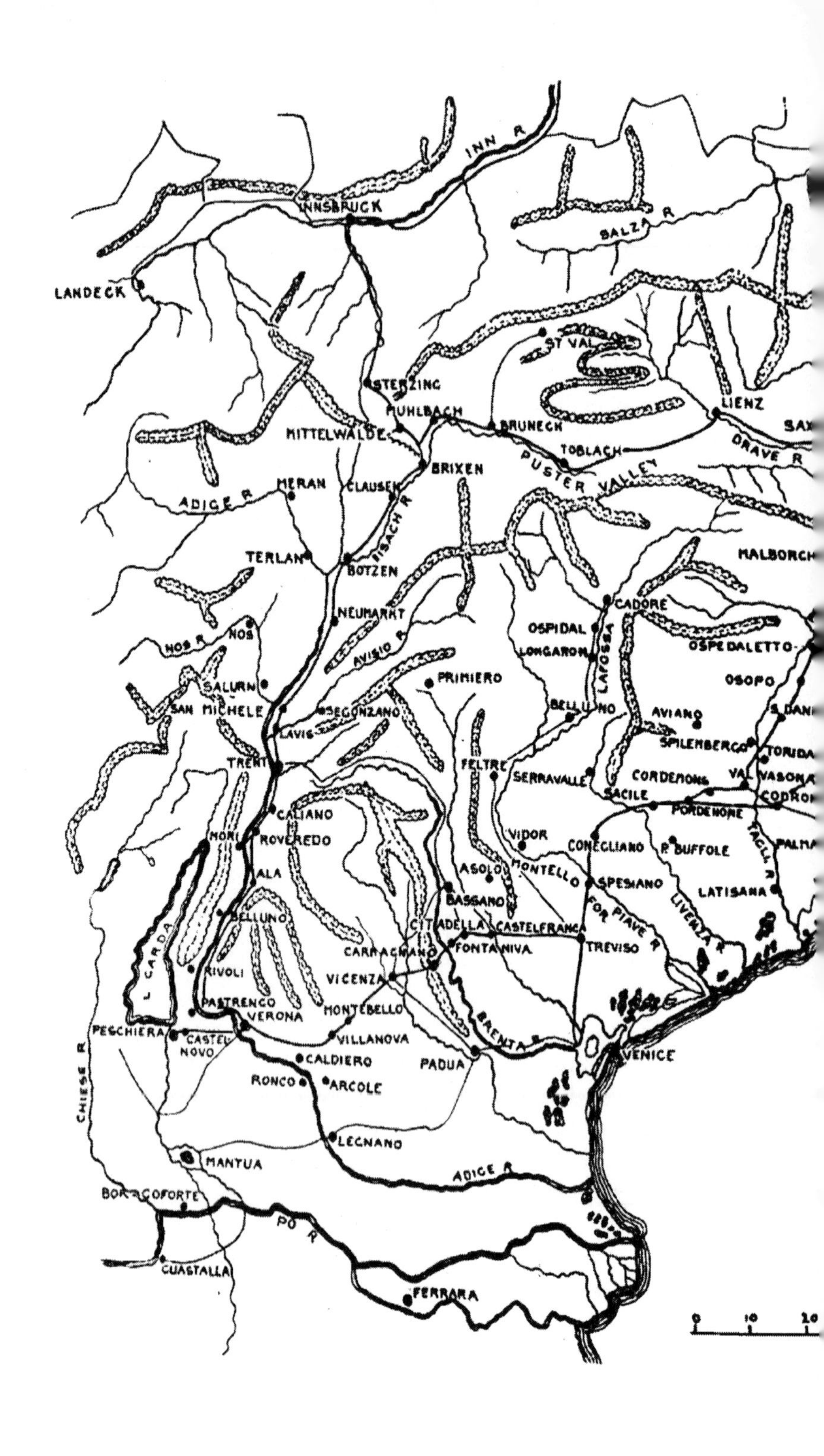

INN R
INNSBRUCK
SALZA R
LANDECK
ST VAL
STERZING
MUHLBACH
MITTELWALDE
BRUNECK
LIENZ
TOBLACH
DRAVE R
PUSTER VALLEY
BRIXEN
MERAN
CLAUSEN
ADIGE R
EISACH R
TERLAN
BOTZEN
MALBORCH
CADORE
NEUMARKT
OSPIDAL
LONGARON
OSPEDALETTO
NOS R
NOS
AVISIO R
LAFOSSA
PRIMIERO
OSOPO
SALURN
SAN MICHELE
SEGONZANO
BELLUNO
AVIANO
LAVIS
SPILEMBERGO
TRENT
FELTRE
SERRAVALLE
CORDEMONS
VALVASONA
SACILE
PORDENONE
CALIANO
MORI
ROVEREDO
VIDOR
CONEGLIANO
R BUFFOLE
ASOLO
MONTELLO
SPESIANO
ALA
BASSANO
PIAVE R
LIVENZA R
LATISANA
BELLUNO
CITADELLA
CASTELFRANCA
L GARDA
CARMIGNANO
FONTANIVA
TREVISO
RIVOLI
VICENZA
PASTRENGO
VERONA
MONTEBELLO
PESCHIERA
CASTEL NOVO
VILLANOVA
CALDIERO
PADUA
BRENTA R
VENICE
RONCO
ARCOLE
CHIESE R
LEGNANO
MANTUA
ADIGE R
BORGOFORTE
PO R
GUASTALLA
FERRARA
0
10
20

TO VIENNA 80 M
BRUCK
AUSSEL
ROTTENMANN
MAUTERN
LEOBEN
RADSTADT
KRAUBAT
MUHR R
JUDENBURG
HUNDSMARK
GRATZ
NEUMARCK
MUHR R
S. MICHEL
DIRNSTEIN
TREISACH
STRASBURG
CURK R
GMUNDEN
SPITHAL
ST VEIT
ST ANDRE
EHRENHAUSEN
KLAGENFURT
MARBURG
DRAVE R
VILLACH
WURZEN
TARVIS
FLITSCH
NEUMARK
RAIBL
PREDEL
CH DI PLOTZ
KRAINBURG
WINDISH FEIBRITZ
CAPORETTO
LITTAY
STUR
CIVIDALE
CANALE
LAYBACH
SAVE R
UDINE
O LAYBACH
CORMONS
CZERNIZA
GORICIA
GRADISCA
SAN P.
PREVALD
TRIESTE
LIPPA
FIUME
QUIETO
50

force) were to cross the Tagliamento, move up to Osopo, and seize the Pontafel pass, thus opening the way to the Drave valley, while Joubert was throwing the enemy back by way of Brixen, and beyond the mountains on Innsbruck, so as to clear his way for an advance down the same river. But, said Bonaparte, first, the Tyrol divisions may be beaten and forced back to Rivoli, or even to the Mincio. Or, second, the enemy may move by way of Feltre and Primolano into the Brenta valley to cut the French communications—a difficult task. Or, third, the Friuli divisions might be turned by right or left, and the enemy reach the Piave or Brenta before the French could come to the right-about and get there. To meet the first hypothesis, Joubert was given command of all forces in the Mantua country and Lombardy, in fact, of everything between the Adige and the Oglio. In any case Mantua, Peschiera, Legnano and Pizzighetone were to be well provisioned and held by good garrisons; Joubert was to maintain himself between Mantua and the Po, so as to feed himself by that river, and be able to debouch on the enemy's rear, should he advance on Milan. Sahuguet was to concentrate and hold himself in Ferrara. Joubert was to use all means to enable the Friuli divisions to fall back on him, his chief says:

> .... as I do not doubt that under all circumstances, you will act in a manner consistent with the spirit of the war we are waging.

The interesting feature about this discussion is the utter calm with which the leader looks at any one of these apparently fatal occurrences. Even if Bonaparte should become completely cut off from Mantua by Joubert's being pushed back on that fortress, yet Joubert should be able, the instructions assume, to hold himself until Bonaparte had beaten the enemy on the Tagliamento, when he would about face on the force which had ventured on his communications, and in connection with Joubert destroy it Unlike the soldiers of his day, this young and bold commander-in-chief did not look on a temporary interruption of his communications as a fatal occurrence. Beat the enemy, thought he, and the communications will care for themselves. This is now a broad and constant maxim; but it was new at the time, and his chief's self-confidence must have had a reassuring effect on Joubert, with the heavy responsibility laid upon his untried shoulders. Another point of interest in this letter is the fact that Bonaparte does not undertake to give directions to Joubert how to act under all possible adverse contingencies. This has been for some time recognized as a bad policy in a captain's instructions to a distant lieutenant; and though the rule had not been formulated in his day, Bonaparte evidently saw the wisdom of leaving Joubert to a certain extent untrammelled, and his letter paid no further heed to the other hypotheses. He relied on Joubert's initiative and discretion to do what might at the time be the wisest thing, and recognized the fact that of this Joubert would probably be a better judge than he.

In the second letter Bonaparte orders him to advance on Botzen by the 28th, and then approves all Joubert has done to procure oil and vegetables for the army.

> You may be persuaded that I approve in advance all you shall do to ameliorate the lot of the soldiers. While you are on the march, have issued to your forces, as much as may be possible, wine in the evening and brandy in the morning.

The Civil Instruction Bonaparte sent was:

> First, to confirm all laws and keep in place all magistrates.
>
> Second, to confirm the public exercise of religion.
>
> Third, to cajole the priests, distinguished theologians and men of science.
>
> Fourth, to speak well of the emperor, but blame his ministers.
>
> Fifth, to protect all Tyroleans who have served the emperor.
>
> Sixth, to see that moneys heretofore paid to the emperor shall go to the army chest.
>
> Seventh, to take no money from the Monts-de-Piété (the government pawnshops), nor from the village treasuries, and to seek to conciliate the people.
>
> Eighth, to disarm the population, take hostages from and fine the villages which resist, or which murder soldiers.

These were substantially the principles he acted on in any new territory he overran.

Although he never gave them great liberty of action, yet Bonaparte insisted on his lieutenants neglecting nothing, and doing their work themselves. In a circular to division generals, March 14, Berthier says:

> The general-in-chief gives you the order to betake yourselves every day at four o'clock in the morning to your vanguard (outposts), to be present at the report of the daybreak patrol, and thus to be equal to giving your orders according to circumstances. The officer of engineers and chief of artillery of your

division are equally to be on hand at the vanguard to receive your orders. You will also order the generals of brigade to remain in camp, that is they must never have quarters more than two hundred toises (a quarter mile) away.

The division artillery park is never to be put in a town, but always near and behind the division. The cannoneers and drivers are to bivouac beside their pieces, the horses to be picketed, or attached to the poles of their wagons. The artillery in the vanguard is never to be unhorsed, except to water the horses at the hour to be indicated by the commander of the vanguard." The generals were also ordered to "forbid expressly that any parliamentarian should be received while troops are engaged. This is a ruse the Austrians have put to use more than once, to give time to execute their retreat.

Such simple precautions are all too often neglected in war. On the 16th the French divisions were headed for Valvasone, in order to cross the Tagliamento. The archduke's right now stretched from Codroipo to Torrida in a position which had been well entrenched; and Guyeux, who was ahead, was destined to move on this wing, while Bernadotte, a few hours behind, should manoeuvre against the Austrian left wing above Latisena, and Serurier remain as reserve, in a general way heading for Codroipo. Speaking of this division on the march, the chief wrote:

> It is assailed by horrible weather; but wind and rain, on the eve of a battle, have always been for the Army of Italy a presage of fortune.

The river was fordable. Bonaparte sent an *aide-de-camp* and twenty-five guides to reconnoitre up to the entrenchments. Having done this, Guyeux and Bernadotte were ordered forward. The light troops as skirmishers were in front, followed by the grenadiers and flanked by cavalry. Each half-brigade had its right and left battalion ployed into close column, the second battalion between them in line. This was a common formation.

The crossing began about 3 p. m.; but the Austrian commander, not purposing to stand here to receive battle, and preferring to wait for the twenty-five thousand veterans coming from the Rhine, as a leaven for his very questionable lump of troops, made only such defence as would enable his army to continue its retreat, already begun, on Palmanova. This place the Austrian army reached at night, with its rear-guard echeloned along the highway. In the Memoirs Napoleon describes much more of a battle than the dispatches written at the time and other contemporary reports and documents lead one to believe was fought on this river. Charles had hoped to gain time here, but Bonaparte afforded him no opportunity to do so. Massena had been delayed by the bad mountain roads over which he had to march, and had not yet reached the main army, but Bonaparte now ordered him to come in rapidly to Spilimbergo. Had the archduke stood for battle, Massena would have been much in demand; as it was, his absence did not prove of consequence. The Austrian army continued its retreat on the 17th towards Gradisca, on the way to Gorizia, and meanwhile Ocskay took over Lusignan's brigade, and making a circuit by the upper Tagliamento, covered the road to Villach at Chiusa Veneta, on the Fella River.

It is to be noticed in this campaign that there are but few roads to determine the strategic manoeuvres, the side roads, where any exist, being merely complementary to the single highway. In a country of broad expanses of ground and many roads, minor strategic manoeuvres can be indulged in on a larger and more interesting scale than here, where Bonaparte was confined practically to a single line of advance along which to follow up the enemy, and could indulge in manoeuvring only partially, as, *e. g.*, to force the enemy to abandon his defence at any given defile or river. While Charles had the poorer army, he had the easier task in defending the approaches to the Austrian capital. Yet the difference in the quality of the troops was marked.

It was not apparent to Bonaparte why the Austrian army had marched on Palmanova, or, indeed, evident whether the mass of it had really taken this southerly direction. He had anticipated that the archduke would retire towards the defile of Tarvis instead, this being—*via* Udine, Ospedaletto, Tarvis, Villach, Klagenfurt—the shorter and more direct road to Bruck and Vienna; and though he was anxious to follow hard on the enemy's heels, yet it consumed some time to reconnoitre the road in his front and ascertain the facts. These two young generals, respectively twenty-five and twenty-eight years old, had gained a hearty respect each for the other, on the score of the successes each had won in 1796 in Germany and Italy. In all his campaigns Napoleon carefully weighed the personal equation as the most important factor in his problem, and he had not at first been able to gauge the archduke. Within a few days, however, he had made up his mind that he had not a dangerous opponent in his front, and wrote the Directory, March 25:

> Up to this hour Prince Charles has manoeuvred worse than Beaulieu and Wurmser; at every step he has made mistakes, and extremely gross ones; these have cost him a great deal, but it would have gone far worse with him had not the repute he has won in a measure deceived me, and had it not prevented my convincing myself of certain errors which I noticed, and which I supposed to be dictated by views that in reality did not exist.

The two men were of types markedly different, and the Frenchman was unquestionably the superior as a soldier; but though here unable to do his best, the Austrian held himself through life a worthy prince of men, and won for himself in future years a high military reputation. Bonaparte's slur is scarcely warranted. Just what had induced Charles to give up the direct road as a first purpose, we do not know, as he shortly reverted to it for a part of his forces. It may have been a rumour of Massena's march on Tarvis, which he feared might anticipate his own, and the path there was readily barred. Yet there was time and to spare for a light column to reach the defile and hold it for the Austrians; indeed, this had already been done from Vienna; and the march *via* Gorizia was an eccentric one.

Some days before, Charles had entertained a purpose of advancing a column down the Fella valley, so as to threaten the French left in its advance on Palmanova, but Massena's smart advance up the same valley had anticipated his plan. The archduke was not now dealing with a general who, like Moreau and Jourdan, would pause after every step; he was facing the most rapid captain of modern days, and that with a force inferior in numbers and morale. All the factors except terrain were against him.

On his side Bonaparte was beginning to appreciate both the value and the growing insecurity of his position. On March 17 he wrote the Directory:

> If the armies of the Rhine cross promptly and enter the lists, the emperor is lost. . . . But if you let me be overwhelmed, I shall have no other resource than to fall back to Italy, and all will be lost.

He never ceased to remind the home authorities of the co-operation they had promised him. On March 25 be wrote to Carnot:

> Has the Rhine been passed? It is clear that in four or five days from now, when my movements will be unmasked, and when the enemy will feel the danger in which he finds himself, he

> will abandon nearly everything on the Rhine to fall upon me. If Moreau does not then march at double speed on the enemy, so as to push him and be able to reach him as soon as possible, I shall be beaten and obliged to return to Italy.

In a dispatch to the Directory of April 1 he said:

> The army has not yet sustained much loss, and is in the best condition. If I had had twenty thousand men more, I would not have been obliged to wait for the passage of the Rhine, and the army would have entered Vienna almost as if travelling by post: a thing which would have so much astonished this great nation that I would have had nothing to fear from the different assemblages which they are making today.

On April 5 he wrote to the Directory:

> I have not yet news as to whether the Rhine is crossed. I presume, nevertheless, that at this hour Moreau is marching at great speed to prevent the Austrians from all falling on me.

And on April 8:

> Our armies have not yet passed the Rhine, and we are already within one hundred miles of Vienna. The Army of Italy is then alone exposed to the efforts of one of the first powers of Europe. The Venetians are arming all their peasants, putting all their priests under arms, and are shaking with fury all the springs of their old government to crush Bergamo and Brescia. The Venetian government at this moment has twenty thousand armed men on my rear.

Retiring, then, behind the Isonzo to Gorizia on March 18, Charles took up a position east of the town, and in accordance with orders of the evening previous, Bernadotte started at early dawn of the same day and reached Palmanova, followed by Serurier and later Guyeux; while Massena filed off by way of San Daniele and Osopo to seize Chiusa Veneta (or Venzone) and the entrance of the Pontafel pass, through which flows the Fella River. The Isonzo, down to Gorizia, runs through a deep valley with few and difficult outlets—for an army practically none. At one moment Bonaparte held the idea that the Austrian army might retire up this river, and that, by manoeuvring with such speed as to seize the lower and upper ends of the river defile, he could prepare for the archduke another Caudine Forks. Massena in the Tarvis region, and Bonaparte, if he could reach the left flank of the enemy near Gorizia, might accomplish this end. But the enemy kept too much in advance for the French to manoeuvre him into the trap. Nor had the archduke harboured any idea of engaging battle until the Rhine troops should have arrived, though Bonaparte did not know it. Thus the French chieftain was disappointed in both his anticipations. Palmanova, evacuated by the Austrians, was occupied March 18, and the French army occupied the right bank of the Torre, which next morning was crossed. On this same day Bonaparte sent orders to Joubert to advance on Brixen.

Bernadotte now led the column, Bonaparte accompanying him, and moved unopposed to near Gradisca; after crossing the Torre, Serurier marched to Villesse; the two divisions then advanced on Gradisca March 19, and surrounding the town, Bernadotte in front and Serurier taking it in reverse by crossing the river at San Pietro after a somewhat prolonged combat, compelled its surrender that evening.

As the Austrian commander expected to find his reinforcements at Villach, he remained of a mind to fall back on these, and continued his retreat on the evening of the 19th. Personally he hurried to Villach to direct movements to hold the Tarvis defile. His army he now divided into two columns, the larger to march by way of Laybach and Krainzburg on the Tarvis pass, which it would thus approach from the rear; and the lesser, under Bayalich, towards the same point by the roads up the Isonzo River. This last column was followed by the most of the artillery and train. Perhaps the archduke feared to lose his hold on the Caporetto road, or he hoped to expedite his march by sending his army along the two roads; and both columns were indeed heading for the same goal; but in case of delay, which would enable the French to attack his Isonzo column, he laid himself open to disaster. Either this was a safe and shorter route for the whole column, or it should not be selected for part of it.

Massena had made some forced marches and thereby re-paired his early delay. He was, moreover, thoroughly at home in mountain warfare. On the 19th he had entered the Pontafel pass, and taken by storm the Casasola bridge, which is one of the strong points in the pass, throwing back the weak Austrian detachment up the Fella. On the 20th the main French column pushed its way up the Isonzo to Gorizia, Serurier on the left bank, Bernadotte on the right, while Guyeux followed an Austrian flanking column on Cormons; but learning that a substantial part of the Austrian army had retired by way of Laybach, Bonaparte altered Bernadotte's direction, March 21, to one towards Czernitza, and this general, forging ahead, soon got into touch with the enemy's rear. This same March 21 Guyeux advanced to Cividale, and Serurier kept on up the river. And meanwhile Massena had, on the 20th, by hard marching, pushed through Pontafel and with his head of column reached Tarvis, and driven the Austrian detachment, which under Ocskay was defending the pass, sharply back to Wurzen. On the 21st, then, Massena was at and near Tarvis, and Bayalich's column was laboriously making its way up the Isonzo from Caporetto on the same point, reaching Predil. Learning here that the French were already at Tarvis, the Austrians determined to cut their way through, and to help in this, the detachment which Massena threw out of Tarvis was ordered to turn back again from Wurzen and join in the attack.

As a matter of fact, Massena had not yet got forward a force sufficiently large to hold the Tarvis pass, and on March 22 the Austrians under Gontreuil were able by a gallant assault to retake the place, Massena's detachment falling back on the main body at Malborghetto. At Tarvis the Austrians concentrated all nearby forces, and sent a detachment out to Seifnitz to hold head against Massena, and another into the Predil pass to keep open the Flitschler-Klause for Bayalich's column. Meanwhile, after driving an Austrian detachment out of Stupizza, Guyeux had reached Caporetto. Serurier's division (now under Chabot, Serurier being sick) was acting as general reserve. He had at first been ordered to follow on after Bernadotte; but was withdrawn before reaching Czernitza, and held as reserve to the Isonzo column.

At and about Tarvis is a network of defiles, on the summit of the Noric Alps. Running east and west is the Tarvis defile, which Massena had approached up the Fella valley; and running south from Tarvis is the Predil defile at the headwaters of the Isonzo, up through which Bayalich was striving to save the Austrian train. This latter pass was shut at the lower end by the Chiusa di Plötz.

After his van had been driven out of Tarvis, Massena shortly recovered himself, again advanced on Seifnitz and Tarvis, took both places after a stubborn fight, in which Brune especially distinguished himself, and forced his way down to Raibl in the Predil pass; and meanwhile Guyeux had sharply followed Bayalich. At the south gate of the pass Guyeux found himself suddenly checked by Köblös, but he cleverly turned this officer's position by scaling the heights and capturing the castle which dominated the entrance of the defile, and captured Köblös brigade almost in entirety. Bayalich and the Austrian train were now shut in between Guyeux, sustained by Serurier, at the southern gate, and Massena, who had got to Raibl in the upper part of the pass. Thus trapped, the Austrians could not even consider resistance, and after a short parley they surrendered four general officers, four thousand men, twenty-five guns and over four hundred wagons.

> A great number of men had been killed, wounded or taken in the different combats since the Tagliamento, and others, in great number, natives of Carniola or Croatia, seeing everything lost, had disbanded in the gorges to regain alone their villages.

The Austrian total had not been large enough to cope with the force assembled by the French. During this active work at Tarvis, which accomplished in a small way what Bonaparte had hoped to inflict on the whole Austrian army, Bernadotte pushed on as far as Prevald, and on the 25th reached Laybach.

A small part of the expected reinforcements had reached Villach, and on this body the Austrian detachment beaten at Tarvis fell back; the archduke proposed to concentrate his army in Klagenfurt, the apex of the two highways along which the French were advancing. On the French side, Guyeux and Massena advanced March 28 on Villach, which was vacated by the Austrians; and here the army paused until Bonaparte could hear from the Tyrol.

Joubert had during all this time been far from idle. He had opposed to him Kerpen with the larger part of the Austrian forces, while a detachment under Laudon was in the Nos valley to protect western Tyrol. So soon as he heard from his chief that the main army had reached the Tagliamento, he broke up March 20, and crossed the Avisio, his main body at Lavis, and a turning column at Segonzano. His left thus imperilled, Kerpen retired,—after a lively combat, but scarcely losing two thousand men killed, as the *Memoirs* report, nor three thousand prisoners,—and was rejoined by Laudon from the Nos valley. The enemy does not appear to have been alert; Joubert surprised them at every turn, and on the 21st threw them back towards Neumarkt with loss of many prisoners, himself moving to Salurn. Thence following them up, on the 22nd Joubert reached Botzen, where he ascertained that a column of eight thousand men under Kerpen had retired up the Eisach valley on Brixen, while the Austrian right wing under Laudon, the roads being crowded and the Austrians scarcely guessing the French intention, had marched up the Adige on Meran. Leaving Delmas behind at Botzen to protect his left and to secure the road back to his base, Joubert followed up the column which had moved up the Eisach valley.

Baraguay d'Hilliers had got back from Primiero, and with his five thousand men took post at Botzen, and later followed Joubert. A detachment was sent up the Adige to Terlan, and Joubert moved on Kerpen at Clausen, where the Austrian general had taken up a strong position, his left leaning on the Eisach, and the right on steep hills. Joubert's first attack on the 24th was repulsed; but his light foot scaled the hills, turned Kerpen's right, and a fresh assault proving successful, the Austrians retired through Brixen to Mittenwalde. The French then entered Brixen, where they seized the big magazines amassed by the enemy for the Tyrol campaign. Next day again the Austrians were pushed towards Sterzing. They had left fifteen hundred men at Mühlbach to hold the entrance to the Pusterthal; but these were captured on the 26th. Having no late news from his chief, Joubert sat down at Brixen to wait for orders.

On the 29th Laudon, who had remained on the Adige, attacked the French left behind at Botzen. These fended off the onset; but when it was renewed April 2 and 3, Baraguay was sent back to aid in holding the river. Still, though Laudon managed to get possession of the bridge-head at Neumarkt, Joubert, on hearing from Bonaparte of his victories, determined to risk any mischief Laudon could do, and started, as ordered, *via* Bruneck, Toblach, Lienz and Sachsenburg to Spithal. Laudon followed Joubert to Brixen, and then returned to Botzen April 7. Kerpen kept slowly on after Joubert.

Daring these days, in the Army of Italy, repeated orders had to be issued against pillaging; and women seemed to be largely at the root of the evil. On March 28 it was:

> . . . . expressly forbidden to the half-brigades to have in their suite more women than the law allows them as washerwomen. The chiefs of half-brigades are held to send the names of the washerwomen of their half-brigade to the chief of staff, and he will have sent to each of them a pass signed by himself. They will be consequently authorized to wear the badge. Every woman who shall be found in the suite of the army without being authorized shall receive public correction, shall be chased out of the army, and sent under guard two marches to the rear.

In an Order of the Day of April 5 all officers were forbidden to have their wives follow the army, and five days were given them to send them away under pain of cashiering. Again, on April 17, it was ordered:

All women who are not authorized by the Council of Administration are held to leave the division in twenty-four hours; failing which they shall be arrested by the chiefs of battalion, smudged with black, and exposed two hours in the public square. The general-in-chief is informed that the disorders which are committed are excited by these abominable women, who urge the soldiers to pillage.

CHAPTER 16

Leoben

March-May, 1797

Bt the end of March Charles had reached Klagenfurt. His forces had melted. Bonaparte followed him up sharply, and March 31 wrote him a letter deprecating the war. Charles made a good retreat, feeling that if he was to fight a battle, he had better do this near the gates of Vienna, where he would be in force. He was growing strategically stronger as Bonaparte was growing weaker. While the apparent gain was on the side of the French, yet their position was questionable, their line of operation being so long. On April 5 Bonaparte was relieved by the arrival of Austrian plenipotentiaries to treat for peace. This was the answer to his letter, and he was wise as well as glad to conclude the truce of Leoben. His advanced position was extra-hazardous. Austria gave up more than France could reasonably expect, and Bonaparte had properly sealed his brilliant march from the Var to within eighty miles of Vienna. He was now the most noted man in Europe. Moreau and Hoche on the Rhine were slow in advancing so as to sustain the forward march of Bonaparte. Finally in April Hoche crossed at Neuwied and pushed the enemy back to the Main, and Moreau crossed at Kehl. But the truce of Leoben stopped their operations. The terms of this truce were eventually embodied in the Peace of Campo Formio. Austria ceded Belgium to France. A Congress was assembled at Rastadt to determine on universal peace. Austria received Venice. The Rhine was the French frontier. France now interfered in the affairs of Switzerland, which would have been more useful to her as a neutral power, and seized some of the treasuries of the Swiss cantons. Bonaparte returned to Paris in triumph, but the time was not ripe for him there, and he determined on an expedition to Egypt.

By the 28th of March the archduke had assembled thirteen thousand men at Klagenfurt, with a body of five thousand men still at Laybach on the Save. By just what means, shrinkage and attrition, garrisons, detachments or otherwise, his forces had so much dwindled, there is no record to show. But beaten armies melt fast. He had learned of the events in the Tyrol. In front of him at Villach stood Guyeux and Massena, and Chabot was coming up. From near Laybach Bernadotte had sent the reserve cavalry as a flying corps to Trieste, to glean news, and to collect any stores useful to the army; and his advance was a threat to the Austrian left. On the 29th Bonaparte advanced on Klagenfurt, and driving in the outlying Austrian detachments, entered the town, the archduke retiring upon St. Veit, where his first Rhine reinforcements reported. But he was still as inferior in numbers as his army was in morale.

Having passed the Drave, the Army of Italy. . . .

> . . . . was in Germany. The language, the manners, the climate, the soil, cultivation, everything, contrasted with Italy. It praised the hospitality of the peasants and their good nature. The abundance of vegetables, the great quantity of wagons and horses were very useful to it, having found in Italy only wagons hauled by oxen, the slow and inconvenient service of which accorded ill with French vivacity.

Bonaparte here issued a proclamation to the inhabitants of Carinthia, Carniola and Istria, in French, German and Italian, which the Memoirs say had a good effect.

On March 31 Bonaparte addressed a letter to Charles, as to a brother soldier, suggesting that nothing could further justify the struggle.

> Headquarters
> Klagenfurt
> 11 Germinal, Year V
> To Prince Charles, commanding the Austrian Army
> *Monsieur le Général-en-Chef*
> Brave soldiers make war and desire peace. Has not this one lasted six years? Have we killed enough men and inflicted enough evils on sad humanity? This implores from every side. Europe, which had taken up arms against the French Republic, has laid them aside. Your nation alone remains, and yet blood is about to flow more than ever. This sixth campaign is ushered in by sinister forebodings; whatever its result, we shall kill on either side some thousands more of men, and yet we must end by some agreement, for everything has a term, even hateful passions.
>
> The Executive Directory of the French Republic has notified H. M. the Emperor of its desire to end the war which is

> desolating the two peoples; the intervention of the court of London opposed this. Is there then no hope of an agreement between us, and must we, for the interest or the passions of a nation foreign to the evils of this war, continue to cut each other's throats? You, Monsieur le Général-en-Chef, who by jour birth approach so near the throne and are above all the little passions which often animate ministers and governments, are you decided to merit the title of Benefactor of all humanity and of Saviour of Germany? Do not suppose, Monsieur le Général-en-Chef, that I understand by this that it may not be possible for you to save her by force of arms; but in the supposition that the chances of war should become favourable to you, Germany would none the less be ravaged. As to me. Monsieur le Général-en-Chef, if the overture that I have the honour to make to you can save the life of a single man, I shall esteem myself more proud of the civil crown that I shall find myself to have merited, than of the sad glory which can come from military successes. I beg you to believe, Monsieur le Général-en-Chef, in the sentiments of esteem and of distinguished consideration, with which I am, etc.
> *Bonaparte*

The archduke replied that he had no power to treat, but that he equally desired to end the calamities of the war; and that he would forward the communication to Vienna. He said

> Assuredly, while waging war, Monsieur le Général-en-Chef, and in following the vocation of honour and of duty, I desire, as do you, peace for the happiness of the peoples and humanity. As, nevertheless, in the post which is confided to me, it does not belong to me to scrutinize nor to terminate the quarrel of belligerent nations, and as I am not furnished by H. M. the Emperor with power to treat, you will find it natural. Monsieur le Général, that I enter on the subject with you into no negotiation, and that I await superior orders with regard to so important a matter, which is not fundamentally within my province. Whatever may be, however, the future chances of war or the hopes of peace, I beg you to persuade yourself, Monsieur le Général, of my esteem and of my distinguished consideration.

On the same day Bonaparte addressed another dispatch to the archduke, protesting against Austrian sick and wounded being left at

Klagenfurt, while the depots of grain had all been destroyed. "This conduct is contrary to the rights of war," said he. In the dispatch it is suggested that, when invalided soldiers of the enemy are left behind to be cared for by the victor, the grain-stores should not be set afire.

On March 30 Bonaparte remained *in situ* to hear from Joubert and Bernadotte, and to let Chabot get his division up. During the last day of the month the main column advanced on St. Veit, and Bernadotte on Laybach. Both bodies of Austrians fell back. This was again the case next day when Massena advanced on the archduke's position behind the Gurk. Charles, not strong enough to fight a battle, withdrew beyond Freisach, which the French then entered. On the 2nd of April Bonaparte reached the Austrian rearguard, and Massena forced the Dirnstein gorge. Bonaparte reported:

> Prince Charles was compelled to bring back from his main body his eight battalions of grenadiers, the same which took Kehl, and who are at this moment the hope of the Austrian army; but the 2nd Light Infantry, which has distinguished itself since its arrival in the army by its courage, stayed not its movement a single moment, threw itself on the right and left flanks, while General Massena, to sweep the gorge, was forming column of the 18th and 32nd of the line. The combat was engaged with fury; it was the élite of the Austrian army which came to fight against our old soldiers of the Army of Italy. The enemy had a superb position, which he had made fairly bristling with guns; but it only retarded a little the defeat of his rearguard. The enemy's grenadiers were put into complete rout, left the battlefield covered with dead and five or six hundred prisoners.

Massena followed, and dealt the enemy another severe blow at Neumarkt and Hundsmarkt. It was at these three places that the Rhine troops were first put into action. The French reached Neumarkt at night, and from here Bernadotte was ordered forward to the main column by forced marches.

Every day brought the archduke closer to his own capital, and that the Vienna authorities did not furnish him with more troops can only be explained on the theory that the Aulic Council preferred, if the Austrians were to fight a battle to save the city, to have it come about nearer the walls, where every man could be put in, and where the French would of necessity be weakened by their excessive marches, and markedly endangered by their long communications. To Bonaparte Vienna must have loomed up as a splendid goal; but before he could call it won, the army in his front must be thoroughly beaten. Charles' retreat was daily making the French situation more difficult. Still Bonaparte never forgot that the enemy's army was the true objective, and that all other matters were subsidiary to beating this. A victory cures a multitude of errors and covers a multitude of risks.

With regard to Joubert, Bonaparte was still in doubt From Freisach, April 3, he wrote him that for the moment the French had not gained enough, nor were they near enough Vienna, to make it certain that the Austrians might not yet resume the offensive in the Tyrol; that in a couple of days things would clear up; and that while he might perhaps order him in to the main body, he need go to no trouble to do more than keep open the road by the Drave valley. Almost immediately after, he was ordered to march to a junction with the army.

The Austrians arrested their backward movement only to ease the troops, continuing the retreat during the night of April 2-3; and the archduke had already instructed the Laybach detachment to move rapidly up to Bruck *via* Marburg and Gratz. Bonaparte was still illustrating the value of his mass theory. Though by calling in Bernadotte he had now opened the road to his rear, by this same way of Gratz, Laybach, Palmanova, Treviso, yet so long as he seriously threatened the Austrian army by his own massed corps, the enemy could not wisely take advantage of the opening, unless commanded by a man of equal skill and boldness with the French commander-in-chief, and well equipped with men and material. This is a risk common to almost all strategic manoeuvres.

A rumour having come in that the column from the Tyrol army which, under Kerpen, had been cut off by Joubert, was marching to join the archduke by the valleys of the Salza and the Muhr, Bonaparte was anxious not only to pursue the retiring Austrians, but hopeful of intercepting this stray force; and with this additional incentive, on the 3rd of April, at early dawn, the tireless advance again began. The report as to Kerpen's column turned out to be an error, but the pursuit of the Austrians was not relaxed. Thus pushed, the archduke retired yet farther, and by the 6th reached Bruck, with rearguard in Leoben. The French army entered Judenburg April 5, and here, to Bonaparte's intense relief, there came to the French headquarters Generals Bellegarde and Meerfeldt as plenipotentiaries from Vienna, prepared to treat for peace. Bonaparte's letter to the archduke had been sent to the capital, with this much-to-be-desired result.

On the 6th Bernadotte had reached Neumarkt, where his advance was checked by Bonaparte. Guyeux had marched forward on Bruck, while Massena had pushed on and taken Leoben the evening of the same day. Serurier was at Gratz, and Joubert, receiving in Brixen his instructions from Bonaparte, had drawn in Delmas, started along the Puster valley on his way down the Drave, and his van was on this day in Lienz. Next day, April 7, a five days' truce was granted, and on April 18 preliminaries of peace were signed at Leoben. These served as a basis for the treaty of Campo Formio.

During the truce, the line of demarcation ran from the sea between Fiume and Trieste, *via* Littay, Wündisch-Feistritz, Marburg, Ehrenhausen, Gratz, Bruck, Leoben, Mautern, Rottenmann, Radstadt, St. Michael, Spithal, Lienz.

The French army shortly started on its return march to Venetian territory. In due season the news of the truce of Leoben reached Joubert, and hostilities were suspended. It was time, for Laudon had driven back Baraguay and the French troops, and followed them down the Adige to Roveredo, and had even pushed a detachment along the left bank towards Verona.

It was just four weeks since the last campaign had opened; it was just a year since Bonaparte had moved on Beaulieu from the shore of the Gulf of Genoa, and he now stood within some eighty miles of Vienna. One can point to few operations as brilliant as this rapid march with a quite small force had been, with its contempt of danger and its many victories; but the apparent success was not founded on a truly solid basis. Bonaparte could not safely advance farther. His numbers were distinctly insufficient for a serious campaign against Vienna. A battle with all the forces the enemy could muster at the gates of the capital would be extra-hazardous. Counting in Joubert and Bernadotte, the Army of Italy again numbered nearly fifty thousand men under the colours; but Austrian troops were coming on from Hungary to Vienna, and for every step back the archduke would grow in numerical strength; and the determination to save the chief city of the country would be universal. The two Rhine armies Bonaparte now learned were still on the left bank in cantonments, accomplishing so little good in the general scheme that he was excusable in suspecting that his enemies at home were striving to isolate the Army of Italy, and destroy it and his reputation at one fell stroke. He could not advance alone into the valley of the Danube. The French communications were already threatened by the regulars and militia under Laudon and Kerpen in the Tyrol, as has just been stated; and the Tyrolese sharpshooter, inflamed by religious hatred of the French, might prove an efficient auxiliary in a winning campaign. Not only had a column advanced down the Brenta and reached Bassano, while another was headed for Verona, but the latter city indeed had risen and murdered the French inhabitants, and driven the garrison of three thousand men under Balland into the citadel, where they were being besieged. Trieste had risen and ousted the French cavalry. Luckily Victor was still on hand, and able to assemble fifteen thousand men to hold Venice within bounds; and joined by Kilmaine and some men from the garrison of the Italian cities, he shortly put down the insurrection in Verona. But in reality, Bonaparte, for all his proud bearing, stood on a volcano.

Under these circumstances, by cunningly taking advantage of the temporary weakening of the Austrian authorities, and by the exertion of that marvellous power which in any other man we should call bullying, the victorious leader was fortunate to sign preliminaries of peace at Leoben, to which place he had moved headquarters. In the negotiations to this end he exhibited as marked a capacity for diplomacy as he had shown for war, and not only made his situation appear sound, but bore down all opposition to the terms he formulated. The *Memoirs* say:

> The Austrian plenipotentiaries had thought to do an agreeable thing in placing for first article that the emperor recognized the French Republic. 'Erase that,' said Napoleon; 'the Republic is like the sun, which shines of its own light; the blind alone see it not!' In effect, this recognition was harmful, because, if one day the French people chose to make a monarchy, the emperor could say that he had acknowledged the Republic.

On April 19 Bonaparte thus sums up the situation to the Directory:

> Moreover, we must not hide from ourselves that, though our military position is brilliant, we have not dictated the conditions. The court had already evacuated Vienna; Prince Charles and his army were falling back on the army of the Rhine; the people of Hungary . . . were rising in mass, and were already on our flanks; the Rhine had not been crossed. . . . Had they been foolish enough to await me, I should have beaten them; but they would have constantly retired, would have joined the Rhine forces and overwhelmed me. . . . I had determined to levy a contribution in the faubourgs of Vienna, and not take a step beyond. . . . Had I, at the opening of the campaign, insisted

> on going to Turin, I should have never crossed the Po; had I insisted on going to Rome, I should have lost Milan; had I insisted on marching to Vienna, I might have lost the Republic. The real plan of campaign to destroy the emperor is what I have done. . . . So soon as I saw that negotiations would seriously open, I sent a courier to General Clarke, who, charged more particularly with your instructions in an object so essential, would have acquitted himself better than I; but when after ten days I saw that he did not arrive, and that the moment began to pass, I had to drop all scruples, and I signed" (the preliminaries). You have given me full power in all diplomatic operations, and in the position of things, the preliminaries of peace, even with the emperor, had become a military operation.

In the opening of this remarkable campaign from Nice to Leoben, Bonaparte had by his operations enunciated and proved the value of the mass theory. In the operation from the Mincio eastward, he had apparently put aside the mass theory, and had divided his forces. This has led to the expression of opinion by some historians that Bonaparte did not believe in or act on his own maxims, that every campaign must open up a new theory of action, and that after all nothing can ever be done by rule. This is in only a narrow sense true. Napoleon wrote to the king of Spain in September, 1808:

> The art of war is an art which has principles which it is never permitted to break.

At St. Helena he truly said:

> All great captains of antiquity, and those who later have most worthily trodden in their footsteps, have only accomplished great results by adhering closely to the rules and the natural principles of the art. . . . The principles of the art of war are those which have led the great captains whose deeds history tells us of.

As a fact, no one adhered more fully to his theory of war than Napoleon; but he knew when to make exceptions, and when to gauge his operations by the character of his opponent. And if we study the situation, we readily see, as has been already explained, that the sending of Joubert up the Adige and down the Drave, while he marched east with the main body, was not a division of forces, but a scrupulous care for his base. Joubert was fending off from it the Tyrol army.

It remains true that few captains have ever utilized so constantly as did Napoleon the rules he had evolved from his study of history, and from the experience he gained in his own campaigns. But it must be remembered that, as Frederick was the first general who wrote down what he practiced in war, so it was Jomini who first put in print the principles on which Napoleon had acted, and which the great man himself jealously guarded as his own. Military critics are wont to forget that Napoleon's able generalship was the result of his study of the campaigns of the other great soldiers in the past, and of his natural acuteness in evolving the secret of their methods, and in again putting their principles into practice. As his theatre grew in extent, he improved his general strategic scheme; and as he never doubted that in force and intelligence he was quite able to cope with any opponent he met, so occasionally he allowed himself to vary from his maxims according as the conditions varied, because he could foresee that in the particular case in hand his opponent would be unable to take advantage of the variation, and because it was safe and convenient to do so. There were, however, for Napoleon certain constant rules which he never forgot without suffering the consequences, and which a lesser captain would violate at his peril.

What especially strikes the student of the 1796-97 campaign is the wonderful personality of the young commander. In his report to the Directory from Milan, December 7, 1796, General Clarke, then Chief of the Topographical Bureau in the Ministry of War, and later Duc de Feltre, visiting the army to represent the Directory, and to inspect the conduct of the military chiefs and the civil commissaries, says:

> The general-in-chief has rendered the most important services. Placed by you in the glorious position he occupies, he has shown himself worthy of it. He is the man of the Republic. The fate of Italy has several times depended on his learned combinations. There is nobody here who does not look upon him as a man of genius, and he is effectively that. He is feared, loved and respected in Italy. All the little means of intrigue fall before his penetration. He has a great ascendant on the individuals who compose the Republican army, because he guesses or conceives at once their thought or their character, and that be directs them with science on the point where they can be most useful. A healthy judgment, enlightened ideas, put him abreast of distinguishing the true from the false. His *coup d'œil* is sure. His resolutions are followed up with energy and vigour. His *sang-froid* in the liveliest

> affairs is as remarkable as his extreme promptitude in changing his plans, when unforeseen circumstances demand it. His manner of execution is learned and well calculated. Bonaparte can bear himself with success, in more than one career. His superior talents and his knowledge give him the means. I believe him attached to the Republic, and without other ambition than that of conserving the glory he has acquired. It would be a mistake to believe him to be a party man. He belongs neither to the Royalists, who calumniate him, nor to the anarchists, whom he loves not. The Constitution is his only guide. And rallying on it and on the Directors who desire it, I believe he will be always useful and never dangerous to his country. Do not think. Citizen Directors, that I am speaking of him from enthusiasm. It is with calm that I write, and no interest guides me except that of making you know the truth. Bonaparte will be put by posterity in the rank of the greatest men.

All contemporary evidence is to this same effect. Nor was Bonaparte lacking in the amenities of life. Harsh and domineering in everything relating to the service, yet his companions testify to his kindly side, and to the marvellous fascination of his society. He had his favourites,—indeed, in a sense, there was far too much favouritism, both in his armies and his government; he kept unworthy relatives, utterly lacking ability, in important posts; and it was often claimed that he recognized moderate services in his dispatches home, and said no word about more important ones rendered by those he did not like, or by those who had once offended him. But this, a merely human weakness, is to be found in every great man's surroundings, and it was in part due to the wonderful individuality he threw into his creation. His work was truly original. Casting aside the narrowness of the old method, he wrought on his own lines. His leading idea was expressed by Bourrienne:

> The art of war consists in having, with a smaller army, more men than the enemy at the point you attack, or at the point where you are attacked.

This is a clear definition of the mass theory, and one on which he uniformly acted. But to do this thing, which a few simple words can describe, requires genius.

After Archduke Charles had himself gone to Italy, and reinforcements had been forwarded to the Noric Alps to stay the progress of

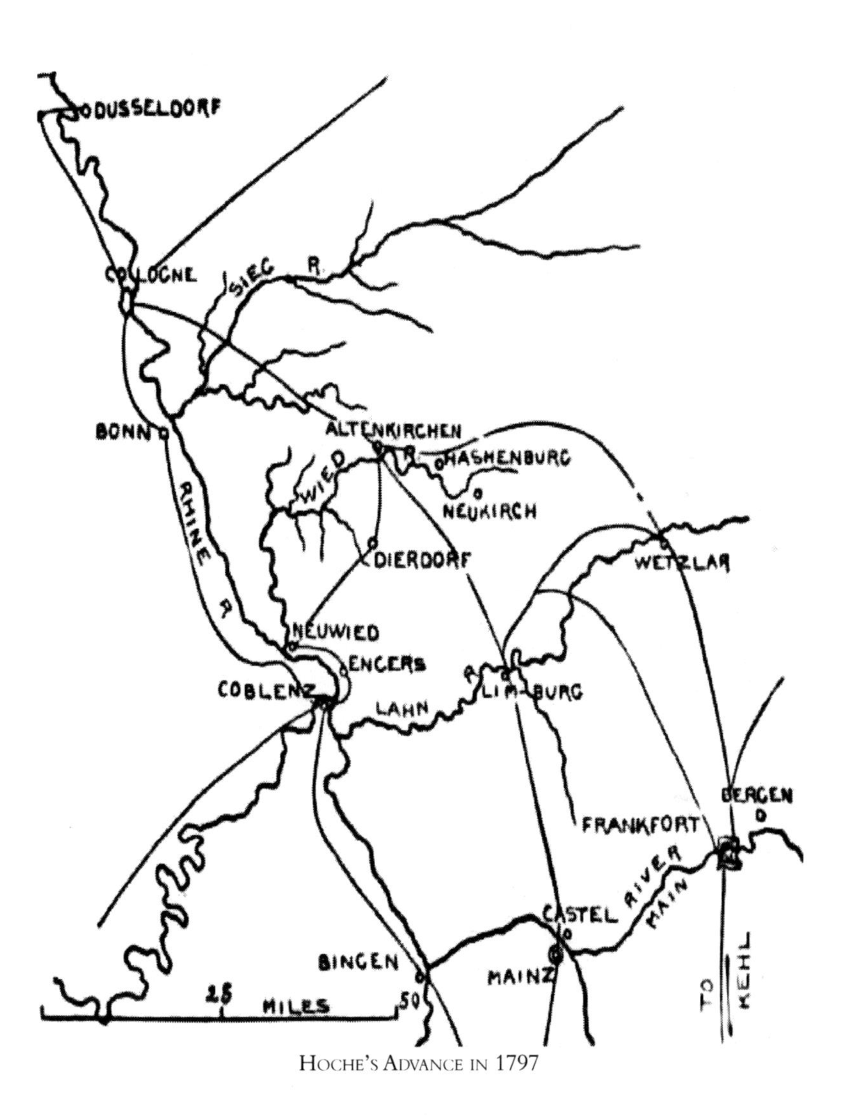

Hoche's Advance in 1797

Bonaparte, there remained on the Upper Rhine a bare forty thousand men under Latour, and on the Lower Rhine twenty-five thousand under Werneck, with some considerable numbers eaten up in garrisons. Facing these forces were respectively Moreau with sixty thousand men, the bulk near Strasburg, and Hoche with seventy thousand men, along the river below Coblenz. Although the Army of Italy sadly needed their cooperation, these armies passed the Rhine only about mid-April, Hoche at Düsseldorf and Neuwied, and Moreau at Kehl. They had been ordered to cross early in March, but there was lack of pontoons and of equipment generally. Vexed at this unnecessary delay, Bonaparte wrote the Directory:

> The armies of the Rhine must have no blood in their veins. . . . If one has the good-will to open the campaign, there is nothing to prevent it.

He had frequently warned the Directory that if he was not supported, it would be impossible for the Army of Italy to hold itself long; but he yet boldly pushed on, and was rewarded by the glorious triumph of Leoben.

Prior to crossing, Hoche sent a division to contain Mainz, and another to pass the Rhine and march on Castel. The rest of his six divisions he assembled in three army corps—Championnet with the left wing at Düsseldorf, Grenier in the centre, and the right wing under Lefebvre near Neuwied. The cavalry was on the right and left. Werneck's plan was to permit Championnet to advance from Düsseldorf to Altenkirchen, hoping to crush him there, and then to turn on the enemy up river; but he divided his forces too much, and Latour and he did not agree as to what the joint reserve they had should do.

It was April 17 when Hoche crossed at Neuwied. Shortly hearing of the truce of Leoben, Werneck offered him an armistice, but the French general gave an uncertain answer, and kept on, beating Kray at Engers, and Werneck at Dierdorf . The latter fell back on Hachenburg; and when Championnet moved from below and crossed the Wied at Altenkirchen, the Austrians again retreated, and the French followed to the Lahn country. Although Werneck had planned to fight at Neukirch, he changed his mind and withdrew to Wetzlar; and Hoche felt encouraged to believe that he could drive the Austrians to Mainz. And despite some slight successes in rearguard combats with the French, yet Werneck later deemed it wise to retire still farther to Bergen, and Lefebvre soon reached Frankfort Here news of the peace came in, much to the relief of the Austrians.

Meanwhile Moreau, with the Army of the Rhine and Moselle, began his crossing at Kehl April 19. He had to force his passage, but cleverly managed it in the teeth of Stzarray. Yet he did not ably use his great superiority to beat the enemy in detail, as he might have done, and the Leoben negotiations arrested the manoeuvres April 24.

The active operations of Hoche and Moreau had lasted only a week. Of how much utility they might have been a month earlier, it is easy to judge. Whether Carnot, or Moreau, or the Directory, or a common jealousy of Bonaparte, was at the root of the delay cannot now be determined.

The hero of Leoben was glad to enter upon the return march, and to this he cleverly lent the air of doing a favour to Austria by evacuating her territory; but in truth he was anxious to regain his own all too distant base, and put an end to the dangerous disaffection which was a real threat to his rear. On May 16, by a *ruse de guerre*, the French army entered Venice, shortly destined to be added to the Austrian territory in exchange for Lombardy and Belgium; and the oligarchy, as a punishment for its opposition to the French, was dissolved. Bonaparte established his headquarters near Udine to await the plenipotentiaries who were to treat of peace, and himself went to Milan to complete the organization of the Cisalpine Republic, and to support the new democratic revolution in Genoa. The Genoese oligarchy was transformed into the Ligurian Republic, and the great fortified city came under the control of the French.

The negotiations at Udine (Passeriano) went on slowly. Every power seemed to strive to influence what was done. It was hoped in France that another expedition to Ireland, aided by the Dutch and Spanish fleets, might be successful. But the battle of Cape St. Vincent, won by Jervis off Cadiz, placed England absolutely in command of the sea. Her ministers were not unwilling to treat for peace, if Austria was to make it; and indeed negotiations to this end were opened at Lille; but they had no result. English demands were not based on French successes on land. The Directory proved unreasonable, and would accede to no acceptable terms.

The Royalist sentiment, fed by the tyranny of the Directory, had long been growing, and the new elections gave the party strength in the Council. Moreau had dallied with the Royalists, but Pichegru was the leader of the movement, which no doubt looked forward to a restoration of the Bourbons. Three members of the Directory, Barras, La Révéllière-Lepeaux and Rewbel, were Jacobins; Carnot and Barthélemy were Moderates. The Council demanded Moderate ministers, but the three Jacobin Directors put strong Republicans in office; and as each party desired an able general on its side, for a few days Hoche was minister of war. Bonaparte was a stanch Republican, and the leanings of the troops were strongly so. But being with the army in the field, he was in a way removed from politics.

On the national fete of July 14, a great celebration was ordered by the general-in-chief in Milan, salvos were fired for all officers of rank killed in action, new standards were delivered, double rations were issued, and races and games ensued. Bonaparte issued the following order:

> Milan
> 26 Messidor, Year V
> To the Army
> Soldiers! Today is the anniversary of the 14th of July. You see before you the names of our companions in arms dead on the field of honour for the liberty of the country. They have given you the example. You owe yourselves wholly to the Republic; you owe yourselves wholly to the happiness of thirty millions of Frenchmen; you owe yourselves wholly to the glory of that name which has received a fresh lustre by your victories.
>
> Soldiers! I know you to be profoundly affected by the ills which threaten the country; but the country cannot run real dangers. The same men who have made her triumph over Europe in coalition are here. Mountains separate us from France; you would cross them with the rapidity of the eagle, if needed, to maintain the Constitution, defend liberty, protect the government and the Republicans.
>
> Soldiers! The government watches the trust of laws confided to it. The Royalists, from the moment they show themselves, will have lived. Be without disquiet, and let us swear by the manes of the heroes who have died beside us for liberty, let us swear on our new flags: Implacable War to the Enemies of the Republic and of the Constitution of the Year III.
> *Bonaparte*

In the same tone Bonaparte wrote the Directory, July 15, that the emperor was waiting to see the turn things would take in Paris; that the army was indignant at the condition of affairs, and that his proclamation of July 14 had produced the best effect; that personally he could not remain insensible to the attacks of the newspapers, or of the Five Hundred, or of the Clichy Club (of Royalists):

> Are there no more Republicans left in France? You can save the Republic with one stroke . . . and conclude peace in twenty-four hours. Arrest the émigrés; destroy the influence of foreigners. If you need force, call on the armies. Break up the presses of the journals sold to England, more bloody than ever was Marat. . . . If nothing can be done to put an end to assassinations and to the influence of Louis XVI., I desire to resign.

And in a letter to Clarke of July 18:

> I confess, however, to you that I much desire to re-enter private life; I have paid my score.

Was this last quite ingenuous? Resignation when he deemed himself essential was always one of Bonaparte's weapons.

Augereau had gone to Paris with the Mantua flags. No one supposed him to be in league with Bonaparte, whose *aide*, Lavalette, was there to represent him. On September 4, the 18th *Fructidor*, by Augereau's aid, the Tuileries, where the Council sat, was surrounded, and Pichegru and Barthélemy were seized. Carnot escaped. A new padded Council upheld the Directory, who selected Merlin and Francois as new members, much to Augereau's disappointment, as he had hoped for the place. Thus the Jacobins triumphed, without Bonaparte's having personally appeared in the affair.

The change had, however, the effect of preventing so much interference with Bonaparte's control of the peace negotiations. He continued the discussion of terms at Udine, and on a fresh interference with his work by the home authorities, he actually handed in his resignation on September 25. This act decided the Directory to favour the man they well knew they could not do without, nor, indeed, dared to place in antagonism to their power. The Army of Italy was reinforced, and Bonaparte given such ample power that he determined to sign a peace at Campo Formio.

The *St. Helena Memoirs* tell the following story of the discussions at Udine. On October 16 Bonaparte recapitulated the conduct of France since the Leoben preliminaries and renewed his ultimatum. Cobentzel, the Austrian plenipotentiary, at whose house the meeting was that day held, argued at length to prove that France was getting too much in the treaty, and would join all Italy to Gaul:

> That the emperor was irrevocably resolved to run all the chances of war, even to flee from his capital, if need be, rather than consent to a peace so disadvantageous; that Russia offered him

armies; that these were ready to rush to his aid, and that people would see what manner of troops the Russians were; that it was very evident that Napoleon was making his character as plenipotentiary cede to his interests as general; that he did not desire peace. He added that he would leave in the night, and that all the blood that would flow in this new conflict would fall upon the French negotiator. It was then that the latter, with coolness, but highly piqued with this outburst, rose and took from a pier-table a little liqueur-set (cabaret) of porcelain of which Count Cobentzel was very fond, as the gift of the Empress Catherine: 'Well, then,' said Napoleon, 'the truce is therefore broken and war is declared! But remember that before the end of this autumn I will break your monarchy as I break this porcelain!' In pronouncing these last words he threw it to earth with vivacity: it covered the floor with its debris. He bowed to the Congress and left. The Austrian plenipotentiaries were astounded. A few minutes afterwards they knew that in entering his carriage he had dispatched an officer to Archduke Charles to notify him that, the negotiations being broken off, hostilities would be begun again in twenty-four hours. Alarmed, Count Cobentzel sent the Marquis of Gallo to Passeriano to carry a signed declaration that he adhered to the ultimatum of France. . . . On the morrow peace was signed.

We must accept this story on the testimony of Napoleon. Many others may have had a foundation far more slender than their present form. But all are like the man, and none lack the interest that anecdotes possess which have grown up about any great character of history.

In the Treaty of Campo Formio, Austria ceded Belgium to France. The Congress of Rastadt was to discuss peace. Austria received Venice to the Adige, with Istria and Dalmatia, and recognized the Cisalpine Republic. Secret articles provided for an Alps-Rhine frontier for France, with possession of Mainz, the navigation of the Rhine to be open to both France and Germany.

There was good reason for signing the peace. The Army of Italy was in excellent condition, but was so placed that the Austrians would be nearer their sources of supply, and be better able to prepare for the next campaign, than could the French. Many questions in the rear of the French army—Naples, Venice, Sardinia—were in a high degree disquieting, and Bonaparte felt the desirability of rounding up by a useful peace the splendour of his campaign. It cannot be said that he exhibited much regard for the promises which had been made to the recently created Italian republics, from which territory was taken in cold blood in order to compass the desired peace. France retained many fortresses until ratification.

The Peace of Campo Formio was clearly the work of Bonaparte. It was glorious for France and not unfair for the enemy. It should have been solid, for Austria got Venice for Antwerp, and Istria and Dalmatia for Belgium—in her present condition a valuable exchange.

There arose during 1797 certain troubles among the Swiss cantons, which led the Directory, in breach of all international law, to interfere in her internal affairs, under the flimsy pretext of establishing a balance between the democratic and monarchical states. This resulted in the establishment of French control in the Alps in the place of Swiss neutrality,—a grievous mistake on the part of France. It seemed to be the idea of the Directory that to protect the political status of the French Republic, it was essential to surround it with a cordon of small democracies—buffer states, as it were; whereas these would but give France a more extended line to protect, instead of the Rhine and the Alps, for French control demanded French protection. The neutrality of Switzerland is one of the political and military necessities of the modern status of Europe. In the case of France this is peculiarly valuable. So long as this great natural barrier remains neutral, it protects her two lines of attack and defence,—the Rhine and Piedmont,—each having the Alps on one of its flanks. With Switzerland no longer neutral, the eastern frontier of France demands greater armies and is but half as well protected.

The designs against Switzerland were hidden under the guise of an expedition to Egypt, and this again was kept secret by ostensible preparations near the English Channel. The Swiss invasion was hurried up by the fact, discovered by Bonaparte, that Berne had in her treasury forty million francs in specie; and France needed the money to equip the army and fleet destined for Egypt. As a pretext to take a hand in the internal affairs of Switzerland, Bonaparte made a demand for the passage of a French detachment from Italy to the headwaters of the Rhone, the shortest road from Milan to France; and to this, as was expected, a courteous refusal was the only answer a neutral state could make. This permitted the Directory to begin covert, and later overt, interference with Bernese affairs; and as a result, a body of French soldiers entered Swiss territory in December, 1797. The Swiss raised troops, and Menard took Lausanne. Fostering revolution against the constituted authorities, the French made such exorbitant demands on the Bernese Senate that the only answer could be the raising of an army. This was placed under Erlach. The Directory then demanded that the several cantons of Switzerland should be made into a republic, one and indivisible, and to Brune was given command of the French army. The Bernese Senate lacked energy. Brune and Schauenburg marched against Erlach early in March, 1798; and by Carnot's ably designed concentric operation from France, Italy and the Rhine (made in anticipation of what actually occurred), coupled with their own really clever work, these generals defeated the Swiss near Berne, March 6; whereupon the French entered the city, and seized on the treasury. Soon Switzerland was overrun by French troops, and the Helvetian Republic, under French protection, was formed by Talleyrand. This invasion of Switzerland made the continuance of European peace impossible.

Revolutionary ideas were growing in southern Italy. Naples was on the eve of an uprising, and the prisons were half full of suspects. Urged on by French partisans, the Roman populace rose to demand a republic. In suppressing this rising, on December 28, 1797, the papal troops charged a mob in front of the French legation, and a French officer was accidentally killed. Of this unintentional violation of diplomatic propriety the Directory at once took advantage. Berthier, with eighteen thousand men, was ordered to Rome; and on February 15, 1798, the Roman Republic was proclaimed from the steps of the Capitol. The Pope left the city for Pisa, and eventually went to France. This interference with papal affairs was a direct blow at Austria. Berthier was succeeded by Massena, and he by Dallemagne. The troops, unpaid and ill-cared for, mutinied, as was not uncommon in these years, and some time elapsed before quiet was restored. All this excessive activity on the part of the Directory was a mistake. It never knew when it had enough. The occupation of Switzerland and Rome tore the treaty of Campo Formio to shreds.

Shortly going to Paris, Bonaparte was received as the hero of the hour. At the opening of 1796 the German emperor had lain on the confines of France with one hundred and sixty thousand men, ready to cross the Rhine. By his activ ity in Italy the young general had called both Wurmser and Archduke Charles from the Rhine with over sixty thousand men, and it was this that had enabled Moreau and Hoche to carry the tricolour to the Lech. Peace forced on the emperor assured that of Europe, for England could have been counted on to make peace if the Directory would be reasonable. Bonaparte had filled the national treasury with money from his forced contributions, and the national museum with works of art; he had covered the French name with a halo of glory.

Though Bonaparte already aspired to a leading role, yet the time was not ripe. He could not well overthrow the Directory at this moment. That must topple of its own weakness, so that he might assume the ever-popular role of Saviour of the Republic. In Paris he ran the danger of becoming allied to one or other party, the last thing he now desired. He could not afford to be a party man; what he needed was to keep the eyes of France and of Europe on his own personality, while entering no entangling alliances. Out of this desire and the then condition of England in India grew the Egyptian expedition, by undertaking which Bonaparte believed he could gain much for France and for himself; and at all events he escaped being at the head of a perilous expedition to England, to the command of which he was at this time appointed.

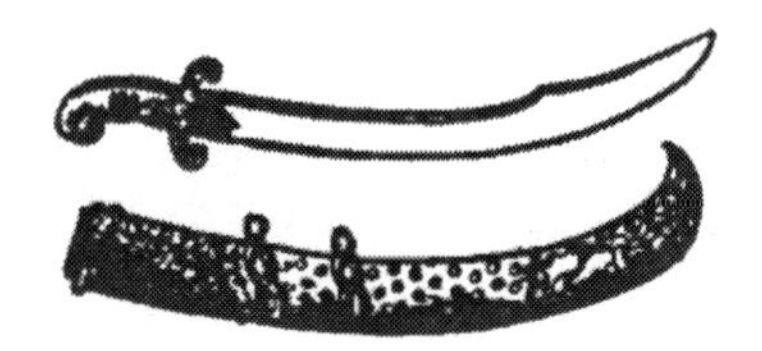

ALSO FROM LEONAUR

AVAILABLE IN SOFTCOVER OR HARDCOVER WITH DUST JACKET

A HISTORY OF THE FRENCH & INDIAN WAR *by Arthur G. Bradley*—The Seven Years War as it was fought in the New World has always fascinated students of military history—here is the story of that confrontation.

WASHINGTON'S EARLY CAMPAIGNS *by James Hadden*—The French Post Expedition, Great Meadows and Braddock's Defeat—including Braddock's Orderly Books.

BOUQUET & THE OHIO INDIAN WAR *by Cyrus Cort & William Smith*—Two Accounts of the Campaigns of 1763-1764: Bouquet's Campaigns by Cyrus Cort & The History of Bouquet's Expeditions by William Smith.

NARRATIVES OF THE FRENCH & INDIAN WAR: 2 *by David Holden, Samuel Jenks, Lemuel Lyon, Mary Cochrane Rogers & Henry T. Blake*—Contains The Diary of Sergeant David Holden, Captain Samuel Jenks' Journal, The Journal of Lemuel Lyon, Journal of a French Officer at the Siege of Quebec, A Battle Fought on Snowshoes & The Battle of Lake George.

NARRATIVES OF THE FRENCH & INDIAN WAR *by Brown, Eastburn, Hawks & Putnam*—Ranger Brown's Narrative, The Adventures of Robert Eastburn, The Journal of Rufus Putnam—Provincial Infantry & Orderly Book and Journal of Major John Hawks on the Ticonderoga-Crown Point Campaign.

THE 7TH (QUEEN'S OWN) HUSSARS: Volume 1—1688-1792 *by C. R. B. Barrett*—As Dragoons During the Flanders Campaign, War of the Austrian Succession and the Seven Years War.

INDIA'S FREE LANCES *by H. G. Keene*—European Mercenary Commanders in Hindustan 1770-1820.

THE BENGAL EUROPEAN REGIMENT *by P. R. Innes*—An Elite Regiment of the Honourable East India Company 1756-1858.

MUSKET & TOMAHAWK *by Francis Parkman*—A Military History of the French & Indian War, 1753-1760.

THE BLACK WATCH AT TICONDEROGA *by Frederick B. Richards*—Campaigns in the French & Indian War.

QUEEN'S RANGERS *by Frederick B. Richards*—John Simcoe and his Rangers During the Revolutionary War for America.

LEONAUR

ALSO FROM LEONAUR

AVAILABLE IN SOFTCOVER OR HARDCOVER WITH DUST JACKET

AFGHANISTAN: THE BELEAGUERED BRIGADE *by G. R. Gleig*—An Account of Sale's Brigade During the First Afghan War.

IN THE RANKS OF THE C. I. V *by Erskine Childers*—With the City Imperial Volunteer Battery (Honourable Artillery Company) in the Second Boer War.

THE BENGAL NATIVE ARMY *by F. G. Cardew*—An Invaluable Reference Resource.

THE 7TH (QUEEN'S OWN) HUSSARS: Volume 4—1688-1914 *by C. R. B. Barrett*—Uniforms, Equipment, Weapons, Traditions, the Services of Notable Officers and Men & the Appendices to All Volumes—Volume 4: 1688-1914.

THE SWORD OF THE CROWN *by Eric W. Sheppard*—A History of the British Army to 1914.

THE 7TH (QUEEN'S OWN) HUSSARS: Volume 3—1818-1914 *by C. R. B. Barrett*—On Campaign During the Canadian Rebellion, the Indian Mutiny, the Sudan, Matabeleland, Mashonaland and the Boer War Volume 3: 1818-1914.

THE KHARTOUM CAMPAIGN *by Bennet Burleigh*—A Special Correspondent's View of the Reconquest of the Sudan by British and Egyptian Forces under Kitchener—1898.

EL PUCHERO *by Richard McSherry*—The Letters of a Surgeon of Volunteers During Scott's Campaign of the American-Mexican War 1847-1848.

RIFLEMAN SAHIB *by E. Maude*—The Recollections of an Officer of the Bombay Rifles During the Southern Mahratta Campaign, Second Sikh War, Persian Campaign and Indian Mutiny.

THE KING'S HUSSAR *by Edwin Mole*—The Recollections of a 14th (King's) Hussar During the Victorian Era.

JOHN COMPANY'S CAVALRYMAN *by William Johnson*—The Experiences of a British Soldier in the Crimea, the Persian Campaign and the Indian Mutiny.

COLENSO & DURNFORD'S ZULU WAR *by Frances E. Colenso & Edward Durnford*—The first and possibly the most important history of the Zulu War.

U. S. DRAGOON *by Samuel E. Chamberlain*—Experiences in the Mexican War 1846-48 and on the South Western Frontier.

AVAILABLE ONLINE AT **www.leonaur.com**
AND FROM ALL GOOD BOOK STORES

07/09

ALSO FROM LEONAUR

AVAILABLE IN SOFTCOVER OR HARDCOVER WITH DUST JACKET

THE 2ND MAORI WAR: 1860-1861 *by Robert Carey*—The Second Maori War, or First Taranaki War, one more bloody instalment of the conflicts between European settlers and the indigenous Maori people.

A JOURNAL OF THE SECOND SIKH WAR *by Daniel A. Sandford*—The Experiences of an Ensign of the 2nd Bengal European Regiment During the Campaign in the Punjab, India, 1848-49.

THE LIGHT INFANTRY OFFICER *by John H. Cooke*—The Experiences of an Officer of the 43rd Light Infantry in America During the War of 1812.

BUSHVELDT CARBINEERS *by George Witton*—The War Against the Boers in South Africa and the 'Breaker' Morant Incident.

LAKE'S CAMPAIGNS IN INDIA *by Hugh Pearse*—The Second Anglo Maratha War, 1803-1807.

BRITAIN IN AFGHANISTAN 1: THE FIRST AFGHAN WAR 1839-42 *by Archibald Forbes*—From invasion to destruction-a British military disaster.

BRITAIN IN AFGHANISTAN 2: THE SECOND AFGHAN WAR 1878-80 *by Archibald Forbes*—This is the history of the Second Afghan War-another episode of British military history typified by savagery, massacre, siege and battles.

UP AMONG THE PANDIES *by Vivian Dering Majendie*—Experiences of a British Officer on Campaign During the Indian Mutiny, 1857-1858.

MUTINY: 1857 *by James Humphries*—Authentic Voices from the Indian Mutiny-First Hand Accounts of Battles, Sieges and Personal Hardships.

BLOW THE BUGLE, DRAW THE SWORD *by W. H. G. Kingston*—The Wars, Campaigns, Regiments and Soldiers of the British & Indian Armies During the Victorian Era, 1839-1898.

WAR BEYOND THE DRAGON PAGODA *by Major J. J. Snodgrass*—A Personal Narrative of the First Anglo-Burmese War 1824 - 1826.

THE HERO OF ALIWAL *by James Humphries*—The Campaigns of Sir Harry Smith in India, 1843-1846, During the Gwalior War & the First Sikh War.

ALL FOR A SHILLING A DAY *by Donald F. Featherstone*—The story of H.M. 16th, the Queen's Lancers During the first Sikh War 1845-1846.

ALSO FROM LEONAUR

AVAILABLE IN SOFTCOVER OR HARDCOVER WITH DUST JACKET

OFFICERS & GENTLEMEN *by Peter Hawker & William Graham*—Two Accounts of British Officers During the Peninsula War: Officer of Light Dragoons by Peter Hawker & Campaign in Portugal and Spain by William Graham .

THE WALCHEREN EXPEDITION *by Anonymous*—The Experiences of a British Officer of the 81st Regt. During the Campaign in the Low Countries of 1809.

LADIES OF WATERLOO *by Charlotte A. Eaton, Magdalene de Lancey & Juana Smith*—The Experiences of Three Women During the Campaign of 1815: Waterloo Days by Charlotte A. Eaton, A Week at Waterloo by Magdalene de Lancey & Juana's Story by Juana Smith.

JOURNAL OF AN OFFICER IN THE KING'S GERMAN LEGION *by John Frederick Hering*—Recollections of Campaigning During the Napoleonic Wars.

JOURNAL OF AN ARMY SURGEON IN THE PENINSULAR WAR *by Charles Boutflower*—The Recollections of a British Army Medical Man on Campaign During the Napoleonic Wars.

ON CAMPAIGN WITH MOORE AND WELLINGTON *by Anthony Hamilton*—The Experiences of a Soldier of the 43rd Regiment During the Peninsular War.

THE ROAD TO AUSTERLITZ *by R. G. Burton*—Napoleon's Campaign of 1805.

SOLDIERS OF NAPOLEON *by A. J. Doisy De Villargennes & Arthur Chuquet*—The Experiences of the Men of the French First Empire: Under the Eagles by A. J. Doisy De Villargennes & Voices of 1812 by Arthur Chuquet .

INVASION OF FRANCE, 1814 *by F. W. O. Maycock*—The Final Battles of the Napoleonic First Empire.

LEIPZIG—A CONFLICT OF TITANS *by Frederic Shoberl*—A Personal Experience of the 'Battle of the Nations' During the Napoleonic Wars, October 14th-19th, 1813.

SLASHERS *by Charles Cadell*—The Campaigns of the 28th Regiment of Foot During the Napoleonic Wars by a Serving Officer.

BATTLE IMPERIAL *by Charles William Vane*—The Campaigns in Germany & France for the Defeat of Napoleon 1813-1814.

SWIFT & BOLD *by Gibbes Rigaud*—The 60th Rifles During the Peninsula War.

LEONAUR

LEONAUR

LEONAUR

LEONAUR

ALSO FROM LEONAUR

AVAILABLE IN SOFTCOVER OR HARDCOVER WITH DUST JACKET

CAPTAIN COIGNET *by Jean-Roch Coignet*—A Soldier of Napoleon's Imperial Guard from the Italian Campaign to Russia and Waterloo.

HUSSAR ROCCA *by Albert Jean Michel de Rocca*—A French cavalry officer's experiences of the Napoleonic Wars and his views on the Peninsular Campaigns against the Spanish, British And Guerilla Armies.

MARINES TO 95TH (RIFLES) *by Thomas Fernyhough*—The military experiences of Robert Fernyhough during the Napoleonic Wars.

LIGHT BOB *by Robert Blakeney*—The experiences of a young officer in H.M 28th & 36th regiments of the British Infantry during the Peninsular Campaign of the Napoleonic Wars 1804 - 1814.

WITH WELLINGTON'S LIGHT CAVALRY *by William Tomkinson*—The Experiences of an officer of the 16th Light Dragoons in the Peninsular and Waterloo campaigns of the Napoleonic Wars.

SERGEANT BOURGOGNE *by Adrien Bourgogne*—With Napoleon's Imperial Guard in the Russian Campaign and on the Retreat from Moscow 1812 - 13.

SURTEES OF THE 95TH (RIFLES) *by William Surtees*—A Soldier of the 95th (Rifles) in the Peninsular campaign of the Napoleonic Wars.

SWORDS OF HONOUR *by Henry Newbolt & Stanley L. Wood*—The Careers of Six Outstanding Officers from the Napoleonic Wars, the Wars for India and the American Civil War.

ENSIGN BELL IN THE PENINSULAR WAR *by George Bell*—The Experiences of a young British Soldier of the 34th Regiment 'The Cumberland Gentlemen' in the Napoleonic wars.

HUSSAR IN WINTER *by Alexander Gordon*—A British Cavalry Officer during the retreat to Corunna in the Peninsular campaign of the Napoleonic Wars.

THE COMPLEAT RIFLEMAN HARRIS *by Benjamin Harris as told to and transcribed by Captain Henry Curling, 52nd Regt. of Foot*—The adventures of a soldier of the 95th (Rifles) during the Peninsular Campaign of the Napoleonic Wars.

THE ADVENTURES OF A LIGHT DRAGOON *by George Farmer & G.R. Gleig*—A cavalryman during the Peninsular & Waterloo Campaigns, in captivity & at the siege of Bhurtpore, India.

AVAILABLE ONLINE AT www.leonaur.com
AND FROM ALL GOOD BOOK STORES

07/09

ALSO FROM LEONAUR

AVAILABLE IN SOFTCOVER OR HARDCOVER WITH DUST JACKET

THE LIFE OF THE REAL BRIGADIER GERARD VOLUME 1—THE YOUNG HUSSAR 1782-1807 *by Jean-Baptiste De Marbot*—A French Cavalryman Of the Napoleonic Wars at Marengo, Austerlitz, Jena, Eylau & Friedland.

THE LIFE OF THE REAL BRIGADIER GERARD VOLUME 2—IMPERIAL AIDE-DE-CAMP 1807-1811 *by Jean-Baptiste De Marbot*—A French Cavalryman of the Napoleonic Wars at Saragossa, Landshut, Eckmuhl, Ratisbon, Aspern-Essling, Wagram, Busaco & Torres Vedras.

THE LIFE OF THE REAL BRIGADIER GERARD VOLUME 3—COLONEL OF CHASSEURS 1811-1815 *by Jean-Baptiste De Marbot*—A French Cavalryman in the retreat from Moscow, Lutzen, Bautzen, Katzbach, Leipzig, Hanau & Waterloo.

THE INDIAN WAR OF 1864 *by Eugene Ware*—The Experiences of a Young Officer of the 7th Iowa Cavalry on the Western Frontier During the Civil War.

THE MARCH OF DESTINY *by Charles E. Young & V. Devinny*—Dangers of the Trail in 1865 by Charles E. Young & The Story of a Pioneer by V. Devinny, two Accounts of Early Emigrants to Colorado.

CROSSING THE PLAINS *by William Audley Maxwell*—A First Hand Narrative of the Early Pioneer Trail to California in 1857.

CHIEF OF SCOUTS *by William F. Drannan*—A Pilot to Emigrant and Government Trains, Across the Plains of the Western Frontier.

THIRTY-ONE YEARS ON THE PLAINS AND IN THE MOUNTAINS *by William F. Drannan*—William Drannan was born to be a pioneer, hunter, trapper and wagon train guide during the momentous days of the Great American West.

THE INDIAN WARS VOLUNTEER *by William Thompson*—Recollections of the Conflict Against the Snakes, Shoshone, Bannocks, Modocs and Other Native Tribes of the American North West.

THE 4TH TENNESSEE CAVALRY *by George B. Guild*—The Services of Smith's Regiment of Confederate Cavalry by One of its Officers.

COLONEL WORTHINGTON'S SHILOH *by T. Worthington*—The Tennessee Campaign, 1862, by an Officer of the Ohio Volunteers.

FOUR YEARS IN THE SADDLE *by W. L. Curry*—The History of the First Regiment Ohio Volunteer Cavalry in the American Civil War.

LEONAUR

LEONAUR

LEONAUR

LEONAUR

Lightning Source UK Ltd.
Milton Keynes UK
UKOW05f2201281113

222046UK00001B/20/P